D1607559

New Partnerships for Innovation in Microfinance

Ingrid Matthäus-Maier

J. D. von Pischke

Editors

New Partnerships for Innovation in Microfinance

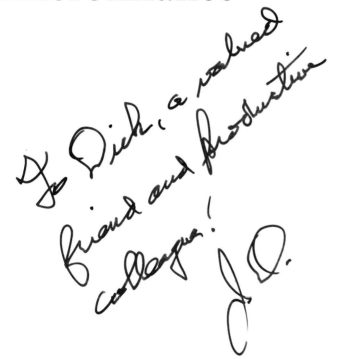

 Springer

Ingrid Matthäus-Maier
KfW
Palmengartenstr. 5-9
60325 Frankfurt am Main
Germany
ingrid.matthaeus-maier@kfw.de

Dr. J. D. von Pischke
2529 Trophy Lane
Reston, VA 20191-2126
USA
vonpischke@frontierfinance.com

ISBN 978-3-540-76640-7   e-ISBN 978-3-540-76641-4

Library of Congress Control Number: 2008923356

© 2008 Springer-Verlag Berlin Heidelberg

Cover design: WMXDesign GmbH, Heidelberg

Printed on acid-free paper

9 8 7 6 5 4 3 2 1

springer.com

The Importance of New Partnerships

Heidemarie Wieczorek-Zeul

Federal Minister for Economic Cooperation and Development

The fight for a dignified life and against extreme poverty is still the most important challenge for mankind. Four billion people in the world live in poverty. Despite recent improvements, around 980 million people – more than a sixth of the world's population – have to survive on less than one dollar a day. Poverty is the reason that 77 million children do not receive any primary education. Women still have significantly fewer opportunities to pursue personal freedoms and live a self-determined life than men. The list of development deficiencies is long and needs not be elaborated any further here. To summarise: we have made some progress towards reaching the Millennium Development Goals, but there is still a long way to go.

Financial sector development has proved to have a strong impact when it comes to achieving sustainable improvements in the living conditions of the poor. A strong and stable financial sector provides the foundations for economic stability and growth. These foundations promote development in other areas, including health, education, and social equality. That is why German development cooperation has consistently supported the deepening and broadening of financial systems in our partner countries.

Building Sustainable Institutions from the Ground up

Supporting microfinance institutions has long been a focus of German development cooperation. The Grameen Bank, which was awarded the Nobel peace prize in 2006, represented by its founder Mohammad Yunus, received support from the German government during the 1980s and 90s. German development cooperation provided this microfinance institution with advisory services for capacity building and funding in order to enable it to expand its micro-lending. An impressive number of microfinance institutions have been founded and supported with contributions from German development cooperation. These include the municipal savings banks in Peru, the fast-growing ProCredit Group serving 3 million women and men in Africa, Latin America and South-East Europe, and microfinance institutions in difficult post-war situations where the population has suffered or is still suffering heavily, for example in Afghanistan, Mozambique or Congo.

Opportunities for Public-Private Partnerships

The future of microfinance is not only about coordinating public donors, but also about mobilising private resources for development purposes. It is estimated that around two billion people still lack adequate access to financial services such as savings, loans and insurance. To reach these people, enormous efforts need to be undertaken – efforts that exceed the possibilities of public development aid by far.

Public-private partnerships are a way to mobilise additional funding and know-how for the poor. Such partnerships – e.g. in the form of microfinance funds or securitisations in the development finance sector – can mobilise private capital for developing and transition countries that are traditionally not considered attractive by private investors. PPPs in the financial sector of developing and transition countries are not only making efficient use of public resources, they also create possibilities for private investors who are new to this sector, i.e. we see a "crowding-in" of private money in a sphere traditionally dominated by public financiers and charities. This opens up opportunities to mobilise significant additional resources for a more effective fight against poverty.

The articles assembled in this book give reason for hope that new partnerships between traditional development finance and private investors will contribute to meeting the Millennium Development Goals.

New Partnerships for Innovation in Microfinance

Ingrid Matthäus-Maier

Spokeswoman of the Board of Managing Directors, KfW Bankengruppe

This publication has a particularly intriguing focus: "New Partnerships for Innovation in Microfinance". Who are the partners we expect to engage for the benefit of microfinance? The universe of microfinance appears to contain a number of different worlds, all of them full of intelligent people, but with very different visions and different cultural backgrounds.

The community-based world of microfinance consists of institutions like the famous Grameen Bank of Nobel Laureate Mohammad Yunus, or BRAC, the Bangladesh Rural Advancement Committee, also based in Dhaka. And there is the fast growing ProCredit Group of professional full-service neighbourhood banks which serve more than 3 million women and men in Africa, Latin America, South East Europe and soon also in Central Asia. In addition, the microfinance world comprises large charitable organisations like the Aga Khan Foundation that establishes and manages institutions that deliver microfinance services in countries like Afghanistan that are shaken by civil war. There is also the universe of commercial banks like Banque du Caire in Egypt, First National Bank in South Africa, or privately owned banks in the Caucasus that have set up microfinance business units with the support of KfW and others. Securitisations and microfinance investment funds are more recent phenomena that support the growth of microfinance institutions by mobilising private capital that can be on-lent to microcredit customers or that provide equity for the foundation and growth of microfinance institutions.

This variety of actors is fortuitous for microfinance. It offers a chance to serve the poor by providing them with adequate financial services. It offers a chance to make an important contribution towards the Millennium Development Goals.

Advances in Microfinance

The International Year of Microcredit in 2005 and the Nobel Prize for Dr. Yunus in 2006 have highlighted the importance of microfinance. Over the last decade microfinance has evolved into an integrated approach that successfully promotes financially viable and stable financial sectors which are accessible and beneficial to low income people and small entrepreneurs. The important contribution of microfinance to poverty reduction and to the realisation of the Millennium Development Goals is now widely recognised. A wealth of studies document that poor people have indeed improved their lives through access to loans, savings and other appropriate financial services.

There are many success stories by institutions supported by KfW that demonstrate how access to financial services helps low income families improve their lives. For example:

- Clients of BRAC, a microfinance institution in Bangladesh, suffered less from severe malnutrition than non-clients.

- In Bolivia, where KfW supported Banco Los Andes ProCredit and PRODEM, micro-entrepreneurs with access to loans doubled their income on average within two years.

- And ProCredit Bank Kosovo helped numerous families to survive post-war crises and rebuild their homes and workshops after the civil war.

To serve clients better and to create access for those who remain beyond the frontier of formal finance, the economic viability of financial institutions is crucial. Without viable institutions, we cannot mobilise the capital necessary for the growth of microfinance. Leading institutions listed in The Microbanking Bulletin[1] demonstrate that financial as well as social returns are produced.

Expanding Outreach

But let us be realistic. Of the ten thousand or so providers of microfinance services only about two hundred are profitable. Many of the ten thousand microfinance institutions are small and reach only a few thousand clients. Yet the market potential is huge, much greater than the current industry can hope to satisfy. Possibly more than 400 million potential clients worldwide still lack access to financial services. According to a recent report by Morgan Stanley, the current worldwide loan portfolios of MFIs amount to about US$ 17 billion, with the potential to grow to US$ 300 billion in the next decade.[2]

This is where the variety of actors in microfinance becomes important. It is imperative to have strong institutions on the ground since only strong microfinance institutions can reach large numbers of clients and gain their trust. It is important to have microfinance institutions that target the urban poor as well as the ones with the know-how and the technology to serve rural clients. Equally important,

[1] http://www.mixmarket.org/; http://www.mixmbb.org/en/

[2] Ian Callaghan et al. (2007): Microfinance on the Road to Capital Markets, in: Journal of Applied Corporate Finance, Volume 19, Number 1, 2007.

there is a role for "Wall Street Finance" in microfinance. Domestic and international commercial banks must engage more deeply with microfinance in order to expand outreach in both volume and quality. It is most important that this is done in a responsible way. Responsible banking is more than informing customers about a bank's products and services. It means educating them about financial services and improving the financial literacy of the small entrepreneurs and less well off people. Moreover, responsible banking means to price deposits and loans transparently, such as by publishing effective interest rates, and to lend responsibly instead of burdening a client with more debt than they can handle.

Microfinance will reach its full potential only if the private sector invests its capital and know-how. The perception of high risk and transaction costs coupled with low transparency has inhibited greater private sector engagement. New forms of public-private partnerships can facilitate private sector entry and the integration of microfinance into the commercial financial sector. Such partnerships offer both socially and financially rewarding opportunities.

KfW has pioneered financial market development for many years – in Germany, in Europe and beyond. Our commitment is to ensure that financial systems continue to deepen and provide financial services to weaker sections of society without requiring continuous donor support. To build a commercial foundation for microfinance – which is absolutely necessary to secure viability and expansion – we emphasise collaboration with our current partners in the microfinance industry as well as with new stars that may rise.

Combining Forces to Increase Impact

KfW's success in microfinance is to a large extent due to strong support by and partnership with the German Federal Ministry of Economic Cooperation and Development (BMZ). This Ministry is the lead agency for international development setting the strategic agenda and influencing the political trends in this arena in Germany.

Together with our partners, we have pioneered successful initiatives in microfinance around the world KfW has contributed equity and long-term funding to these programmes as well as results-oriented advisory services. Among them are partnerships with widely differing players to combine their respective strengths for optimum impact. Examples of such initiatives include:

- To reach out to the poorest in a war-torn country, KfW worked with the IFC, FMO, and Triodos to transform ACLEDA Bank in Cambodia from an NGO into a full-fledged microfinance institution.

- IPC's know-how and our early support to FEFAD in Albania helped to pioneer a microbanking model which was later taken up by a number of ProCredit banks that today form the ProCredit Group, a network of twenty-one microfinance institutions worldwide. They now serve more than 3 million microfinance clients. Incorporating private and public investors it is an out-standing example of a public-private partnership.

- In close cooperation with IFC, FMO and other partners, we facilitated the founding of several microfinance investment funds including the Global Microfinance Facility, Access Microfinance Holding, Acción Investments in Microfinance and Advans.

- As a landmark initiative, we have used structured finance techniques to create the European Fund for Southeast Europe (EFSE). This microfinance investment fund provides long-term financing and technical assistance to qualified financial institutions in Southeast Europe. These institutions provide credit to micro and small businesses, and housing loans to small salary earners. Investments by public and private players go hand-in-hand here.

- Last but not least, KfW has supported a number of securitisation transactions of microfinance portfolios. These enabled microfinance institutions to tap international capital markets. Institutions such as BRAC Bank or ProCredit Bank Bulgaria, for instance, are among those that participated and benefited – also stimulating the development of their domestic capital markets.

Recent developments in world financial markets following difficulties in the US mortgage market have demonstrated the importance of transparency and good governance for the stability of financial sectors. The German Federal Ministry of Economic Cooperation and Development and KfW put considerable emphasis on the institutional strengthening of the microfinance institutions we partner with. Furthermore, we support the development of an enabling environment in our part-ner countries to foster the development of transparent and stable, pro-poor finan-cial systems.

Partnerships for Innovation

"New Partnerships for Innovation in Microfinance" is more than a book title, it is a credo. Let me re-emphasise: Microfinance can reach its full potential only when several conditions converge. Microfinance institutions on the ground must be ready to increase outreach by offering new products in an economically sustain-able manner and by going beyond the client groups already served. We must con-vince the private sector looking for a double bottom line investment that it pays off in the long run to contribute capital and know-how to the microfinance sector. To attract and leverage private capital, public development finance institutions should contribute their risk-bearing capacity, country know-how, banking knowl-edge and political clout when private actors alone would not yet step forward to meet the challenges we face.

I am certain that this book will engage its readership and will stimulate discus-sions among microfinance practitioners as well as in academia. The theme of this book stems from the recognition that microfinance innovation and expansion requires three simple but essential ingredients:

- mobilising savings and managing risks,

- technologies that scale up outreach – especially in rural regions of Africa and Asia, and

- mobilising private capital through intelligent use of donor funds.

The chapters in this book are built on the results of a conference which KfW organised in cooperation with our colleagues from the German Federal Ministry for Economic Cooperation and Development (BMZ) together with our partners from the Agence Française de Développement (AFD), the U.K. Department for International Development (DFID), the Netherlands Development Finance Company (FMO) and especially our colleagues in the Consultative Group to Assist the Poor (CGAP). I would like to thank all of them for their contributions.

Special thanks are due to Wolfgang Kroh, Norbert Kloppenburg, Doris Köhn, Hanns-Peter Neuhoff and Klaus Glaubitt for their relentless promotion of microfinance and their enthusiasm for expanding the boundaries of financial sector development. As editor of this book I am grateful to Hanns Martin Hagen and Mark Schwiete for their efforts in developing the central concepts and themes and for engaging partners and sponsors for the conference and for the realisation of this publication. The organisation and logistics of the conference were superbly managed by Hanns Martin Hagen and his team: Jana Aberle, Tim Cao, Rosa Eckle, Lauren Day and Valerie Karplus. Tina Butterbach's outstanding organisational and managerial talents were invaluable throughout, from planning the conference through to her support in assembling the book's manuscript.

Each chapter in this book presents a fascinating perspective for microfinance development. Challenges and potential hindrances are outlined and promising solutions proposed.

We look forward to seeing many more partnerships in microfinance that foster innovation in products, technologies, financing and risk management. The potential demand that can be satisfied by innovative approaches is enormous.

Table of Contents

CHAPTER 1

New Partnerships for Sustainability and Outreach

J.D. von Pischke

President, Frontier Finance International, Inc.

Some Early Building Blocks in the Structure of Microfinance

Microfinance has developed steadily and rapidly over the last 20 years. Its antecedents include co-operative and community endeavours in the 19th century in Germany and elsewhere in Europe. Today these institutions and their offspring around the world continue to provide a very large volume of credit and other financial services to households and tiny businesses. These early inspirations are reflected in the objectives of microfinance, which include the use of credit and savings to create better lives for the poor and others of modest means, and a certain style of leadership and concern by activists and social entrepreneurs.

In other respects, comparison with this past is at best indirect. Microfinance became possible on a broad scale through a convergence of events. The most important was the liberalisation of financial markets in the 1980s and beyond (Shaw 1973, McKinnon 1973, WDR 1989). Of overwhelming importance, liberalisation made it possible to set interest at rates that cover the costs of dealing in finance at the frontier, providing a window for experimentation in the commercialisation that could ensure sustainability. Liberalisation also facilitated the emergence of new types of formal financial institutions dedicated to the bottom end of the market. The burdens of co-operatives that failed to operate on a commercial basis and the losses incurred by dysfunctional state-owned development or promotional banks in the great majority of countries around the world no longer had to be shouldered by those who wanted to provide financial services to people of modest means (Schmidt, Kropp 1987). Alternatives emerged.

Another positive factor was a new emphasis on helping the poor, especially the rural poor, most notably expressed by a change in policy at the World Bank in 1973. A third feature was a focus on women that energised many microfinance institutions and their supporters. Finally, the participation of bilateral and multilateral development co-operation and technical co-operation agencies, formed from the mid-1940s onward, became more effective and refined over time.

Successes in the early 1980s on the social front of microfinance in Bangladesh (Hossain 1988, Bornstein 1996) and on the commercial front in Indonesia (Robinson 1998 2001 2002) provided basic institutional models: respectively, the maximalist or "finance plus" and the minimalist or "finance only" schools that continue to contest. Shortly thereafter, officially-sponsored German efforts among others in Latin America helped to shape a concept that integrated microfinance into the larger world of finance: posed as a question, could microfinance supplied on a competitive, commercial basis make financial markets more efficient? (Schmidt, Zeitinger 1996 1998). If so, possibilities could quickly leap from frontiers to horizons. Enormous numbers of people around the globe could benefit from more efficient financial markets. Direct benefits would arise in the form of private goods for savers, borrowers and investors. More importantly, indirect benefits would create a social good in the form of more robust, productive institutions and better economic conditions that bubble up and also hopefully ooze down (Gonzalez-Vega 1998, WDR 1989).

Commercialisation as the Path to Sustainability

New services attracted new clients among the poor and others who had not had prior access to formal financial services. A breakthrough occurred when ACCION, a US-based NGO network active in Latin America, spun off part of its operations in Bolivia to form a specialised microfinance bank that got off to a dynamic start (Otero, Rhyne 1994). The commercialisation of microfinance became a fact, which imposed the discipline of sustainability. Public sector development agencies set the pace by providing funds, and remain the largest promoters of microfinance (Ivatury, Abrams 2006).

Large scale efforts have been made by donor-investors to downscale commercial banks. The goal is to modify banking infrastructure in order to serve new classes of clients at the bottom end of the market (Schmidt, Zeitinger 1996 1998). German co-operation has supported downscaling as part of its market-based strategy to work with different types of institutions in national markets, which creates competition and the opportunity to compare the performance of different institutional forms. Downscaling has had varying degrees of success – in a number of markets specialised microfinance banks have performed better – but recent results indicate scope for optimism (Wallace 2004).

Early in the new millennium a major microfinance network based in Germany, now known as ProCredit, had attracted a large share of the foreign funding invested in microfinance banks in developing countries and transition economies (Ivatury, Abrams 2006). Its strategy focuses on synergies produced by a readily replicable operational format structured as a public-private partnership (Schmidt, Moisa 2005). Its example encouraged other networks to do likewise.

The powerful vision of microfinance as mainstream finance fulfilled the dreams and passions of economists and political economists who, since the early 1970s, had advocated financial market liberalisation. One school of thought worked on implications for the macroeconomy (McKinnon 1973 1992, Fry 1988 1995). Another defined a commercial view of credit as a vehicle for development, beginning with research on the financing of small farms (von Pischke, Adams, Donald 1983; Adams, Graham, von Pischke 1984). Yet another developed the case for institution building (Krahnen, Schmidt 1994; Schmidt, Zeitinger 1998). In each context, the conclusion was that liberalisation would produce superior economic results that would improve welfare broadly. The literature grew rapidly, adding buoyancy and legitimacy to an exciting new movement or industry, depending upon the perspective. Development and technical co-operation agencies supported much of this research.

Principles and Lessons

These different approaches proved to be complementary, and a broad consensus emerged through the engagement of scholars, practitioners, and policy makers. Major realisations from this eclectic endeavour can be unambiguously summarised:

- *interest rates* matter in institution building – interest rates are high in inefficient financial markets and should be assaulted, most easily by introducing new, competitive institutions that lower costs.

- *transaction costs* are of critical importance in defining a market – relentless efforts to reduce these costs are required to enlist the poor as clients.

- *refining valuation processes* (that is, changing what lenders think they are lending against) creates exciting new paradigms – the poor will meet the conditions of appropriately structured loan contracts, and collateral recedes to being simply a collateral issue.

- *information and incentives* are of paramount importance in governance – attention to these two foundations of New Development Finance at every level of institution building is essential to growth and survival.

- *economies of scope and scale* can be achieved by networks with coherent business models, which are likely to attract public sector and private investors.

And, the poor can indeed benefit from it all. Empirical evidence assembled by KfW, the World Bank and many others indicates that better performing financial sectors are consistent with better performing economies. A deepening of financial sectors occurs when the financial sector grows faster than the rest of the economy. This benefits the poor. Research that included World Bank economists (Beck, Demirgüç-Kunt, Levine 2004) found that financial intermediary development (financial system development) reduces income inequality by *disproportionately* boosting the income of the poor, thereby reducing poverty while improving income distribution. More efficient economic systems lead to development, in part because the working poor can use finance wisely. Economic efficiency produces two effects: improved welfare directly from enterprise at the household level and through spread effects from greater activity in the community.

Microfinance Attracts New Friends

As microfinance became integrated into financial markets and into the larger world of services, new apex and peripheral supporters quickly appeared. The World Bank, a late starter in microfinance, enlisted official and private donors to form CGAP (Consultative Group to Assist the Poor), a co-ordinating body. Other network organisations appeared, producing an explosion of acronyms. Specialised training courses, a post-graduate degree course, seminars, symposia, conferences, rating agencies, regulators and others have become part of an effort to define and encourage best practice among microfinance institutions (MFIs) and networks.

Public sector investors became curious about new possibilities that would vault microfinance into capital markets, the pinnacle of the financial sector. Private investors, some with the dual objectives of financial return and development impact, quickly followed. It became clear that the future of microfinance would depend upon tapping private capital – because public sector finance is relatively scarce – although a catalytic role remains for official donor-investors. Private capital is increasingly forthcoming, with more than 50 microfinance investment funds (MFIFs) currently in operation. Some are network captives, others are structures designed independently by capital market pros.

New insights in understanding behaviour were also important. Commercial microfinance got a legitimising boost at the Frankfurt Seminars held from 1997 to 2001, which were organised by Frankfurt University and Ohio State University. These meetings attracted considerable attention, placing microfinance within the structure of the New Institutional Economics, which in Frankfurt inspired an offshoot called the New Development Finance. Each views human behaviour, in this case focusing on the effectiveness of institutions, as a function of information and incentives. In fact, institutions are viewed as bundles of incentives and bundles of information. The better the information and the clearer and more relevant the incentives, the greater the productivity that results. As competitive markets generate information and create incentives that increase productivity, inefficiencies are driven out. The New Development Finance provides a comprehensive format for examining and managing risk at all levels.

Further refinement in policy and in the exploration of issues resulted from the three annual KfW Financial Sector Symposia that began in 2002 in Berlin. The first focused on Southeast Europe, the second on EU accession, and the third on microfinance funding and the role of microfinance investment funds (MFIFs). This book records the fourth and largest in this series, held in Frankfurt in 2005. (Each of these meetings, hosted by KfW, had additional sponsors. Those supporting the 2005 Conference were AFD, BMZ, CGAP, DFID, FMO and Hewlett Packard.)

New partnerships, the theme of this book, expand the impact of microfinance even further. Our focus is overwhelmingly on microfinance on a commercial scale.

Three types of partnerships are examined, each consisting of a thematic part. Part I focuses on equity investments in microfinance, especially the possibilities for engaging private investors through innovative measures. Structures based on emerging market private equity funds are establishing microfinance equity as a new asset class that can be related to benchmarks, providing transparency that will make microfinance investment more attractive. Rating agencies are part of this process; development impact ratings are an interesting challenge for specialised microfinance rating agencies. The three topics of part I are:

- Raising MFI Equity through Microfinance Investment Funds

- Market Transparency: Benchmarking and Rating of MFIs

- MFIFs and MFI Equity: An Investment Opportunity for the Broader Public?

Part II focuses on collaboration among MFIs, governments, private investors and technology companies that help MFIs to integrate new technologies into their business models and practices, reducing costs and increasing outreach. Partners include international money transfer services and multinational IT firms providing cutting-edge technologies that cut costs and serve clients better. Traditional credit scoring models are being adapted to help MFIs reduce costs by avoiding risky clients and favouring reliable ones. Part II topics are:

- Cross-Border Ventures: Money Transfers and Remittances

- IT Innovations to Scale Up Outreach in Rural Microfinance

- Credit Scoring: The Next Microfinance Revolution?

Part III concentrates on how partnerships between microfinance institutions and commercial banks, pension funds and insurance companies can mobilise capital and manage risk in developing countries and transition economies. Specific topics include the debut of micro-pensions; the role and characteristics of savings for and by the poor, so that savings may be encouraged; and securitisation of microcredit portfolios so that refinancing could be widely distributed among insurance companies, pension funds and banks. Throughout, development of strategic partnerships and sophisticated financial instruments are examined to facilitate microlending and more complex products at the bottom end of the market. Part III topics explore:

- Micropensions: Old Age Security for the Poor?

- Microinsurance: Sustainable Risk Management for the Lower-Income Market?

- Securitisation: New Funding Opportunities for MFIs?

Drivers of Change

These themes are all about expanding the frontier of sustainable microfinance. What are the drivers that make it work and enable it to improve? Globalisation coupled with technology is certainly a driver. Information becomes cheaper and more valuable as communications improve, which in turn opens markets of all sorts, creating economies of scale and scope that make things easier and cheaper. These markets may be entirely new, in rural areas, and across all kinds of borders.

Increasing disaggregation of risk is sweeping through financial markets, making them more efficient. One result is that microfinance will increasingly obtain funds directly from capital markets, again reducing costs while expanding sources of funding. Efficient provision of debt, equity and contingent contracts at the wholesale level is increasingly important, although a continuum remains, driven by capital markets at one end and by subsidies at the other.

Institutional transformation is also important as a driver of progress through microfinance. Transformation occurs as microcredit becomes microfinance, which becomes microbanking, which in turn becomes microfinance risk management. In this progression, NGOs with a commercial outlook are transformed into banks, which become sustainable and expand their range of services. A parallel shift occurs in funding: from grants to short-term debt, to long-term debt, to equity, and to contingent and derivative contracts.

On a larger scale in financial markets, new structures emerge. For example, banks and insurance companies offer similar products that compete and overlap in the market. The complexity that this produces requires financial supervision, not simply banking and insurance oversight. As this process continues, as it surely will, global risk management systems are appearing on or are just over the horizon. Microfinance is part of this trend.

What Business Are We in?

The conference clearly confirms that our relationships, centred on microfinance, grow rapidly and in many directions simultaneously. This explosion of links or networking provides an opportunity to reassess the way in which we define ourselves. In other words, how should we answer the question, "what business are we in?"

Some observers would say that we are in the money business, but money is only a useful medium of exchange and not necessarily a dependable store of value. In fact, our core business is finance – a very special type of finance. The difference between money and finance is that finance has structure that permits it to have a tremendous capacity for good generally and for harm occasionally. The good (Gonzalez-Vega 1998):

- transfers purchasing power from low-return to higher-return activities – an important part of finance is the decision to say "No," to reject unremunerative transactions and relationships. Of course, the art of deciding when to say "Yes" is also important.

- improves inter-temporal choices and decisions governing savings, asset accumulation and investment – lengthening term structure along the normal yield curve suggests a better future.

- reduces costs of managing liquidity and of the accumulation of stores of value – facilitating transactions, accumulating usefully large lump sums and cushions against uncertainty, which increase choice and improve welfare.

- improves ways to deal with risk in economic activities – quantifying, pooling, assuming and shedding risk also increases choice and improves welfare by matching the capacities, strategies and preferences of different parties.

These characteristics are obvious to all of us who work within the structure of finance, but remain insufficiently understood outside our circle. Given this, what business are we in? Microfinance and poverty alleviation are parts of a single formula. But we comprise a special category that transcends poverty alleviation, as finance transcends money. And, we should be able to hold ourselves to a higher, more precisely defined standard that is more amenable to measurement and also directly related to our contribution.

From this perspective, our business is the creation of wealth, especially and precisely creating wealth where there is little wealth (Kloppenburg 2006). Wealth creation is made possible through the structure of finance. We should promote wealth creation as empowerment among the poor, as a positive, uplifting construct.

Why should we define ourselves and our objectives in this way?

- We are proficient at creating wealth, defined as the accumulation of productive assets. (Wealth may in some degree be measured in terms of money, but should not be confused with money.)

- We help to create wealth more broadly by expanding the volume of remunerative transactions made possible by the structure of finance at the small end of the market.

- The poor benefit – increasingly.

- The process of wealth creation – described as enterprise – can go on forever.

At the same time, we need to do a little work on our vocabulary. We need to discard the word "need," as in "credit needs," "capital needs," or in "meeting needs." Needs convey no information useful to finance, such as the ability or willingness to repay a loan, prospects for remunerative transactions, or the management of risk. Need, at worst, is a con-man's pitch or a political contrivance. Need is infinite, a bottomless pit: when all financial needs are met, the financial sector will have been destroyed by defaults and wasted resources.

The real drivers of wealth creation are expressed by terms such as "potential," "innovation" and "opportunity." These are also infinite, with the sky as the limit. In our passion to create wealth in places where there is little wealth, we should use terms with positive, functional connotations. Finance, being based on trust and confidence, is an intensely probing, profoundly optimistic business.

Reconsideration of Mission Drift and Other Opportunities

As microfinance finds more ways to be useful, further opportunities arise. Finance is flexible, and how can we ensure that we remain focused on the poor? Three types of institutional strategies can be identified that relate to our fidelity in cultivating the poor as a target group. The first of these is *mission stability*, which consists of the continued provision of a limited range of services to the poor.

Mission enhancement is the second possibility. New services are offered, new target groups are engaged, while the original target group continues to be served – often better. Mission enhancement is consistent with the objective of serving those who have not had prior access to formal finance, or who have not had access to specific financial instruments or products. These additional opportunities are numerous and include small businesses and professionals as clients, payments and savings facilities as services, and risk management tools such as insurance. This strategy is consistent with the mission of making financial sectors more efficient by continuing to engage those beyond the frontier of formal finance, such as women microentrepreneurs, and by catering to others not well served by mainstream finance, such as small businesses.

Mission drift is the third possibility: the institution that once served the poor moves up-market, abandoning the poor. This occurs most dramatically with a change in the ownership of an institution, but it can also happen slowly, by creeping out of the small end of the market.

The important point is that mission enhancement should not be confused with mission drift. Enhancement is not drift – it is outreach and it is development. Most of us are working hard on enhancement in our own competitive self-interest. As a result, financial sectors become more efficient as indicated by finer spreads, lower risk premia, new products, lower transaction costs, more participants, and service to an expanded array of clients. Accordingly, this expanded, three-part paradigm should be applied in the evaluation of service to any specific target group. Mission stability is unlikely to be a viable business strategy except in very small scale operations or in sluggish or stagnant markets.

Micro-savings and Micro-pensions: A Cautionary Note

Risk management assumes greater importance as the term structure of contracts lengthens. Micro-insurance and even micro-pensions are increasingly available to the poor, and these extremely important financial services can promote welfare generally while diminishing anxiety at the household level. However, the long time periods over which these instruments are outstanding are not without challenges.

The most intractable is the protection of value, which requires close scrutiny. Does it pay to save over the long-term, especially in the form of pensions, which may have a time horizon of 35 years or more? Two simple tests apply: What would 100 deposited in a savings vehicle in 1971 be worth in 2006? What would 100 deposited in a savings vehicle annually since 1971 be worth in 2006?

Anecdotal evidence suggests that local currency values have collapsed in a number of countries since 1971 because of factors such as macroeconomic shocks, war, and opportunistic governance. That old vintage, large denomination banknote that was once someone's life savings may not even buy lunch today. In some affected countries those who saved in financial form may have been left worse off by movements in interest rates and in consumer prices. When this risk occurs, saving is discouraged. These forces retard the emergence of a middle class that can look forward to a reasonably secure old age, and of a peasant or working class that can send its children to school rather than committing them to the labour force before they reach puberty. Encouraging savings should therefore be undertaken with some caution.

A useful research priority that would address this concern consists of testing the historical durability of long-term financial contracts in domestic currencies in poor countries over periods of 35 or more years. Financial statistics produced by the IMF provide a useful base for research. If analysis indicates that this problem occurs frequently, is of significant magnitude, or is concentrated in certain regions or groups of countries, remedial efforts may be in order. One response to the threat posed by currency collapses would be a global facility to protect the value of long-term savings in financial form, denominated in local currency, and accumulated by the poor and middle classes in non-OECD countries.

Of course, this protection should not be extended to cover the idiosyncratic failure of local banks or savings institutions because that is a local supervisory matter and because of moral hazard. If the idiosyncratic failure of local financial institutions that collect long-term savings is a significant problem, alternatives should also be considered.

Outlook

Our business is to innovate in ways that make it possible for the poor to create wealth. Our conference is a testimony to this effort, as suggested by the synergies of the three thematic pillars. We shall surely succeed. Our pace will be determined by market and non-market forces that propel and restrain innovation in finance. (Those who do not understand the difference between money and finance are unlikely to be enthusiastic partners. We should engage them.)

Finance innovates in three ways: reducing transaction costs, lengthening term structures and refining valuation processes. The nature of the challenges posed by these three ways and the social benefits they produce deserves explanation:

- Reducing transaction costs – the admission tickets to financial markets – is the first mode of innovation in finance. At the retail level these costs include the transaction costs of savers, intermediaries and borrowers. These costs are often major constraints at the small end of the market. However, they can be dealt with in a number of ways. For example, highly successful co-operatives and group credit arrangements may pass many of these costs on to borrowers, who in fact believe that these costs are benefits – benefits from being involved in new activities that make a difference in their lives. Commercial financial institutions probing the frontier may attract clients by assuming greater costs, but in ways that lower clients' costs relative to the next best alternative, which is often informal finance. This formula relies on market-based pricing and economies of scale and scope that make it possible for formal institutions to cover the greater costs of dealing at the bottom end of the market. Transaction costs play a large role in defining financial market segments.

- The second way in which financial markets innovate is by lengthening term structure.[1] Longer term structures denote confidence and produce accumulations of long-term funds that can be applied to useful projects of all sorts that take a long time to generate income. (To borrow from Stuart Rutherford (2000), a long normal yield curve is society's "usefully large lump sum.") Lengthening term structure is the most difficult mode of innovation because finance is delicately tuned to, and often has little power over, the larger determinants of term structure – confidence, moods and how society generally views the future. Information and incentives have a large role to play. But when crises occur and term structure collapses, finance is often blamed, sometimes rightly so. However, term structures lengthen as confidence grows, assisted by good contracts that protect creditors' rights, and when projected rates of inflation are stable. Microfinance investment funds lengthen term structures in microfinance.

These two forms of financial innovation are well-trod paths – the new quickly becomes routine and sometimes boring, but always important. The third is of a different order with transcendental features that are created by what sellers of financial contracts think they are buying.

---

[1] Loosely put, term structure is defined by the most distant maturities available oncredit-instruments, and by the volume of credit and the interest rates prevailingondifferent maturities, from the present into the future. Term structure isusually plottedfor government securities on a yield curve that is normally steeper in theverynearterm and relatively flat in the long term.

- The third way in which finance innovates is by refining valuation processes – which are determined by views of risk. Finance creates value by pricing contracts, based on estimations of risk and confidence. When the foundation of this process changes with better information and constructive incentives, opportunities arise for introducing new ways of managing and quantifying risk. How else did Muhammad Yunus make it possible through Grameen Bank to monetise the promises of very poor women who had never before held a coin or banknote in their hand? Broad leaps occur as valuation processes are refined. In credit markets the key variable is "what are you lending against?" In equity markets the question is "what are you buying?" In contingent contract markets the concern is "what is being guaranteed?" Credit scoring, explored in this volume, is a dramatic example of a refinement of valuation in credit markets.

These three modes of innovation in finance will be used relentlessly to do what finance can do, which is to transfer purchasing power from lower yielding to higher yielding activities; to expand, across time, the range of choices governing savings, asset accumulation and investment; and to improve risk management in economic activities. An important example is the increasing involvement in microfinance by venture capital/private equity investors, and from other segments of capital markets. A related trend is based on a proliferation of support systems that include technology, information and risk management systems, funding/refinancing vehicles, fiduciary norms and institutions, ratings, and credit scoring.

Microfinance will continue to be driven by donors and public sector investors, but less so as integration into capital markets gathers steam. Donors and public sector investors continue to play an essential role in attracting private investors to microfinance through financial engineering, by pioneering new products, by promoting competition, by bolstering confidence through support for supervision and regulation, and by using their influence to reduce predation and corruption that stymies innovation in difficult markets. An exciting challenge that is receiving greatly increased interest is exit. How will donors reap their well-earned gains on their microfinance investments in ways that do not destabilise microfinance institutions or weaken their mission? It seems reasonable to predict a smooth landing for efficient institutions.

In summary, our innovative task is:

- To create wealth where there is little wealth by using finance to facilitate productive activities at the bottom end of the market. Mission enhancement is essential for the realisation of this objective.

- To create institutions that are structured to generate the information and the incentives to drive inefficiencies out of financial markets so that more people can be served with a greater choice of deals at better prices.

- And, if justified by research results, to consider the feasibility of a global long-term savings guarantee mechanism that would to some degree protect poor people in non-OECD countries who save in instruments denominated in local currency. How might it be possible to insulate them from macroeconomic shocks or trends that unwind their efforts to save over their lifetimes so that they could realise their dream of a more secure future?

References

Adams, D.W, D.H. Graham and J.D. Von Pischke, eds. (1984) *Undermining Rural Development with Cheap Credit*. Boulder CO: Westview Press.

Beck, T., A. Demirgüç-Kunt and R. Levine (2004) "Finance, Inequality, and Poverty: Cross-Country Evidence." Working Paper 10979, National Bureau of Economic Research, Cambridge MA.

Bornstein, D. (1996) *The Price of a Dream: The Story of the Grameen Bank and the Idea that is Helping the Poor to Change their Lives*. New York: Simon & Schuster.

Fry, M.J. (1988, 1995) *Money, Interest, and Banking in Economic Development*. Baltimore and London: The Johns Hopkins University Press.

Gonzalez-Vega, C. (1998) "Do Financial Institutions Have a Role in Assisting the Poor?" in Kimenyi, M.S., R.C. Wieland and J.D. Von Pischke, eds., in *Strategic Issues in Microfinance.* Brookfield VT: Ashgate.

Hossain, M. (1988) "Credit for Alleviation of Rural Poverty: The Grameen Bank in Bangladesh," Research Report 65. Washington DC: International Food Policy Research Institute.

Ivatury, G. and J. Abrams (2006) "The Market for Microfinance Foreign Investment: Opportunities and Challenges," in I. Matthäus-Maier and J.D. von Pischke, eds., *Microfinance Investment Funds – Leveraging Private Capital for Economic Growth and Poverty Reduction.* Berlin: Springer.

Kloppenburg, N. (2006) "Microfinance Investment Funds: Where Wealth Creation Meets Poverty Reduction" in I. Matthäus-Maier and J.D. von Pischke, eds., *Microfinance Investment Funds – Leveraging Private Capital for Economic Growth and Poverty Reduction.* Berlin: Springer.

Krahnen, J.P. and R.H. Schmidt (1994) *Development Finance as Institution Building: A New Approach to Poverty-Oriented Banking*. Boulder CO: Westview Press.

McKinnon, R.I. (1973) *Money and Capital in Economic Development*. Washington DC: The Brookings Institution.

McKinnon, R.I. (1992) *The Order of Economic Liberalization: Financial Control in the Transition to a Market Economy*. Baltimore and London: The Johns Hopkins University Press.

Otero, M. and E. Rhyne (1994) The New World of Microenterprise Finance: Building Healthy Financial Institutions for the Poor. West Hartford CT: Kumarian.

Robinson, M.S. (1998) "Microfinance: The Paradigm Shift from Credit Delivery to Sustainable Financial Intermediation" in Kimenyi, M.S., R.C. Wieland and J.D. Von Pischke, eds., in *Strategic Issues in Microfinance*. Brookfield VT: Ashgate.

Robinson, M.S. (2001) *The Microfinance Revolution: Sustainable Finance for the Poor* (Vol. I). Washington DC: The World Bank.

Robinson, M.S. (2002) *The Microfinance Revolution: Lessons from Indonesia* (Vol. II). Washington DC: The World Bank.

Rutherford, S. (2000) *The Poor and Their Money*. Delhi: DFID.

Schmidt, R.H. and E. Kropp (1987) *Rural Finance: Guiding Principles*. Eschborn: BMZ, GTZ, DSE.

Schmidt, R. and N. Moisa (2005) "Public-Private Partnerships for Financial Development in Southeast Europe," in I. Matthäus-Maier and J.D. von Pischke, eds., *EU Accession – Financial Sector Opportunities and Challenges for Southeast Europe*. Berlin: Springer.

Schmidt, R.H. and C.-P. Zeitinger (1996) "The Efficiency of Credit-Granting NGOs in Latin America," in *Savings and Development*. Vol. 20.

Schmidt, R.H. and C.-P. Zeitinger (1998) "Critical Issues in Microbusiness Finance and the Role of Donors," in Kimenyi, M.S., R.C. Wieland and J.D. Von Pischke, eds., in *Strategic Issues in Microfinance*. Brookfield VT: Ashgate.

Shaw, E.S. (1973) *Financial Deepening in Economic Development*. New York: Oxford University Press.

Von Pischke, J.D., D.W Adams and G. Donald, eds. (1983) *Rural Financial Markets in Developing Countries*. Baltimore and London: The Johns Hopkins University Press.

Wallace, E. (2004) "EBRD's Micro and Small Enterprise Lending Programmes: Downscaling Commercial Banks and Starting Greenfield Banks," in I. Matthäus-Maier and J.D. von Pischke, eds., *The Development of the Financial Sector in Southeast Europe: Innovative Approaches in Volatile Environments*. Berlin: Springer.

WDR (1989) *World Development Report*. New York, Oxford University Press for The World Bank.

PART I:

Partnerships to Leverage Private Investment

Introduction to Part I

Part I of this book focuses on the role of private investment and the benefits it can offer in the promotion of sustainable microfinance. This theme is tremendously important – especially to sponsors such as KfW – because the volume of private funds is greatly larger than public funding. This implies that an important role of public funding is as a catalyst at the frontier, experimenting with new concepts and ideas that will attract private capital.

Patrick Goodman's contribution in Chapter 2 continues the theme he pioneered in the 2004 Berlin Symposium. His earlier piece was contributed to *Microfinance Investment Funds: Leveraging Private Capital for Economic Growth and Poverty Reduction*, by the same editors and publisher as this volume. Goodman's theme at the 2005 conference was the role of investment funds that invest all or part of their assets in the equity of MFIs (microfinance institutions). As of 2005, 23 funds had contributed a total of USD 725 million in equity to MFIs. These funds had a range of motives and investment styles, from the developmental to the fully commercial. Goodman notes that most MFIs are under-leveraged, offering possibilities for growth in equity participation. Valuation and exit issues are explored, as are the motives, objectives and expectations of different types of investors.

Sanjay Sinha is an entrepreneur in the field of microfinance ratings. He explains in Chapter 3 the importance of rating as a means of providing information that can attract investors. The newness and novelty of microfinance deter many investors and investment companies from participating in microfinance equity. Ratings can provide comfort and assurance, but only if the ratings are credible. Specialised microfinance raters seek to provide this credibility. Three market leaders have emerged, using similar procedures. Innovations in rating processes include calculations of MFI debt capacity – specific amounts of new investment that an MFI could comfortably handle – plus specific recommendations to the management of rated institutions. Competition with mainstream raters, or more broadly the advantages and disadvantages of specialised raters by potential users, remain as challenges. Social ratings – fiduciary ratings of social investment funds -- by specialised microfinance ratings agencies are on the horizon.

Microfinance will reach its potential only when it becomes an asset class that attracts mainstream investors. In Chapter 4 Kylie Charlton explores the potential role of equity investment by the broader investing public. Private equity (venture capital) is taking an interest in microfinance, which implies that investors could or will provide strategic direction, and that the exit of these investors is to be expected. More investors are expected to be attracted because of the rapid growth of microfinance as a vehicle for financial returns as well as for social or environmental ends. Their numbers can be accelerated by better matching of investment goals with investor goals, and by fiscal dispensations or incentives.

K.V. Kamath in Chapter 5 reflects on insights from India concerning the relationships between microfinance and economic growth. He contrasts the types of services that are required for mainstream financial institutions to gain access to the poor. A multitude of very small transactions challenges the attitudes, traditions and systems commonly associated with mainstream banking. Simply opening branches in rural areas is not sufficient. Financial innovation is required. Linkages of microfinance institutions with mainstream finance are being used in India, with incentives in the form of risk sharing and provision of wholesale funds for successful providers at the grass roots. These new instruments and structures create opportunities for both microfinance and traditional commercial finance, contributing to development.

Mark Schwiete and Jana Hoessel Aberle deal with an issue of strategic importance in Chapter 6. They explore the valuation processes that can be used to determine the value of MFI equity or of MFIs themselves. For a number of reasons MFIs are hard to price. IFRS (International Financial Reporting Standards) is their reference point and ascertaining "fair value" is their quest. Many considerations are required to determine fair value, but alternatives exist – at the level of definitions as well as at the technical level that arrives at a fair price. Through a process of elimination they conclude that "value at cost" is the most transparent and reliable way of measuring MFI value.

CHAPTER 2:

Raising MFI Equity Through Microfinance Investment Funds

Patrick Goodman

Consultant

Introduction

Microfinance institutions (MFIs) are increasingly addressing the traditional financial market to fund their continued growth and to better serve their clients. In its early days, the microfinance sector was essentially driven by non-profit organisations and official development agencies. Over the last few years, these institutions, together with a few new entrants in the sector, have set up an increasing number of investment structures to fund MFIs.

Common usage in the microfinance industry is "microfinance investment fund" as the generic term to identify all corporate investment structures (such as holding companies for example) which have been set up to provide equity and/or debt financing to MFIs, with investors acting as shareholders or as lenders.[1]

This paper builds upon a study prepared by the author on microfinance investment funds (MFIFs) for the 2004 KfW Financial Sector Development Symposium held in Berlin in November 2004. This initial study presented an overview of microfinance investment funds with their main features and characteristics. This paper focuses on those investment funds which invest all or a part of their assets in the equity capital of MFIs.

A number of investment structures were initially created as vehicles to provide funding to development initiatives, such as MFIs. Oikocredit was for example established in the Netherlands in 1975 to make development-oriented investments in church-related institutions. It was only in the mid-1990s that the first commercially focused investment structures emerged, targeting MFIs such as Profund, launched in 1995. The original promoters of these investment vehicles were development agencies and non-profit organisations. All these initiatives had a com-

---

[1] Donor institutions such as foundations and NGOs would not qualify as structures set up for an investment purpose. Development agencies are also not considered as investment funds as their structure and mission extend far beyond those of such vehicles.

mon goal: to increase the development impact by investing collectively in a diversified pool of MFIs. This approach afforded clear advantages to these development investors, notably the sharing of costs and experience.

Today the investors in these funds are still mainly the original participants in the microfinance industry: non-profit organisations and development agencies. Institutional investors such as pension funds and insurance companies remain largely absent while private individuals have shown some interest, but this is still quite limited.

Recently, though, an increasing number of MFIFs are being set up to mobilise the traditional capital markets, clearly targeted to these commercial investors. It is interesting to note that the most commercially oriented investment funds invest almost exclusively in debt instruments of MFIs, whereas the funds promoted by development-oriented institutions have a greater mix of investments with equity as well as debt products.

Microfinance Investment Funds' Status in 2005

In mid-2005 there were 23 investment funds that provided equity to MFIs.[2] As Table 1 shows, their total assets amounted to € 536 million (or $725 million at the relevant exchange rate for each fund at the time of the survey).

Many of these funds do not invest exclusively in MFIs but also provide equity and debt to others such as trade finance organisations. To have a better picture of the actual investments of these microfinance investment funds into MFIs, non-microfinance assets such as trade finance and other investments, and cash positions have also been excluded. On this basis, the total microfinance portfolio of these investment funds amounted to € 262 million (or $ 355 million) of which € 132 million ($ 179 million) was invested in equity participations of MFIs. Concentration is very high: 44% of the total equity provided by these funds originate from a single structure: ProCredit Holding.

Table 1. Investments of the 23 microfinance investment funds investing in equity

Total assets	€ 536 million	$ 725 million
Total investments in microfinance	€ 262 million	$ 355 million
Investments in equity	€ 132 million	$ 179 million

---

[2] Based on surveys conducted for the KfW Financial Sector Development Symposium organised in November 2004 (Goodman 2005), there were 38 microfinance investment funds providing equity, loans and guarantees to MFIs.

An element to consider when analysing these numbers is the unclear border between microfinance and small business lending. An increasing number of MFIs are up-scaling their lending operations to small and medium-sized enterprises (SMEs). Traditional SME banks are also starting to provide microfinance services, while some microfinance investment funds are also funding financial institutions focusing on SMEs. In most cases these amounts are classified as part of the microfinance portfolio.

In addition to the 23 MFIFs, two funds invest almost exclusively in other microfinance funds: Oikocredit Nederland Fonds and Gray Ghost Microfinance Fund. They indirectly participate in the equity financing of MFIs and thus their investments are already taken into account in the 23 funds. They are mentioned here because they channel funds from private investors to MFIs and actively participate in increasing private investors' awareness and understanding of microfinance.

The full list of all these microfinance investment funds can be found in Appendix 1 together with their main characteristics such as total assets and investments in microfinance equity, debt and guarantees.

The Three Main Types of Microfinance Investment Funds

There is a very wide diversity of investment structures targeting MFIs. A key differentiating factor is the balance between the social returns of these vehicles and their financial returns. Three broad categories of microfinance investment funds can be identified based on the following criteria:

- Targeted MFIs and the terms offered

- Products proposed to the MFIs

- Shareholder structure, targeted investors and the returns offered

- Structure and objectives of the vehicle

- Role of the investment fund in the governance of the invested MFIs

- Availability and form of technical assistance (TA)

The three categories identified are the following:

- Microfinance development funds

- Quasi-commercial microfinance investment funds

- Commercial microfinance investment funds

The following Table 2 and Figure 1 summarise the total assets and the total amount of MFIs' equity for each of these three categories:

Table 2. Assets and MFI equity portfolio by category of microfinance investment funds[3]

	Microfinance Development Funds	Quasi-commercial Microfinance Inv Funds	Commercial Microfinance Inv Funds	Total
Total Assets ($ million)	460	215	51	725
% of Total	63%	30%	7%	100%
Total Equity in MFIs ($ million)	62	115	3	179
% of Total	34%	64%	1.5%	100%
Number of funds per category	12	7	4	23

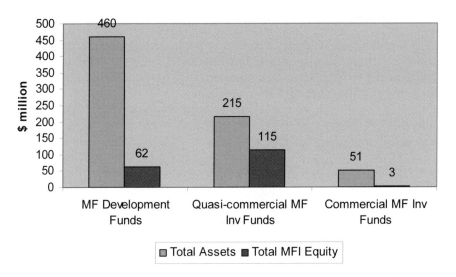

Fig. 1. Assets and MFI equity portfolio by category of microfinance investment funds

---

[3]   Based on surveys conducted between March and June 2005.

Microfinance Development Funds

These were the first structures set up to fund MFIs. They typically put more emphasis on development aspects than on financial return. Their objective is indeed usually to make capital available to MFIs through sustainable mechanisms that support their development and growth without necessarily seeking to maximise the financial return.

As shown in Table 2 above, these funds constitute the largest portion of the total assets (63%) of all the MFIFs but have a significantly lower share of these funds' total equity portfolio (34%). This category of funds has a widely diversified portfolio, not only between equity and debt investments but also in their funding of fair trade organisations and other investments. The investors in these structures essentially seek a social return with the protection of the real inflation-adjusted value of their original capital. This objective usually translates into favourable terms to the MFIs, typically below market conditions. The MFIs targeted are also usually not the most profitable nor the most mature. Such a structure offers a very good fit between investors willing to accept a lower financial return on their investment and the MFIs which benefit from these favourable conditions.

Oikocredit is a very good example of this approach. It is one of the oldest and it is also the largest MFIF, with total assets of € 245 million and € 8.5 million of equity investments in MFIs at the end of 2004. It is also one of the largest investment fund providers of microfinance equity originating from private capital. Most of its shareholders are private individuals and church-related institutions. Oikocredit[4] is well known in the microfinance industry for its wide outreach to less mature MFIs on favourable conditions. It also makes local currency loans[5] which are in high demand by MFIs.

Some microfinance development funds, usually non-profit organisations, are restricted to a limited number of shareholders, sometimes to only one investor. The purpose of several of these funds, also called "funds with a network approach",[6] is to invest in a group of MFIs, usually providing equity only, and to participate actively in the management and the governance of the MFIs in which they invest. Examples are the Accion Gateway Fund and Opportunity Transformation Investments, both fully owned by their mother NGO. Other structures dedicated to essentially one investor are two Desjardins funds, and the Hivos-Triodos and Triodos-Doen Foundations. These latter two funds have relatively widely diversified investments and are not dedicated to a specific network of MFIs.

---

[4] Oikocredit Nederland Fonds, targeted at private individuals, is essentially a microfinance development fund but is not listed here because it invests around 90% of its assets in Oikocredit shares. Including its assets would result in double counting.

[5] These loans represent approximately 20% of Oikocredit's total approved portfolio: Oikocredit Financial Statements 2004 available on www.oikocredit.org.

[6] Köhn and Jainzik (2005), p328.

Microfinance development funds often provide and finance technical assistance from their own resources. This is a cost to these funds that limits the financial return to their shareholders, but this is acceptable given their overall philosophy.

The following microfinance investment funds investing in equity can be classified as microfinance development funds:

- Accion Gateway Fund
- Alterfin
- Développement Int'l Desjardins – Partnership Fund
- Dvt Int'l Desjardins – FONIDI Fund
- Hivos-Triodos Foundation
- Incofin

- Kolibri Kapital ASA
- Oikocredit
- Opportunity Transformation Investments (OTI)
- Sarona Global Investment Fund
- SIDI
- Triodos-Doen Foundation

Quasi-commercial Microfinance Investment Funds

The microfinance equity funds which can be classified as quasi-commercial microfinance investment funds as of mid-June 2005 are:

- Accion Investments in Microfinance
- Africap
- Investisseur et Partenaire pour le Développement

- La Fayette Participations
- ProCredit Holding
- Profund
- ShoreCap International

Three other quasi-commercial microfinance investment funds have been launched since the surveys were conducted for this paper:

- Balkan Financial Sector Equity Fund (launched in December 2005)
- La Fayette Investissement (launched in August 2005)
- MicroCred (launched in July 2005)

These investment funds (called "commercially-oriented microfinance investment funds" in a previous study[7]) have had a considerable impact on the development of microfinance. Funds in this category have clearly stated financial objectives including returns larger than those in the previous category. They nevertheless have

---

[7]   Goodman (2005).

a clear development mission and the determination to pursue it. They are usually not actively distributed to new investors, unlike the more commercially oriented investment funds. These funds are essentially owned by development finance institutions, NGOs or by other institutions close to the development world. In many cases, a few private investors have joined these funds, motivated by the presence and the experience of these development finance institutions.

In general these funds tend to be very equity-focused. Table 2 and Figure 1 show that although their total assets are smaller than those of the microfinance developments funds, their equity portfolio represents 64% of the total equity of the 23 microfinance equity funds. 53% of their assets consist of equity investments. Investment in debt instruments is undertaken for two main reasons: either the investment fund provides loans (usually on a long-term basis) to the institutions in which it has equity stakes or loans are provided in anticipation of a future participation in the MFI's capital. This is the case for Africap: a convertible debenture constitutes 20% of its disbursed portfolio.

Profund was the first microfinance equity fund. It was launched in 1995 with a 10-year life. Bilateral and multilateral organisations[8] owned 76% of its capital. 16% were held by NGOs and 8% by private investors. It invested in what became the success stories of microfinance (Compartamos, BancoSol, MiBanco, etc.) but, as is common for such funds, losses were incurred on some other investments.[9] Overall it demonstrated that it is possible to invest in the capital of MFIs and make a decent return on investment. Profund is expected to have an annualised internal rate of return of between 6 and 7%[10] by the time all the expected receivables have been collected. The exit strategy is key to ensuring that potential capital gains are transformed into realised gains for the original investors.

The development finance institutions (DFIs) have to strike a difficult balance. They are criticised by a number of microfinance professionals for excessively favouring mature MFIs and for not providing enough funding to less mature MFIs. But they also have a role as promoters and participants in investment vehicles through which commercial investors can learn about the business of microfinance.

Private investors are increasingly interested in the business potential of banks focusing on micro, small and medium enterprises. Recent evidence is the share purchase agreement signed on 21 April 2005 which transferred the majority of the shares of the Russian Small Business Credit Bank, KMB, to Banca Intesa, a large Italian bank.[11] The DFIs involved (DEG and EBRD) successfully transferred to

---

[8]   www.profundinternacional.com – shareholder structure.

[9]   Silva (2005).

[10]   According to Alejandro Silva, Profund.

[11]   The shareholders that sold their shares are Triodos-Doen Foundation, Soros Economic Development Fund and DEG, a member of the KfW banking group. The European Bank for Reconstruction and Development (EBRD) retained a 25% plus 1 share ownership of KMB with a put-call option exercisable from 2010.

the private sector the bank which they launched and supported. In a similar manner, quasi-commercial MFIFs can facilitate the transition of ownership of MFIs from NGOs and development actors to the commercial sector.

Attracting private investors to microfinance through investment funds started only recently. For example, three recently launched investment structures promoted by development actors (Africap, AIM and ShoreCap International) and essentially targeting equity investments have almost 88% of their equity originating from NGOs, foundations and official development finance institutions (DFIs). The remaining only about 12% of fund capital invested originates from private investors, including ShoreBank (the promoter of ShoreCap International describes itself as a community development bank). As these three funds invest primarily, at least for the time being, in mature institutions, a larger participation by private investors could have been expected. One of the few truly traditional commercial investors to venture into microfinance, ABN Amro, is a shareholder of ShoreCap International. By participating in such a collective investment scheme, this Dutch bank is learning about microfinance while sharing the risks and opportunities with other, more knowledgeable players in this field.

The percentage of private capital in this kind of fund has grown since Profund was launched. It is a question of time before (1) the amounts committed by the current investors are placed, and (2) additional, probably more commercial, investors are sought. (The valuation of investment funds when new investors enter will be explored in a later section.)

ProCredit Holding is an example of a successful public-private partnership (PPP) in which both the private and the public sector play sizeable roles.[12] It is 59% owned by private capital.[13] This includes 29.5% owned by the founding members of ProCredit Holding – IPC and IPC Invest – while a further 27.4% is held by Doen Foundation and by an NGO, Fundasal. Little capital has been forthcoming from commercial sources outside these investors close to the world of microfinance, and has not been necessary so far: 2.2% of the total equity is owned by the responsAbility Global Microfinance Fund, a Luxembourg-based commercial microfinance investment fund, and by Andromeda, a private equity fund that also invests in AIM.

Not only is ProCredit Holding a true PPP, but it has also attracted a sizeable commercial investor, Commerzbank, to co-invest in a number of MFIs in the Pro-Credit Group. This experience shows that if an investment is properly structured

---

[12] Schmidt and Moisa (2005) and Alexander (2005).

[13] www.procredit-holding.com – shareholder structure as of 15th April 2005. The remaining capital (41%) is held by five DFIs: BIO, DEG, IFC, FMO and KfW. In mid-June 2005, ProCredit Holding was in the process of acquiring the shares of IFC, FMO, DEG and KfW in the various ProCredit Banks. At the end of this process, these DFIs will only own shares of ProCredit Holding (conversation with Helen Alexander, ProCredit Holding – 27 May 2005).

and managed, there is interest not only from the public sector but also from the private sector.

Further evidence of this interest is shown by Ivatury and Abrams (2004).[14] Their study shows that the 18 ProCredit institutions at the time of their research had received 60% of the total equity invested by public investors (defined in their study as nine investment arms of bi- and multilateral development agencies) and 58% of the total equity invested by private funds (defined as 45 privately managed investment funds and foundations). Ivatury and Abrams also point out a high concentration of DFIs in the funding of the ProCredit Group, either directly or through investment funds. The reason lies in the very high funding needs of the Group which the private sector is not yet willing to meet.

As more commercial investors become interested in microfinance, DFIs will quite probably move towards less mature MFIs. This is demonstrated by a new investment fund which was launched in August 2005 in Luxembourg as a SICAR (venture capital investment company) with an unlimited duration. The aim of La Fayette Investissement (LFI) is to invest a controlling interest in the creation of new MFIs, primarily in Africa and Asia. LFI may also participate in the equity of MFIs transforming from a non-profit or a mutual status to a joint stock company. The initial investors were Horus Development Finance in France and its existing investment company, La Fayette Participations (LFP), which was founded to invest in existing MFIs or in start-ups. Five DFIs[15] have joined these investors in establishing this new venture capital company with € 14.1 million of committed capital, to be drawn down over five years.

In this structure, the DFIs play their role fully as financiers of greenfield or transforming MFIs, which they also did at the beginning of the ProCredit[16] venture. The challenging task for the DFIs is to find the right balance between exiting a financially sustainable institution in order to finance the next generation of MFIs and staying on board to ensure that the institution maintains the development mission it was intended to pursue.

Two new quasi-commercial microfinance investment funds were launched shortly after the 2005 Financial Sector Development Conference (Frankfurt, June 2005). Each one targets a combination of development-oriented investors such as DFIs, socially responsible investors and commercial investors. The first is the Balkan Financial Sector Equity Fund promoted by Oikocredit and Opportunity International. It was launched in December 2005 and has raised about € 25 million. It aims to collect a further € 25 million in additional commitments. This fund's objective is to invest in the equity of MFIs in the wider Balkan region.

The second fund, MicroCred, was launched in July 2005 and is promoted by PlaNet Finance. It expects to raise € 31.5 million. It will invest in equity participa-

---

[14] Ivatury and Abrams (2004).

[15] AfD, EIB, FMO, IFC and KfW.

[16] ProCredit Holding was formerly IMI AG.

tions. Half of its assets will be in Africa. Technical assistance may be provided by PlaNet Finance to the MFIs funded.

In fact, virtually all quasi-commercial investment funds have some form of TA attached. In a few cases it is provided by the fund. For instance, I&P pour le Développement provides tailor-made assistance on financial planning and strategy. TA can also be provided by an entity specifically set up by a donor to assist MFIs in capacity building. For example ShoreCap International is supported by ShoreCap Exchange, a US-based NGO, and Africap is assisted by a grant facility, the Technical Services Facility. TA can also be provided directly by development-oriented investors in the fund or by related donor agencies. This is probably one of the key differences between the commercial microfinance investment funds, discussed below, which operate without TA, or at least without TA connected to the fund or its investors.

Commercial Microfinance Investment Funds

These funds are new, they are the most commercial and they are the most heterogeneous of the three categories. They also are by far the smallest: with only 7% of the total assets of microfinance investment funds investing in equity, they represent only 1.5% of these funds' equity portfolio, as shown in Table 2. The main distinction between commercial microfinance investment funds and the previous category of funds is the nature of the investors targeted. These funds tend to target private investors and usually invest primarily in the most mature MFIs. They favour loans, with equity representing no more than 10 to 20% of their portfolios. These funds provide investors a relatively stable return based on the loan portfolio and hope to achieve an additional return with limited investments in MFI equity.

The first microfinance investment fund with the objective of targeting private investors was the Dexia Micro-Credit Fund. It was launched in Luxembourg in 1998 by the bank Dexia-BIL. It grew rapidly, reaching $58.3 million as of 30th April 2005 with a MFI loan portfolio of $46.4 million,[17] outpacing many older donor and development agency-sponsored funds. Most of the original seed money of $10 million advanced by Dexia-BIL has been withdrawn: the owners are private individuals and a few commercial institutional investors.

This fund demonstrates that a microfinance vehicle specifically targeted to private investors can attract sizeable amounts of money. This fund invests primarily in microfinance loans.

Other similarly structured microfinance investment funds that target private investors that include some equity positions in their portfolios have recently been launched. These are the responsAbility Global Microfinance Fund (rGMF – launched in November 2003) and the Triodos Fair Share Fund (TFSF – launched in December 2002). Each has about 10% of their microfinance portfolios invested

---

[17] BlueOrchard Finance S.A. Monthly Newsletter May 2005.

in MFI equity. These two funds (as well as the Dexia Micro-Credit Fund) have monthly net asset valuations which enable investors to subscribe to or redeem these funds each month.

Thus four vehicles can be considered as commercial microfinance investment funds with an equity portfolio in MFIs:

- Impulse
- MicroVest
- responsAbility Global Microfinance Fund
- Triodos Fair Share Fund

Although these funds were still rather small at the time the surveys were made, they are among the fastest growing in the industry and will soon count among the largest microfinance investment funds. The rGMF reached € 9.8 million ($12.6 million) in April 2005 and the TFSF reached € 9.1 million ($11.8 million) at the end of March 2005. Their modest size has had a detrimental impact on their profitability, with net returns for the rGMF of 1.55% on the US dollar share class in 2004 (but an annualised 3.2% in the first four months of 2005) and a net return of 2% for the TFSF in 2004.[18] The larger Dexia Micro-Credit Fund, with no equity positions, netted 3.95% on the US dollar share class and 4.4% for the Euro share class in 2004. As these funds grow, their fixed costs will weigh less on their profitability, enabling investors to enjoy higher returns with at least the same social impact.

Although launched by three NGOs – CARE, MEDA and Seed Capital Development Fund – MicroVest I is a commercial microfinance investment fund targeted at private and commercial investors, of which there are currently 70, including two mutual funds. It is a ten-year vehicle which has collected $15 million in committed funds. As of December 2004, $9.1 million had been placed with mature MFIs. Although it can hold up to 50% of its assets in equity, MicroVest I's equity position stood at 8% (December 2004). In addition to the social return it offers by investing in microfinance, it aims to provide between 7 and 8% net on average per annum over its 10-year life. In contrast to rGMF and TFSF, which are not leveraged, MicroVest I will be, with a projected debt/equity ratio of 1.82.

As it is structured as a US Limited Partnership, MicroVest I is limited in the number of investors it can attract. The targeted private individuals are therefore high net-worth individuals. By contrast, the TFSF and the rGMF accept much smaller investors. The minimum amount to invest in the rGMF, for example, is $1,000.

---

[18] Funds in the Netherlands which are recognised as socially responsible investment funds benefit from an additional 2.5% fiscal bonus in addition to the net return of the fund. The TFSF benefits from the fiscal bonus, as does Oikocredit Nederland Fonds, already mentioned, and ASN-Novib, which currently invests only in loans although it may also invest in equity. Other governments should consider this tax incentive for households to invest in microfinance.

Impulse is a recently-created commercial microfinance investment fund, launched by Incofin, a Belgian cooperative company investing in microfinance as a
commercially focused vehicle. Impulse, founded in December 2004, is a closed-
ended 12-year investment company under Belgian law. Its shareholders are Incofin and other Belgian financial institutions, including KBC, one of Belgium's
largest banks. This € 10 million fund will primarily provide loans to medium-
sized, commercially viable MFIs, but may also invest up to 20% of its portfolio in
equity positions.

Gray Ghost Microfinance Fund, founded in 2003, does not directly invest in the
equity of MFIs, but it is the first microfinance fund of funds. As such, it invests in
microfinance funds, including funds which invest in equity. The goal of Gray
Ghost Microfinance Fund is to assemble a $50 million microfinance portfolio by
2008 and to attract at least another $200 million from private investors as co-
investments and linked transactions in microfinance funds.[19] By the end of May
2005, $17.8 million had been committed of which $8.5 million was disbursed. A
further $15 million was then being negotiated with investment funds. The portfo-
lio includes funds such as AIM or MicroVest I. Gray Ghost also supports funds
such as the Emergency Liquidity Facility which acts as a lender of last resort that
provides immediate short and medium term loans to pre-qualified MFIs con-
fronted with a liquidity crisis stemming from natural or man-made disasters.[20]
Gray Ghost may also serve as a source of seed capital for new investment funds.

We would have expected to see some venture capital microfinance investment
funds in this category of investment funds. Out of the 360 MFIs considered for
comparison by the Comparative Analysis tool of the MixMarket database, 59
earned a return on equity (ROE) greater than 20% in 2003.[21] The average return of
57 of them was just under 39%.[22] These kinds of returns would seem to be sufficient to attract commercial capital.

Microfinance is, however, a novel business for private investors; gaining their
interest is taking longer than some had anticipated. Commercial investors need
investment structures to invest in, but when none are available, it does not necessarily mean that commercial or private capital is not interested in equity participations in MFIs. The success and rapid growth of some of the commercial microfinance investment funds show that, whenever an investment fund is appropriately
structured for its targeted audience, there is no lack of capital.

---

[19] Paper dated 6th Dec. 2004 – Gray Ghost Microfinance Fund, LLC – A microfinance
portfolio company.

[20] SECO website: http://www.seco-cooperation.ch/entwicklungsarbeit/00618/?lang=fr.

[21] Comparative Analysis tool of the MixMarket used on 16th May 2005 with the selection:
Return on Equity for MFIs for 2003 (www.mixmarket.org/).

[22] The two largest ROEs of over 150% were not taken into account to avoid distortion of
the average.

A trend seems to be getting underway that will lead to a greater number of equity microfinance investment funds being targeted at private investors. Except for a few early movers, institutional investors will require some sort of track record and a minimum fund size before even contemplating investment in such funds. The process may well be slow for these investors. Private individuals are already showing a greater interest in participating in such funds, especially in diversified funds (for example with a maximum 20% equity component) rather than in funds that invest essentially in equity. Microfinance venture capital funds are also likely to appear, but will initially appeal only to a limited number of private investors who are aware of the social impact of microfinance and seek to support it.

Challenges Facing Microfinance Investment Funds Investing in Equity

The following sections outline some of the challenges facing microfinance investment funds that invest in equity. Recent publications offer a comprehensive view of these challenges in the wider context of the transition from a donor-driven environment for the MFIs to that of the private capital markets.[23]

Most MFIs Are Under-Leveraged: Does This Mean Little Demand for Equity?

According to Gautam Ivatury and Julie Abrams (2004), "Regulated MFIs' continuing high levels of equity capital will lead them to increase their liabilities rather than raise new equity". They mention NBFIs (non-bank financial institutions) reporting to the *MicroBanking Bulletin* (No. 9) as having a 2.9x (2.9-to-1.0) average debt-to-equity ratio, with specialised microfinance banks maintaining a 5.6x average ratio. Unregulated MFIs usually have far lower debt-to-equity ratios, around 1-to-1. According to MicroRate's analysis of the 11 Peruvian MFIs in the MicroRate 30 in 2003, there is a clear correlation between debt-to-equity ratios and ROEs.[24] These findings should encourage unregulated MFIs to transform, which would enable them to have higher leverage and higher profitability.

Even regulated MFIs could increase their leverage: levels of between 5 and 8-to-1 are viewed as being reasonable in the industry. The problem is in fact more profound than these ratios imply, as even the best performing MFIs still need guarantees to support their access to commercial loans.[25] It seems that the reliance of most MFIs on non-commercial capital is part of the problem. MIX Market data from August 2004 indicate that the following sources of funding are sought by MFIs, in order of priority: (1) local currency loans, (2) capacity building grants,

---

[23] Among those: de Sousa-Shields and Frankiewicz (2004).

[24] MicroRate (2004).

[25] de Sousa-Shields and Frankiewicz (2004).

(3) donations, (4) loans in USD, (5) equity, and finally (6) guarantees. The issue is that as long as non-commercial funding is available, there is little incentive for MFIs to run their business as efficiently as possible and within the parameters of its earnings. As Gert van Maanen puts it: "It is much easier to go overseas and to ask for renewal of a grant, than to increase earnings and reduce costs".[26] Another view, which is not necessarily contradictory, is that in the long run NGOs have little other choice if they want to survive, because grant money is volatile and can very well disappear.

A paper issued by the Council of Microfinance Equity Funds in 2004[27] reports that eight general managers of MFIs were questioned regarding their institutions' appetite for equity capital within the next three to five years. Seven indicated that they would not require additional equity capital because they had just raised capital, were counting on internally generated revenues or planned to increase their deposit base. The eighth manager was reported to be searching for a strategic partner who could substantially raise his or her institution's capital base.

These reports indicate that equity capital is not the highest priority among the types of funding sought by MFIs. Deposits are the preferred source of funding for MFIs that can take deposits, but only on the condition that the maturities and deposit accounts are correctly structured. Debt funding, preferably from domestic sources or at least in local currency, is the next priority but is limited by the unwillingness of the borrowers and the lenders to increase the MFI's leverage beyond prudent levels. When these levels are reached or whenever the institution is going through transformation, equity capital will again be in demand.

Different types of investment funds have different roles with respect to providing equity capital to an MFI. If the MFI wants a strategic partner, quasi-commercial microfinance investment funds or venture capital equity funds – both focussing on equity and prepared to take relatively large stakes – would be appropriate partners depending on the maturity of the MFI. Venture capital equity funds are more likely to invest in the most mature MFIs whereas quasi-commercial microfinance investment funds should probably invest increasingly in less mature or start up MFIs in addition to investing in mature MFIs. A very good example of the latter is La Fayette Investissement already mentioned above. Other types of investment funds with a more balanced portfolio could provide equity to a lesser extent without necessarily playing an active role in the MFI's governance.

[26] van Maanen (2004).

[27] Kaddaras and Rhyne (2004).

Valuation of Equity Participations and Exit

Valuation was never much of an issue for many closed-ended investment funds as the initial investors remain in the fund until its termination. Capital gains or losses are realised whenever the positions are sold. All the investors benefit or loose at the same time.

However, valuation of equity participations, other than at cost, is becoming an increasingly important issue. Three situations require the determination of the "fair value" of equity positions:

- When new shareholders enter or some existing shareholders exit an investment fund

- When accounting rules require fair value determination (such as the International Financial Reporting Standards – IFRS)

- When a fund is terminated

New or exiting shareholders: Whenever investors move in and out of an investment fund, a "fair value" of the equity participations ensures that all shareholders are treated equally. In contrast, if an equity position is undervalued, it benefits the new investors to the detriment of the existing shareholders. An entry by an investor (or in some cases an exit) can occur at periodic closings or whenever a net asset valuation is calculated for an open-ended fund. As noted earlier, amongst microfinance investment funds holding equity participations, two[28] have monthly valuations, allowing subscriptions and redemptions. The assessments of the "fair value" of the equity positions are conducted at the same intervals. Since these two funds' equity positions constitute no more than 10-11% of their assets, a thorough review of the fair value of their equity holdings does not have to be conducted every month, but at least a simplified assessment of fair value has to be provided. As another example, ProCredit Holding has accepted new investors over the last few years. Each time a new shareholder came on board or when an existing shareholder increased their participation, a thorough valuation of the equity positions had to be conducted to ensure that new and existing investors were treated fairly.

Accounting rules: Some accounting rules require that equity positions be reported at "fair value". The British Venture Capital Association (BVCA) and the European Venture Capital Association (EVCA) issue guidelines to assist in this valuation. In 2001, EVCA issued new guidelines for valuing unquoted investments in two ways:

- Conservative value: unquoted investments should be valued at cost unless a new financing round or a partial sale has occurred, in which case the transaction price should be used. An investment should also be written down if there has been a material and permanent reduction in the value of the investment below cost.

---

[28] Triodos Fair Share Fund and responsAbility Global Microfinance Fund.

- Fair market value: the most appropriate indication is likely to be an independent third party transaction within the valuation period. In the absence of such third party transaction, for companies generating profits, multiples of comparable companies should be used, with a discount to cater for illiquidity. The conservative value would apply in case of losses.

Many private equity funds used conservative value, resulting in significant differences in valuation upon exit. Microfinance investment funds essentially applied the same rules, with most equity participations being valued at cost.

Changes will occur with the recent introduction of the new IFRS rules which require that all investments be valued at "fair value". The 2004 Annual Report of Africap nicely illustrates the implications of these new rules. Two of its investments were valued at cost, as they were either recent or were not subjected to any new events which would justify changing their valuation. A third investment, in Equity Bank Ltd, was revalued following a new share issue in December 2004. The new issue price more than doubled the value of Africap's investment in that MFI in less than two years.

Microfinance investment funds will increasingly be required to value their equity participations at fair value, even in the absence of new share issues by MFIs or of recent transactions.

The two main methods used to value the equity of MFIs are the discounted cash flow (DCF) method and the application of multiples,[29] with the multiple of book value (BV) as the main one. According to interviews conducted for this chapter, the DCF method may be more appropriate for fast growing MFIs. However, the book value of a company is the result of its history, which may be a more appropriate basis for more mature and more stable MFIs. The main disadvantage of the DCF method is its extreme sensitivity to discount rates, which can produce a wide array of results. The microfinance industry still seems reluctant to pay for an MFI at high multiples to BV, even for a high growth company. As there are few cases in which such companies are sold at high multiples, potential buyers are still wary about paying too much over BV.

The multiples for five MFIs sold by Profund ranged from 0.9 to 1.4 of BV, with an average multiple of 1.12. Another sale, Compartamos, commanded a multiple of 2.2,[30] almost double the average of the other five. This MFI has unique features justifying such a multiple. KMB in Russia is rumoured to have been sold at a multiple of between three and four times the bank's BV. In both cases the features that supported a high multiple was that the company was unique in its market, its market was growing rapidly, and its staff were particularly skilled and well-trained.

---

[29] Clay O'Brien and Ken Vander Weele from Opportunity International are thanked here for sharing their presentation on the valuation of MFIs which was discussed at the meeting of the Council of Microfinance Equity Funds in May 2005.

[30] Conversation with Alex Silva, Profund.

Exit or divestment: These examples touch upon the third reason for valuing an equity position: at the time of an exit. The experience of Profund is particularly interesting[31] because it was the first microfinance investment fund to go through such an exit. Profund used a number of exit strategies for its investments, but the mode of exit does not reduce the importance of a thorough valuation of the MFI at the time of exit. Profund's exit strategies are not unique – all other investments funds use them in one way or another – but Profund is the first case in which these strategies were actually tested for an entire investment fund that was wound up when its 10-year life expired.

The most commonly used strategy was to require put options as a condition for investment in an MFI. These put options (option to sell the equity positions) were granted by the sponsors or the initiators of MFIs. The exit prices were usually a function of the MFI's performance. Therefore the puts would not guarantee an exit price but would ensure that the holder of the put would always have a buyer.

A second method involves shareholders in an MFI acting in concert, especially when a controlling block of shares is concerned. These situations are usually covered in shareholders' agreements that require the same treatment for all shareholders: drag along rights enable a shareholder to force other shareholders to join in a sale with uniform conditions for all, while tag along rights enable a shareholder to join in a sale of equity with the same conditions if another shareholder is selling their shares.

As of May 2005, Profund had sold or had agreed to sell almost all its investments through a combination of selling through put options, drag along or tag along rights, a management buy-in process, and through self-liquidating provisions for its quasi-equity investments.

Equity positions are increasingly likely to be valued at "fair value". In the absence of recent transactions, valuation of equity will most likely continue to be made using a combination of the DCF and the multiple of BV methodologies, with an increasing acceptance of multiples to BV that will probably be higher than in the past.

The Paradox of Dividend Distribution vs. Retained Earnings

There is a paradox in the dividend policy which microfinance investment funds, and therefore MFIs, must follow in order to attract private capital. The first view is that an MFI will find no better source of funding than from its own earnings. Why would an institution distribute a dividend if retained earnings can fuel its expansion? And why would an investor's point of view differ? Could the investor generate a better return on investment on the dividend rather than leaving the proceeds in the institution? For example, why would a European pension fund generating a return of between 5 and 10% per annum require a dividend from an MFI

---

[31] Silva (2005).

that generates a return on equity (ROE) of over 20%? This was the case in 2003 for 14 of the 30 Latin American MFIs in the MicroRate 30.[32]

International institutional investors such as pension funds and insurance companies generally expect some form of dividend on an investment in microfinance, at least until they become more familiar with microfinance and begin to appreciate the real potential of MFIs. Although a portion of their portfolios may be invested in venture capital funds with returns that are uncertain until liquidation, these institutions generally require a steady flow of income to match their liabilities. When institutional investors consider acquiring shares of a traditional company, they will analyse the potential for the company's share price to rise but they will also look at the dividend policy and its track record in paying dividends.

Triodos, for example, requires a dividend from the MFIs in which the Triodos Fair Share Fund invests. This fund has a monthly financial target to reach. Although it mainly invests in debt instruments, it also requires a regular income flow from its equity investments.

MFIs typically have not paid dividends. Their traditional shareholders or owners, first NGOs and then development agencies, did not ask for dividends. It made more sense from a financial point of view to retain these earnings in the MFI. But if private capital is to be tapped in any significant way, MFIs will be requested to pay dividends so that the microfinance investment funds investing in them can also pay a dividend to their own investors.

Microfinance venture capital equity funds normally do not want to receive dividends because their investors seek an overall return at the maturity of the fund. But more balanced funds with a periodic valuation will look favourably on MFIs that pay a regular dividend.

Governance or Investment?

Most microfinance investment funds require some sort of involvement in the governance of the MFIs they invest in. Köhn and Jainzik[33] identify two main approaches used by investment funds. Investment funds using the outsider approach look for good investment opportunities independently of a network of MFIs. But even in this category, quasi-commercial microfinance investment funds usually seek an active role in the MFIs they invest in, as would most of the development microfinance funds if justified by the size of their equity investment. Funds using the network approach are deeply involved in the networks in which they invest. A number of microfinance development funds (such as the Accion Gateway Fund) and quasi-commercial microfinance investment funds (such as AIM, ProCredit Holding and OTI) follow this approach.

---

[32] MicroRate (2004).
[33] Köhn and Jainzik (2005).

The commercial microfinance investment funds would logically be the least involved in the governance of MFIs. But probably because these funds are relatively new and also because they have very few equity investments, they also demand involvement in the governance of the MFIs in which they invest equity capital. The more commercial funds are likely to assume a more passive role, focusing essentially on the potential for a financial return in addition to the social return. Playing an active role in the governance of an MFI is costly and may not be justified considering the focus and objectives of these more commercial funds and also the relative size of their investments. In these cases governance would be left to the main owners of the MFIs and to other categories of funds.

Potential Financial Returns for Microfinance Investment Funds with an Equity Focus

According to many microfinance specialists, the potential returns for a microfinance investment fund with a 10-year life invested essentially in equity could range from 8 to 14% per annum (without leverage) in US Dollars or Euros. This return is substantially below what private equity investors would expect in emerging markets (30-40% p.a.), which may explain some of the reluctance of these investors to invest in microfinance. They view it as a low return activity that carries the high risk of emerging markets.

As private investors become familiar with microfinance and understand the risk-return dynamics of the business, investment structures may be created that cater to these investors. Private investors with a dual objective – social and financial – are likely to be the initial investors in such commercial private equity funds. In the meantime the quasi-commercial funds will play a role in familiarising private investors with the microfinance business.

Seed Capital and Critical Mass

Many microfinance investment funds are too small to be sustainable on their own. Small funds require subsidies one way or another, if only by investors willing to accept a lower return due to the fund size. Setting up an investment fund requires seed capital, usually provided by the promoter of the fund. DFIs have a role to play here and some DFIs do that by facilitating the creation of new structures. Similarly, one of the aims of Gray Ghost is to provide seed capital to new funds.

A traditional stand-alone investment fund with assets below € 20 million which is not growing significantly would be terminated by many traditional investment fund promoters. Many small microfinance investment funds, however, have survived because their owners or investors were more concerned about their social impact than maximising the return on their capital. Larger investment funds can increase their financial returns while simultaneously increasing the social impact.

With a total balance sheet of € 245 million, Oikocredit clearly benefits from economies of scale. The total expense ratio (TER) is used to measure the efficiency of traditional investment funds. The TER is the sum of the annual operating expenses (the largest portion being management fees) divided by average net assets. A simple calculation of the TER of Oikocredit (by eliminating the impact of grant income which comes as a reduction of expenses in their 2004 financial statements) amounts to 2.3%, which compares favourably to smaller funds. Smaller microfinance investment funds very often have management fees of between 2% and 4%, to which further expenses such as custodian, legal and auditor expenses have to be added.

Of the 23 microfinance investment funds investing in equity in the sample described above, 19 have total assets below € 20 million while 4 have total assets greater than € 20 million. A number of funds have grown considerably over the last few months, such as the two most actively distributed commercial microfinance investment funds investing in equity: the Triodos Fair Share Fund grew by 49% in 2005 to reach € 12.2 million at the end of that year; and the responsAbility Global Microfinance Fund that grew to $43 million in just over two years from its creation in November 2003 until the end of 2005 (a 424% increase over December 2004!).

The growth of an investment fund benefits all participants. Investors benefit from a lower TER and therefore from a higher financial return. The fund manager benefits from increased revenues stemming from increased assets under management. Finally, the MFIs benefit from increased volumes of funding, potentially on better conditions.

An additional advantage for a growing investment fund is that it becomes increasingly interesting as an opportunity for commercial institutional investors. These private investors would not even engage in research on microfinance if they knew they could place only a small amount. Some pension funds, for example, will not make investments of less than € 5 million. Such investors may also refuse to invest in a small fund because it is unlikely to have sufficiently diversified sources of funding[34] (which may also be a regulatory requirement) and because redemption could cause liquidity problems and therefore a delay in receiving the proceeds. The effects of these two criteria strongly limit these investors' willingness to participate in many microfinance investment funds.

There are nevertheless a few early movers among pension funds that are attracted to commercial microfinance investment funds by their social aspect, despite the limited size of their investment. They hope to make further investments in these funds as they grow, while in the meantime becoming acquainted with microfinance.

---

[34] Similarly to the checks an investor would perform for an MFI.

Distribution: Shifting the Funding of Mature MFIs from DFIs to "You and Me"

Distribution is an essential condition for investment fund growth. The key to success for a traditional investment fund is its distribution, that is, its access to the final investor. Sponsors of traditional investment funds constantly examine the trade off between keeping their own smaller funds and selling comparable but larger funds managed by others. A small fund would be kept only if it has a chance to be distributed actively by other institutions. This industry is moving increasingly towards an open architecture, where promoters sell each other's funds. This benefits the largest and the most profitable funds and thus also the final investors in such funds.

A fund can be distributed actively only if it is structured appropriately for its target audience. ProCredit, for instance, is structured very differently from the responsAbility Global Microfinance Fund. ProCredit may certainly be attractive to institutional investors, which would be accepted on a negotiated or case-by-case basis. It is not structured for active distribution, nor would ProCredit want it to be at this time. responsAbility is specifically structured for private individuals and institutional investors. It was among the first funds to integrate the active distribution in its structure with external distributors organised when the fund was launched.

There are many high net worth individuals as well as less wealthy people who would be willing to allocate a part of their savings to microfinance, attracted by the social and financial returns offered. However, many do not know how to proceed. Microfinance investment funds targeting them should be created in greater numbers and distributed more actively.

Investment funds actively distributed to commercial investors, via a bank network for example, would most probably invest only a small proportion of their assets in the equity of MFIs. It is therefore unlikely that commercial investors will soon displace DFIs as investors in the capital of the more mature MFIs. The debt funding of these mature MFIs could certainly come primarily from commercial investors through commercial microfinance investment funds as these continue to grow. Minority equity stakes could also be taken by these investment funds for the diversification of their investments and to obtain greater involvement in MFIs.

Another paradox concerns the more active distribution of the more commercial microfinance investment funds. On the one hand, DFIs and NGOs regret that commercial capital is not yet ready to replace their funding of the most mature MFIs or that it arrives only in meagre amounts. On the other hand, some commercial players are willing to take a more active role in distributing commercial microfinance investment funds, but they are being told that there may be capacity problems in absorbing large inflows into MFIs. What is required is a greater number of these commercial investment funds, promoted by a greater number of fund managers, combined with an expanding distribution by commercial actors. These funds will gradually absorb a greater portion of the equity and debt financing of mature MFIs.

Conclusions

Microfinance investment funds enable different types of investors to join in a single structure in order to invest in a diversified set of MFIs. Investors can learn from each other and from the investment fund by participating in the debt or equity funding of MFIs, while committing amounts smaller than would be required if they funded MFIs directly. Microfinance investment funds can therefore be powerful tools in the continued growth of MFIs.

Quasi-commercial microfinance investment funds will probably continue to hold the bulk of the equity of MFIs that is held by investment funds. They are also most likely to continue to be ordinarily focused on equity, with debt products being provided mainly to the MFIs in which they hold equity or to those with which they want to establish long-term relationships. These funds will continue to act as true public-private partnerships which attract private capital while ensuring that the development mission of the MFIs they invest in is maintained. DFIs and other development-oriented players are likely to continue to play a very important role in steering these quasi-commercial microfinance investment funds.

Microfinance development funds will continue to attract funding from socially responsible investors who want both a social and financial return on their investment, and who are willing to allocate part of their resources to microfinance and other development activities such as Fair Trade. These funds are likely to maintain their wide diversification with most of their microfinance portfolio invested in debt instruments.

Commercial microfinance investment funds are and will continue to be the fastest growing category. As commercial actors become familiar with microfinance, more microfinance investment funds targeted to private investors will be set up. They are very likely to be distributed actively by institutions other than the promoter.

Most commercial institutional investors such as pension funds and other mutual funds will consider investing in microfinance investment funds when a proven track record is available. Institutional investors which have taken the step to invest in a microfinance investment fund are still few and far between. Although institutional investors are likely to remain hesitant to invest substantially in microfinance, they will gradually do so through structures that are built to respond to their needs and objectives. These investment structures will most probably invest predominantly or only in debt instruments of MFIs.

Private individuals of various sorts (high net worth individuals and others less wealthy) are the most promising investors in microfinance. Those attracted first will seek financial returns as well as development impact. Financial institutions should not underestimate the capacity of individual investors to make "good use" of their money. Many individuals are willing to invest a small portion of their portfolio in development-oriented projects such as microfinance, especially if they realise that the financial returns are decent.

Promoters of microfinance investment funds should target the investment port-folios of individuals. These portfolios are potentially much larger than their alloca-tions to investments producing a clear social return but only a modest financial return. Microfinance development funds will always attract individual investors because these investors can feel good about these investments. They are likely to invest larger amounts if they can make a slightly higher return.

Will these individuals find suitable investment funds? Including those investing exclusively in debt instruments, at the time of the surveys, only five commercial microfinance investment funds attract a large number of private individuals. Three are in the Netherlands, mainly geared towards Dutch investors. The other two are in Luxembourg, targeting international investors. All five are growing rapidly. At least four other commercial microfinance investment funds have been set up since then, thereby contributing to widening the range of commercial investment vehi-cles in microfinance available to individual as well as institutional investors.

Commercial microfinance investment funds will almost certainly continue to be essentially debt driven with potentially a small portion of their assets in equity investments, which corresponds to the risk profile of the private investors targeted. They are likely to be an important source of debt financing in hard currencies for the most mature MFIs. This will encourage DFIs and other development oriented investors to focus on less mature MFIs and on local currency funding. As the eq-uity portion of these funds will remain small and certainly well diversified, they are likely to co-invest in the equity of MFIs either with quasi-commercial microfi-nance investment funds or directly with DFIs or NGOs, without taking an active role in the governance of these MFIs.

This activity will constitute a new form of public-private partnership in the field of equity investment in MFIs, between DFIs (and potentially NGOs) on the one hand and commercial microfinance investment funds on the other. The former will provide expertise in microfinance and the checks and balances required to maintain the development mission of these MFIs. The latter will hopefully provide funding in much needed far larger amounts by giving MFIs access to the wider capital market.

Annex A

Microfinance Investment Fund Legal Name	Country of Incorporation	Legal status	Sponsor	Total Fund Assets USD Million	Total Fund Assets EUR Million	As of Date	Microfinance Portfolio USD Million	Microfinance Portfolio EUR Million	Fund Manager	Category of Microfinance Investment Fund	Shareholders	Equity	Loans, debt	Guarantees
ACCION Gateway Fund	USA	LLC	ACCION International	6,6	4,8	31. Dez 04	6,6	4,8	ACCION International	Microfinance Development Fund	ACCION International	100%	0%	0%
ACCION Investments in Microfinance (AIM)	Cayman Islands	Portfolio company	ACCION International	12,9	9,5	31. Dez 04	11,7	8,6	ACCION Investment Management Company	Quasi-commercial Microfinance Inv Fund	Social Inst. Investors and private individuals - Min. $ 250,000	100%	0%	0%
Africap	Mauritius	Private Equity Fund	Calmeadow	13,3	9,7	31. Dez 04	5,1	3,7	AfriCap MicroVentures Ltd, Dakar	Quasi-commercial Microfinance Inv Fund	Social Inst. Investors	80%	20%	0%
ALTERFIN	Belgium	Société coopérative à responsabilité limitée	NA	11,2	8,2	31. Dez 04	3,7	2,7	Alterfin	Microfinance Development Fund	Social Inst. Investors and private individuals	11%	89%	0%
Développement International Desjardins - FONIDI Fund	Canada	Limited Partnership	Développement International Desjardins	4,2	3,1	31. Dez 04	0,5	0,4	Gestion FONIDI Inc.	Microfinance Development Fund	Four wholly-owned subs of the Desjardins Group	100%	0%	0%
Développement International Desjardins - Partnership Fund	Canada	Part of Développement International Desjardins	Développement International Desjardins	6,6	4,8	31. Dez 04	2,0	1,5	Développement International Desjardins	Microfinance Development Fund	NA	35%	65%	0%
Hivos-Triodos Foundation	Netherlands	Foundation	Hivos Foundation and Triodos Bank	22,6	16,6	31. Dez 04	20,7	15,2	Triodos International Fund Management B.V.	Microfinance Development Fund	NA	32%	61%	8%
Impulse	Belgium	Investment Company	Incofin	12,3	10,0	31. Mai 05	1,2	1,0	Incofin	Commercial Microfinance Inv Fund	Institutional Investors	0%	100%	0%

Microfinance Investment Fund Legal Name	Country of Incorporation	Legal status	Sponsor	Total Fund Assets		As of Date	Microfinance Portfolio		Fund Manager	Category of Microfinance Investment Fund	Shareholders	Financial products actually offered (in percentage of microfinance portfolio)		
				USD Million	EUR Million		USD Million	EUR Million				Equity	Loans, debt	Guarantees
Incofin	Belgium	Co-operative Company	NA	5,7	4,6	31. Mai 05	3,2	2,6	Incofin	Microfinance Development Fund	Institutional Investors (mainly commercial) and private individuals	42%	58%	0%
Investisseur et Partenaire pour le Développement	Mauritius	Investment Company	NA	11,0	8,5	30. Mrz 05	2,2	1,7	I&P Etudes et Conseils	Quasi-commercial Microfinance Inv Fund	Mainly private individuals + 1 listed company	31%	69%	0%
Kolibri Kapital ASA	Norway	Public Limited Liability Company	Korsvei	0,4	0,4	30. Sep 04	0,4	0,3	Kolibri Kapital ASA	Microfinance Development Fund	Private individuals & Church-relatd inst. Investors	100%	0%	0%
La Fayette Participations	France	Société par actions simplifiée	Groupe Horus	0,5	0,4	31. Dez 04	0,5	0,4	Horus Development Finance	Quasi-commercial Microfinance Inv Fund	Social Inst. Investors	100%	0%	0%
MicroVest I, LP	Delaware USA	Limited Partnership	MEDA, CARE & SEED	15,0	11,0	31. Dez 04	9,1	6,7	MicroVest Capital Management LLC	Commercial Microfinance Inv Fund	Mainly private investors incl. 2 mutual funds	8%	92%	0%
Oikocredit	Netherlands	Co-operative Society	NA	332,5	245,3	31. Dez 04	80,8	59,6	Oikocredit	Microfinance Development Fund	Essentially church-related organisations incl. local parishes	14%	85%	1%
Opportunity Transformation Investments Inc. (OTI)	USA	Investment company	Opportunity International	21,9	16,1	31. Dez 04	21,8	16,0	Opportunity International	Microfinance Development Fund	Opportunity International	91%	9%	0%
ProCredit Holding AG	Germany	Bank Holding Investment Company	Initiative of IPC	135,1	99,0	31. Dez 04	108,3	79,4	ProCredit Holding AG	Quasi-commercial Microfinance Inv Fund	Social and commercial Inst. Investors	74%	26%	0%

Microfinance Investment Fund Legal Name	Country of Incorporation	Legal status	Sponsor	Total Fund Assets		As of Date	Microfinance Portfolio		Fund Manager	Category of Microfinance Investment Fund	Shareholders	Financial products actually offered (in percentage of microfinance portfolio)		
				USD Million	EUR Million		USD Million	EUR Million				Equity	Loans, debt	Guarantees
PROFUND	Panama	Investment Fund as an S.A.	Calmeadow	13,4	9,8	31. Dez 04	13,4	9,8	Omtrix S.A., Costa Rica	Quasi-commercial Microfinance Inv Fund	Mainly Social Institutional Investors	97%	3%	0%
responsAbility Global Microfinance Fund	Luxembourg	Fonds Commun de Placement	Crédit Suisse	12,6	9,8	29. Apr 05	11,7	9,1	Credit Suisse MF Fund Mgt Cy (responsAbility Social Inv Ser. as Advisor)	Commercial Microfinance Inv Fund	Social Inst. Investors and private individuals	11%	81%	0%
Sarona Global Investment Fund, Inc.	USA	Nonprofit Corporation	MEDA	5,5	4,5	30. Sep 04	2,2	1,7	MEDA Investments, Inc.	Microfinance Development Fund	MEDA as shareholder and inst. and private ind. as lenders	32%	68%	0%
ShoreCap International	Cayman Islands	For-profit Investment Company	Shorebank Corporation, Illinois	28,3	20,7	31. Dez 04	5,5	4,0	ShoreCap Management Ltd	Quasi-commercial Microfinance Inv Fund	Mainly Social Institutional Investors + Financial Inst.	86%	14%	0%
SIDI (Solidarité Internationale pour le Développement et l'Investissement)	France	S.A.	Comité Catholique contre la Faim et pour le Développement	7,2	5,3	31. Dez 04	6,4	4,7	SIDI	Microfinance Development Fund	Social Inst. Investors and private individuals	55%	43%	2%
Triodos Fair Share Fund	Netherlands	Mutual Fund	Triodos Bank	11,2	8,2	31. Dez 04	7,0	5,1	Triodos International Fund Management B.V.	Commercial Microfinance Inv Fund	Social Inst. Investors and private individuals in Holland	10%	90%	0%
Triodos-Doen Foundation	Netherlands	Foundation	Triodos Bank and Doen Foundation	35,1	25,7	31. Dez 04	30,8	22,6	Triodos International Fund Management B.V.	Microfinance Development Fund	Doen Foundation	31%	69%	0%
Total for existing Microfinance Investment Funds				**725,2**	**536,0**		**354,9**	**261,6**						
					Of which Equity		**179,0**	**131,5**	The term Social Institutional Investors refers to Development Agencies, Private Donors and other such institutional investors					

Annex B

Microfinance Investment Fund Legal Name	Country of Incorporation	Legal status	Sponsor	Total Fund Assets		As of Date	Microfinance Portfolio		Fund Manager	Category of Microfinance Investment Fund	Shareholders	Financial products actually offered (in percentage of microfinance portfolio)		
				USD Million	EUR Million		USD Million	EUR Million				Equity	Loans, debt	Guarantees
Gray Ghost Microfinance Fund LLC	USA	Limited Liability Company	Robert Patillo	50,0	40,5	30. Mai 05	8,5	6,9	Gray Ghost	Commercial Microfinance Inv. Fund	Private indiv.	-	-	-
Oikocredit Nederland Fonds	Netherlands	Mutual Fund	Oikocredit	39,4	29,1	31. Dez 04	27,4	20,2	Oikocredit	Microfinance Development Fund	Retail investors in the Netherlands	2%	98%	0%
Total for existing Microfinance Investment Funds				89,4	69,6		35,9	27,1						

Annex C

Microfinance Investment Fund Legal Name	Country of Incorporation	Legal status	Sponsor	Total Fund Assets		As of Date	Microfinance Portfolio		Fund Manager	Category of Microfinance Investment Fund	Shareholders	Financial products actually offered (in percentage of microfinance portfolio)		
				USD Million	EUR Million		USD Million	EUR Million				Equity	Loans, debt	Guarantees
La Fayette Investissement (launched in August 05)	Luxembourg	Venture Capital Investment Company (SICAR)	Horus Development Finance	17,4	14,1				Horus Development Finance	Quasi-commercial Microfinance Inv Fund	Social Institutional Investors	-	-	-
Balkan Financial Sector Equity Fund (launched in December 05)	Netherlands	Limited Partnership	Opportunity/ Oikocredit	30,9	25,0				Development Finance Equity Partners	Quasi-commercial Microfinance Inv Fund	Social Institutional and Private Investors	-	-	-
MicroCred (launched in July 2005)	France	Investment Company	PlaNet Finance	38,9	31,5				PlaNet Finance	Quasi-commercial Microfinance Inv Fund	Social Institutional and Private Investors	-	-	-
Total for new Microfinance Investment Funds				87,2	70,6									

References

Alexander, Helen: Sustainable Microfinance Banks – IMI as a PPP in Practice, in Matthäus-Maier and von Pischke (2005)

De Sousa-Shields, Marc and Frankiewicz, Cheryl: Financing Microfinance Institutions: the Context for Transitions to Private Capital – (Accelerated Microenterprise Advancement Project – USAID – Dec 2004)

Goodman, Patrick: Microfinance Investment Funds: Key Features, ADA, February 2005, originally presented at the KfW Financial Sector Development Symposium, Berlin (November 2004)

Ivatury, Gautam and Abrams, Julie: The Market for Microfinance Foreign Investment – Opportunities and Challenges, CGAP, KfW Symposium (November 2004)

Kaddaras, James and Rhyne, Elisabeth – Characteristics of Equity Investments in Microfinance – Council of Microfinance Equity Funds (April 2004)

Köhn, Doris and Jainzik, Michael: Microfinance Investment Funds – An Innovative Form of PPP to Foster the Commercialisation of Microfinance, in Matthäus-Maier and von Pischke (2005)

Matthäus-Maier, Ingrid and von Pischke, J.D. (eds.), EU Accession – Financial Sector Opportunities and Challenges for Southeast Europe, Springer (2005)

Microrate: The Finance of Microfinance (September 2004)

Silva, Alejandro: Investing in microfinance – Profund's story (2005)

Schmidt, Reinhard H. and Moisa, Nina: Public-Private Partnerships for Financial Development in Southeast Europe, in Matthäus-Maier and von Pischke (2005)

van Maanen, Gert – Microcredit – Sound Business or Development Instrument (2004)

CHAPTER 3:

Market Transparency: The Role of Specialised MFI Rating Agencies

Sanjay Sinha

Managing Director, Micro-Credit Ratings International Limited

The Rationale for MFI Rating

Two recent studies, one by CGAP in 2003[1] and the other, in 2004 by Patrick Goodman (sponsored by ADA)[2] show the substantial volume of international investment funds available for microfinance. The latter study indicates that there are now over 40 investment funds supporting microfinance institutions (MFIs) and that some 75% of the funds available are allocated to debt financing with virtually all the rest being allocated to equity financing. However, as the CGAP study indicates, overall foreign investment is only a small proportion of the global total of microfinance lending – $1 billion out of an estimated global total of $15 billion in microfinance loans at end-June 2003.

This substantial amount of microfinance lending has taken place because of a significant shift in the financing of microfinance portfolios from being almost exclusively donor-funded to significantly investor-financed. Finance is now being sourced from domestic sources (apex-level NGOs, development banks and even from commercial banks) as well as from the international investment funds referred to above. Prominent amongst the institutions lending to MFIs in Asia are the Palli Karma Sahayak Foundation (PKSF) of Bangladesh, Permodalan Nasional Madani (PNM) in Indonesia, People's Credit and Finance Corporation (PCFC) in the Philippines and the Small Industries Development Bank of India (SIDBI). The encouraging experience of these institutions in revolving wholesale funds for microfinance has accelerated interest in microfinance investment. As a result, more

---

[1] CGAP. Foreign Investment in Microfinance: Debt and Equity from Quasi-Commercial Investors. Focus Note No. 25. Washington DC: Consultative Group to Assist the Poor, January 2003.

[2] Goodman, Patrick. Microfinance Investment Funds: Objectives, players, potential. Paper presented at the 2004 KfW Financial Sector Development Symposium. Berlin: 11-12 November 2004.

domestic apex institutions (as wholesale lenders) as well as domestic commercial banks, such as ICICI Bank in India and Bank Mandiri in Indonesia, have become active in this field. In addition, international funds have also shown increasing interest in investing in microfinance.

Investment inevitably generates concerns about the borrower's cash flows, profitability and sustainability, making the availability of skills for MFI appraisal and risk analysis an increasingly important issue. The response of the domestic apex organisations that wholesale development funds to MFIs has been to attempt to develop these skills internally. PKSF (Bangladesh) and RMDC (Nepal) are in this category. Banks – such as Sonali Bank of Bangladesh and SIDBI and ICICI Bank in India – with large portfolios but relatively minuscule exposure to the microfinance sector have been more reluctant to undertake appraisals as purely internal exercises.

There are two reasons for this. First, as custodians of commercial rather than development funds, their risk analysis is more sophisticated than is customary in the development sector. Second, a bank with a loan portfolio of a billion dollars or more, invested in a diverse range of activities, may find it difficult to persuade many of its staff to specialise in MFI appraisals when they expect the microfinance portfolio to be no larger than $20-30 million in the immediate future. Yet, the potential for microfinance lending in India alone is estimated to be between $6-8 billion if the substantial liquid resources of the banking system could be channelled in this direction.

The microfinance funding situation can therefore be characterised as one of information asymmetry. Commercial banks and international investors have funds but not the specific expertise to assess and analyse microfinance operations. MFIs have a high demand for funds but in many cases doubtful records on systemic strength, sustainability and profitability. While apex institutions financing MFIs have preferred to develop their own appraisal systems with varying success, the development and commercial banks – along with many international funds – have preferred to use the services of specialised MFI raters that have entered the field since 1997.

The Progress of Microfinance Rating

Microfinance rating started around 1996-2000 with the advent of three specialised raters – MicroRate in Washington DC, Planet Rating in Paris and Micro-Credit Ratings International Limited (M-CRIL) near New Delhi.[3] MicroRate and M-CRIL grew out of microfinance assessment and appraisal expertise developed by a team assembled by Damian von Stauffenberg in the US and EDA Rural Systems

---

[3]   MicroRate was the first actually to be established and to undertake a commercial rating assignment – in 1997.

in India. Planet Rating was set up in 2000 by Planet Finance, a French NGO that promotes the development of microfinance.

These three agencies have become the market leaders, accounting for over two-thirds of some 900 ratings of MFIs. As Table 1 shows, these three had undertaken 600 ratings (according to the website of the IDB-CGAP Rating Fund) through end-March 2005, covering all regions of the world with significant microfinance activity. By 2005, M-CRIL emerged as the market leader in numbers of ratings (accounting for over 30% of the total) with a volume of 50-60 a year.

Using M-CRIL as an example, in the six and a half years following the launch of its rating service in 1998, M-CRIL assembled a team of 8-10 professionals. It has an active Board of Directors made up of professionals and academics with intimate knowledge and experience in microfinance. These professionals are part of its Rating Committee to provide independent oversight of the ratings process. This vetting mechanism has served to mitigate the risk of prejudice, conflicts of

Table 1. Ratings undertaken by agencies recognised by the Rating Fund

Rating agency	Area(s) of operation	Microfinance ratings			All ratings during 12 mos. to March 05
		Total conducted	% of total	Financed by Rating Fund	
Specialist raters					
ACCION	Worldwide	56	6.3%	2	9
M-CRIL	South/SE & Central Asia	269	30.3%	16	58
Microfinanza	Worldwide	50	5.6%	45	25
MicroRate	Latin America, Africa, E. Europe	203	22.9%	56	37
Planet Rating	Worldwide	130	14.6%	66	28
	Sub-total	708	79.7%	185	157
Corporate raters					
Apoyo & Asociadas	Latin America	86	9.7%	1	282
Class & Asociadas	Latin America	20	2.3%		100
CRISIL	South Asia	18	2.0%	8	400
Equilibrium	Latin America	13	1.5%	1	55
Feller Rate	Latin America	8	0.9%		310
Fitch Ratings	Latin America	20	2.3%		25,000
JCR-VIS	South Asia	5	0.6%		113
Pacific Credit Rating	Latin America	7	0.8%		80
Standard & Poor's	Latin America	3	0.3%	1	50,000
	Sub-total	180	20.3%	11	
	Total	**888**	**100%**	**196**	

Source: CGAP-IDB Rating Fund website www.ratingfund.org.

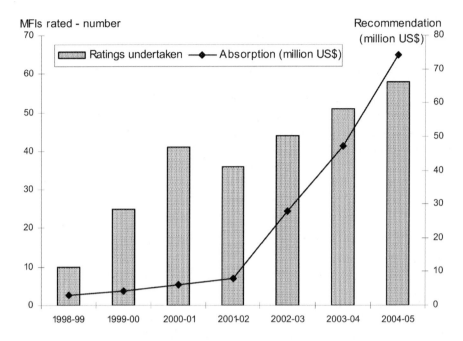

Fig. 1. MFI ratings undertaken by M-CRIL and lending recommendations *(financial years from April to March)*

interest or sins of omission that might otherwise cloud the judgements made by M-CRIL's analysts. As a result, M-CRIL's MFI ratings are accepted as a highly reliable assessment of the creditworthiness of institutions engaged substantially in providing financial services to low-income clients.

Ratings are based on intensive visits of 3-6 days (depending on the size and spread of an MFI) by a team of at least two analysts to MFI head offices, branches and clients. The analytical reports emerging from these visits provide detailed, independently verified information on MFI operations that financial institutions and investors require in order to make lending/investment decisions and judgements of creditworthiness. M-CRIL rating reports are normally accompanied by projections of the MFI's growth. Based on these projections, M-CRIL makes a recommendation for the level of investment that would be appropriate (in M-CRIL's opinion) for external investors in the rated MFI.

Table 1 lists rating agencies financed by the Rating Fund that are active in different regions and provides the total number of their rating activities. Corporate rating agencies have made a few ratings of microfinance institutions, which are included in the overall numbers of ratings made by these large agencies.

Figure 1 shows the progress of M-CRIL's rating activity over the six and a half years through end-March 2005. It had undertaken 269 MFI ratings in Asia resulting in a cumulative lending recommendation ("absorption") equivalent to US$171 million.

The professional opinions emerging from the risk analysis and capacity assessment of MFIs undertaken by M-CRIL have served as a key factor in the lending and other investment decisions of a number of investors in microfinance. M-CRIL's rating service has greatly accelerated the rate at which commercial (or near-commercial) investment has become a source of funds for MFIs in Asia. It is the author's understanding that MicroRate's work in Latin America and South and East Africa and that of Planet Rating and others in the CIS and north Africa has had a similar effect. Though precise figures on the investment stimulated by the other rating agencies may not be available, it is likely that these numbers – in terms of funds invested – would exceed those of M-CRIL since average MFI portfolios (as opposed to client numbers) in Latin America and Eastern Europe tend to exceed those of Asian MFIs by significant multiples.

Use of Ratings for the Financing of Microfinance

Internationally the demand for microfinance rating services has grown slowly but steadily as an increasing number of ratings are being commissioned by a variety of clients. These clients include donors such as USAID, DFID, Swiss Development Cooperation, HIVOS, and CGAP. Also, MFIs seek ratings directly at the request of investors such as Blue Orchard Finance representing the Dexia Micro-Fund and others, as well as by social funds such as Unitus and MicroVest. Again using M-CRIL as an example, this section discusses how rating services play a role in the funding of international microfinance (Annex 1). The various ways in which rating services have been used can be broadly classified as:

- initiatives to raise international financing,
- facilitation of seed capital finance for emerging MFIs,
- demonstration to commercial banks of the utility of the rating service, and
- benchmarking of performance and identification of institutional weaknesses.

MFI Initiatives to Raise International Financing

MFIs that want to raise funds from international investors use the opportunity offered by their donor supporters and/or by the CGAP Rating Fund to obtain a rating – paying part of the cost from their own resources. MFIs use the rating reports provided by a rater such as M-CRIL as independent assessments to attract investors – whether donors or lenders. In Asia, MFIs/banks in Cambodia (Amret, Hatha Kaksekar), Indonesia (the erstwhile Bank Dagang Bali), the Philippines (CRBBI, NWTF, TSKI) as well as in India (SHARE Microfin, Spandana) have used M-CRIL's ratings in this way. Blue Orchard Finance, Deutsche Bank, Citibank and a number of private Indian banks have used M-CRIL's rating reports as part of their appraisal for lending to these MFIs.

Facilitation of Seed Capital Finance for Emerging MFIs

The Dutch NGOs, Hivos and Cordaid, have gone further and used M-CRIL's rating for their programmes that provide seed capital to emerging MFIs. Ratings have been used to advise on the suitability of MFIs for support under the programme and for determining appropriate capitalisation levels over a three year period. Such ratings have covered an MFI in Kazakhstan, another in Timor-Leste and three MFIs in Indonesia. Following the investment phase, M-CRIL was asked by Hivos to undertake quarterly desk reviews (based on information provided by the MFI) and periodic rating updates. The object of this process is to enable the MFI to obtain near-commercial funding. The Kazakhstan Community Loan Fund was the first to graduate in this way from a seed capital partner of Hivos to a borrower of Triodos Bank.

In Myanmar, M-CRIL's rating methodology was used to recommend the future capitalisation of three UN-funded microfinance initiatives. At the request of UNOPS,[4] no ratings were assigned to the MFIs but detailed projections were made to determine the capitalisation requirements of the three projects. In addition, the analysis of performance identified areas for capacity building and institutional development of the projects.

Demonstrating the Utility of Rating to Banks

A Bank Indonesia pilot initiative in 2002 funded by USAID/Asia Foundation rated three BPRs (licensed micro-banks) to determine the suitability of M-CRIL's rating methodology as a basis for obtaining commercial bank funding for BPRs. This exercise led to a discussion about the establishment of a joint venture rating agency focused on BPRs. The revenue model for this proposed joint venture was based on the expectation that the commercial banks and the BPRs would share the cost of the rating.

In Nepal, the technical support network, the Centre for Microfinance, commissioned four ratings by M-CRIL in 2000 to determine the utility of the rating exercise for the local microfinance industry.

Benchmarking Performance and Identification of Institutional Weaknesses

Others have used rating for benchmarking and to identify shortcomings in MFIs' capacity to provide services in an effective and cost-efficient manner. Essentially, benchmarking compares the performance of the rated MFI with "best practice" norms emerging either from the specialised raters' own databases or by comparison with international averages available from the MicroBanking Bulletin. This

---

[4]   United Nations Office for Project Services – the executing agency for the UNDP-funded programme.

exercise requires no extra effort on the part of the rater since benchmarking against the performance of best practice institutions is an essential component of the rating exercise.

- Friends of Women's World Banking, India (FWWB) – a wholesale lender to MFIs in India – has used the rating service to verify appraisals conducted by its own staff and to identify problem areas in the operations of its MFI partners.

- The Asian Development Bank has used M-CRIL's services to benchmark the performance of its microfinance initiative in Timor-Leste, to identify its weaknesses and to chart a growth path for the organisation.

- A few large MFIs in Sri Lanka and India have used M-CRIL's ratings to benchmark their own performance and to identify and accelerate institutional development initiatives.

Overall, ratings in microfinance are driven largely by investment motives. Most of the specialised raters' activities have contributed to the policy objective of financial market deepening[5] adopted by apex lending agencies, international investors and commercial banks that use the rating service to inform their lending decisions. Much of the rest of the work – whether through the CGAP Rating Fund, or donors such as USAID or the Swiss Agency for Development Cooperation (SDC) – has either promoted or experimented with the promotion of relationships between commercial investors such as banks or funds and MFIs. To the significant extent that these efforts augment the flow of finance to MFIs, these initiatives also deepen financial markets for low-income clients.

Results and Impact – Contributing to Financial Market Deepening

Most analysts agree that the microfinance sector makes a contribution to economic growth at the macro level by expanding and deepening financial markets. MFIs offer organised financial services to large numbers of un-banked low-income clients. They can:

---

[5] Financial market deepening occurs when the financial sector, or in this case a specific part of the financial sector, grows faster than the "real" or nonfinancial sectors of the economy. Where financial market deepening is constrained by policy limitations or other barriers, the financial sector may remain too small, not able to play a significant role in economic progress. Initiatives that deepen financial markets or specific parts of financial markets promote growth by reducing costs and expanding access to financial services.

- provide a range of financial products for a variety of clients and purposes, and

- enable investors to get reasonable returns from the operations of sustainable MFIs by financing their activities increasingly via investment channels that value efficiency.

However, the outreach of microfinance is still relatively low in many countries – other than in Bangladesh (>90% of poor families) and Indonesia (50-60%). If the microfinance industry is to cover a substantial proportion of the un-banked low income families in the developing world it must be able to construct the systems and processes required for a dramatic expansion. The contribution of MFI rating to this process – in facilitating the financing of the activity and in improving MFI performance – is discussed in this section.

Facilitating Financial Flows

Table 2 provides the distribution by country of the 178 MFIs rated by M-CRIL through March 2005 and the cumulative investment recommended in these institutions. (The 269 ratings/assessments undertaken by the agency include one or more updates of 49 MFIs.)

Table 2. Ratings by country and by amount recommended for investment *(through end-March 2005)*

Country	Number of ratings undertaken	Investment recommended (million US$)
Bangladesh	20	6.8
Cambodia	6	7.7
East Timor	3	0.5
India	217	128.0
Indonesia	8	17.0
Kazakhstan	2	0.7
Nepal	4	0.8
Pakistan	1	0.8
Philippines	4	5.9
Sri Lanka	1	1.3
Myanmar	3	1.2
Total	269	170.8

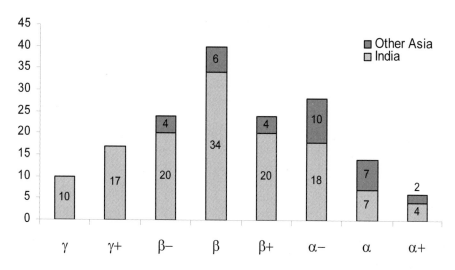

Fig. 2. Distribution of M-CRIL grades awarded

The grade distribution resulting from the latest rating of 163 of the 178 MFIs is shown in Figure 2. M-CRIL's rating symbols range from α+++ (alpha triple plus – the highest grade) to γ (gamma – the lowest grade awarded). All institutions achieving β+ (beta plus) or above qualify as creditworthy and receive a lending recommendation. Institutions achieving a β (beta) grade usually – but not always – also receive a lending recommendation. This is the cut-off point between investment grade and high risk institutions. As the figure shows, around two-thirds of the rated MFIs are investment grade. The short track records in this nascent industry are reflected in the large number of investment grade (creditworthy) MFIs that fall on the margins in the β grade. At the other end of the range, none of the MFIs rated by M-CRIL through mid-2005 achieved the highest two grades, α++ and α+++.

As discussed earlier, the rating service has been successful in terms of the number of ratings undertaken. It has also made a substantial contribution to the flow of funds to MFIs. As indicated above, the cumulative value of the recommendations made through the end of March 2005 exceeds US$170 million, though the actual investment made is probably higher. Most lenders/donors appear willing to provide more support to investment grade institutions than the amounts suggested by M-CRIL, which in retrospect may be relatively conservative. The foremost objective of the rating service – facilitating the flow of finance to MFIs – is being substantially fulfilled. Other raters such as Micro-Rate and PlanetRating do not make lending recommendations but their reports are used in this way.

Contributing to Capacity Enhancement

Improving the performance of the industry and enhancing the capacity of MFIs to expand and increase the volume of financial services provided has become an important secondary goal of rating exercises undertaken by specialised raters. M-CRIL's rating reports have, from the start, provided not only more description of products, programmes and systems than a rating traditionally undertaken by a corporate rating agency. They have also provided an analysis of the strengths, weaknesses, opportunities and threats (SWOT) of the MFI's operations. This has enabled progressive MFI managements to treat M-CRIL rating reports as management consultancy inputs providing substantive pointers to improvements in their operations. Leading institutions that have used M-CRIL reports in this way include BURO Tangail in Bangladesh, Spandana, SHARE and SIFFS in India, ARDCI/Vision Bank in the Philippines and Amret in Cambodia.

The use of the rating process and report for capacity building purposes has gathered momentum. Annex 1 shows that a number of MFIs have obtained ratings purely for benchmarking purposes and for promoting internal learning. A prime example of this is the use of M-CRIL's rating by FWWB for verification of the findings of its appraisal mechanism and for identifying weaknesses in the operations of their partner MFIs.

To reinforce these benefits, M-CRIL has taken the initiative to aggregate and present MFI level information in its database. An analysis of the performance of the first 50 MFIs rated through end-2000 was published in 2001; a second analysis of 120 MFIs rated through June 2003 was published as the M-CRIL Microfinance Review in 2004; the third is to be published in 2006. The M-CRIL Review has played an important role in setting benchmarks for the rating process in the Asian region, and has also been used by networks (particularly Sa-Dhan in India) to make their members more conversant with industry standards. Comparison of performance indicators like portfolio at risk, operating expense ratio and return on assets, with averages for the best performers from M-CRIL's database, has increased the awareness of standards in the industry. This has reinforced the impact of the SWOT analysis by encouraging and enabling the design of capacity building and systems improvement programmes by the MFIs themselves and by their donors/investors. (MicroRate also produces an analytical review of the performance of MFIs it rates in a periodic publication, The Finance of Microfinance.)

During 2002, M-CRIL expanded and documented its accumulated knowledge on systems and best practices in microfinance, starting in India. This was undertaken for a selection of leading MFIs using good practice in various aspects of microfinance operations.[6] The practices covered include governance and institutional linkages, operational strategy, products and delivery mechanisms, management information systems, and internal control for risk management, financial management, accounting policies and human resource management. The docu-

---

[6] Supported by End Poverty Foundation, California.

ment that emerged was published in a user-friendly format and disseminated through a national-level workshop attended by a large number of MFIs from South Asia, and followed by extensive mailing. Feedback from users indicated that the report was well received, making a significant contribution to learning about good practices in microfinance operations.

Challenges in Contributing to Financial Market Deepening

Specialised microfinance raters have clearly made an important contribution to the deepening of the financial sector in developing countries by

- providing investors with a professional appraisal tool that facilitates the flow of funds to MFIs, and by

- enabling MFIs to improve their performance by benchmarking, identifying areas of weakness and improving awareness of standards and best practices, enhancing their capacity to provide financial services and thereby enabling them to serve larger numbers of low income clients.

This section covers some of the key challenges that arise in efforts to enhance this contribution.

Frequency and Cost-Effectiveness

A key concern for a domestic or international investor is that an MFI's portfolio can break down rapidly. A higher frequency of rating would naturally improve the investor's level of comfort with the MFI investment. However, repeated ratings multiply the cost of the investment, either to the investor or to the MFI, depending on who pays. The Rating Fund website indicates that ratings can cost from $2,000 to $25,000, depending on the rating agency and the location, size and spread of the MFI.

In practice, the cost can be controlled while maintaining a reasonable frequency if, following an initial rating visit, quantitative and qualitative performance is monitored via quarterly reporting by the MFI. Key indicators include portfolio quality, profitability, operating cost, client drop-outs, staff turnover, management concerns and other operational challenges. This model is currently being implemented by M-CRIL in the case of MFIs in Indonesia and East Timor (for Hivos) and SIDBI in India also now asks for mid-year reviews of some of its leading MFI borrowers.

It is essential that the information be reviewed by the same rating agency to ensure consistency of cross-checking based on first hand knowledge. The quarterly review could be supplemented by annual visits by the rater to validate information and reporting systems and to update the agency's assessment of governance and management capacity. More frequent monitoring in the form of monthly desk reviews and six-monthly visits on a routine basis is redundant, increasing costs without reducing risk substantially. Clearly, these procedures work best if the rater has a stable rating team with low staff turnover. M-CRIL's experience has shown that if the senior management of the rating agency is constant, problems resulting from turnover at the analyst level can be overcome.

Rating Methodology and Criteria

There is apprehension amongst investors that criteria for rating MFIs are varied in type and purpose and that there is little consensus on the interpretation of financial ratios. This has apparently created a barrier for donors and especially for the emerging private, socially responsible investment funds for MFIs. This sub-section addresses some of these questions.

What Are the Different Criteria Used to Rate MFIs?

Microfinance rating began as separate initiatives by the three main specialist companies. But, a convergence in the criteria and definitions used has resulted from a series of formal and informal consultations amongst these raters. The key parameters assessed relate to:

- portfolio quality
- financial performance
- products and delivery systems
- information and accounting systems
- the control environment
- governance and
- strategies for expansion and competition

There are no longer major differences in the ratios used by the various agencies: all rely on the Technical Guide on ratios in microfinance, initiated by MicroRate and published by the SEEP Network in 2003. Competition amongst the specialised raters and a concern for quality has ensured that the approach to analysis also has substantial similarities. The main differences amongst the specialised raters are in the format of their reports. The extent, detail and style of the presentation of information and analysis may be different but the approaches of the agencies are similar, with allowances for differences in context in different regions.

What has not yet emerged is a single standard judgement, rating scale and grading system for rating MFIs. Such a rating scale could facilitate comparison among MFIs rated by different agencies. There has been some progress in discussions between M-CRIL and MicroRate, with the latter adopting the Greek alphabet scale used by M-CRIL. Recent discussions between these two agencies indicate that the judgements represented by each grade are similar.

How Are Rating Tools Being Improved with Experience?

Broadly, experience with the tools of the specialised raters has been very good from the start. An indication of the positive nature of this experience is provided by M-CRIL's long term relationships with its investor clients – Small Industries Development Bank of India (SIDBI), Hivos, Cordaid and SDC – but also by an analysis of the performance of MFIs it has rated.

Table 3 and the related Figure 3 presents an analysis of the growth and portfolio quality of 27 investment grade MFIs rated more than once by M-CRIL between 2002 and 2005. These data show the relative performance of MFIs with various rating grades. Clearly, the β+ rated MFIs have grown the least between their last two ratings and also have the worst portfolio quality. The α– MFIs have

Table 3. Analysis of the performance of investment grade MFIs

Rating grade (number)	Average Portfolio		Borrowers		Portfolio at Risk	
	Amount (US$)	Growth*	Number	Growth*	Previous	Latest**
β+ (8)	718,000	41%	7,764	11%	17.8%	11.0%
α– (8)	2,648,000	89%	30,433	109%	4.0%	3.3%
α (8)	3,939,000	103%	41,865	66%	3.5%	2.1%
a+ (3)	12,286,000	78%	145,893	78%	1.9%	0.6%

* % growth between ratings   ** end-March 2005

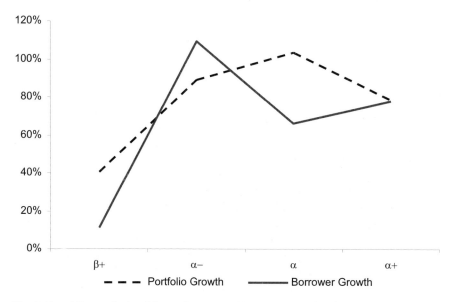

Fig. 3. Trend line analysis of the performance of investment grade MFIs

grown substantially faster, both in portfolio size and number of borrowers, while α rated MFIs have grown even faster in portfolio size but not so rapidly in terms of numbers of borrowers (which exceed 40,000). The best rated $\alpha+$ MFIs grow more slowly than $\alpha-$ MFIs in terms of portfolio and client size, reflecting their far higher base. Across the 27 MFIs, there has been consistent improvement in portfolio quality between their last two ratings. There were just two downgrades, each by one level, and eight upgrades between ratings. This is partly because of stricter M-CRIL standards introduced over several years to reflect a more mature microfinance sector in Asia.

Only one investment grade MFI rated by M-CRIL failed: the well known closure of Bank Dagang Bali by the Indonesian central bank due to governance failure. In fact, M-CRIL's rating pointed to governance risk as the one risk factor limiting the Bank's performance.

To the extent that improvements in microfinance rating tools may be necessary, they should include a sharpening of focus on specific risk factors in MFI operations – governance, cash flow monitoring, portfolio tracking and the control environment – and a greater emphasis on the rater's perception of the extent of risk relating to such factors.

How Does Microfinance Rating Affect Investor Confidence and Behaviour?

The issue in investor confidence is presently investors' perceptions of the credibility of specialised raters. Contrary to social investment funds like Unitus, MicroVest and Dexia Micro Fund, most conventional international investors, such as large pension funds and mutual funds, regard specialised raters as "unproven". This view reflects the investment funds' lack of familiarity and experience with the specialised rating agencies.

Neither the attempt to obtain greater sophistication in analysis and understanding of MFIs, nor the issue of investor confidence, has been helped by the Rating Fund's approach. The tendency, particularly of CGAP, has been to encourage a proliferation of 'instant raters.' These raters have suddenly become interested in microfinance only because of the lure of the Rating Fund's subsidy. They have been accredited by the Rating Fund without adequate evidence of their understanding and experience with microfinance issues and operations.

A more discerning approach by the Rating Fund could have helped to distinguish the proven from the unknown. The Rating Fund could have served as an internationally respected filtering mechanism, ensuring that only competent and experienced specialised raters could obtain accreditation. However, over-anxiety on the part of CGAP and the Rating Fund to gain recognition for microfinance as an economic activity has led to an approach that welcomes all and sundry, resulting in as many as 14 raters, big and small, being listed on the Rating Fund website. Many of these do not have significant experience or knowledge of microfinance. This disregard for the specialised agencies' combination of technical competence and dedication to microfinance is most unfortunate. Except for one local agency in Peru, the traditional, corporate rating agencies listed on the website have undertaken only a few ratings of MFIs, as indicated in Table 1 above.

This is, perhaps, not surprising. Most MFIs in Asia have fewer than 5,000 to 10,000 clients with portfolios of little more than $0.5 million. For corporate raters, such institutions are too small to deal with. They also subscribe to the ultimate heresy, lending to the poor. Corporate raters view MFIs as "essentially risky" propositions due to the widespread but standard misperception that lending to the poor is inherently risky.

Innovative Services for Private Social Investors

The presumed social and ethical basis for microfinance as an activity creates an opportunity to rate and benchmark peer groups in an ethical dimension. For instance, peer groups can be developed on the basis of

- depth of outreach in terms of the proportion of clients who belong to the poor and the extremely poor groups in society,

- those whose mission addresses the typical "development values" of concern to ethical investors, and/or in terms of

- improving access to financial services by poor women or microentrepreneurs.

However, there are far greater methodological and definitional issues here than there are in peer group benchmarking based on size, clientele and modes of delivery, presenting a highly complex challenge. The ratio of average outstanding loan to per capita GDP is sometimes used as a proxy for depth of outreach. But it is a weak indicator because of inter-country differences in income distribution and also because it primarily reflects the supply side. Impact studies undertaken by M-CRIL's parent organisation (EDA Rural Systems) and under the ImpAct programme, hosted by IDS Sussex, have shown that small loan sizes do not necessarily deter the non-poor due to their limited access to alternative credit.

Recent microfinance research has begun to focus on developing a clearer understanding of social performance and defining relevant indicators and methodologies for assessment. Rating agencies can respond by providing a separate assessment of an MFI's social performance which can be viewed side by side with the credit rating, as indicated in Box 1.

Is there a need for fiduciary ratings of social investment funds and are such ratings necessary to build trust amongst social investors in the emerging market for microfinance investment funds? The private social investor's concern is likely to be the safety of the invested funds. The microfinance investment funds that have been established to attract private social investors are largely using specialised raters. These ratings contribute to and inform investment appraisal and due diligence in selecting MFIs for investment. Therefore, fiduciary ratings of such funds will largely duplicate the work of the raters at the MFI level.

Box 1

Social rating is a tool to determine whether an MFI is achieving or is likely to achieve its social mission, and whether its social objectives are in line with wider development values. The social rating process is designed to assess whether an MFI adheres to its (explicit or implicit) social mission and has systems in place to ensure this; has substantive depth and breadth of outreach to the poor and underprivileged groups in their target areas; and is geared to respond effectively to its clients through appropriate products and delivery systems. This assessment is undertaken via staff discussions, systems review, field-level sample surveys and focus group discussions carefully designed to provide a socio-economic profile and substantive feedback from clients. This is the approach developed by M-CRIL.[7]

Social ratings require a unique set of research and assessment skills. M-CRIL has launched such a product based on the impact research experience of EDA Rural Systems, its parent organisation. The first social rating was undertaken by M-CRIL/EDA in December 2004. The report is posted on the CGAP website[8] and the social rating service is now available to MFIs, donors and investors in conjunction with credit rating or as a stand-alone assessment.

A similar type of assessment (but without independent field work) is being tested by other specialised raters based on work by CGAP's social indicators programme.[9] The case for developing a consensus around standards and methods for credit rating can now be applied to social rating. M-CRIL is working with other rating agencies under the CGAP programme to build such a consensus on relevant indicators and method of assessment.

Can Specialised Microfinance Raters Survive the Entry of Traditional Rating Agencies?

There is a clear distinction between traditional rating agencies and specialised rating agencies. From an MFI's perspective the distinction between them is as follows:

- The specialised agencies are more likely to understand the *dynamic issues* in financial service delivery to the poor; that lending to the poor is NOT inherently risky and is, indeed, inherently *less risky* in a developing country than lending to politically influential classes who can manipulate and obtain

---

[7] Details are posted on the M-CRIL website, www.m-cril.com.

[8] See Social Rating of Bullock-Cart Workers Development (BWDA) on www.ratingfund.org.

[9] A project undertaken by CERISE.

favourable treatment from local financial service providers; and that historically poor performance is likely to continue if MFI's products and systems are weak, but is more than likely to improve if the MFI's governance and management systems are strong and improve over time.

- While most donors and development banks are willing to accept a rating by a specialised agency, many more traditional investors such as pension funds, private investment funds, large corporations and individual investors are not yet willing to do likewise. Such investors are more accustomed to using ratings by corporate agencies for making "traditional" investments in international equity and debt markets but are unfamiliar with the products and the skills of specialised rating agencies for MFIs.

For this reason it is possible that, as MFIs improve and professionalise, they may increasingly use public credit risk rating services offered by corporate raters. In this case, the positioning and viability of specialised MFI rating agencies could become an issue. However, the main reason MFIs may increasingly use public credit risk rating services is that the ratings of the specialised agencies are not accepted by international commercial investors and by regulators. Similarly, the response by the international microfinance support agencies, such as CGAP, has been to devote development resources to encourage traditional agencies to rate MFIs.

Yet, the commercial logic of this luring strategy is doubtful. The traditional rating agencies are large organisations with turnover in hundreds of millions of dollars, while the microfinance rating business – with about 200 ratings conducted per year – is currently worth perhaps no more than $2 million a year. It is difficult to see the corporate agencies treating microfinance rating as anything more than a niche service offered for "social" rather than commercial reasons and, therefore, treated as peripheral, rather than as a mainstream activity with minimal resources devoted to understanding microfinance. The logic of accrediting 14 agencies for a $2 million market is baffling. If each employed an average of just 4 microfinance analysts, there would be about four ratings per analyst-year to go round! As it is, even some specialist raters undertaking ratings by the dozen find it difficult to break-even...

For specialised agencies, microfinance is their main or even only activity. As a result, such agencies make an intensive, undiluted effort to understand microfinance and its risk profile. Further, since rating is an ethics and confidence-based business, the leading specialised MFI raters have been careful to build confidence in their product and go out of their way to deliver high quality, trustworthy assessments with careful analytical orientation and independent rating committees as described earlier. On this basis, CGAP and other development support institutions would do well to use their resources to encourage regulators and commercial investors to accept the assessments of specialised raters that have demonstrated commitment to and skills for microfinance rating. This would be a far better fulfilment of their development mandate than chasing the elusive goal of persuading traditional raters to take the very small microfinance rating market seriously.

Furthermore, the specialised MFI rating agencies are targeting the same market as the corporate raters. As discussed above, these rating agencies may soon be in a position to offer social ratings in addition to credit risk ratings. This represents another contribution to serving microfinance investors – a matter that is better understood by specialised raters.

To conclude regarding the sustainability of specialised raters: The main problem is not the possibility of a takeover of the MFI rating market by corporate raters. On the contrary, the current state is a market caught in limbo: specialised raters being unacceptable to private investors largely because of the latter's lack of knowledge and familiarity with the former's commitment and skills, while corporate raters drag their feet over an unviable market scenario of "inherently risky" MFIs. The solution must be a concerted effort by the specialised raters – and as a public service by microfinance support organisations like CGAP – to increase the familiarity of investors, central banks and regulators with specialised raters who have clearly demonstrated their knowledge of and commitment to microfinance market development.

Important Links in Setting Standards for Disclosure and Accountability

In the absence of significant coverage in most Asian countries, the microfinance industry in the region is still largely self-regulated although some countries such as the Philippines (through microfinance-oriented rural banks) and Cambodia (through licensed MFIs) are starting to put a regulatory mechanism in place. Disclosure requirements for MFIs are minimal and poorly enforced so that the information available in the public domain is mostly self-reported by individual MFIs. This is true even for the most broadly circulated and widely used documents relating to the industry, such as the MicroBanking Bulletin.

In this situation, the role of rating agencies in bringing about qualitative change on disclosure and accountability issues is paramount. Some efforts have been made with the support of the specialised rating agencies that have significant databases, primarily M-CRIL and MicroRate. Some national networks in Pakistan and India in particular and the CGAP-IDB Rating Fund have made progress on setting disclosure standards, but much remains to be done. While the CGAP-IDB Fund insists on disclosure as a minimum condition for its support of a rating exercise, the nature of the activity is such that in many other cases the availability of M-CRIL's reports for public use is dependent on the wishes of the client, often an investor who has paid for the rating specifically for private decision making. MicroRate and PlanetRating, on the other hand, do manage to retain proprietorship of many of their rating reports.

In any case, in the absence of mandatory requirements in most countries, the large majority of MFIs remain unrated. Information about their operations has no credible independent verification. This lack of authentic information is a challenge for the microfinance industry to address. The rating agency's role here is to foster a common appreciation of this challenge among MFIs and investors, including specialised funds, lending institutions and donors.

Conclusions

Specialised microfinance rating agencies play a role in increasing the flow of funds – mainly loan funds – into financial institutions that work primarily with low income clients. These institutions include banks and specialised microfinance institutions. This role may be defined by the experience of three of the leading specialised microfinance raters: MicroRate, Planet Rating and M-CRIL. The latter is used here as the primary example.

Rating of microfinance institutions by specialised rating agencies has produced improvements in microfinance operations. This has occurred by drawing attention to weaknesses in individual MFIs, fostering knowledge and understanding of standards to be achieved and disseminating information about best practices in microfinance. This process has made a significant contribution to the deepening of financial markets in ways that serve low income families. Specialised rating of MFIs is poised to enhance MFI governance and performance by developing social rating, an entirely new product specifically developed for the microfinance sector that should also be of great interest to dual-objective investors in microfinance who seek social or developmental returns as well as financial returns.

The major issues facing specialised ratings for MFIs are:

- The incomplete harmonisation of the grading systems used by the different raters leads to confusion about the comparability of ratings made by different agencies. This complexity sends mixed signals to potential investors and complicates due diligence.

- Specialised microfinance rating should benefit international social investors. Promotion by public entities such as CGAP is warranted. Emphasising these raters' substantial commitment to, knowledge of and experience with microfinance should enhance the acceptability of specialised ratings. The relevance of specialised ratings and raters contrasts with the relative lack of microfinance knowledge and experience in the large corporate rating agencies.

- The social and ethical concerns and objectives of microfinance investors require the design of a social rating that could be offered in conjunction with or in addition to the fiduciary rating undertaken by microfinance raters at present. M-CRIL has launched such a product which will probably require greater sophistication as social investment markets become more discerning – in part through the existence of specialised rating services.

Above all, for financial services to reach a large proportion of low income families in developing countries, an increasing focus on professionalisation and efficiency is essential. This focus is a pre-condition for linking MFIs with social investors initially, and then with commercial markets. Only through these markets can the vast resources required be realised. The efforts of specialised raters in providing rating services for microfinance have made and will continue to make a substantive contribution to this process.

Annex: Ratings Directly Financed by Donors/MFIs

Country	MFI	Rating financed by ..	Purpose
Bangladesh	Ashrai	SDC Novib	loan fund & operating cost: Determination of investment in loan fund and operating cost subsidy
	BURO Tangail	DFID SDC	creation of special purpose funds
	Shakti Foundation	SDC	provision of guarantee
Cambodia	CEB, EMT TPC	MPDF CGAP	fund raising
India	RGVN – Orissa	Hivos	financing loan fund and operating cost
	8 MFIs	FWWB-USAID	cross-verification
	ASA Trust DCCB Bidar SHARE Spandana Shepherd	CGAP	benchmarking and fund raising
	BASIX	Ford Foundation	fund raising
	SEWA Bank	SEWA Bank	benchmarking
Indonesia	3 BPRs	USAID Asia Foundation	demonstrate utility of rating to banks
	Ganesha Found'n Pokmas Mandiri Ysn Mitra Usaha	Hivos	loan fund and operating cost
	Bina Swadaya	Cordaid	loan fund and operating cost, fund raising
Kazakhstan	Kazakhstan City Loan Fund	Hivos	(1) loan fund and operating cost (2) graduation to commercial funding
Myanmar	Grameen Trust GRET PACT	UNDP	loan fund and operating cost
	Nirdhan Utthan Bk NSSC RRN VYCCU	CECI-CIDA	benchmarking, demonstrate utility of rating to banks
Pakistan	Urban Poverty Alleviation Project	CGAP	benchmarking
Philippines	ARDCI CRBBI NWTF TSKI	CGAP	benchmarking fund raising
Sri Lanka	SEEDS	CGAP	benchmarking
Timor-Leste	Moris Rasik	Hivos	loan fund and operating cost
	Institute for Microfinance TL	ADB	benchmarking

CHAPTER 4:

MFI Equity: An Investment Opportunity for the Broader Public?

Kylie A. Charlton

Vice President – Capital Markets, Unitus

Introduction

Microfinance institutions (MFIs) provide financial products to the economically active poor (EAP), a market segment underserved by mainstream financial institutions. Traditionally, credit in the form of livelihood (or business) loans has been the focus for MFIs. In recent years some MFIs have extended their product offering to include savings accounts, home improvement loans, education loans and a range of insurance products.

Having the EAP as their target market, MFIs have been largely confined to governments and international donors for funding. MFIs have been unable to access the broad range of funding available to mainstream financial institutions from the debt and equity capital markets. Despite this limitation microfinance has proven to be an important, financially sustainable, even profitable instrument for economic development when sufficient capital is available in combination with sound business practices. However, continued dependence on capital from government and donor sources will prevent the microfinance industry from closing a supply-demand gap estimated at 420 million people and an annual demand for capital of between $2.5 billion to $5.0 billion[1] (de Sousa Shields and Frankiewicz 2004). The ability of MFIs to attract large amounts of new capital on a commercially sustainable basis, without an erosion of their original development goals, is critical to the future growth and success of the microfinance industry.

This chapter explores one aspect of the capital dilemma faced by the microfinance industry: the role of equity investment from the broader public. Equity is the cornerstone on which regulated, for-profit MFIs can build sustainable liability structures to support growth. Many parallels can be drawn between the investment opportunity presented by equity in early stage or "second generation" MFIs and private equity, or more precisely venture capital. Microfinance investment funds

---

[1] All figures are in US dollars unless otherwise stated.

(MFIFs) focused on equity investment in second generation MFIs present a potentially attractive investment opportunity not dissimilar to that of emerging market venture capital funds. The corollary is that such MFIFs appeal to niche investors. The challenges faced by MFIFs across the investment lifecycle in part mirror those of emerging market private equity funds, but are in some respects unique. Despite these challenges, MFIFs are increasingly taking ownership in MFIs around the world, providing clear evidence of a continuing evolution of microfinance away from philanthropy towards a sustainable commercial industry.

Role of MFI Equity

Portfolio growth and increasing the number of clients served depend on an MFI's ability to generate retained earnings and attract external capital. Since the mid-1990s, internal capital sources have expanded beyond the traditional charitable grants or subsidised debt. Many MFIs are beginning to seek commercial debt and private equity. This transition reflects two changes. First, the microfinance industry recognises that retained earnings and traditional funding sources cannot satisfy the long-term funding requirements of MFIs. Second, the well-publicised success of a number of MFIs that have transformed from not-for-profit organisations to regulated, for-profit financial institutions is changing investors' perception of microfinance from that of charity to a profitable commercial venture.

The current universe of MFIs structured as regulated, for-profit institutions is limited. A study commissioned by the Council of Microfinance Equity Funds[2] identified a total of 124 regulated, for-profit MFIs in the developing world, inclu-

Table 1. Regulated, for-profit MFIs in the developing world

Regions	No. of MFIs Identified	No. of MFIs Providing Sufficient Information	Total Assets (USD millions)	Gross Loans (USD millions)	Number of Clients	Total Equity (USD millions)
Latin America & Caribbean	47	35	1,032.4	826.7	965,668	159.5
Eastern Europe & NIS	25	21	874.5	377.3	145,988	82.7
Asia	24	17	248.7	130.2	1,077,808	47.8
Africa & the Middle East	28	19	335.9	214.4	706,839	76.7
TOTAL	**124**	**92**	**$2,490.8**	**$1,548.6**	**2,896,303**	**$362.6**

Source: Kaddaras and Rhyne (2005)

[2] The Council for Microfinance Equity Funds is a group of 19 private equity funds with joint social and financial missions that invest in MFIs (www.cmef.org).

ding nine government-controlled institutions (Kaddaras and Rhyne 2005). A significant increase in this number is expected as three trends accelerate: (1) "upgrading" or transforming not-for-profit MFIs into regulated, for-profit financial institutions, (2) "downscaling" or the entry of mainstream financial institutions into microfinance services, and (3) "greenfielding" or founding new MFIs as regulated, for-profit financial institutions.

Equity is the critical cornerstone for regulated, for-profit financial institutions. Equity is required to meet the minimum capital requirements set by the local central bank. Moreover, equity provides the capacity to: (1) leverage an institution's balance sheet through debt, mezzanine debt and quasi-equity instruments; and (2) mobilise local savings. Together, equity, debt and savings deposits form the essential components of a sustainable liability structure that over time can be fully integrated into international and local capital markets and substantially increase MFIs' access to capital and thus their ability to expand outreach to target clients. Diversification across these funding sources will lower MFIs' cost of funds.

Equity's expansionary role is as important as its role in corporate governance. Equity entails ownership: shareholders' active presence at the board level influences the strategic direction and ultimate performance of an MFI.

Second Generation MFIs: A Subset of Private Equity?

"Private equity" denotes investment in illiquid, unregistered securities of firms. It describes all venture, buyout and mezzanine investing. This chapter focuses principally on venture capital and the many parallels it has with investment opportunities presented by second generation MFIs. "Private equity" and "venture capital" are used interchangeably.

Venture capital bridges the gap between the sources of funds for innovation (chiefly corporations, government bodies, an entrepreneur's friends and family or "angel investors") and lower-cost sources of capital available to going concerns. Venture capital funds typically:

- Invest in high-growth industries at the middle of the classic industry S-curve when companies begin to commercialise their innovations;

- Support rapid growth in portfolio companies (that is, companies represented in an investor's portfolio) by dedicating funding to building these companies' infrastructure in ways that drive and sustain growth;

- Provide equity finance and also add value through active participation in the management of portfolio companies;

- Seek some control over portfolio companies by, for example, taking an equity stake large enough to buy a board seat or to reserve the right to replace management;

- Realise returns for investors through exit mechanisms such as a trade sale, management buy-back or initial public offering; and

- Thrive when invested in illiquid, difficult-to-value firms in environments with substantial uncertainties and information asymmetries.

Successful private equity transactions occur when market inefficiencies are identified and exploited. This can mean searching for sectors lacking capital, investing in misperceived or out-of-favour industries and asset classes, identifying companies with significant franchise value, barriers to entry and other competitive advantages, or taking advantage of government or tax policies that skew the risk/return trade-off decidedly in favour of investors.

The microfinance industry is characterised by factors that would typically attract private equity. First, as noted above, microfinance is estimated to have a substantial supply-demand gap and an annual demand for capital of between $2.5 billion to $5.0 billion. Second, there is a wide misperception that microfinance is nothing more than a philanthropic endeavour. Few in the global investing community are aware that some MFIs have attained self-sufficiency and are profitable, providing strong returns on assets and on equity, while performing better than commercial banks operating in the same market (Tucker and Miles 2004). Third, favourable regulatory changes in many countries are creating environments that promote microfinance.

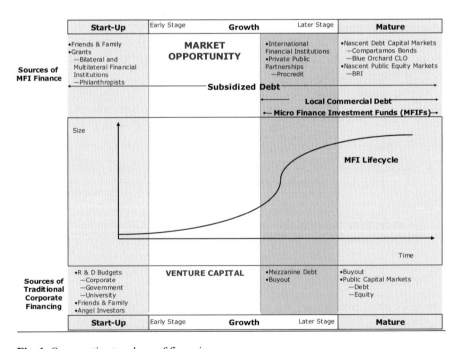

Fig. 1. Comparative typology of financing sources

Governments, development banks and international donors have provided grants to fund innovation in microfinance and have demonstrated its power as an economic development tool. Mature MFIs have arisen as a result and are increasingly attractive to nascent debt and equity capital markets. However, equity for transforming, downscaling and greenfielding MFIs is as vital for the commercialisation and scale of microfinance as venture capital is for traditional industries. MFIF managers conversant with both traditional investment processes and microfinance understand the latter's close parallel to venture capital when they select high-potential institutions and add value through active ownership. The challenge for many MFIFs is to ensure that the scope of their investment target allows them to reach second generation MFIs, opening opportunities in which they can participate for the benefit of their investors.

An Attractive Investment Opportunity

CGAP[3] and others state that microfinance is a more stable investment than commercial banks in emerging markets (Littlefield and Rosenberg 2004). During the Asian crisis in the late 1990s commercial bank portfolios imploded, but loan repayment among the 26 million microfinance clients of Bank Rakyat Indonesia declined much less. During the Bolivian crisis the quality of MFIs portfolios fell, but by less than commercial bank portfolios. Developing World Markets[4] identifies four highlights in investing in MFI equity via MFIFs:

- Microfinance industry growth forecasts are substantially higher than GDP growth in emerging markets.

- Portfolio quality and loan default rates are usually more favourable than those of most major global banks.

- Organic growth drives high internal rates of return on investment.

- Volatility is lower than for traditional emerging market equities or bonds.

MFI investment extends beyond quantitative factors. For Bob Pattillo, founder of Gray Ghost, investment in MFIFs includes the opportunity to participate in and drive innovative financing techniques. Such innovation is rewarded with a "double bottom-line" consisting of a financial and a social return. Participation by investors in MFI equity helps to build a full service financial system for those beyond the frontier of formal finance, directly contributing to alleviation of poverty. Pattillo (2004) observes that:

---

[3] The Consultative Group to Assist the Poor (CGAP), a microfinance support and research organisation chaired by the World Bank.

[4] Developing World Markets was the co-structuring agent on an $87 million securitisation issue for BlueOrchard Microfinance Securities.

> *...when it comes to really making a dent in world poverty in a pow-*
> *erful, sustainable way, none compare to the promise of the social*
> *investment fund.... A fund recycles capital, well beyond a person's*
> *lifetime if that is their intention.*

MFIFs managed by experienced microfinance fund managers using disciplined investment practices enable investors to participate in a portfolio of MFIs. Such funds provide asset diversification by asset class and geographic region along with a double bottom-line return. Viewed as venture capital in emerging markets, MFIFs could also be considered as a class of alternative assets[5] that offer portfolio diversification and build returns by reducing volatility and risk. This is particularly true for double bottom-line investors who seek less volatility than in traditional equities or bonds in emerging markets.

Ethical Double Bottom-Line Returns

What double bottom-line return can investors expect from MFIFs? First, are financial returns from investment in MFI equity ethical? The simple justification for a double bottom-line return is that the funding required for the microfinance industry to reach its potential as a highly positive social and financial force cannot be satisfied from traditional donor or government sources. In short, capital markets must be tapped. The challenge is to produce a financial return for investors without drifting away from the development objective of poverty alleviation.

The success of large scale microfinance programmes is often credited to three key elements: social collateral, borrower participation, and charging a fee for services that exceeds costs. But success is more directly attributable to strong credit risk management skills, innovative credit technology and the operational focus of microcredit lenders. Careful attention to strategic fundamentals means keeping transaction costs low; matching loan repayment schedules to borrowers' income and savings potential, finding ways to obtain good performance from large and widely dispersed field staff, addressing basic client expectations efficiently with innovative products; and, above all, managing the risk of borrower default. Focus on these fundamentals creates financially sustainable MFIs able to attract commercial capital.

Microfinance industry specialists advocate a financially sustainable model as imperative for long term success. For example, PROFUND, a ten-year closed fund that was dissolved on schedule in 2005, explicitly stated that it "does not perceive a conflict between poverty alleviation and profitability....It believes that financial viability is a necessity for the long term success of poverty alleviation efforts in microfinance" (Silva 2005). Participants in a panel discussion on "International

---

[5] Alternative assets are non-traditional asset classes, such as private equity, venture capital, hedge funds and real estate. While alternative assets are generally more risky than traditional asset classes and therefore offer an accompanying higher return, their primary attractiveness lies in their lack of correlation with traditional assets.

Microfinance: A New Investment Opportunity" at the Milken Institute's Global Conference in 2003 stated that there was "no contradiction between making a profit and having a social impact given that a sustainable impact can only be achieved on the social side of your business if it is indeed profitable and able to remain in business continuing to provide financial services to the people it serves". One participant noted that unless the industry generates reasonable returns acceptable to patient capital, it is destined to fail.

Accepting that a financial return on MFI equity is ethical and essential, what level of double bottom-line return is required to attract investors? Dual-objective investors want to maximise their internal rate of return (IRR) on investment and simultaneously promote the greatest socioeconomic benefit possible. Conversations with investors suggest that their return expectations range from 7 percent to greater than 25 percent. Lacking detailed research on investor demand and return requirements, this range does little more than demonstrate a wide discrepancy in expectations. It poses a challenge for MFIFs that typically target an IRR on equity of 8 percent to 12 percent to investors after fund management costs. IRR, a financial measure, does not capture social return. A challenge for MFIFs is to develop metrics for social return that are comparable to the way IRR is used to evaluate financial performance.[6]

PROFUND was incorporated as a for-profit investment fund with the aim of achieving superior financial returns for its investors by supporting the growth of regulated, efficient financial intermediaries in Latin America and the Caribbean. It invested equity and quasi-equity in eligible financial institutions to improve their operations while expanding their scale. The fund's all-inclusive, final annualised IRR is believed to have ranged between 6 percent and 10 percent. As with any private equity fund, PROFUND losses on some investments were offset with good returns on others. The performance of its portfolio companies more than offset currency losses from MFIs in countries that devalued against the US Dollar.

Private equity funds in emerging markets in Latin America over the same period averaged single digit returns. PROFUND performed well against this standard. Moreover, foreign exchange risk and unclear exit strategies are little different from those faced by private equity funds generally in emerging markets. PROFUND demonstrated that it is possible to build successful financial institutions to serve the entrepreneurial poor, and that investing in such institutions can be attractive compared to other private equity opportunities in emerging markets.

Defining the Broader Public

Having established the critical role of equity in closing the global supply-demand gap for microfinance and that investment in MFIFs presents an attractive investment opportunity, who should be the target investors for MFIFs? Can MFIFs be-

---

[6] See Sinha, Chapter 5 in this volume.

come an alternative asset class that appeals to the broader public? Or are MFIFs a
niche investment? As of June 2003, MFIFs had invested $250 million – a small
percentage of the estimated $15 billion global microfinance portfolio (CGAP
2004). Public funds provide approximately half the capital invested in MFIFs.
Only $125 million was committed by private investors, primarily high net-worth
individuals and private foundations, followed by minor participation by pension
funds, insurance companies and other financial firms. Furthermore, investment in
MFIFs is mostly debt with equity attracting just 20 percent of investment dollars

Table 2. Investor characteristics and MFI equity

Sophisticated	There is no independent rating or benchmarking of MFIFs to which investors can look for assistance in determining their choice of investment. Investors must make their own assessment of the strengths and weaknesses of respective MFIFs. The absence of any widely accepted measure for double bottom-line returns means investors have no single benchmark against which the combined financial and social performance of MFIFs can be easily compared in a manner they are accustomed to, such as IRR for traditional fund investments.
Risk seeking with appetite for emerging markets	Investment in MFIFs investing in emerging markets expose investors to country risk (regulatory, political, settlement and foreign exchange); management risk given a limited pool of qualified human capital; and dysfunctional capital markets and high illiquidity.
Patient	Regulated, for-profit MFIs with performance track records over a significant time are only beginning to evolve. Investment opportunities are few. Management efforts to negotiate and close investments time consuming. Traditional exit options available for companies in private equity portfolios in developed economies are not available in emerging markets. Patience is required throughout the investment cycle, along with a highly flexible time frame. MFIFs must act creatively to source investment opportunities and orchestrate profitable exits in dysfunctional capital markets.
Able to absorb high transaction costs	Costs associated with investing in MFIs are high given the time and management effort absorbed in identifying and closing investment deals, combined with active ownership throughout the investment period. Management fees for MFIFs, especially if small in size, may need to be higher than those of traditional private equity funds.
Unregulated	Investor participation in traditional private equity progressed from high net worth individuals to institutional investors with the relaxation of regulatory constraints. The regulatory environment must be conducive for MFIFs.
Socially motivated	Investors in MFIFs must be motivated by a double bottom-line objective. They must clearly accept that the objective of an MFI is to optimise financial and social return.

(CGAP 2004). To attract increased equity investment MFIFs must target investors having a unique set of characteristics based on the market for MFI equity.

Investment in MFIFs has the characteristics of both venture capital and philanthropy as illustrated in Figure 2. If the trajectory of investor participation in venture capital is any indication of investor participation in MFIFs, it can be hypothesised that the long-term definition of the broader public for MFIFs will be a niche market comprising socially responsible (dual-objective), high net worth individuals and socially motivated institutional investors, especially those with an appetite for emerging markets. Moreover, early evidence suggests that the timing of investor participation in MFIFs is likely to follow a path similar to that of venture capital, which was the domain of wealthy individuals and families before attracting institutional investors.

Reaching such investors is not, however, without challenge. First, the current structure of most MFIFs providing equity opportunities to investors, especially those in the US, is a legal structure that limits participation to a narrowly defined set of high net worth individuals recognised as "accredited investors".[7] Second, institutional investors, while having a risk appetite for illiquid long-term investments (as demonstrated by their investment in venture capital) do not typically

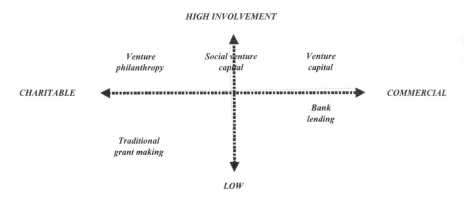

Fig. 2. Typology of social financing (adapted from John Kingston, Venturesome)

---

[7] MFIFs developed in the US have typically been structured as limited liability partnerships with limited partnership interests offered through private placements not registered under the Securities Act 1933. Such investors are required to meet the definition of an "accredited investor", which for an individual requires net worth exceeding $1,000,000; annual income exceeding $200,000 in the last two calendar years plus a reasonable expectation of income in excess of $200,000 during the current year; or joint income with their spouse of more than $300,000 in the last two calendar years plus a reasonable expectation of income in excess of $300,000 during the current year. The use of limited liability partnerships mirrors the accepted structure of traditional private equity funds.

have investment policies and asset allocation strategies that incorporate a measure for double bottom line returns.

Finally, international financial institutions (IFIs), both bilaterals (such as FMO and KfW) and multilaterals (such as EBRD, IFC, and IADB), are expected to continue as an important subset of the target investor market for MFIFs.[8] Their task is to "crowd-in" private investors who are hesitant to commit capital in countries with highly uncertain risk/return trade-offs and with which they are unfamiliar (Leeds and Sunderland 2003; Rhyne 2005). IFIs risk crowding out private investors if they take long term positions in MFIFs supporting mature MFIs without continually reallocating capital to second generation MFIs.

Life Cycle for Microfinance Equity Funds

MFIFs' investment cycle closely mirrors that of private equity: fundraising, investing, monitoring and exiting. Fund managers for MFIFs recognise, however, that they cannot blindly apply traditional private equity investing tools and processes without taking into account the characteristics of the microfinance sector. MFIFs preparing to approach investors have learnt a number of important lessons which differentiate the investment cycle for MFI equity from that of private equity firms. These lessons include the challenges of creating an environment conducive for investment in MFIFs.

Fundraising

Structures. Fund structures for MFIFs have attempted to mirror those of traditional private equity, providing a look and feel familiar to seasoned investors. Some of these structures have been established using for-profit entities, while others have combined for-profit and non-profit entities. Combinations usually result from a not-for-profit microfinance organisation with an established history that expands its operations to act as fund manager of a for-profit investment vehicle. For-profit, not-for-profit and combined structures all present varying complications and limitations under different investment jurisdictions. Policy makers could greatly assist the attractiveness of MFIFs to investors by simplifying procedures for structures that straddle the for-profit and not-for-profit worlds or by establishing regulation that favours the emergence of blended for-profit and not-for-profit structures.

---

[8] FMO (Nederlandse Financierings Maatschappij voor Ontwikkelingslanden NV), KfW (Kreditanstalt für Wiederaufbau), EBRD (European Bank for Reconstruction and Development), IFC (International Finance Corporation, part of the World Bank Group), IADB (Inter-American Development Bank).

Investing

Types of Investments. Perhaps the greatest challenge facing investment in MFIFs is MFIs' capacity to absorb equity. As noted above, the Council for Microfinance Equity Funds identified only 124 regulated, for-profit institutions with an ownership structure able to absorb foreign equity investment. This universe is further restricted by the investment criteria of most MFIFs favouring mature MFIs. The challenge of expanding the pool to second generation MFIs requires balancing the increased risk associated with early stage investment with the higher potential returns of attractive entry valuations and growth rates. However, the greater challenge for MFIFs may be the costs of providing advisory assistance to optimise the potential investment return of second generation MFIs. Unless investors accept higher management fees, or unless substantial growth in the average size of MFIFs increases management fee income, MFIFs working with second generation MFIs will continue to rely heavily on donor funds to cover the cost of technical assistance to their portfolio companies.

Deal Structuring. The form of equity financing by MFIFs ranges from ordinary shares, preferred shares, warrants to convertible debt. For MFIs that become regulated, for-profit institutions, convertible debt gives MFIFs the right to participate in equity as soon as the ownership structure allows. The key consideration in ownership structure is that rights of control, combined with community ownership and carefully defined management incentives, drive the MFI to deliver double bottom-line returns.

Valuation. Pricing is one of the greatest challenges for MFIFs. First, developing countries typically lack timely and accurate macroeconomic and financial information which, when combined with political and regulatory risk, makes it difficult to construct reasonable projections for an investment in an MFI. Uncertainty is compounded by the absence of audited financial statements or, if audited, by accounting principles and practices that differ from accepted international standards. Second, few benchmarks are available to assist in determining price. The low volume of MFI equity transactions, combined with the lack of public information about many such transactions, makes it difficult for MFIFs to find benchmarks or other points of reference.

Valuation challenges are not confined to the purchase and divestment of equity. They also apply to MFIFs' portfolios. Lack of benchmarks and consistency in valuation methodology throughout the investment cycle make it difficult for investors to compare MFIFs and contrast this to other portfolio investments.

Investment Management

Active Ownership. Perhaps the most important and challenging role for MFIFs is the value they add as active owners. Active ownership contributes significantly to an institution's corporate governance through participation at the board level and possibly advisory assistance. A recent study by McKinsey & Company revealed strong correlation between active ownership by private equity firms and superior performance by portfolio companies (Heel and Kehoe 2005). Emerging market private equity funds have also recognised that value created by management is the most important part of their business (Leeds and Sunderland 2003). Active ownership by MFIFs to nurture their portfolio companies is, however, a costly endeavour consuming valuable professional resources that need to be carefully factored into management fees.

Exiting

Exit is the most vexing problem for MFIFs, as it is for emerging market private equity funds. Mapping an exit strategy and ensuring that company management is fully committed to it is essential in investment negotiations. Strategies may include guaranteed exits and divestment mechanisms such as put options, controlling blocks, management buy-in and liquidation. These mechanisms do not ensure successful exit. Successful exit requires the financial well-being and strong performance of the MFI, which also depends on the economic situation of the country in which the MFI operates.

Traditional exit through an initial public offering (IPO) is not a reliable option because few developing countries' equity markets have sufficient depth. Most MFIFs consider that private sale to strategic local investors, including commercial banks wanting to acquire microfinance operations, provide the most probable exits. The continuing evolution and increasing sophistication of the national securities exchanges, regulatory agencies, banking systems, and capital markets in developing countries is also expected to open up exit opportunities. MFIFs must be willing and able to experiment with new, more creative approaches to exit.

Going Forward

MFIFs that bring together microfinance professionals and the specialised knowledge and experience of finance provide a clear opportunity for catalysing investment participation. Participation will increase as the microfinance industry sheds its charity image and adopts commercial investment practices, and as regulatory hurdles are lowered. Acknowledgement of the benefits of structuring MFIs as regulated, for-profit institutions with equity as the cornerstone of their capital structure is beginning to emerge.

The many challenges for MFIFs in expanding this investment opportunity to the broader public can be distilled into four main themes that have the potential to shape investment opportunity:

1. Expanding MFIFs' investment targets to include second generation MFIs and fulfilling the role of venture capital for the microfinance industry, positioning themselves as a subset of private equity in emerging markets.

2. Lobbying emerging market governments for favourable treatment of venture capital-type investments in MFIs. US Government regulation and tax policies (changes in capital gains tax rates, tax treatment of stock options, regulations on pension funds' asset allocations, regulation of investment advisors) drove the creation and growth of the domestic private equity and venture capital industry in the US (Fenn et al. 1996). A recent Cambridge University study of private equity in 15 countries found that the legal and tax environments matter as much as the depth of capital markets in the development of private equity, and that more lenient bankruptcy laws spurred "entrepreneurial demand" for private equity (Armour and Cumming 2004).

3. Incorporating social venture capital, and more precisely MFIFs, into the asset allocation models of socially motivated institutions and individuals. Social venture capital should comprise a small percentage of these investors' portfolios in the same way that investment is allocated to high-risk assets. This challenge is as much about the development of appropriate financial theory to encapsulate the concept of a double bottom line as it is about building support for the alleviation of global poverty. Investment advisers and private bankers should increasingly present MFIFs as offering double bottom-line returns to dual-objective investors. Advisers to philanthropists should indicate that donations are not the only way to participate in a cause – social investment instruments are also available. Within an overall giving strategy, these may offer a superior sustainable, long-term social benefit.

4. Lobbying developed country governments to adopt regulations conducive to development of and investment in social venture capital funds, such as MFIFs, by the broader public. Consideration should be given to monetary incentives that would encourage investors to participate in social venture capital, such as through reduced tax on income and capital gains. Such incentives could be incorporated in developed nations' strategies towards poverty alleviation and the achievement of the Millennium Development Goals defined by the United Nations. It would not be the first time that investment incentives were offered for direct investment in projects having a development impact. Municipal bonds' tax-exempt status in the US promotes private investment in public infrastructure. Favourable tax policy was applied to infrastructure bonds in Australia in the mid-1990s for the same purpose; the Netherlands promotes social investment through tax incentives to investors; and Community Investment Tax Relief (CITR) investors in the United Kingdom can invest in accredited community development finance institutions (CDFIs) which provide finance to qualifying profit-distributing enterprises, social enterprises or community projects.

A number of research topics follow directly from these themes:

- Empirical studies to explore the largely anecdotal comparisons between emerging market private equity and MFIFs.

- Recommendations for regulatory changes in emerging markets to promote investment in MFIs.

- Asset allocation tools encapsulating measures to assess double bottom-line investment opportunities provided by social venture capital funds.

- Assessment of the options that governments could consider to promote investment in social capital venture funds.

Concluding Remarks

For microfinance to reach its potential, poverty must be viewed as an investment opportunity. It is essential that MFIFs work collectively to relay this message to lenders, private equity, investment bankers, fund managers, capital market specialists, large and small investors, philanthropists, financial advisers, regulators and policy makers. The investment opportunity presented by MFI equity will not be seized by the broader public until the investment community and policy makers in developed and developing nations refine their approaches. This convergence is critical to providing MFIs with capital sources similar to those available to mainstream financial institutions, with equity as an essential component, to build full service financial systems for the entrepreneurial poor.

References

Armour, John and Cumming, Douglas (2004) 'The Legal Road to Replicating Silicon Valley', ESRC Centre for Business Research, University of Cambridge Working Paper No. 281

CGAP (2004) 'Foreign Investment in Microfinance: Debt and Equity from Quasi-Commercial Investors', Focus Note 2004, No. 25

EMPEA (Emerging Market Private Equity Association) (2005) 'Emerging Markets Private Equity', A quarterly newsletter of the Emerging Markets Private Equity Association, Vol.1, Issue 1, Q1 2005

Fenn, George, Liang, Nellie and Prowse, Stephen (1996) 'The Economics of the Private Equity Markets', Federal Reserve Bulletin, January 1996

Heel, Joachim and Kehoe, Conor (2005) 'Why some private equity firms do better than others', The McKinsey Quarterly, No. 1

Jain, Pankaj and Moore, Mick (2003) 'What makes microcredit programmes effective? Fashionable fallacies and workable realities', ISD Working Paper 177

Kaddaras, James and Rhyne, Elisabeth (2004) 'Characteristics of Equity Investment in Microfinance', Council of Microfinance Equity Funds, 2004

Leeds, Roger and Sunderland, Julie (2003) 'Private Equity Investing In Emerging Markets', Journal of Applied Corporate Finance, Vol. 15, No. 4, Spring 2003

Littlefield, Elizabeth and Rosenberg, Richard (2004) 'Breaking Down the Walls between Microfinance and the Formal Financial System', CGAP

Pattillo, Bob (2005) 'Commercial Investment in Microfinance: Fears and Fulfillment', Ingrid Mattäus-Maier and J.D. von Pischke (eds.), Microfinance Investment Funds – Leveraging Private Capital for Economic Growth and Poverty Reduction Berlin, Springer Verlag, pp. 227-230

Rhyne, Elisabeth (2005) 'Perspectives from the Council of Microfinance Equity Funds', Small Enterprise Development, Vol. 16, No. 1

Silva, Alex (2005) 'Investing in microfinance – Profund's story', Small Enterprise Development, Vol. 16, No. 1

Sousa-Shields, Marc de and Frankiewicz, Cheryl et al. (2004) 'Financing Microfinance Institutions: The Context for Transitions to Private Capital', USAID Microreport #8

Tucker, Michael and Miles, Gerard (2004) 'Financial Performance of Microfinance Institutions: A comparison to Performance of Regional Commercial Banks by Geographic Region', Journal of Microfinance, Vol. 6, No. 1

VentureOne (2005) 'Quarterly Venture Capital Report'

CHAPTER 5

Microfinance and Economic Growth – Reflections on Indian Experience

K.V. Kamath

Managing Director & CEO, ICICI Bank

Introduction

Achieving balanced and inclusive economic growth is a key challenge faced by policymakers in countries around the world. The gains of economic growth are accessible to a greater extent by the relatively advantaged, who find it easier to participate in the growth process. Poorer people, who are separated by distance from the urban areas where economic activity is concentrated, have to wait much longer to reap the benefits of economic growth. Engaging these sections of society in the economic mainstream is essential to achieve balanced growth, which is critical for the long-term sustainability of social development and economic prosperity.

Access to financial services is a key element of the process of socio-economic empowerment. Only by delivering financial services to people in rural areas and lower income strata can they be brought within the ambit of economic activity. Only then can the full potential of the country's physical and human resources be realised. The rural economy represents a large latent demand for credit, savings and risk mitigation products like insurance. Governments and regulators the world over have articulated the expansion of financial service delivery to this segment of the population as a priority objective.

The Importance of Financial Services

The delivery of financial services to lower income households in rural areas, however, presents a unique set of challenges. This customer segment has a high volume of low value transactions and requires doorstep services, flexibility in timing as well as simple procedures and documentation . These require a set of skills completely different from those deployed by mainstream financial intermediaries. At the same time, traditional modes of outreach, like physical branch networks, prove to be inappropriate because of their high costs. Microfinance is a model which seeks to provide financial services to the rural population in a viable and sustainable manner.

Microfinance

Microfinance encompasses the provision of a broad range of services such as deposits, loans, payment services, money transfers and insurance products to poor and low-income households and microenterprises. Microfinance allows replacement of high-cost debt from informal sources, thereby increasing disposable income. It inculcates financial discipline, resulting in ownership of assets, and enhances the ability to withstand shocks due to access to savings products, credit and insurance. In lower income countries with inadequate institutional infrastructure, microfinance is an important development tool and has helped expand the depth of financial services.

The Indian Context

With a population of over 1 billion and estimates of the number of poor people ranging from 300 to 400 million, India is one of the largest markets for microfinancial services. It is estimated that a large part of the demand for credit in this stratum is currently met by informal sources.

The twentieth century saw large-scale efforts to improve the quality of life in rural India. Different approaches were adopted by government agencies and non-government organisations (NGOs) to improve the condition of the rural population. These included land redistribution, building economic and political awareness, technology transfer and delivery of a variety of services. Credit in the rural sector was largely supplied by co-operative societies till the mid-1960s with the commercial banks' rural operations centered around agri-businesses and marketing. One of the objectives of bank nationalisations in 1969 and 1980 was to increase the flow of rural credit. However, merely expanding physical presence in rural areas did not achieve the desired results, given the need to overlay mainstream financial service delivery models with the social mobilisation skills that were essential to meet developmental objectives.

The self-help group (SHG)-bank linkage programme was the initial microfinance initiative launched by the National Bank for Agriculture and Rural Development (NABARD) in 1992. While this model of partnership between the banking sector and voluntary organisations achieved reasonable success, it continued to depend on the creation of an extensive banking network. Challenges in scaling up this model led to the introduction of financial intermediation by microfinance institutions (MFIs) that provide microfinance services to the poor, especially in rural areas.

Microfinance Institutions

MFIs borrow from commercial sources and on-lend to clients (groups/individuals). Most MFIs in India started with grants and concessional loans and gradually made the transition to commercial funding. While much of the growth in the initial years was financed by concessional loans from funding agencies, this was followed from 2001 onwards by raising equity from domestic as well as international agencies and by borrowings from the banking sector.

MFIs have been observed to administer risks better than the traditional banking sector. There may be two explanations for this:

- MFIs have developed specialised systems of evaluation, supervision, administration and recovery of credits attuned to their clientele, and

- the clients have developed an appropriate financial culture.

Since 2003, several banks have entered the microfinance sector with innovative scaling-up strategies. In addition to term loans, some of the innovative structures offered by banks in India to create access to financial services in the rural areas are:

- Partnership: Several MFIs have an excellent base and infrastructure in their specific markets. However, they lack access to product knowledge, funding and technology platforms. In the partnership model, the bank provides mezzanine equity and technology to the NGO/MFI and lends directly to clients with risk-sharing by the NGO/MFI. The bank also provides loan funds for the MFI's own investment requirements.

  The MFI undertakes loan origination, monitoring and collection. The advantage of this structure is that it separates the risk of the MFI from the risk of the portfolio. Here the intermediary or the MFI assumes a fraction of the credit risk (to the extent of risk sharing), leading to a reduction in capital required. It combines the core competence of NGOs/MFIs with that of banks – social mobilisation skills with finance.

- Securitisation: In this model the commercial bank identifies a portfolio based on fulfillment of minimum criteria and past portfolio performance. Though the MFI continues to collect receivables from the borrowers, its leverage is reduced which enables it to originate further assets. This product gives the bank the advantage of differentiating between the financial and operational risk of the MFI while credit enhancement improves the rating of the portfolio and enables competitive pricing.

  The product has highlighted the potential for creating a large secondary market in India for microfinance receivables. Bonds may also be issued against securitised microfinance assets, creating linkages between MFIs and capital markets.

- On-Tap Securitisation: In this product the bank provides the MFI advance funding with which the MFI can build assets. Once created, assets are assigned to the bank. The MFI can continue to build assets and assign them to the bank on a regular basis.

Microfinance provides a credit delivery channel to rural households. The main impacts of microfinance are increased access to credit for those at the 'Bottom of the Pyramid' with easy and door-step delivery of institutional credit, and, where available, the provision of risk cover for financial losses through a range of insurance products.

Way Forward – Scaling up Microfinance

Scaling up the MFI model would involve the following:

- Delivery of services at appropriate costs: Reduction in the cost of intermediation would have a direct impact on the profitability of MFIs. This could be achieved through increased efficiency in operations and through greater outreach.

- Serving a wider set of clients: In addition to financing poor households, MFIs could extend their services to individuals with larger loan capacity to set up enterprises, purchasing farm equipment and housing. This would involve a shift from acting as an MFI to acting as an LFI (local financial institution).

- Increasing profitability through cross-selling: MFI branches in unbanked areas provide significant opportunities to bundle services like insurance and collection of savings. Income from cross-selling would lead to an increase in the profits of MFIs.

Summary

In every country, development takes place over time, but its level and pace may not be adequate to maintain a satisfactory standard of living for the less advantaged. In such situations, intervention is in order to speed up the natural pace of development.

Microfinance is an intervention which tries to speed up this process in a two-pronged manner – improving household income by providing timely and adequate support for economic activities, and sharing the responsibilities of the government and of the mainstream financial sector. In India, microfinance is at a nascent stage with a vast potential for growth. While the sector has begun to grow, challenges must be addressed to make this growth both effective and sustainable. Microfinance needs to become more accessible, more customised and more comprehensive. To scale up activity in this area, we must build financial skills in microfinance institutions and establish linkages to the debt and equity capital markets. Microfinance can then truly contribute to transforming rural India into an engine of economic growth.

CHAPTER 6:

Microfinance Investments and IFRS: The Fair Value Challenge

Mark Schwiete[1] and Jana Hoessel Aberle[2]

[1] Principal Sector Economist, KfW Entwicklungsbank
[2] CFA, Consultant

Introduction

Demand for microfinance products clearly exceeds supply: over 2.5 billion people, or 83% of the global market, lack access to financial services.[1] One constraint that prevents microfinance institutions (MFIs) from reaching more customers is their lack of access to refinancing. Given the scarcity of donor funds and the limits of long-term domestic funding sources, MFIs seeking funding are increasingly turning to international private capital markets.

The hurdles MFIs face in attracting private capital are complex and profuse.[2] Industry-specific characteristics, including size, a dearth of regulation, lack of internationally-recognized ratings, and location in developing and transition countries impede MFI access to international capital markets. MFIs must also overcome the challenges of attracting private capital to a new asset class. Microfinance does not fit neatly into institutional investment mandates, few institutional investors have microfinance expertise in-house, and the perception of microfinance as a risky asset class, as well as the high cost of thorough analysis relative to investment size, may discourage due diligence. Moreover, the total potential volume of institutional investors' portfolios of microfinance instruments is very large relative to the limited number and small size of such investments. This may limit institutional investors' ability to reap the benefits of diversification – and may contribute to prohibitively high transaction costs.

Yet for investors, the challenges of investing in microfinance as an asset class do not end once the investment is made. A different type of challenge may then arise:

---

[1] CGAP "Financial Institutions with a Double Bottom Line," 2004, cited in the presentation "The State of Microfinance: A Snapshot," October 2006.

[2] For a discussion of these challenges see Glaubitt, Hagen, Feist, Beck, "The Future of MFI Funding: Structured Finance" in this book.

International Financial Reporting Standards (IFRS) require that investments be reported at fair value. For microfinance debt instruments, fair value is used primarily for informational purposes in the supporting balance sheet notes (see box 1). On the other hand, determining fair value for microfinance equity investments in the absence of reliable earnings and transaction data can be quite complex.

The purpose of this paper is to identify these challenges and to discuss how KfW approaches these issues on its way to full adoption of IFRS at year-end 2007. We begin with an overview of the current state of MFI funding and trends, focusing on equity and mezzanine funding. Next, we provide a brief background of IFRS, followed by a comparison of standard setters' fair value definitions. We examine the options for determining fair value, including those based on market prices, and of most relevance to the case of microfinance, methodologies recommended for use in the absence of active markets. Finally, we conclude with a brief summary.

Microfinance and Foreign Equity Investment

Current MFI Funding Sources

The largest overall source of MFI financing is domestic, including commercial loans, savings deposits for institutions with banking licenses, and retained earnings. Yet domestic sources also pose the greatest bottleneck, which is the dearth of long-term domestic funding sources in emerging markets. The lack of developed pension systems and institutional investor funds are the primary missing links.

At the same time, only a small proportion of total MFI funding comes from foreign investment, defined by CGAP as "quasi-commercial investment in equity, debt, and guarantees, made by private-sector funding arms of bilateral and multilateral donor agencies (*development investors*); and by socially-motivated, privately-managed investment funds financed by both public and private capital (*social investment funds*)."[3]

Yet it is difficult to make generalisations about MFI funding sources, as they vary significantly with type of institution and maturity, among other variables. One way to categorise these differences is through a "tiered" approach. We regard first tier MFIs as those that are sustainable on both a financial and operational basis. The 2nd tier is comprised of promising MFIs on track toward becoming 1st tier institutions. Institutions seeking to retain their primary social objective, or unable to make the leap to financial and operational sustainability for other reasons, may prefer (and may be limited to) financing their operations through grants and donations – these institutions would be regarded as the 3rd tier.

[3]   CGAP FocusNote No. 25. "Foreign Investment in Microfinance: Debt and Equity from Quasi-Commercial Investors." January 2004. Available online at www.cgap.org.

First tier institutions have the greatest access to domestic and international funding sources. They tend to be more mature and often have banking licenses, allowing them to fund themselves partially through deposits. Their "formalisation" also subjects them to a higher level of regulatory oversight, in turn requiring a higher level of management, operational and systems competency – all of which decrease their credit risk, which makes them more attractive to domestic commercial funding sources. Because of their financial sustainability, the interest of private foreign investors focuses almost exclusively on this group.

We began this paper by stating that one of the reasons 2.5 billion people lack access to financial services is that the institutions that would serve them lack funding – particularly long-term funding. So where are these funding gaps? They lie in the 2nd tier MFIs. Third tier institutions have limited possibilities to attract foreign investment given their lack of operational and financial sustainability. Some may have little interest in taking on quasi-commercial funding as their founders may presume that commercial funding would compromise the institution's social mission. The prospects for foreign investment in 2nd tier institutions, however, are promising. These institutions, often not licensed to accept deposits and deemed too high a credit risk for commercial loans, may not be attractive to domestic funding sources.

This situation is a challenge for – as well as the duty of – development financiers: they may provide support in the form of long-term refinancing as well as technical assistance for institutional improvement necessary to promote a 2nd tier institution to 1st tier status – while retaining the institution's reach and avoiding "mission drift".[4] Expanding the 1st tier means more institutions will be able to access private capital, decreasing these institutions' reliance on funding from development finance institutions (DFIs).

Tapping International Capital Markets

Determining fair value for equity investments tends to be more complex than for debt investments. The extent to which equity valuation issues will arise is a function of the percentage of equity and quasi-equity funding relative to debt: as MFIs tap international capital markets, what form will this funding take? According to a 2004 CGAP study, debt and equity accounted for 73% and 20% respectively of the USD 167.3 million in foreign investment in microfinance surveyed in the study.[5]

---

[4] See Doris Köhn and Michael Jainzik: "Sustainability in Microfinance – Visions and Versions for Exit by Development Finance Institutions," in Ingrid Matthäus-Maier and J.D. von Pischke, eds., *Microfinance Investment Funds: Leveraging Private Capital for Economic Growth and Poverty Reduction*, 2006.

[5] Kadaras, James and Elisabeth Rhyne, "Characteristics of Equity Investment in Microfinance," April 2004. Cited in CGAP FocusNote No. 25. "Foreign Investment in Microfinance: Debt and Equity from Quasi-Commercial Investors." January 2004. Available online at www.cgap.org.

Some pundits have questioned a narrowing of this gap: a 2006 Council of Microfinance Equity Funds (CMEF) study identified just 199 MFIs as eligible for foreign equity investments,[6] underpinning the limited number of potential investees, making it more important to support 2nd tier institutions.

Other opportunities for equity investment do exist. Two of the most salient are the upgrading of 2nd tier to 1st tier institutions, discussed above, and greenfield investments in newly established MFIs – both of which require equity. The minimum capital adequacy requirement (CAR) under Basel I is 8% of risk-weighted assets, though an appropriate minimum capital level may be deemed to be much higher – indeed, as high as 20% in the case of start-up banks in some developing countries. Whether upgrading an existing institution into a bank or establishing a new one, risk capital is necessary, and its most likely source is donors.

Box 1: The MFI Perspective: Relative Advantages and Disadvantages of Equity Investments

Advantages

- **Meeting minimum capital requirements:** Equity investments provide a capital base for MFIs to meet regulatory capital requirements.

- **Cash flow timing:** Equity investments do not require regular repayments, simplifying cash flow planning or freeing up liquidity for other purposes.

- **No collateral required:** Though many MFI loans are unsecured, the lack of collateral is often compensated for through credit enhancement techniques. These considerations do not arise for equity investments.

- **Decreased rollover risk:** Debt investments are limited to a specific time period and require careful planning on the part of the MFI to ensure that funding is either renewable or that new funding sources will be available after current credit lines mature. Equity investments, in contrast, are not limited to a specific time period.

- **Reduction in foreign exchange risk:** The vast majority of foreign debt investment in MFIs is denominated in hard currency, creating a currency mismatch for the MFI. This problem does not occur in equity investment.

---

[6]   Rhyne, Elisabeth and Brian Busch, "The Growth of Commercial Microfinance: 2004-2006", September 2006. Available online at http://cmef.com/CMEF%20Growth%20of%20Commercial%20MF%202006.pdf. 222 MFIs are defined as regulated, commercial shareholder-owned entities, of which 199 make sufficient information publicly available.

Disadvantages

- **Unwillingness to cede control:** This may be particularly true of potential profit-maximizing equity investors. An MFI may foresee conflicts between the goal of pure profit maximisation and the MFI's efforts to balance social and profit goals.

- **Greater disclosure:** In return for taking on residual risk or ownership, equity investors will require greater disclosure from MFIs.

- **"Mission drift":** Profit-oriented equity investors may increase the danger of "mission drift" – that less profitable business segments which benefit the poor may be cut back in favour of more profitable business in other markets.

Financial innovations have made the juxtaposition of debt and equity a false dichotomy. What lies in between – quasi-equity, or mezzanine investment – may represent the future of microfinance funding. Because mezzanine instruments are often highly customised using structured finance techniques, their flexibility may enable them to best match MFI funding appetite with those of potential investors. (For a more detailed discussion of structured financing options for MFIs see Glaubitt, Hagen, Feist, Beck: "Reducing Barriers to Microfinance Funding: The Role of Structured Finance" in this book.)

Box 2: The Investor Perspective: Relative Advantages and Disadvantages of Equity Investments

Advantages

- **Control:** Investors may seek influence or partial control of an MFI's business. While this is an advantage of equity investments in general, it may be particularly salient in the case of microfinance. First, equity investments may allow investors greater insight into an MFI, improving transparency. Second, taking partial control over an MFI may decrease the risk of the MFI's business decisions which could adversely affect the performance of the equity investment. Given generally low levels of regulation in the microfinance sector and the perception of microfinance as a "risky" asset class, gaining influence or control may reduce investors' perceived risk.

- **Higher risk/reward profile:** Equity investors may share in profits only after all claims to debt holders have been paid. Empirical evidence demonstrating good average MFI performance in repaying debt, combined with strong growth potential given the enormous unmet demand for microfinance services, may encourage investors with higher risk/reward appetites to make equity investments. For example, social investment funds are willing to take greater risk for less reward, ceteris paribus, than an average profit-maximising investor.[7] Their phenomenal growth may help shift the trend of microfinance investing toward equity.

Disadvantages

- **Difficult investment exit:** From an investors' perspective, the lack of exit opportunities may impede investment. In contrast to the fixed maturities of most debt instruments, equity investments provide no fixed exit date. The lack of a liquid secondary market further limits potential exit possibilities.

- **Combination of non-profit and for-profit owners:** Profit-maximising investors may hesitate to invest in MFIs with other non-profit owners, fearing that their expected return may suffer as non-profit owners strive to meet social goals rather than profit targets. Non-profit investors may also fear that MFI poverty reduction efforts may be impaired by the pursuit of profit.

Valuing Microfinance Investments

Before discussing the challenge of valuing equity and mezzanine investments according to IFRS, we provide a brief background of IFRS, current standard setters' definitions of fair value, and an overview of accepted methodologies for calculating fair value.

Defining Fair Value

According to the International Accounting Standards Board (IASB), IFRS is comprised of the standards and their corresponding interpretations adopted by IASB, an independent and privately-funded accounting standards organisation. Standards include International Accounting Standards (IAS), issued from 1973 to 2001 by

---

[7]   CGAP FocusNote No. 25. "Foreign Investment in Microfinance: Debt and Equity from Quasi-Commercial Investors." January 2004. Available online at www.cgap.org.

the International Accounting Standards Committee,[8] and IFRS issued by the IASB. Standards and topics range in scope and depth from the presentation of financial statements to financial reporting in hyperinflationary economies.

The standard relevant to valuing investments in MFIs is IAS 39, entitled "Financial Instruments: Recognition and Measurement." The objective of IAS 39 is "to establish principles for recognising and measuring financial assets, financial liabilities and some contracts to buy or sell non-financial items." It requires that a financial asset or liability be recognised at fair value at initiation, including related transaction costs.[9] Thereafter, equity instruments and embedded derivatives[10] should be stated at fair value whereas debt instruments are usually held at amortised cost depending on their classification into one of the categories defined in IAS 39.9 (see box 3). There is an important exception that is relevant to microfinance: "equity investments that do not have a quoted market price in an active market and whose fair value cannot be reliably measured ...."[11]

Box 3: IFRS and Debt Investments

Debt investments are usually classified as loans and receivables, and according to IFRS are therefore stated at amortised cost. When debt investments are held at amortised cost, the fair value of the investment may be referenced in the balance sheet notes for informational purposes.

In certain circumstances IFRS does allow for the valuation of debt instruments at fair value (see IAS 39.9 for more detail). For example, if an investor holds both a debt investment and an equity investment in the same entity, or if the investor holds a convertible bond, it may make sense to report the debt investment at fair value, rather than amortized cost. This approach would treat both debt and equity in the same manner and any changes to the fair value of either the debt or equity investment at remeasurement would flow through the income statement.

Whether held at amortized cost or at fair value, debt investments are subject to impairment tests.

---

[8] The International Accounting Standards Committee is no longer in existence and has been effectively replaced by the IASB. Most of the standards issued by the International Accounting Standards Committee were adopted, either in original or revised form, by the IASB. See the IASB web site at www.iasb.org for more details.

[9] IAS 39.43: Transaction costs are excluded in the case of financial assets or liabilities at fair value through profit or loss.

[10] IAS 39.11.

[11] IAS 39.46 (c).

IASB states its mission as "developing, in the public interest, a single set of high quality, understandable and enforceable global accounting standards that require transparent and comparable information in general purpose financial statements."[12] Indeed, great progress toward this goal has been made: seventy-four countries, about two-thirds of which are developing countries, require domestically-listed companies to report according to IFRS.[13]

Standard setters, including the IASB and FASB, have made significant efforts to align standards. A good example of recent efforts is the convergence of definitions of fair value, listed below.

- **IAS 39**: *The amount for which an asset could be exchanged, or a liability settled, between knowledgeable, willing parties in an arm's length transaction.*[14]

- **International Private Equity and Venture Capital Valuation Guidelines (IPEVCVG):** *The amount for which an asset could be exchanged between knowledgeable, willing parties in an arm's length transaction.*[15]

- **Global Investment Performance Standards (GIPS):** *The amount at which an asset could be acquired or sold in a current transaction between willing parties in which the parties each acted knowledgeably, prudently, and without compulsion.*[16]

- **Financial Accounting Standards Board (FASB):** *An estimate of the price that could be received for an asset or paid to settle a liability in a current transaction between marketplace participants in the reference market for the asset or liability.*[17]

In a November 2006 press release, the International Private Equity and Venture Capital (IPEV) Valuation Board reported that changes to its guidelines "will en-

---

[12] From IASB's web site, www.iasb.org.

[13] See Deloitte and Touche's IAS Plus web site: www.iasplus.com.

[14] IAS 39, IN18, IAS 32.11.

[15] IPEVCA were developed by the Association Français des Investisseurs en Capital (AFIC), the British Venture Capital Associate (BVCA) and the European Private Equity and Venture Capital Association with input and endorsement from numerous international private equity and venture capital associations. 1 January 2005. Available online at http://www.privateequityvaluation.com/documents/International_PE_VC_Valuation_Guidelines_Oct_2006.pdf.

[16] Global Investment Performance Standards. Revised by the Investment Performance Council and Adopted by the CFA Institute Board of Governors. February 2005. Available online at www.cfainstitute.org.

[17] Financial Accounting Standards Board. Fair Value Team. Minutes of the June 29, 2005 Board Meeting – Definition, Transaction Price Presumption, and Hierarchy. Available online at http://www.fasb.org/board_meeting_minutes/06-29-05_fvm.pdf.

sure full consistency of the IPEV Guidelines with both FASB and IASB standards."[18] Moreover, in the amended version IPEV explicitly notes that their definition of fair value is "...congruent in concept with alternately worded definitions such as 'Fair Value is the price that would be received for an asset or paid for a liability in a transaction between market participants at the reporting date'."

Yet much work remains: alternative accounting standards, such as U.S. GAAP, continue to be used around the globe. Though differences in standards are not as large or numerous as they once were, differences remain, and they create ambiguity for those responsible for financial reporting. The fair value case provides a salient example: while standard setters share similar views of the definition of fair value, the recommended methodologies which may be employed to calculate fair value for investments which lack an active market are inherently subjective and are specified differently among standards. These are discussed in detail below.

Market Prices and Microfinance Investments

Determining fair value at investment initiation – when the first funding transaction is made for a de nove entity – is usually a simple task: according to IFRS, the transaction price is normally considered the fair value of an investment. The initial transaction price for a debt, equity or mezzanine investment in an existing microfinance institution or the subscription price for an equity stake in a greenfield transaction would be considered fair value. At remeasurement, the determination of fair value can be more complicated and a fair value hierarchy, discussed below, must be applied.

Market prices, when available, are considered the best gauge of fair value. According to IFRS, "The existence of published price quotations in an active market is the best evidence of fair value and when they exist they are used to measure the financial asset or liability."[19] Usually the current bid price in the most advantageous market is used as a basis, adjusted for necessary considerations such as differences in the credit risk profile of the counterparty.

Yet market prices require active financial markets, which creates a problem in valuing MFI Investments. Markets for MFI investments are neither active by any definition, nor do transactions occur on an arm's length basis. (See below for more detail on microfinance secondary markets.) According to IFRS, "A financial market is quoted in an active market if quoted prices are readily and regularly available from an exchange, dealer, broker, industry group, pricing service or regulatory agency and those prices represent actual and regularly occurring market transactions on an arm's length basis,"[20] this term referring to independent third-party transactions.

---

[18] International Private Equity and Venture Capital Valuation Board Press Release, "Valuation of Private Equity Investments: Changes Ensure Consistency with Recent Fair Value Standard", Brussels, November 15, 2006. http://www.privateequityvaluation.com/.

[19] IAS 39.71.

[20] IAS 39.7.

KfW's internal definition of a market price in an active market provides additional guidance:

- Investment shares are available from a stock exchange, or through a broker or trader.

- The share price reflects the arm's length principle (e.g that parties to the transaction are equal and independent and there is a market price).

- The free float of the shares comprises a minimum of 5% of total share capital.

- There are no restrictions on the maximum turnover or trading volume of the shares.

- On at least one-third of the trading days in the last year trades were registered, and on at least five days in each calendar month shares were traded.[21]

In cases where current market prices are unavailable, the task of determining fair value becomes more complicated. In such a case, the starting point for determining fair value is the price of the most recent transaction – providing that no "significant change in economic circumstances" has taken place since that transaction's settlement.[22] If such a change has occurred, or if the reporting organisation can prove that the price of the most recent transaction does not accurately represent fair value, then the market price is adjusted accordingly to arrive at fair value according to IAS 39.

The initiation price of the investment itself may be used as the fair value, or the price of a recent investment in the same entity by a different investing party may be used. The International Private Equity and Venture Capital Valuation Guidelines (IPEVCVG) provide specific guidance as to events which may materially reduce current fair value in relation to the investment initiation value: (1) the performance or prospects of the underlying business has significantly deteriorated relative to expectations at investment initiation; (2) a significant adverse change in the underlying business or business milieu has occurred; (3) market conditions have declined; and (4) the underlying business is raising capital and evidence exists that future financing will take place under conditions materially different from the investment in question.[23]

KfW has chosen to define the "recent" prices which may be used under IAS 39 as prices of transactions taking place within one year of the valuation date. In order to use the price of the last transaction as the "fair value," none of the following conditions can be true:

---

[21] KfW Internal Draft Document. "Konzernvorgaben zur Bewertung von Finanzinstrumenten ('Investments') durch Geschäftspartner der KfW-Bankengruppe für den Bereich Beteiligungsfinanzierung" ("KfW banking group valuation directives for investments in participatory financing").

[22] IAS 39.72.

[23] Paraphrased from IPEVCVG. Page 15.

- Parties to the transaction were exclusively management or employees of the investment entity investing their own funds.

- A minimum of one investor is a related party of the investment entity.

- Restructuring financing has been undertaken by existing investors.

- The last transaction was a strategic financing round (defined below).

KfW guidelines also provide for extraordinary events which alter the value of the investment and preclude the use of the last market transaction as a basis for determining fair value.[24]

The above caveats to the use of recent transaction prices are loosely based on those of IPEVCVG:

1. "a further Investment by the existing stakeholders with little new Investment;

2. different rights attached to the new and existing Investments;

3. a new investor motivated by strategic considerations;

4. the Investment may be considered to be a forced sale or 'rescue package;' or

5. the absolute amount of the new Investment is relatively insignificant."[25]

The third point is of particular importance to microfinance investments and is relevant to both new and existing investors. Many microfinance investors are motivated by strategic considerations, including sustainable development and more specific social goals in addition to profit. If, as pundits predict, MFIs tap into private capital markets in the future, more profit-oriented investors may join the ranks of the current social/mixed or dual objective investors in MFIs. In the future, profit-driven equity holders in a particular MFI may have to adjust for the dual or mixed goals of other investors in the same MFI when considering using the most recent transaction price as the fair value.

Markets for MFI investments are neither active by any definition, nor do transactions occur on an arm's length basis: though the number of microfinance investors is growing, the number remains limited and many transactions take place between "related parties". Data on transactions among related parties, clearly violating the "arm's length" principle, cannot be used as a basis for determining the fair value of a "comparable" transaction. The lack of an active secondary market for MFI investments precludes the use of published price quotations or recent transactions as a basis for calculating fair value.

---

[24] KfW Internal Draft Document. "Konzernvorgaben zur Bewertung von Finanzinstrumenten ('Investments') durch Geschäftspartner der KfW-Bankengruppe für den Bereich Beteiligungsfinanzierung."

[25] Quoted directly from IPEVCVG, Page 14.

Estimating Fair Value: Valuation Methodologies

According to IFRS, and confirmed by other standard setters such as FASB and EVCA, in the absence of an active market an alternative valuation technique must be used to determine fair value.[26] FASB has outlined a three-level system for determining fair value, referred to as the "fair value hierarchy". This hierarchy, supported by IASB as well, is depicted in the following diagram.

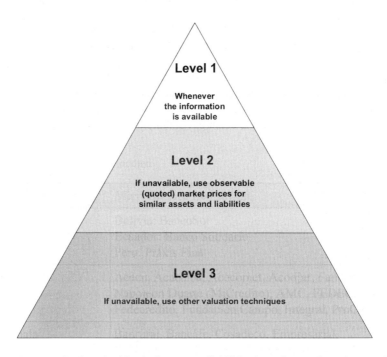

Fig. 1. Use quoted prices for identical assets or liabilities in active markets. Source: From "How Fair is Fair Value?" published by Ernst & Young, adapted from Exposure Draft, Proposed Statement of Financial Accounting Standards, Fair Value Measurements, FASB, June 2004.

International Private Equity and Venture Capital Valuation Guidelines (IPEVCVG) do not have a valuation hierarchy per se, but specify that in the absence of an active market, fair value must be estimated using one of the specified valuation methodologies.

Given the lack of market prices for microfinance investments, how then can one determine "what the transaction price would have been on the measurement

---

[26] IFRS. IAS 39. AG74. Page 1778.

date in an arm's length exchange motivated by normal business considerations"?[27] IAS 39 guidance on methodologies for calculating fair value in the absence of an active market begins with the idea that a valuation "incorporates all factors that market participants would consider in setting a price" and that it "is consistent with accepted economic methodologies for pricing financial instruments."[28] A valuation methodology which is used for measuring the fair value of an unquoted equity instrument is considered reliable when "the variability in the range of reasonably fair value estimates is not significant for that instrument" or "the probabilities of the various estimates within the range can be reasonably assessed and used in estimating fair value."[29] When a valuation methodology is not deemed reliable, the unquoted equity instrument shall be measured at cost.[30]

Valuation options set out in IAS 39 include those based on recent transactions, the current fair value of a similar investment, option pricing models, or discounted cash flow analysis (DCF).[31] While not discussing the methodologies in detail, IAS 39 outlines inputs to valuation techniques that should be taken into consideration, including the time value of money, credit risk, foreign currency exchange prices, commodity prices, equity prices, volatility, prepayment risk and surrender risk, and the servicing costs for a financial asset or a financial liability.[32]

More specific guidance on the methodologies for calculating the fair value of equity investments are contained in the IPEVCVG.[33] These guidelines emphasise the role of judgement in choosing a valuation methodology, rather than setting out a hierarchy of preferred methodologies as in GIPS. Factors to be considered when choosing a methodology include the following: "the relative applicability of the methodologies used given the nature of the industry and the current market conditions; the quality, and reliability of the data used in each methodology; the comparability of enterprise or transaction data; the stage of development of the enterprise; and any additional considerations unique to the subject enterprise."[34]

The methodologies set out in the IPEVCVG include:

1. price of recent investment,

2. earnings multiple,

---

[27] IAS 39.75.

[28] IAS 39.76.

[29] IAS 39.80.

[30] IAS 39.46 (c); in this case an entity shall assess at each balance sheet date whether there is any objective evidence that this asset is impaired (IAS 39.58 ff.).

[31] IAS 39. 48A.

[32] IAS 39.82.

[33] These guidelines were developed by AFIC, BVCA and EVCA with input from international venture capital and private equity associations. The guidelines were endorsed on June 28, 2006.

[34] IPEVCVG. Page 13.

3. net assets,

4. discounted cash flows or earnings (of the underlying business),

5. discounted cash flows (from the investment), and

6. industry valuation benchmarks.[35]

Considering the methodologies used to value microfinance investments, half may be quickly disregarded. We have already considered that based on the price of recent investment in the previous section. Industry valuation benchmarks will not be further considered here as the use of this methodology is extremely limited and applies to industry-specific indicators, such as "price per subscriber" in the telecommunications industry. A similar argument holds for the net assets approach, which values a business by its underlying assets when the liquidation value of the business is greater than its value as a going concern, which is not applicable to MFI investments and is not discussed further.

The earnings multiple approach merits consideration. Its greatest problem is the lack of comparable data in microfinance. Equity and quasi-equity transactions tend to be discrete and highly structured, and MFIs vary significantly in terms of business model, geography, source of revenue and maturity, among other factors. The dearth of published transaction data as well as the lack of reliable earnings data, impede the use of recent transactions as a reference for determining the appropriateness of a multiple. Even if reliable data were available, a multiples approach is often backward-looking and more appropriate for businesses with steady, predictable earnings. For a young growth industry like microfinance, earnings tend to be highly volatile, and will be affected by organisational and staff changes, reorganisation and consolidation phases, and changes in provisioning policies, to name just a few discontinuities. This volatility will thwart attempts to predict earnings even within a given range.

Finally, in using this approach, the IPEVCVG recommends that a marketability discount be considered. This may be challenging for all microfinance investments, but may pose particular challenges for investments lacking an exit strategy.[36] According to IPEVCVG, "…if the underlying company were not considered saleable or floatable at the reporting date, the questions arise of what has to be done to make it saleable or floatable, how difficult and risky that course of action is to implement and how long it is expected to take …."[37] These considerations complicate the subjectivity of any valuation based on earnings multiples.

---

[35] IPEVCVG. Page 14.

[36] For a more detailed discussion of exit strategies within the context of microfinance investments see Doris Köhn and Michael Jainzik, "Sustainability in Microfinance – Visions and Versions for Exit by Development Finance Institutions." In Ingrid Matthäus-Maier and J.D. von Pischke, eds., *Microfinance Investment Funds: Leveraging Private Capital for Economic Growth and Poverty Reduction.* (2006).

[37] IPEVCVG. Page. 19.

Is DCF the Solution of Last Resort?

The final option, with two variations, is the discounted cash flow method (DCF). DCF can be based either upon the projected cash flows of the underlying business or on the projected cash flows of the investment (though for pure equity investments the two would yield the same net present value). DCF based on projected cash flows from the investment may be more reliable relative to those based on the projected cash flows from the underlying business when investment pricing is fixed or when there is only a short period of time until the investment exit. However, DCF based on projected investment cash flows yields a more reliable fair value for MFI equity investments with fixed exit strategies – especially for mezzanine investments, which typically have more structured terms and conditions including fixed maturities and exit conditions.

Flexibility is the primary benefit of DCF: it "enables the methodology to be applied in situations that other methodologies may be incapable of addressing."[38] Yet the flip side of flexibility is subjectivity. DCF requires a choice of inputs: cash flows for the underlying business or investment must be projected; the terminal value of the business or investment must be estimated; and the discount rate, including the risk-free rate and the market risk premium at which to discount the cash flows must be specified.

The variables most relevant to our discussion are the discount rate (r), comprised of a risk-free rate plus a risk premium, and the terminal value of the investment. The sensitivity of a DCF model to small changes in these variables is quite high. For example, in a recent DCF MFI model, a 1% change in the discount rate yielded a 6.3% change in the net present value of the MFI being valued.

In applying DCF to microfinance equity investments, the challenge regarding the discount rate lies in estimating the risk-free rate. In developed markets, the risk-free rate is commonly estimated using the interest rate of a sovereign bond of the country of investment. The risk-free rate should not reflect reinvestment risk, therefore the yield of a sovereign bond of similar maturity to that of the expected cash flows should be used as a benchmark rate.

The risk-free rate for emerging market countries is in some sense a misnomer. In contrast to developed markets, even emerging sovereign bonds carry default risk, as the cases of Russia in 1998 and Argentina in 2002 demonstrate.

For foreign investors in emerging markets, the reference instrument from which the risk-free rate is estimated should be denominated in the same currency as the expected cash flows (often in EUR or USD), and it should match the maturity of the expected cash flows. The rates of Euro-denominated bonds or Brady bonds would be the first choice as a reference rate to estimate the risk-free rate for foreign investors in emerging markets receiving Euro or dollar cash flows.

Interest rates are the market prices of bonds. Price quotations are reliable indicators of current bond value only if markets are active – and many emerging mar-

---

[38] IPEVCVA. Page 21.

ket countries lack active sovereign bond markets and some lack any sovereign bond market at all. Another obstacle is the problem of similar maturities.

Moreover, using spreads of a similarly-rated country (the "an AA is an AA" approach) to estimate the risk-free rate is not a fully satisfactory substitute. Even if one could assume that two countries rated "AA" have the same default probability, their spread over that of a AAA-rated sovereign bond may differ because of differences in their loss given default.[39]

The default risk in emerging market sovereign bonds raises an important question regarding the market risk component of the discount rate. Might an MFI pierce the "sovereign ceiling"? Experience suggests that in many cases, a 1st tier MFI is a better risk, ceteris paribus, than the sovereign risk of the country in which it is located. IAS 39 allows reference to the interest rates of the highest-rated corporate bonds of a particular country in estimating the risk-free rate for cases where "the central government's bonds may carry a significant credit risk and may not provide a stable benchmark interest rate for instruments denominated in that currency." Yet in emerging market countries, corporate bond markets are even less active than sovereign bond markets. In addition, the debate continues as to whether "real sector" corporates and financial institutions alike can and should pierce the sovereign ceiling

The second variable is the "terminal value", which is required in a DCF model to calculate the present value of future cash flows. While mezzanine investments may have a specified time horizon and defined terminal value (the future value of the investment at the end of the time horizon), pure equity investments do not. Calculating the "terminal value" for an equity investment requires an assumption of the indefinite future growth rate beyond the time horizon for which cash flows are forecasted.

A DCF model relies upon assumptions regarding the macroeconomic environment, interest rates, exchange rates, markets and business development. Getting the assumptions for the DCF model "right" for an institution in a young growth industry characterised by highly volatile earnings located within highly volatile markets is, to say the least, a difficult task. Besides the lack of earnings history or reliable earnings data as a basis for extrapolation, macroeconomic conditions in volatile markets are notoriously difficult to predict, as is forecasting cash flow in a accurate and robust way.

Cash flow planning, and business planning more generally, is another challenge. Few MFIs have the capability and resources at hand to develop a detailed and systematic business plan including cash flow forecasts – not only for the next few months, but for a period of five years. In one recent case, the attempt to calculate the fair value of an MFI failed because management simply lacked the experi-

---

[39] The earlier mentioned cases of Russia and Argentina showed that defaults don't lead to complete losses for investors but to partial losses (loss given default). As LGD exerts a significant influence on spreads, the latter differs between countries even if default probabilities are similar.

ence and know-how in business planning to provide business forecasts plausible enough for a DCF valuation. Moreover, if business plans are available, their cash flows projections are often outdated within a few months given the industry's fast development. Projections for business plans generated in early fall of one year are often inaccurate or outdated when they are discussed in February of the following year.

Business plans are important and useful tools. They provide the framework and discipline to outline the specific operational measures necessary to meet the strategic goals of management and owners for the development of the MFI. But for many MFIs, the cash flow forecasts in business plans may not be sufficiently robust or up-to-date to generate a plausible value from a DCF model.

In the case of one recent MFI DCF model, stress testing the exchange rates by 10% yielded a 10% change in the net present value of the MFI. While a pro rata change may not seem large at first glance, given the high volatility of exchange rates in developing countries, a 10% fluctuation in exchange rates is a conservative estimate. This simple case suggests cause for concern regarding the accuracy of assumptions of a DCF model.

The objective of the use of valuation techniques, according to IAS 39, is clear: "to establish what the transaction price would have been on the measurement date in an arm's length exchange motivated by normal business considerations." However, the valuation techniques themselves are inherently subjective. Some experts, including Ernst & Young, have questioned the appropriateness of the use of valuation methodologies for determining fair value: „…we consider it inappropriate to refer to such calculated values as 'fair value'. And this is not just a matter of semantics: the term 'fair value' implies active and liquid markets with knowledgeable and willing buyers and sellers and observable arm's length transactions – not values calculated on the basis of hypothetical markets, with hypothetical buyers and sellers."[40] In the case of microfinance equity investments, as we have demonstrated above, it is often difficult to reliably determine fair value using a valuation technique. How then should an equity investment be valued if a reliable estimate of fair value cannot be determined? The next section addresses this question.

When to Use "At Cost" Measurement?

According to IAS 39, "A valuation technique would be expected to arrive at a realistic estimate of the fair value if (a) it reasonably reflects how the market could be expected to price the instrument and (b) the inputs to the valuation technique reasonably represent market expectations and measures of the risk-return factors inherent in the financial instrument."[41]

---

[40] Ernst & Young. "How Fair is Fair Value?" 2005. Available online at http://www2.eycom. ch/publications/items/ifrs/single/200506_fair_value/en.pdf#search=%22How%20Fair%20 is%20Fair%20Value%3F%22.

[41] IAS 39.75.

Indeed, achieving reliability in calculated fair values for microfinance investments is in practice often not possible. The example of greenfield investments in MFIs is instructive. Greenfield institutions have no history of cash flows upon which to extrapolate. Because of their early growth stage, earnings volatility will likely be high – it is unlikely that a reliable business plan exists for such an institution in such a market. Moreover, the location in emerging or transition markets adds to the complexity of forecasting macroeconomic conditions – most importantly, the discount rate. And how can a terminal value for such an institution be reliably estimated?

Standard setters provide varying depth and detail in guidance regarding when to use cost as a basis for valuation:

- **IFRS**: Cost basis should be used "if the range of reasonable fair value estimates is significant or the probabilities of the various estimates cannot be reasonably assessed, an entity is precluded from measuring the instrument at fair value."[42]

- **GIPS**: "Cost as a basis of valuation is only permitted when an estimate of fair value cannot be reliably determined." GIPS further stipulate that a fair value basis should always be attempted, and that when not used, the firm must disclose justification of its choice to use a cost basis.[43]

- **IPEVCVG**: According to these standards fair value cannot be reliably measured when four situations apply: „(1) the range of reasonable Fair Value estimates is significant, (2) the probabilities of the various estimates within the range cannot be reasonably assessed, (3) the probability and financial impact of achieving a key milestone cannot be reasonably predicted, (4) there has been no recent Investment into the business."[44]

The guidance given above is clearly subjective and relies heavily upon judgement as to what constitutes, for instance, a "significant" range or "reasonable" prediction.

KfW's decision-making process with regard to the use of cost to value an investment may provide an instructive example. The diagram below is a visual representation of this process.

---

[42] IAS 39.81.

[43] GIPS. Page 40.

[44] IPEVCVA. Page 11.

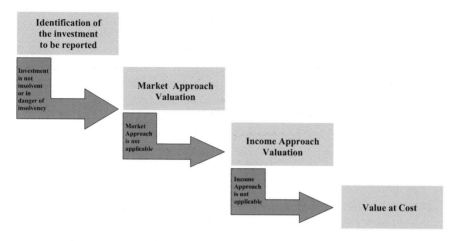

Fig. 2. KfW's valuation decision tree

Conclusion

Microfinance institutions are generally young entities in immature growth sectors located in developing and transition countries. Given the challenges to plausibly estimate the inputs to a DCF model (risk free rate, terminal value, and cash flow forecasts), a cost approach to valuation might yield a result that is as reliable or even more reliable than a DCF model, ceteris paribus.

Even if a valuation at cost and a DCF model for an investment in an MFI yield similar results, valuation at cost (plus an impairment test) for microfinance investments has the advantage of transparency, avoiding the assumptions required by the DCF model which are particularly challenging to estimate for MFIs.

A "cost plus impairment" approach is of course subject to human error because every impairment test requires at least a rough estimate of the future cash flows of the investment. This estimate for determining fair value requires assumptions, but to a much lesser extent and for a different purpose than in a DCF model.

While IFRS poses a challenge for microfinance equity investors today, this may not be the case in the future. The industry is developing quickly. More and more MFIs are improving their business planning capacity, both through dedicated technical assistance provided by IFIs and through experience. The quality of financial data provided by MFIs is improving, as institutions upgrade their reporting and IT systems, and more MFIs undergo annual audits. It is probable that as MFIs and the microfinance industry develop, so will secondary markets for MFI investments. Early portents indicate that the availability of transaction data is improving. These developments will facilitate the valuation of MFI investments. Much more importantly, they will facilitate MFI access to refinancing, allowing these institutions to extend their reach to some of the 2.5 billion clients who lack access to microfinance services.

References

Association Français des Investisseurs en Capital (AFIC), the British Venture Capital Associate (BVCA) and the European Private Equity and Venture Capital Association (2006): *International Private Equity and Venture Capital Guidelines,* June 2005, amended October 2006. Online at http://www.private-equityvaluation.com/.

CFA Institute Board of Governors (2005): *Global Investment Performance Standards,* February 2005. Online at www.cfainstitute.org.

CGAP (2004): "Focus Note No. 25, Foreign Investment in Microfinance: Debt and Equity from Quasi-Commercial Invesors", January 2004. Online at www.cgap.org.

Deloitte. IAS Plus Website: www.iasplus.com.

Ernst & Young (2005): "How Fair is Fair Value?", Online at http://www2.eycom.ch/publications/items/ifrs/single/200506_fair_value/en.pdf#search=%22How%20Fair%20is%20Fair%20Value%3F%22.

Financial Accounting Standards Board, Fair Value Team (2005) : "Minutes of the June 29, 2005 Board Meeting – Definition, Transaction Price Presumption, Hierarchy". Online at http://www.fasb.org.

Kadaras, James and Rhyne, Elizabeth (2004): "Characteristics of Equity Investment in Microfinance". Available online at http://www.accion.org.

Kreditanstalt für Wiederaufbau (KfW) (2006): Internal Draft Document, "Konzern-vorgaben zur Bewertung von Finanzinstrumenten durch Geschäftspartner der KfW-Bankengruppe für den Bereich Beteiligungsfinanzierung" ("KfW banking group valuation directives for investments in participatory financing").

Köhn, Doris and Jainzik, Michael (2006): "Sustainability in Microfinance – Visions and Versions for Exit by Development Finance Institutions", in: Matthäus-Maier, Ingrid and von Piscke, J.D., eds., *Microfinance Investment Funds: Leveraging Private Capital for Economic Growth and Poverty Reduction,* Berlin/Heidelberg/New York: Springer.

International Accounting Standards Board (IASB). Website: www.iasb.org.

IASB (2006): *International Financial Reporting Standards.* Bound volume.

International Private Equity and Venture Capital Valuation Board Press Release, "Valuation of Private Equity Investments: Changes Ensure Consistency with Recent Fair Value Standard", Brussels, November 15, 2006. Online at http://www.privateequityvaluation.com/.

Rhyne, Elisabeth and Busch, Brian (2006): "The Growth of Commercial Micro-finance: 2004-2006". Available online at http://cmef.com/CMEF%20Growth%20of%20Commercial%20MF%202006.pdf

Unitus (2005): Annual Report 2005. Online at http://www.unitus.com/sections/media/media_dl_main.asp.

PART II:

Technology Partnerships to Scale up Outreach

Introduction to Part II

Three forces have forever altered the financial landscape. The first of these is financial liberalisation, which releases market forces as government-imposed restrictions on financial market structure and on transactions are relaxed or redesigned to increase efficiency. The second is the disaggregation of risk, which makes the pricing of financial assets and services more accurate. The third is communications technology, which expands the sources, volume and speed of information transmission. This part focuses on such technology: In a connected world, information transfer is rapid, cheap and dependable. But what about "the last mile," the frontier beyond which these three global developments have not yet conquered? And what is required to meet the challenges posed by small volume transactions?

Remittances from richer countries to poorer countries amount to very large sums, although the individual sums sent are usually quite small. Remittances are commonly from workers in richer countries to their families in their countries of origin. While the senders have their own private agendas, the development community is increasingly engaged in efforts to leverage the flow in ways that could reduce remitters' costs and facilitate their efforts to build assets. Chapter 7 by Cerstin Sander deals comprehensively with these issues, exploring the opportunities presented by remittances for the broader development of microfinance. Her perspective centres on financial sector development – integrating poorer clients into financial systems by designing new instruments for this purpose and by facilitating conducive regulation.

Chapter 8 by Manuel Orozco and Eve Hamilton is an empirical study of remittances to Latin America. They deal with the large international money transfer networks and MFIs that provide retail services to recipients. They compare cost structures and the relatively modest extent, at the time of their study, to which their sample of MFIs used remittances as platforms for bundled or integrated services to their clients.

The focus of Chapter 9 by Gautam Ivatury is the use of technology to build financial systems capable of serving large numbers of low income clients. He finds that commercial banks in some emerging markets are pioneering technical solutions that reduce their costs to levels that make microfinance an attractive proposition. In these cases, transaction volumes must be substantial for innovations to be viable. A variety of transactions can be undertaken using these technologies. ATMs and POS devices are used, along with internet banking and mobile phone banking. Technological advances that provide convenient retail services increasingly involve a variety of providers other than banks.

In Chapter 10 Laura Frederick describes and addresses the magnitude of the challenges and complexities that arise in the provision and use of information technology. Her objective is to create and serve very large numbers of rural micro-finance clients. Realisation of this objective requires frameworks that enlist the collaboration of a large number of parties and a comprehensive understanding of all aspects of service provision. She describes and compares several models and explains the risks each carries.

Chapter 11 by Janine Firpo explores issues that confront efforts to design and deliver financial services for the poor. Her examples are based on pilot projects undertaken in Uganda. She concludes that the introduction of technology com-bined with business process change yields the greatest return; that innovative technologies that can be scaled up are essential for successful delivery in emerging markets; and that the costs of building the necessary infrastructure are beyond the capacity of individual MFIs. These three imperatives indicate that collaboration is essential, even among competitors. The introduction of credit card technology in the US several decades ago provides instructive lessons.

Mark Schreiner describes credit scoring in Chapter 12, applying it to microfi-nance. Scoring consists of giving weights to various characteristics in credit proc-esses, and using these to calculate probabilities. He argues that credit scoring, done correctly, provides more accurate results at lower cost than other risk evalua-tion techniques because it quantifies risks to a high degree. Credit risk can be specified to include, for example, probable losses and likely periods of delin-quency. The risks concerned extend beyond credit risk to include borrower behav-iour in general, such as the probability of the borrower's not taking another loan. In order to introduce credit scoring successfully, considerable attention must be devoted to dealing with loan officers and others suspicious of new techniques or who fear (often wrongly) loss of status or employment.

Chapter 13 by Christoph Freytag suggests that credit scoring is not a panacea. Operational risks, described as inefficient systems or insufficient attention to in-formation and procedures, are common in many microfinance institutions: these factors cannot be corrected by scoring. Borrowers often fail to repay because of crises of large and small, including civil unrest. Fraud is also not predictable. Scoring may lead to overindebtedness because the debt capacity of the loan appli-cant is not rigourously quantified. Scoring requires information infrastructure capable of handling large data bases and works best when behaviour is highly predictable, which is not necessarily the case in microfinance. However, scoring may help at the margin and may be useful as a guide, as Schreiner acknowledges.

CHAPTER 7:

Remittance Money Transfers, Microfinance and Financial Integration: Of Credo, Cruxes, and Convictions

Cerstin Sander

Project Manager, KfW Entwicklungsbank[1]

Ever spent a month without transferring money? Money transfer for payments or remittances is among the foremost financial services demanded along with current or deposit accounts. Such transactional banking is part of a set of basic financial services which are essential for any private individual, rich or poor, and any business, big or small.

Wherever the regulated financial sector leaves gaps or creates bottlenecks in service coverage, businesses and people find 'workarounds' through informal or proprietary systems. Traders and migrants have for long sent or received monies using informal ways before banking existed; they are using them to this day whenever regulated financial systems fail them or when their own solutions strike them as more attractive, often for reasons of trust, convenience, or familiarity. Examples are hawala or hundi, informal money transfer systems originally developed amongst Asian and Arab traders, respectively, many centuries ago.[2] In recent years these have received much attention due to concerns about anti-money laundering (AML) and counter-terrorist financing (CTF).

Concomitantly, migrant remittances have attracted much interest, partly due to the informal systems still commonly used. But mainly this attention seems due to a new awareness of the magnitude of the flows: an estimated US$ 170 billion to developing countries in 2005.[3] The significance of these flows has been highlighted, especially for poor people and poverty reduction or more broadly for their

---

[1] Unless other sources are specified, this article draws on the author's research on remittances since 2001 which is partly captured in a number of articles and publications, selectively listed in the bibliography. The author also teaches on the subject at the annual Boulder Microfinance Training Program (www.bouldermicrofinance.org).

[2] See, for example, El Qorchi et al. 2002.

[3] World Bank 2006.

welfare effects.[4] Also, remittance receipts typically rise in times of need or crisis.[5] For recipients, remittances are often an important addition to household finances for basic consumption, education or health, to finance consumer goods and also to generate savings or facilitate investments. Both effects – income smoothing or investment in human capital as well as investment in business or assets – are substantial. Some countries' economies are strongly characterised by remittance inflows, especially small or island nations with large migrant populations such as Albania, Moldova, Jamaica or Cape Verde. Remittances can surpass one fifth or more of GDP in a few cases such as Lesotho, Tonga or Lebanon and can also serve as a key source of foreign currency reserves.[6]

The following explores the credo (belief) that microfinance providers (MFPs),[7] because they are closer to the target clientele than other providers, are well placed to offer money transfer services and can thus contribute to financial service integration of low-income groups. While perhaps intuitively obvious at first, a closer look at some cruxes (puzzles) MFPs tend to encounter leads to a quite differentiated picture on MFPs' potential suitability as a service provider and their contribution to financial integration. I conclude that integration of low-income groups in financial systems through money transfer products is possible, though far less obvious and developed than might be assumed, and so far to no greater degree when MFPs provide the service. Only MFPs that are strategically located and possess sufficient institutional capacity can greatly contribute to filling gaps in the service patchwork for the benefit of their low-income clientele. Such opportunities exist and should be pursued using a multi-pronged approach to regulation, systems, and products.

Credo: Integration

> *It has become a common credo in discussions among the financial sector development community that migrant remittances offer the opportunity to integrate hitherto unbanked migrants and recipients of their remittances back home into the financial system. For obvious reasons it is an intuitive and also not entirely unfounded credo. How much integration has occurred or can be achieved?*

---

[4] See, for example, Adams 2006.

[5] See, for example, Rapoport et al. 2005.

[6] See, for example, Spatafora in IMF World Economic Outlook, April 2005.

[7] MFP is used here to encompass financial service providers with primarily a low-income clientele, typically providing loans but increasingly also savings or other financial products; they can be unregulated, regulated within specific microfinance legislation, or licensed as a bank or a non-bank financial service provider.

Financial integration of remittances has two distinct but related aspects: One is the integration of the remittance funds into the formal financial system by attracting migrants to services which are recorded within the system (typically transfer products offered by regulated services or banks). The other is the integration of money transfer clients into the financial system – of a migrant as remittance sender, of the recipient of the funds, or of both – for instance by opening an account.

'Cash in, cash out' is still the most common way independent of whether remittances are transferred via banks or specialised services such as Western Union or MoneyGram. Senders as well as receivers of remittances are often 'unbanked'. Recipients typically take a full cash payout to finance personal or business expenses. Any remaining cash finds its way into piggy banks or under mattresses. While this can do the job of storing cash, it has risks and limitations: the money is idle capital while it sits there and is at risk through theft, fire, other damage, or ad hoc spending demands such as relatives' claims for financial support.

Typically, where the banking sector is relatively stable and reliable, financial institutions provide a safer place for the money and they contribute to the financial integration of remittances. Such institutions can offer a broader range of services to their clients with savings or loans, for instance, in addition to money transfers. Moreover, they have the added advantage of pooling and intermediating funds through loans which facilitate investments.

Attracting migrants and their families as clients of financial services beyond money transfer is thus a useful goal. For the client the benefits can include safety, interest accrual, income smoothing through use of savings, and access to a broader range of basic financial services. For the service provider the benefits can include opportunities for cross-selling of products and, if licensed to take deposits, access to the typically lowest cost refinancing for lending. For the financial market, the transparent flow of funds as well as greater intermediation contributes to stability and leveraging of capital for investments.

Commercial banks however, mostly show limited interest in this client segment and its opportunities. Banks, especially in recipient countries, still have corporates, wealthy individuals, and the salaried as their target clientele. Exceptions can be observed in some remittance corridors such as between the USA and parts of Latin America (e.g. Mexico) where high volumes and competition have led a few banks to recognise the opportunities and enter the market.[8] Corridors such as those between Germany and Turkey, for instance, are more developed with branches of Turkish banks in Germany. In addition, a very active market in future flow securitisations of remittances originated by Turkish banks to refinance their lending business indicates the contributions of these funds to capital market development and financial intermediation.

---

[8]   See, for example, Migrant Remittances 1(1), 2004; an internet search also yields numerous examples.

Microfinance providers as well have increasingly shown interest. At first glance they would seem very well placed to offer money transfers. Serving clients whom commercial banks would rather not serve is part of their mission. Providing clients with a range of key financial services has also become much more salient in microfinance. The initial almost exclusive focus on loans has made way for a range of savings products and more recently also for a number of MFPs offering money transfer services.

The benefit to the customers could also translate into a benefit for the MFP if they manage to attract more clients through money transfer services, increase customer loyalty, and cross-sell their products such as savings or loans. In addition, earning fees through money transfers is an attractive complement to interest generated by loans. If licensed to take deposits, client savings offer the MFP the cheapest source of refinancing and extending their loan portfolios.

Microfinance and Money Transfer Clients – Living up to the Credo of Integration?

A first order question is how common are money transfer services through MFPs? Exact numbers are elusive but attempts to identify MFPs with such services have indicated that, while the numbers are growing, only a few offer the service. Typically they are regulated MFPs and often they possess a full banking licence, though a few exceptions exist, including NGOs or cooperatives.[9] Many act as sub-agents for branded money transfer services. The growing competition among the brands broadens the opportunities for MFPs to become agents.

MFPs that offer the service typically do so as an ancillary product which generates fee income, significantly so for some. Very few advertise the service (for instance to attract new clients) beyond the general marketing that comes with brand name products such as Western Union. Cross-selling is not common but exists, for instance, with mortgage loans.

The contribution they or the product makes to better integrate unbanked money transfer clients to become banked, such as migrants and their families, is still mainly anecdotal or based on scant and scattered data accumulated by individual MFP managers.[10] But the information is fairly consistent and indicates the following effects:

- increases in savings

- indirect links to loans

- direct packaging e.g. with mortgage finance

---

[9] For examples, see Migrant Remittances 2(2), 2005.

[10] Author's interviews with MFP managers; see also experience of WOCCU's IRnet, e.g. in Migrant Remittances 2(2) 2005.

What would it take to have more MFPs offer money transfer services? Is it desirable? And what would entice money transfer clients to use other financial services such as savings or loans?

Cruxes – A Few ...

> *Transactional banking such as money transfer for remittance purposes is a product with requirements that are different from MFPs' core business of lending. Among the key factors which account for the differences are: i) the market for money transfers and access to clients in the originating and the receiving markets along with ii) the institutional set up required for the product as well as the regulatory context.*

Regulatory Context

'Heed thy regulator' is a bitter truth, as some in the money transfer business have learned the hard way – and were shut down for at least some time. Ascertaining whether the regulatory context is conducive is key. It can also determine which market(s) an MFP could realistically target – especially whether it is a cross-border remittance market or a domestic market. In-country migrant remittances and money transfers for payment purposes more generally can be in higher demand than international transfers.

The regulatory context for microfinance and also for money transfer services varies widely by country. For money transfer services, regulators typically require either a full banking licence or a separate money transfer licence. Fees and requirements of either minimum equity and/or bonds incur direct costs. Recording and reporting requirements which depend on adequate IT systems incur additional indirect costs. Some regulators will not authorise money transfer services by unregulated MFPs. Often as a result of tightened regulations related to AML and CTF, regulators appear to have become conservative and risk-averse in their assessments. This reduces the likelihood of approval, particularly for non-regulated MFPs. As domestic products avoid foreign exchange and cross-border transactions, authorisation can be easier to obtain than for a cross-border product.

A related issue is whether an MFP can take deposits. This determines whether it can offer accounts and transfer remittances into accounts as well as whether cross-selling opportunities with deposit products are feasible. An MFP without a deposit product is little more than a pay out point in a money transfer system, as opportunities to cross-sell are limited.

MFPs that offer money transfer services are thus usually regulated financial institutions. Many of them have a full bank licence, some are licensed as non-bank financial institutions, others operate under specific microfinance regulations, such as the Microfinance Deposit Taking Institutions (MDIs) in Uganda. A very few non-regulated MFPs also offer money transfers; their outreach is typically restricted to members of the MFP which they usually serve with a proprietary product operating in a single corridor between only one bank in the originating market and the MFP. As transaction volumes are very low, they tend to remain below the regulatory radar screen.

Markets – Global, Regional ... Local

Given the regulatory options, how much of a market is there for remittance transfers? Globally, migrants sent close to US$ 170 billion home to developing and transition countries in 2005 according to World Bank data. Remittance volumes (as recorded by central banks) have nearly doubled since 2000.[11]

These figures are stunning and grow each year, suggesting a sizeable overall market. Major players, such as Western Union, anticipate substantial growth in remittance flows based in part on migration forecasts by the United Nations that project an increase from 190 million migrants in 2005 to 280 million in 2050.[12]

Yet, while the data gives an indication, it does not show the full picture. The data is in fact quite messy and provides only approximations:

'Guesstimates' of informal flows not captured by official statistics add between 50 and 100% at an aggregate level.[13] But some claim that informal flows have diminished as tighter regulations related to AML and CTF in the wake of the attacks in the United States in September 2001 have led to more transfers being transacted through formal, regulated services. This would also account for some of the growth in officially recorded volumes rather than constituting real growth.

There are also entire blanks on the data map – e.g. for two thirds of Sub-Saharan African countries – so data is significantly underreported. Moreover, data quality is very mixed due to weaknesses in recording.[14]

Such aggregates also mask much relevant detail.[15] For example, the readily available data does not identify the corridors of the flows: the sending and receiving markets. Some are well known, such as the United States and Mexico, or the

---

[11] World Bank 2006. The IMF's figures of about US$100 billion are more conservative using a narrower definition than the World Bank. (Spatafora in IMF World Economic Outlook, April 2005).

[12] Western Union, Investor Presentation, 18 September 2006.

[13] Freund et al. 2005 suggest between 20 and 200% depending on the country.

[14] Efforts to improve remittance data have followed the recommendations of the G8 2004 Sea Island Summit and are led by the World Bank in close collaboration with the Committee on Payment and Settlement Systems (Bank for International Settlement), and the IMF.

[15] As a notable sidebar, while East Asia and Latin America receive the largest volumes, the flows are economically more significant for the Middle East and North Africa and South Asia where the levels compare to 4.1 and 3.6% of the region's GDP, respectively, compared to 2.1% of GDP for Latin America.

UK and India; others perhaps less so, such as South Africa and Mozambique or the United Arab Emirates and the Philippines. It also does not identify where within those markets the senders and receivers live – for instance Kenyans in the United States cluster partly in Minneapolis, Indians in the UK cluster in London and in the Midlands (Manchester area). As money transfer is a volume business – requiring high transaction volumes to generate profits out of often narrowing fee margins as competition grows – being at either end of a high volume corridor is preferable. Finding out where the 'migrant stock' of potential senders has settled is part of assessing the market and its potential.

The market is also quite dynamic. Competition has been growing and has in some parts become reasonably fierce.[16] New regional providers have entered and captured significant market shares, creating enough pressure to lower fees in several high volume markets. For instance, in North and Latin American markets many smaller regional services have made a mark.[17] Anelik Money Transfer (also known as Anelik System) is an example in the CIS region. Competition is now such that even in a small market the number of brand name products has roughly tripled in the last 5 years: Moldova, the poorest nation on the European continent,[18] has a population of 4.4 million and an estimated 1 million migrants. The country received some US$ 300 million in remittances, equalling a quarter of its GDP (2005 figures). In addition, an untold amount arrives via informal channels. Moldova's banking industry offers 15 different dedicated money transfer products from global brand names to lesser known regional ones – with few of them operating in this market for more than five years.

The actual client fee charged is only one aspect at the retail end. The terms of an agency agreement, such as fee splitting, that can connect a new service with desirable partner banks offering strong retail capacity through their branch network may be a more powerful determinant. For instance, a young, aggressively growing regional money transfer service provider quickly signed up a large number of banks by offering same day settlement of transfer balances, fees, and commissions.

This brief and partial sketch of market features illustrates a greater complexity than one might anticipate. Understanding their potential money transfer market and how to tap into it is a main crux or challenge for MFPs. Whereas they are used to selling a microloan or also a savings product in their home market, money transfer, and especially migrant remittances, requires a network of points of sale (PoS) in the originating and in the receiving markets. As they are generally situated in receiving markets, MFPs need to know whether they are located close to

---

[16] Of the remittance transfers to developing countries, the top competitors – Western Union and MoneyGram – are estimated to hold about one fifth of the market. (Aite 2005).

[17] See, for instance, Andreassen 2006; Migrant Remittances 1(1), 2004 and 2(2), 2005.

[18] Comparable to Mongolia and Nicaragua on the UN Human Development Index Scale.

remittance recipients and where the money they receive originates so they can find a link to the originating market. To cast the widest and most readily available net, MFPs therefore often seek access to existing networks of money transfer services, several of which operate globally.

Experience shows that basic homework on the market, including clients and competition, is well worth the effort and can save an aspiring MFP from some headaches later on. One MFP, for instance, proudly became a sub-agent to a global brand name service – presumably on the assumption of an overall strong remittance receiving market with recipients among their clientele as well as within reach of their branches. These assumptions basically held, but within the first year they found that business was far less buoyant than they had hoped. Transaction volumes and commission income were not as high as they had thought. Moreover, their situation was unlikely to improve due to increasing competition as more sub-agents were rapidly signing up.

A different and perhaps more manageable proposition for MFPs are money transfer services in their domestic market. They are a potentially very attractive alternative to cross-border transfers and have some immediate similarities and differences: Data is generally scarce here as well – in this case because domestic transactions are not usually captured in readily available statistics whereas cross-border remittances are a standard part of reporting in the balance of payments of the IMF. For domestic transfers the MFP again needs access to a sufficient network of points of sale – either its own (e.g. branches) if they are in locations with high volume potential, or by linking up with others to form a service network.

The path of first offering domestic transfers to provide a complementary client service and build the systems and experience is fairly typical for MFPs offering money transfers. Examples include ACLEDA Cambodia, XAC Bank Mongolia, NMB Tanzania, Apex Bank Ghana, and ProCredit Bank Bulgaria using their own branch or member bank networks. As they evolved, they took up international transfer services, typically becoming part of a brand name network. Despite some qualms about their choice, given their mission and desire to offer a lower priced product, they saw no real alternatives in terms of ready feasibility, best access to originating markets, reliability and consistency.

Institutional Capacity

Money transfer is a product quite different from lending or from deposit taking. MFPs are not typically set up with the requisite basics of transactional banking and often do not directly handle cash, unless they already operate as a fully licensed bank. Essential capacities for a money transfer service in back and front office operations require systems, procedures and skill sets of management and staff. These create changes and demand investments, as highlighted in the following examples:

Ancillary costs – costs accrue across a range of factors such as set-up costs for systems and staff training. Security deposits or bonds may have to be held, depending on the service agreement or the licence. Handling cash incurs insurance and security costs (e.g. armoured cars for money transport and guards). Fraud and theft prevention are essential.

Liquidity and liquidity management – for many MFPs loans and repayments, and often savings, are managed through client accounts with local banks: the MFP handles no cash and has no cashiers. Paying out remittances requires a fair amount of cash. Clients seek their cash partly at regular intervals but also with peaks around festive seasons, when school fees fall due, or when calamity strikes in the form of failed harvests, severe weather, or natural or economic shocks. Reliability in immediate payout is essential for the acceptance and continued success of a money transfer service. Sufficient liquidity needs to be on hand when and wherever clients may request their money. This requires learning clients' patterns quickly and being prepared for deviations. It also requires the transfer of cash to branches or service outlets which have remittance traffic. In reality this tends to mean physically moving cash. Bank transfers to a nearby bank branch may not be possible and access to cash centres of the central bank is given only if the MFP is a licensed bank. It also means safekeeping of significant volumes of cash in branches.

MIS and back-office systems – money transfer systems are quite different from systems created for credit. As previously indicated in discussing regulation, recording and handling must comply with a range of regulatory requirements stipulated to prevent money laundering and terrorist financing. Also required is the capacity to identify and report suspicious transactions or patterns. Depending on the regulatory requirements and the transaction volume, this can range from a very few to more than a thousand reports filed a day. MFPs can circumvent much of this by using a system provided by an established money transfer service.

Convictions ...

> *The integration of low-income groups in financial systems through money transfer products is possible, though far less obvious and developed than might be assumed. The hope that MFPs could be a significant part of better financial integration through money transfers has not yet been realised to any great degree. Opportunities to engender major developments in the market that would achieve greater integration contribute first to better access to money transfer services, second to greater financial inclusion of low income clients, and third to the integration of remittances into the financial systems. These outcomes hinge in many respects on changes in three areas: regulations, systems and products.*

Integration of remittances in financial systems has partly been achieved through a combination of stricter regulation and more competition in the money transfer market.[19] Thus more of the funds are transacted through the formal financial system and can be used for refinancing (intermediation).

Recent research shows that remittances have an aggregate positive effect, increasing levels of deposits and credit to the private sector relative to GDP.[20] Thus they contribute to financial sector development.[21]

The analysis and criteria used, however, do not assess whether or how low-income groups have in fact been better integrated in financial systems. Statistical evidence is lacking, but illustrative observation of markets and actors provides a useful indicative picture:

The integration of low-income groups in financial systems through money transfer products is possible though far less obvious and developed than might be assumed. Commercial banks' interest in attracting this clientele has grown but is still lagging. Cross-selling does not appear to be much pursued where money transfer is offered and could be coupled with or used to attract clients to ancillary financial services. In part it is hampered by insufficient training and incentives for retail staff as well as by the absence of interfaces between money transfer systems and core banking systems, especially links to accounts.

The hope that MFPs could be a significant part of better financial integration is not yet realised to any great degree. They are not currently the predestined service providers for money transfers. For MFPs it makes good business sense and has the potential to be a good service where regulations and the market permit and the service network and institutional capacity are conducive. When MFPs offer money transfer services they often still display the lag in integration of this client segment in financial services generally, e.g. as savers, as do commercial banks.

Opportunities to engender major developments in the market – which contribute to better access to money transfer services and also to greater financial inclusion – hinge in many respects on changes in three areas: regulations, systems and products.

---

[19] Stricter regulations have, however, limited the access to financial services for some individuals and small businesses who have not been able to comply with identification or other requirements under the new, tightened rules, or by banks, that rated them as too costly to serve or too high a risk. This has to some extent hampered competition in the money transfer business as some small licensed service providers have found that banks refuse to open an account or that their bank asked them to move their accounts.

[20] Aggarwal et al. 2006.

[21] In weak financial sector contexts (cash-based, weak service levels and financial infrastructure), however, research suggests that remittances alleviate credit constraints on the poor and substitute for the weak financial sector development. (Giuliano et al. 2006).

Enabling Regulations

Whether business models, technologies or partnerships can be made to work in a certain market is often a matter of the regulatory environment. A market where a full bank licence is a prerequisite for offering money transfer services (MTS) tends to have fewer service providers and points of sale than a market where a money transfer service can be licensed separately. Licensing of MTS is quite new in most markets and, where it exists, has often been introduced in the context of AML and CTF measures. The UK is an example where a separate license and regulation was put in place in 2002.

Cost and simplicity of licensing is another factor that tends to affect the demand for licenses. The United States is one of the most cumbersome markets to licence an MTS: federal licensing requirements coupled with separate State licensing requirements have to be fulfilled wherever the service is to be offered. The concomitant costs for fees and bonds are high.[22]

Where non-banks and non-financial services such as retailers can be part of the point of sale network, the opportunities for outreach are much greater. Grocery stores, petrol stations, or similar businesses which have high client traffic and cash on hand are well placed. Thus, for instance, in the United States, supermarkets or large retail chains are part of the agent network of money transfer companies, especially in locations where migrants shop regularly. In Brazil, the regulator allows retail stores to join an agency network and similarly in Peru. How it is done varies – for instance, Banco do Credito del Peru operates cashless ATMs (automated teller machines) in retail stores. The client uses it like any other ATM except that the ATM provides a printed record based on which the client receives the money from the store's till.[23] Allowing sub-agents of money transfer services that pay out only in local currency is another factor which facilitates the growth of a service network.

Combining mobile phone technology with money transfer services is a very compelling idea.[24] As those who have tried know, the technology or software is less of an issue than regulation. Regulators looking after banking and financial services and those in charge of telecommunications need to be convinced in cases such as G-Cash and SMART in the Philippines, or CelPay once active in Congo, Zambia, and South Africa. These are products of mobile phone companies or their subsidiaries using the short messaging system (SMS) to make payments in stores

---

[22] For US State licensing requirements see, for instance, a list at www.westernunion.com/info/aboutUsStateLicense.asp.

[23] For a recent presentation of the agent model, see www.nfx.nl/binaries/conference-website/presentations/microfinance/bcp-microfinance--nfx-format-.ppt#289,10, Slide 10.

[24] For examples see Migrant Remittances 2(1) April 2005; for a recent presentation by G-Xchange detailing their G-Cash business model, see www.nfx.nl/binaries/conference-website/presentations/mobile-banking/gcash-nfx-11-01-06rev.ppt#256,1,Mind the Gap: Bankable Approaches to Increase Access to Finance.

or for utilities, or to make transfers between individuals, such as for remittances. Often the company initiating such a product finds itself paving the regulatory way by bringing together the different regulators to find a solution which allows the service to operate. Solutions include developing business processes whereby a financial institution holds all the clients' funds to account for compliance with prudential rules in case the regulators view these as deposits. Alternatively, the funds are not considered as deposits but held in stored-value-accounts analogous to the prepayment accounts customers hold for mobile phone charges. Regulators respond differently – in the Philippines positively or at least constructively and the services operate; in South Africa the regulator eventually required CelTel to separate its payment product from the mobile phone service leading to the sale of CelPay to a bank.

In general, better financial service regulations or even just a better application of existing regulations can facilitate the range of service providers, products, and geographic accessibility of money transfers. In addition, improved interplay of different regulatory regimes can open the way to new business models which can greatly increase outreach to new, previously unserved clients as well as allow for better services to current money transfer users in terms of lower cost, speed or accessibility.

Better Systems

Payment systems are the backbone of any financial sector. They are key to transactional banking such as money transfer. Availability, access and quality of the payment system affect the availability of money transfer services and their cost. Systems have been developed largely without international standards, leading to low compatibility and high costs for transactions across payment systems.

Money transfer service providers often use their proprietary systems to transact client transfers. This puts transaction cost and time within their control and reduces their need to connect to other existing payment systems to settling their accounts with agents. Such stand-alone systems also typically lack a link to the main account and client information systems of banks or other financial service providers such as MFPs. Client remittance information is thus typically delinked from client account information, limiting the prospects for a more integrated financial service to the client. In interlinked systems remittance information could become part of the clients' financial track record when considering a loan application.[25]

---

[25] At least informally, credit officers often take into account remittance receipts as part of their overall loan approval assessment. Based on bank supervision requirements, however, remittances typically can not be counted as regular income and part of the basis for loan approval.

Attractive Products

A migrant's choice to send money via formal services is largely a question of whether the formal service is sufficiently attractive compared to the informal alternative. Market research indicates that familiarity and trust are often as important or more important than the cost of the service. Some banks serving migrant neighbourhoods have staff of that diaspora working in their branches. Being within ready physical reach of the sender as well as the recipient is another factor, such that branches or points of sale in neighbourhoods with migrants or with remittance recipients tend to show high transaction volumes. Each client group can differ, however, so that blueprint assumptions based on market research done elsewhere are not always valid. While proximity to the client is typically an attractive feature, recipients in Moldova preferred to use a payout point away from their village or neighbourhood for fear that others would learn about the arrival of cash.

Informal services also indicate some of the product features which regulated services have lacked. Among them is the ability to specify a set of payments to be made from a single money transfer such as a payment to a builder or supplier of construction materials, an insurance or a utility payment, and a remittance to a family member. In contrast, money transfer products offered in the regulated market are typically limited to a single instruction, i.e. payout to a specific recipient.

Also worth considering is how accessible and attractive saving or investment is for migrants and remittance recipients. Access to money transfer, even if through a bank, does not coincide with access to other financial services such as a current or savings account because minimum balances or account fees often deter low-income clients. Even where access to an account is not a barrier, concerted strategic efforts to cross-sell savings or other products to migrants or remittance recipients are still the exception rather than the norm. Targeting migrants especially as clients and savers or investors is becoming more common – for instance Indian government bonds specifically targeting the Indian diaspora.

In Closing …

Market observers concur that more accessible and cheaper money transfer services have come about in markets where competition has increased. This has typically been fuelled by new services entering the market as they realised the potential, partly due to growing remittance flows. It has also been fuelled where regulatory systems have set clear rules for money transfer licences and reasonable compliance and cost thresholds. Similarly, regulatory contexts which are open to new business models regarding point of sales networks, and new types of service providers taking advantage of technologies such as mobile phones, have provided opportunities for competition that results in more and better services.

Though remittance money transfer services are not a panacea for banking the unbanked, some direct effects can be seen. Moreover, the integration of remittances in financial systems is progressing and contributes to financial sector development by increasing deposits and credit to the private sector. More is possible through attractive products, better systems and conducive regulations.

Bibliography

Adams, Richard H. 2006. 'Do Remittances Reduce Poverty?' Id21 insights no. 60, Institute of Development Studies, University of Sussex.

Aite Group. 2005. 'Consumer Money Transfers: Powering Global Remittances'.

Aggarwal, Reena, Aslı Demirgüç-Kunt, and Maria Soledad Martinez Pereira. 2006. 'Do Workers' Remittances Promote Financial Development?' Policy Research Working Paper Series 3957, The World Bank, June 2006.

Andreassen, Ole. 2006. 'Remittance Service Providers in the United States: How remittance firms operate and how they perceive their business environment'. Financial Sector Discussion Series – Payment Systems & Remittances, The World Bank, June 2006.

CGAP. 2004. 'Crafting a Money Transfers Strategy: Guidance for Pro-Poor Financial Service Providers'. CGAP Occasional Paper.

El-Qorchi, Mohammed, Samuel M. Maimbo and John F. Wilson. 2002. 'Hawala: How does this informal funds transfer system work, and should it be regulated?' *Finance and Development*, 39(4), December 2002.

Freund, Caroline and Nikola Spatafora. 2005. 'Remittances: Transaction Costs, Determinants and Informal Flows'. World Bank Policy Research Paper 3704.

Giuliano, Paola and Marta Ruiz-Arranz. 2006. 'Remittances, Financial Development, and Growth'. IMF Working Paper No. 05/234, June 2006.

Migrant Remittances. Newsletter. USAID and DFID, various issues, published since 2004.

Rapoport, Hillel and Frédéric Docquier. 2004. 'The Economics of Migrants' Remittances.' In Handbook on the Economics of Reciprocity, Giving and Altruism, ed. L.-A. Gerard-Varet, S.-C. Kolm, and J. Mercier Ythier. Amsterdam. Elsevier North-Holland.

Sander, Cerstin. 2005. 'How money moves in cash-based markets: money transfer services in Kenya, Tanzania and Uganda.' in Shaw, Judith (ed.). *Remittances, Microfinance and Development: building the links*, Volume 1: a global view, The Foundation for Development Cooperation, Brisbane, 2005.

Sander, Cerstin, Doina Nistor, Andrei Bat, Viorica Petrov, and Victoria Seymour. 2005. 'Migrant Remittances and the Financial Market in Moldova'. Study prepared for USAID (BASIS/CRSP), February 2005.

Sander, Cerstin and S.M. Maimbo. 2005. 'Migrant Remittances in Africa – A Regional Perspective'. In Samuel Munzele Maimbo and Dilip Ratha (eds.): *Remittances – Development Impact and Future Prospects*. World Bank, Washington, D.C.

Sander, Cerstin. 2005. 'Migrant Remittances: A Profitable Proposition for the Financial Services Sector'. *Developing Alternatives*, 10 (1), winter 2005.

Sander, Cerstin. 2004, 'Capturing a Market Share? Migrant Remittances and Money Transfers as a Microfinance Service in Sub-Saharan Africa'. *Small Enterprise Development Journal*, special issue on migrant remittances, March 2004.

Sander, Cerstin, Issa Barro, Mamadou Fall, Mariell Juhlin et Coumba Diop. 2003. 'Etude sur le transfert d'argent des émigrés au Sénégal et les services de transfert en microfinance'. Working Paper / Document de Travail No. 40, Employment Sector, Social Finance Unit / Le Programme Finance et Solidarité, International Labour Office (ILO/BIT), Geneva.

Sander, Cerstin. 2003. 'Migrant Remittances to Developing Countries – A Scoping Study: Overview and Introduction to Issues for Pro-Poor Financial Services'. Prepared for DFID.

Spatafora, Nikola. 2005. 'Two Current Issues Facing Developing Countries'. IMF World Economic Outlook, chapter 2, April 2005.

World Bank. 2006. *Global Development Finance: The Development Potential of Surging Capital Flows*, Volume I: Review, Analysis and Outlook.

CHAPTER 8:

Remittances and MFIs: Issues and Lessons from Latin America[*]

*Manuel Orozco[1] and Eve Hamilton[2,**]*

[1] Senior Associate, Inter-American Dialogue
[2] Project Director, Chemonics International

Introduction

Remittance flows to Latin American and the Caribbean reached $45 billion in 2004. For countries such as El Salvador, Nicaragua, Jamaica and others, remittances represent 10 percent or more of GDP and are one of the most important sources of foreign currency (IAD 2004). At the household level, remittances are a critical source of income for families living in poverty. Poor households receiving remittances have significant purchasing power relative to peer households that do not receive them (Orozco 2004). However, recipient households have limited access to financial institutions that provide financial services such as secure remittance delivery, safe interest-earning savings instruments, and loans.

The recent entry of microfinance institutions (MFIs) into the remittance market has increasingly been advocated as a mechanism for leveraging remittance flows in ways that would achieve development goals.[1] Donors have begun to provide technical assistance to help MFIs develop linkages with formal money transfer organisations (MTOs) and have enthusiastically supported such partnerships. Donors' underlying assumption is that, due to their close proximity to recipient communities and experience in serving low-income households, MFIs are in a unique position to reach recipients with low-cost transfer services and other finan-

---

[*] A similar paper by these authors was published earlier as "Remittances and MFI Intermediation: Issues and Lessons," in Judith Shaw, ed., *Remittances, Microfinance and Development: Building the Links*. Vol. 1, The Foundation for Development Cooperation. Brisbane: 2005.

[**] The authors thank the UK Department for International Development for funding part of this research.

[1] Microfinance institutions (MFIs) are organisations that provide financial services, including savings and/or credit facilities to small and microentrepreneurs and other low income groups with limited or no access to traditional commercial bank services.

cial products. Moreover, by providing these services — often through partnerships with MTOs — MFIs can expand their operations and increase their revenues.

Despite these assumptions, little empirical evidence has been collected on the practices and performance of MFIs in the remittance market. Are MFIs located in areas where current or potential remittance recipients reside? Can they effectively compete with MTOs? Do remittance recipients obtain a broader range of financial services? To begin answering questions such as these, we present a framework for assessing the development impact of MFI entry into the remittance market. We then propose a series of indicators linked to that framework and provide an initial analysis of the performance of the 27 MFIs and two credit union federations we studied.[2] We conclude with suggestions for further research.

The findings presented here are based on interviews with 27 MFIs and 2 credit union federations operating in Latin America and the Caribbean. The institutions were asked approximately 25 questions relating to their presence in communities receiving remittances, their remittance transfer services, cross-selling efforts, information technology, and management information systems. The information gathered was quantified to get a sense of overall trends, and to serve as a basis for future research and identification of best practices. Due to the sample size, comparisons and conclusions are tentative.

Microfinance Institutions and Remittance Markets

Empirical analysis requires a preliminary working definition of the intersection between remittances and microfinance, accompanied by measurable indicators that relate to development. We define this intersection between remittances and microfinance as *a condition in which microfinance institutions offer remittance transfers in underserved areas through an effective market presence, selling tailored financial services based on a systematic understanding of the remittance recipient market.* These factors are summarised in Box 1, explained below and used as bases for analyses.

Geographic Presence: For remittances and microfinance to intersect, MFIs must at a minimum operate near remittance recipients. The first factor to explore, which is perhaps the most taken for granted, is the presence of MFIs in or near communities receiving remittances.

Market Position refers to the ability of MFIs to compete effectively in the remittance market. At a minimum, this is achieved through a combination of partnerships with money transfer companies, the offer of low-cost transfers, and distribution capacity inferred by the number of transfers completed.

---

[2]   To our knowledge, there were fewer than 100 MFIs in Latin America and the Caribbean offering remittance transfers in 2005.

Box 1: Factors That Build MFI Capacity to Increase the Development Impact of Remittances

Geographic Presence

- Relative position of MFI vis a vis competitor branches

Market Position

- Type of MFI-MTO partnership

- Branch transaction rate

- Transfer cost

Financial Service Provision

- Existence of cross selling

- Design of remittance-linked products

Management Information System

- Data management linked to remittance market base

Transfer Technologies

- Basic back end transfer system

Provision of Financial Services: MFIs' commitment and capacity to provide a broad range of financial services to low-income people who are often ignored by traditional commercial banks is at the heart of the link between MFIs, remittances, and development. Institutions that offer a range of financial services such as savings accounts, loans, and insurance to remittance clients create opportunities for cross-selling. Successful provision of these services by MFIs, however, depends on the existence and/or design of financial products attractive to customers and the effectiveness of marketing strategies.

Systematic Information Management: Effective data management is another critical factor that improves the link between remittance transfers and other financial services. Among other benefits, efficient data management systems strengthen the decision-making capacity of financial institutions by facilitating access to market and client information that informs marketing strategies. Marketing is important to the successful expansion of broader financial services as well as to the growth of MFI remittance services.

Technology provides a conduit for data gathering, organisation and transmission. MFIs increasingly rely on technology to improve their effectiveness and efficiency in managing and delivering services. To compete in the remittance market, MFIs must adopt back end technologies that ensure efficient wire transfers as well as adaptable data transmission to the institution's information management systems.[3]

Analysing the Intersecting Issues

Based on an initial framework for analysis, using a few key indicators and available data, we provide preliminary indications of MFIs' successes in leveraging the development impact of remittances. The analysis that follows is based on interviews with MFIs operating predominantly in El Salvador and Guatemala. However, MFIs in other countries, including Mexico, Paraguay and Haiti, were also considered (Table 1). Subjects were selected randomly, but an effort was made to include large and small MFIs, including regulated and credit-only institutions.

Table 1. Countries and MFIs studied

Region or country	Microfinance Institution
Andean	Bolivia: BancoSol Ecuador: Banco Solidario Peru: Praxis Fina
El Salvador	Acacu, Acacciba, Acocomet, Acodjar, Fundación Napoleon Duarte (MiCrédito), AMC, FEDECACES, Fedecrédito, Fundación Campo, Integral, ProCredit
Guatemala	Banrural, Bancáfe, Cosadeco, Empresarial, FENECOAC, Genesis Guayacán, Salcajá
Mexico	AMUCCS (Xuu Nuu), BANSEFI (Red de la Gente), Credemich, Fincoax
Southern Cone	Paraguay: El Comercio
Other	Haiti: Fonkoze Honduras: ODEF

Note: Annex 1 contains statistics as of 2004 or 2005 for each of these entities.

---

[3]   Another important consideration is the regulatory or legal environment. Some countries do not allow unregulated institutions to transfer funds. This element goes beyond our research framework.

These MFIs represent a wide array of organisations. Three have more than 200,000 members (Banrural, Bancafe and FENECOAC), and five have between 40,000 and 90,000. The remaining MFIs have fewer than 20,000 clients. Ten MFIs started their business prior to 2000 (six in 1998), and five in 2004. Most of these MFIs (60 percent) have over 70 percent of their branches in rural areas.

Geographic Presence

Where data are available, we would evaluate an MFI's geographic presence by comparing the geographic distribution of remittance recipients with the MFI's area of operation and that of all MTO competitors in those areas. To get such information, in addition to the MFI's information, two datasets are necessary: the size of the remittance recipient community and the number and outreach of MTO competitors where the MFI operates. This kind of extremely useful information is rarely available. Alternatively, we can estimate the ratio between the distribution of MFI branches and competitor MTO branches in the same location, such as a district or city.[4]

Employing this alternative approach in El Salvador and Guatemala, we compare the number of branches of each MFI offering remittance transfers with the number of outlets of a large company like Western Union, a major competitor on the distribution side. A ratio is obtained by dividing the total number of an individual MFI's branches by the number of Western Union branches in that city. Since MFIs generally operate in underserved areas, a minimum ratio of 30% was selected as a threshold of significant presence in that area because it seems reasonable to expect an MFI to be one-third as strong as a major competitor in the same area.

Using Western Union (WU) as a proxy for MTOs has advantages and limitations. The two major advantages of using WU are that data are available and that WU is the world's largest and most ubiquitous MTO. As such, WU can serve as a reference point for the industry. The obvious limitation is that WU is not equally important in all markets and in some (and possibly all) markets it would be helpful to include other companies. This latter approach requires greater resources than were available for this survey, but remains a desirable goal for continued research.

The geographic presence of these institutions is not necessarily related to their relative size nationwide. For example, Salcajá in Guatemala has only four branches. Similarly, AMC, which operates solely in rural areas, is smaller than ProCredit, yet has a stronger position vis-a-vis Western Union.

An important limitation of this approach is its assumption that a large MTO is present where remittances are received. However, an MFI may be located in an area where there is no large MTO. Consequently, the most comprehensive measure of an MFI's geographic presence would use national survey data to compare the

---

[4] This alternative approach could be improved by calculating this ratio for lower income remittance recipient households. However, obtaining data for such fine-tuning is difficult.

Table 2. MFI ratio to WU agents

El Salvador	(%)
FEDECACES	51
AMC de RL	44
Banco ProCredit	36
Apoyo Integral	29
Fundación Jose Napoleon Duarte	22
Fundación Campo	14
Guatemala	**(%)**
Salcajá	47
FENACOAC	41
Genesis Empresarial	36

Source: MFI information and Western Union.

institution's operating zone with geographic data on the volume of remittances sent, but such data are not always available. The alternative approach described above serves as a proxy. An MFI analysing its remittance recipient base in the community can use this procedure to compare its branches vis–a-vis the recipient community and competitor companies.

Market Position

MFI-MTO partnerships: Most of the institutions analysed have a partnership with an MTO, and many types of partnerships exist. Some MFIs work with large companies like Western Union whereas others choose mid-level companies like Vigo Corporation. Partnerships result in part from an institution's efforts to identify a viable partner, but also from companies seeking to expand their network. Many companies look primarily for commercial financial institutions that can provide payment points for recipients of remittances. More recently, MTOs have looked for MFIs operating in areas where other payers would not normally be present. This is the case of Western Union's partnership with rural financial institutions such as Banrural in Guatemala, El Comercio in Paraguay, and ProCredit in El Salvador. Another example is MoneyGram's partnership with Bancafe, and Vigo Corporation's with FEDECACES and FENACOAC. What these institutions have in common is their strong presence in rural areas (greater than that of commercial banks) as well as a tested payment capacity. As discussed below, the choice of partner(s) appears to have important implications for the number of transactions processed and transfer fees offered.

Transaction Rates: Achieving effective involvement in the remittance market has been a major challenge for MFIs. One measure of market involvement is the transaction rate per branch.

Large competitors like Western Union or MoneyGram may have more than 100 branch agents in a given country and process an average of more than 200 transactions per branch per month. This indicator helps compare small and large institutions. For example, the Guatemalan cooperative Salcajá's 4 branches process a branch average of 250 transactions a month, a rate similar to that of the larger Western Union agents. Only two institutions monitored in this study process more than 1,000 transactions a month: Bancafe and Banrural in Guatemala, which are agents of MoneyGram and Western Union, respectively. Credit unions in Guatemala and El Salvador range in the middle, processing between 250 and 1,000 transactions monthly. Table 3 provides a distribution of transaction rates.

Table 3. Percentage distribution of transactions per branch per month

Number of transactions	%
Fewer than 50	48%
51 to 200	7%
201 to 400	14%
More than 400	31%
Total	100%
n=18	

Table 4. MTO partnerships and number of transfers per month

Transfers per month	No partner	One partner	> 1 partner or a large MTO as partner
0 to 50	50.0%	60.0%	27.3%
51 to 200	50.0%	6.7%	
201 to 400		26.7%	
Over 400		6.7%	72.7%
	100.0%	100.0%	100.0%
n=29			

One possible explanation of high volumes is an institution's partnership with one or more large MTOs. A second explanation may be that the longer the institution has been active in the remittance market, the higher its volume of transfers. Indeed, in our sample, most institutions processing more than 400 transactions per month have partnerships with large or multiple MTOs (Table 4). Furthermore, 70 percent of the MFIs that initiated operations before 2000 make over 400 transactions a month, compared to 11 percent of those that started after 2000, 67 percent of which have fewer than 50 transactions a month (Table 5). These two elements suggest that a critical MFI strategy may be to view remittance transfer as a long term venture that can be assisted by establishing agreements with several partners.

Costs, Fees and Charges of Remittances: The analysis of the cost of transfers produces mixed results.[5] One fifth of MFIs charge higher than average transaction fees — three of these institutions work with Western Union and MoneyGram. Sixty percent of all MFIs charge rates below average (Table 6).

Table 5. Number of transactions per month by processors offering remittance services before and since 2000

Transactions per month	Year service began		Total
	Before 2000	**Since 2000**	
0 to 50	10%	66.7%	46.4%
51 to 200	10%	5.6%	7.1%
201 to 400	10%	16.7%	14.3%
More than 400	70%	11.1%	32.1%
	100%	100.0%	100.0%

Table 6. MFI consumer transaction cost relative to the market average

Above average	21%
Equal to average	10%
Below average	59%
Total	100%
n=29	

---

[5] Costs to customers receiving remittances result from two prices; the fee on the transaction and the commission on the exchange rate when cashing the remittance. Data on transfer costs are elaborated elsewhere by one of the authors (Orozco, June 2004).

Those offering some of the lowest fees to recipients of remittances are small MFIs as well as credit unions that have forged partnerships with either smaller or non-traditional money transfer companies (Tables 7 and 8). Further analysis of the cost structure of MFI remittance services is required to understand the diverse cost reduction strategies of those institutions in our sample that offer lower prices and to identify what – if any – additional trade offs exist, and if the subset mentioned above can achieve both scale and lower costs.

Table 7. Transactions by branch and transfer cost

Transactions per branch per month	Above or below transfer cost			Total
	Above average transfer cost	Equal to average transfer cost	Below average transfer cost	
0 to 50	8.3%	16.7%	75.0%	100.0%
51 to 200			100.0%	100.0%
201 to 400	100.0%			100.0%
More than 400	30.0%	10.0%	60.0%	100.0%
Total	23.1%	11.5%	65.4%	100.0%

Table 8a. Transfer cost and type of MTO partner

Relative transfer cost	Type of MTO partner		
	> 1 partner of a large MTO partnership	Engaged with one partner	No partner
Above average	33.3%	66.7%	
Equal to average	66.7%	33.3%	
Below average	41.0%	47.0%	11.7%
Total	42.3%	50.0%	7.7%

Table 8b. Transfer cost and type of financial institution

Transfer cost	Institution type				Total
	Commercial bank	Credit union	Microfinance institution	Transformed MFI	
Above average		36.4%	10.0%	33.3%	23.1%
Equal to average	50.0%	9.1%	10.0%		11.5%
Below average	50.0%	54.5%	80.0%	66.7%	65.4%

Financial Service Provision

Converting the recipients of remittances into bankable clients with savings accounts and access to other financial products is critical to leveraging the development impact of remittance transfers. Two-thirds of the surveyed MFIs in our sample have sought to provide financial services to clients, whether through the opening of bank accounts (particularly savings accounts) or diverse loan products.

Some institutions have specifically tailored financial products to remittance recipients. Two examples are Banco Solidario and Salcajá. Banco Solidario's main
strategy has been to provide financial products designed for both remittance senders and recipients. As part of its Enlace Andina, Banco Solidario created a special
account called "My Family, My Country, My Return" which offers clients bundled savings options. This package most frequently uses credit lines, housing and
home buying credits, savings accounts and insurance. Banco Solidario's other
banking products include the Chauchera smart card that allows clients to make
transactions through the POS (point of sale) network used by established providers. After less than two years of operating in the remittance market, Banco Solidario holds a 5 to 8 percent market share and expected to attain an 8 to 12 percent
market share by the end of 2005 (Table 9).

Table 9. Banco Solidario remittance transfer and financial services (2002-2004)

Year	Transfers	Volume	Deposit accounts		Loans issued	
2002	1,800	$6,000,000	270	$150,000	50	$70,000
2003	14,000	$23,000,000	860	$670,000	230	$525,000
2004	60,000	$50,000,000	4,000	$3,500,000	1,700	$4,000,000

Source: Banco Solidario, interviews in January 2004 and 2005

To reach clients, Salcajá has taken advantage of 'word of mouth' marketing, and it
ensures that its branch tellers and representatives are well informed and capable of
explaining the remittance services and other products it offers. This institution is
formalising a cross-selling strategy, and plans to install at least one client-service
window at each branch, dedicated solely to serving remittance recipients. Salcajá's
goal is to expand its current base of nearly 15,000 clients by offering recipients
other financial services including pension funds, life insurance, medical insurance,
small business credit, home equity funds, and various savings packages such as
the Infant/Youth Savings Plan which encourages parents to invest in their children's schooling over the long-term.

Other institutions such as FEDECACES, a credit union, have targeted remittance
recipients directly as potential members. Approximately 25 percent of recipients

Table 10. Additional products offered by MFIs to remittance recipients

None yet	41.5%
Basic/standard services	41.5%
Tailored package	14.0%
No data available	3.0%
Total	100.0%
n=29	

who choose FEDECACES to process their remittances are also FEDECACES clients. To determine how best to tap the other 75 percent, FEDECACES commissioned an assessment with funding from the Inter-American Development Bank (IDB). This exercise revealed that many recipients do not understand what it means to own a savings account because they have never been offered one. FEDECACES is significant because, like Salcajá, it is an alternative savings and credit institution with a commitment to work with low-income households and in rural areas.

Box 2: Successful Cross-Selling in Mexico

Operating in the Mixteca region in Oaxaca, the microbank Xuu Ñuu Ndavi (Money of the Poor People) provides a basic remittance service to residents from relatives living abroad. With fewer than 200 clients during the first year of its remittance service, the microbank received $170,000 in remittances, capturing $160,000 in savings (IAD, 2004).

The effectiveness of financial service provision is arguably the most important indicator of development impact, but it is the area in which the least data are available for analysis. Ideally, the percentage of remittance clients that become clients using other financial services would provide this information. But few institutions track this development. Interviews indicate that many institutions are having difficulty persuading remittance recipients to use other financial services. One possible explanation is that many of the institutions referred to here as MFIs — because they serve low-income target groups, including microenterprises — are not using microfinance methodologies such as non-traditional collateral, solidarity guarantees, etc., that have proven most effective in reaching the poor. This may be particularly true for some cooperatives, since they tend to serve a slightly higher income client than do NGO MFIs. In other words, although it is assumed that these institutions know how to serve remittance recipients, they may actually be operating up market and need assistance to move down market effectively. However, as Table 11 shows, the conversion rates are comparable among NGO MFIs and cooperatives.

But possibly those receiving remittances — or some segment of this group — are fundamentally different from traditional microfinance clients, or it may be a case of inadequate marketing. More research is needed to understand this situation.

Table 11. Number of accounts opened among households receiving remittances (2005)

Institution	New accounts opened	Monthly transfers	Acceptance rate
Red de la Gente	2500	25000	10%
Guayacan	533	5426	10%
El Comercio	80	800	10%
Coosadeco	529	4780	11%
FEDECACES	4375	22000	20%
Acocomet	800	2383	34%
Salcajá	500	1000	50%
Banco Solidario	4000	5000	80%
Acacu	2703	2703	100%

Information Management for the Demand Side

Information management is central to developing an effective strategy to design and market a financial service. Improved management tools provide input to enhance the decision making capacity of institutions. To be considered minimally effective, an information management system should enable an institution to determine the percentage of its current clients who receive remittances and the services they use.

Few if any of the MFIs studied were able to use their MIS to track which of their remittance recipients were also clients of other financial services and vice versa. Moreover, only two of the MFIs studied, Financiera El Comercio in Paraguay and Genesis Empresarial in Guatemala, could determine how many of their clients receive remittances and what other financial services they do or could use. El Comercio, an agent for Western Union, discovered that 20 percent of its clients received remittances, while Genesis Empresarial learned that 30 percent of its clientele received money from abroad.

According to El Comercio's analysis of 500 clients, remittances are predominantly from Argentina. Seventy-seven percent received remittances within the past three years. This information helped the MFI learn more about its clients' income sources and the other services it could provide. El Comercio's data base provided profiles of senders and was continually refined for marketing purposes: for example, Paraguayan migrants are typically women from poor, rural areas engaged in domestic work in the informal sector.

This type of information is useful for making decisions on the investment and funding required to cater to various communities. This issue is particularly important because, aside from these two institutions, no other MFI surveyed had actually done systematic market research on the trends of remittances received in the communities in which they operate. Market research is essential in designing and implementing packages of financial products.

Technology Tools

An increasing number of institutions argue that "technology solutions are the current frontier in remittances" (Migrant Remittances, April 2005).[6] In fact, current technologies can offer at least four advantages to the remittance and MFI industries: functionality, innovative value-added competences, business and development impact, and cost-effectiveness. The functionality of the technology is such that, whether for the back or front end of the business or institutions, technologies are easily adapted to the current transfer platforms most institutions have. Although 95 percent of the leading companies remitting to Latin America and the Caribbean use agent based cash-to-cash transfers, the increasing flexibility offered by technology offers the choice of adopting attractive mechanisms for account-to-account transfers.

Technologies include data payment transmission systems through typical automatic clearing house (ACH) software platforms; prepaid, debit, or fully functionally multipurpose credit and debit cards; cell phones; and online transfers. These technologies permit firms to shift and transform their business into fully electronic-based transfer systems with both back and front end capabilities.

MFIs currently have a basic back end remittance transfer mechanism which is usually installed by the money transfer company. Some MFIs are considering modernising their technology platforms to process international wire transfers and other important features such as card processing, regulatory compliance, telecommunication via voice over internet protocols (VOIP), and online data management.

---

[6] Often using technologies to the best benefit is, however, not as straightforward as one might wish: 'The greater challenges lie in two areas: ensuring that regulations enable financial services and technology providers to roll out new service solutions, and moving from closed platforms or networks to interoperable, open platforms that broaden access and lower costs. (Migrant Remittances, April 2005).

Table 12. Functionality of technology in remittance transfers

Data payment transmission applications	Back end	Front end
ACH* Software platforms	International payment processing, settlement and data management	Card issuing (for closed or open networks)
Online platforms		Card issuing (for closed or open networks), online customer transfer
Payment system cards (prepaid, debit, store value)		Card issuing (for closed or open networks)
Wifi** for closed and open networks		NA
Other (SMS,*** etc.)		Data transmission by cellular phone

* Automated Clearing House
** Wireless Fidelity: high-frequency wireless local area network
*** Short Message Service

However, the investment, administration, maintenance and training costs of such a task are often beyond the reach of some institutions processing remittances. Adopting such platform technology costs approximately $250,000, excluding hardware expenses (computers, network lines, communication devices, among others). Moreover, the decision to adopt the technology depends on the size of the target market and the commercial partner on the sending side. Specifically, MFIs must analyse who among recipients currently has access to financial institutions and uses cards, the financial and commercial preferences of that market segment (such as making phone calls), and must identify possible retail partners who could adopt a card or retrieve information for payment processing. With respect to the first issue, available data suggest that use of debit or credit cards among remittance recipients is generally low (Table 13).

The low penetration of payment cards raises two issues: first, there are obstacles to entering the market with an alternative transfer mechanism; second, in order to transform these customers into users of card-based instruments, the financial institution needs to implement a marketing programme that includes knowledge of preferences, product design, and commercialisation. None of the MFIs studied currently provided card-based transfers. Bancafe, a bank that offers microfinance in Guatemala, has been able to get 5 percent of its remittance recipients to use cards.

Table 13. Remittance recipients having debit and/or credit cards in selected Latin American and Caribbean countries

	No card yet	Debit, credit, or both
Colombia	51.1%	49.0%
Guyana	61.3%	38.7%
Dominican Republic	67.9%	32.1%
Ecuador	76.8%	23.2%
El Salvador	77.0%	23.0%
Nicaragua	83.4%	16.6%
Guatemala	86.1%	13.9%
Cuba	93.3%	6.7%
Eight countries above	70.8%	29.2%

Source: Orozco, Manuel 2005.

Preliminary Conclusions

Microfinance institutions are positioned as potentially important agents in leveraging remittances for local development. A look at the trends as observed in this preliminary survey of 27 institutions finds, first, that most MFIs have a moderately effective presence vis-a-vis major competitors. The positive aspect of this finding is that it suggests that at least some of the remittance customers of these institutions have greater access to a wider range of financial services than they might otherwise. But this may still be the exception rather than the rule.

A second major finding is that the majority of the most active MFIs surveyed that deal in remittances offered transfer charges that are below the market average. For recipients of remittances at costs below the market average, these MFIs provide can provide valuable incentives to increase the volume of remittances by decreasing the cost of transferring funds. With lower costs, marginally more money is available to senders or recipients, and the lower price may solidify or strengthen the emerging role of the MFI. The challenge for at least some of these MFIs is to reach scale.

Finally, only a third of the MFIs offered tailored financial services to their clients, suggesting that while MFIs can and do provide some of the development functions they seek to achieve, this role should not be assumed as a given. Much work needs to be done to help MFIs expand their financial service offerings.

Taken together, these results suggest that, in general, MFIs are moving forward in processing remittance transfers, often at a low cost, while experiencing difficulty in providing tailored financial products to recipients of remittances. Additional research is needed to understand better the challenges MFIs face in the remittance industry and in implementing emerging best practice. This research should include analyses of:

- the challenges institutions face in convincing remittance clients to use additional financial services;

- cost reduction strategies employed by MFIs charging less than traditional MTOs, and any trade-offs between cost reduction, scale, or other factors;

- financial concerns and preferences of remittance senders and receivers; and

- the legal and regulatory environment governing remittances in developing countries.

References

Cruz, Isabel. Remesas y microfinanzas rurales. EL FINANCIERO, 1o de febrero de 2005, p. 31

IAD (2004). All in the family: Latin America's Most Important International Financial Flow, Washington DC, January. Report of the Inter-American Dialogue Task Force on Remittances

Migrant Remittances Newsletter, Volume 2, Number 1, August 2005

Orozco, Manuel (2005). Transnational Engagement, Remittances and their Relationship to Development in Latin America and the Caribbean, Institute for the Study of International Migration, Georgetown University, Washington DC July 2005

Orozco, Manuel (2004). The Remittance Marketplace: Prices, Policy and Financial Institutions, Washington DC: Pew Hispanic Center, June

Orozco, Manuel (2004). Remittances to Latin America and the Caribbean: issues and perspectives on development, Report commissioned by the Office for the Summit Process, Organization of American States

Orozco, Manuel (2004). International Financial Flows and Worker Remittances: A best practices report, Report commissioned by the Population and Mortality division of the UN

Robinson, Scott (2004). Remittances, Microfinance and Community Informatics – Development and Governance Issues paper presented at the Remittances, Microfinance and Technology Conference: Leveraging Development Impact for Pacific States, FDC – Brisbane, 10 June 2004

Annex 1: Latin American Microfinance Institutions: Key Indicators and Data Sources

Organisation	Type*	Clients (000)	Average Transactions per branch per month	Branches	Rural Presence	Monthly Transfers	Annual Volume (000)	Accounts Opened by Remittance Recipients	Year of Inception of Remittance Services	Partner Company**
Acacciba	CU	NA	508	3	100%	2657	11,032	NA	1998	VG, VI
Acacu	CU	10	391	4	90%	2703	14,790	3000	1998	VG, VI
Acocomet	CU	2.2	437	2	80%	2383	10,489	800	1998	VG, VI
Acodjar	CU	4.9	422	3	95%	2125	9,816	NA	1998	VG, VI
AMC de RL	MFI	6	10	9	100%	88	38	NA	2004	MP
Bancéfe	CB	250	1500	50	50%	75000	270,000	NA	1998	MG
Banrural	CB	200	1267	150	70%	190000	684,000	NA	1998	WU, VG, others
BancoSol	TMFI	47	135	37	20%	5000	14,100	NA	2002	CX, QS
Banco Solidario	TMFI	100	45	110	60%	5000	50,000	4000	2000	EA
Caja Solidaria	CU	NA	20	1	100%	20	84	NA	2004	RG
Coosadeco	CU	66	367	13	70%	4780	22,944	529	2000	VG
Credemich	MFI	NA	50	1	85%	50	210	NA	NA	UG, MA
El Comercio	MFI	7	67	12	73%	800	2,400	80	2003	WU
FEDECACES	CU	90	412	29	60%	22000	80,000	4375	1998	VG, VI
Fedecrédito	CU	450	31	90	40%	2778	10,000	NA	1998	VI, CR
FENACOAC	CU	563	288	125	90%	35000	178,800	NA	2001	VG, MG
Fincoax	MFI	NA	6	7	.	40	168	NA	2003	DC
Fonkoze	TMFI	60	177	13	80%	2300	7,000	NA	1998	OS
Fundación Campo	MFI	3.8	1	86	100%	12	2	NA	2004	MP
Fundación José Napoleon Du-arte (MiCrédito)	MFI	3.5	33	6	100%	200	15	NA	2004	MP
Genesis Empresarial	MFI	40	NA	50	75%	NA	NA	NA	2004	MP
Guayacán	CU	51	543	10	70%	5426	26,045	533	2000	VG
Integral	LMFI	20	9	16	70%	150	100	NA	2004	MP
ODEF	MFI	12	2	21	80%	45	122	NA	2004	MP
Praxis Fina	MFI	NA	2	NA	30%	45	91	NA	2004	RI
ProCredit	TMFI	52	600	20	60%	12000	25,200	NA	2002	WU
Red de la Gente (BANSEFI)	MFI	3800	21	1200	50%	25000	99,000	2500	2002	MG, VG
Salcajá	CU	15	250	4	100%	1000	3,600	500	1998	VG
Xuu Nuu, Oaxaca	MFI	0.3	30	1	100%	30	1189	NA	2000	OS

* CB= Commercial Bank; CU= Credit union; MFI= Microfinance institution; TMFI= Transformed microfinance institution

** CR= Cor; CX= La Caixa; DC= Dinero a Casa; EA= Enlace Andino; MA= Mercha; MG= MoneyGram; MP= Mi Pueblo; OS= Own System: QS= Quisqueyana; RG= La Red de la Gente; RI= Remesas Instant; UG= Unigram; VG= Vigo; VI= Viamericas; WU= Western Union

CHAPTER 9:

Using Technology to Build Inclusive Financial Systems[*]

Gautam Ivatury

Microfinance Specialist, The Consultative Group to Assist the Poor (CGAP)

Providing financial services to poor people is costly, in part because they have small amounts of money, often live in sparsely populated areas, and rarely have documented credit histories. During the past few decades, specialised microfinance institutions[1] (MFIs) have begun to solve the latter problem by developing techniques that permit safe lending in the absence of borrowers' credit histories. Still, MFIs must charge relatively high interest rates to cover the administrative costs of handling small transactions.[2] MFIs with operating costs of 12–15 percent of assets are considered efficient, while the similar ratio for banks rarely exceeds 5 percent.[3]

Despite significant inroads in microfinance in recent years, such as through widespread wholesale lending to MFIs, most commercial banks still view microfinance as unprofitable.[4] Unlike MFIs, many commercial banks cannot compensate for high costs by charging high interest rates. Banks in many developing countries

---

[*] This article is based on an earlier version which was published as Focus Note No. 32. January 2006. More information is available on the CGAP Web site: www.cgap.org.

[1] The term "microfinance institution," as used here includes nongovernmental organisations (NGOs), cooperatives, banks, and licensed nonbank institutions that focus on delivering financial services to microentrepreneurs and other low-income clients, generally using new lending techniques that have been developed during the past 30 years.

[2] Ninety-six mature MFIs report a median ratio of financial revenue to average total assets of 27.4%, and a median ratio of operating expenses to average total assets of 15.3% (*MicroBanking Bulletin*, Issue 11).

[3] The median ratio of noninterest expense to total assets for the world's largest 492 banks (by assets) is 1.66% according to Bankscope.

[4] According to results of an informal poll of representatives from 25 financial institutions (mostly U.S. banks and credit unions) attending a session on banking the un- and underbanked, 60% of respondents cited the small margins and profitability as an obstacle to serving the underbanked. Forty percent cited risk and potential fraud as obstacles, and others, the lack of proven examples. Poll conducted by Center for Financial Services Innovation at BAI's Retail Delivery Conference and Expo, Las Vegas, November 2004. www.cfsi.org.

are legally required to limit interest rates on loans to low-income and rural borrowers, particularly when they use government funds. In India, most commercial banks cannot charge more than their prime lending rate (roughly 11%) for loans below Rs 200,000 (US$ 4,500). Public-sector banks are particularly sensitive to the political implications of charging poor borrowers relatively high interest rates.

Public agricultural, development, and savings banks do serve poor clients in many developing countries,[5] but their objectives are largely political or social rather than commercial. Private and public banks devote resources and attention to a smaller set of wealthier retail and corporate customers, while a majority of people remain without access to formal financial services.[6] Banks will not aggressively target the poor as a market until they find ways to serve these customers profitably. This will require delivery channels that are inexpensive to set up, a wider range of financial services for poor customers, and the ability to handle transactions at low cost.

Some of the innovations commercial banks need to serve poor clients may be found in information and communications technologies (ICTs). In developed countries, low-cost "direct banking" technology channels, such as Internet banking and automated teller machines (ATMs), process transactions at only one-fifth the cost of a branch teller. Banks in Brazil use point-of-sale (POS) terminals such as bankcard readers at retail and postal outlets to deliver bill payment, savings, credit, insurance, and money transfer products in nearly every municipality in the country. These terminals can be set up at a cost of less than 0.5 percent of the cost of setting up a typical bank branch.[7]

Can banking technologies, applied innovatively in developing countries, make microfinance profitable for formal financial institutions? Will they reduce costs to such an extent that banks could profitably serve even those whom MFIs have mostly excluded to date, such as very poor and remote rural customers? Will these customers be comfortable using technology? CGAP addressed these questions by surveying the use of technology to deliver financial services to poor people in developing countries:

- Are financial institutions using ICTs as a delivery channel for poor people? *Yes. In a CGAP study, 62 banks and MFIs report using ATMs, POS terminals,[8] and mobile phones to deliver services.*

---

[5] Christen, Rosenberg, and Jayadeva, "Financial Institutions with a 'Double Bottom Line': Implications for the Future of Microfinance," CGAP 2004.

[6] See Basu, "A Financial System for India's Poor," *Economic and Political Weekly*, September 10, 2005, for how banks in India have responded to the government's social banking mandate.

[7] Kumar, Parsons, and Urdapilleta, Expanding Bank Outreach Through Retail Partnerships: Correspondent Banking in Brazil, World Bank Discussion Paper 2006, World Bank.

[8] "POS terminals" refers to devices connected to a telephone or other telecommunications network and placed at retail outlets for payments and disbursements. The device may

- How are banks benefiting from using these technology channels?
  A handful of banks are reaching new customers by using ICTs to deliver services through retail outlets. But most banks simply attract their existing customers to technology channels to reduce costs.

- Will technology channels make microfinance profitable for banks?
  It is uncertain. Banks still have to build transaction volume and find ways to lend profitably in the informal sector using ATMs or POS channels.

- Are poor people gaining access to services through these technologies?
  Probably yes, at least in Brazil and South Africa, but the service quality is uncertain. We do not know if poorer and remote areas are benefiting.

- What lessons have emerged from early experiments with these technologies?
  Innovative channels are not possible without the right policies and adequate financial sector infrastructure in place. Managing cash security and liquidity in a wide network of terminals is the main operational hurdle.

Are Banks Using Technology to Deliver Financial Services to Poor People?

In a recent CGAP survey, 62 financial institutions in 32 countries reported using technology channels to handle transactions for poor people.[9] (These technologies, including ATMs, POS devices, and mobile phones, are described later in this chapter.) Nearly 75 percent of the respondents (46) were banks[10] that operate in large markets (e.g., India, Brazil, and South Africa) and in small markets (e.g., Malawi, Namibia, and Guatemala). (See tables 1 and 2.)

Table 1. Technology channels used by financial institutions (62 institutions responding)

Technology Channel	Number of Institutions
ATMs	46
POS	35
Internet Banking	26
Mobile Phone Banking	10

read debit or credit cards or barcodes, or the device itself may be a mobile phone that can accept information transmitted by another mobile phone through short messaging service or another protocol.

[9] See Annex I for a complete list of the financial institutions participating in this study.

[10] Most MFIs are not well suited to develop technology delivery channels. They lack the strong core information systems, the substantial financial and management resources, and the membership in electronic payment associations required for such initiatives.

Table 2. Services offered through technology channels (26 institutions responding)

Services Offered via Technology	Number of Institutions
Cash withdrawal	24
Bill payment	20
Money transfer	19
Deposit	15
Loan repayment	14
Balance inquiry	12
Account statement	10
Account opening	10
Loan disbursement	9
Insurance premium payment	8
Remittances	5
Benefit payments	5
Credit card advances	4
Checkbook request	2
Payroll payment	2
Cash back[11]	1

What Technologies Are Used?

Most poor people, particularly those working in the informal economy and in rural areas, earn and spend in cash. To handle a cash transaction where there is no bank branch, banks have at least two ICT options. They may use an ATM that can accept, store, and dispense cash, or they can use a POS device placed at an outlet where cash is kept on hand.

These technologies are becoming increasingly available in developing countries because of falling hardware costs and growing support infrastructure. At one time the erratic supply of telecommunications and electricity could not support ATMs or POS devices, particularly in rural areas. Now, however, telecommunications and electricity infrastructure is more widespread and reliable. From 1999 to 2004, the number of mobile phone subscribers in Africa grew from 7.5 million to 76.8

---

[11] Cash-back transactions take place when a customer makes a purchase from a retailer using a debit card and requests a limited amount of cash in addition to the cost of the item purchased. Cash back is different from a withdrawal because it takes place only during a purchase.

million, an average annual increase of 58 percent.[12] There are now more users than mobile phone owners: entrepreneurial subscribers in rural South Africa receive text messages and deliver them verbally to those who are illiterate.[13]

Technology has also made advances. In cooperation with hardware manufacturers, Visa International developed a battery-powered wireless POS device suitable for rural areas. The device costs US$ 125;[14] most POS devices in developed countries cost about US$ 700.

ATMs

Widespread use of ATMs in these developing country markets face additional challenges. For example, the fact that most survey respondents use ATMs suggests that they target customers in urban and semi-urban areas. These locations are more likely to have reliable electricity and "always-on" telecommunications connections that most ATMs require to connect to a bank's central server. In addition, because ATMs must regularly be manually refilled or emptied of cash, it is most cost effective to place them in densely populated areas. ICICI Bank in India is pilot testing a low-cost ATM that can withstand high temperatures and handle soiled and crumpled notes.

POS Devices

POS devices typically are used to handle payment transactions. The device can be a card reader, mobile phone, personal computer (PC), barcode scanner, or any hardware that can identify customers and receive instructions for the transfer of value. Where transaction volume is expected to be high, or where wireless Internet access is available, PCs may be used, although most POS devices are card-reading terminals.

Each POS device uses a telephone line, mobile phone connection, or the Internet to send instructions for transferring value from one account to another. For example, after swiping a card through the POS device, the merchant presses a button on the terminal authorising payment from the customer's line of credit (credit card) or funds available in the customer's current account (debit card). If the POS device is a mobile phone, the customer uses her mobile phone to send a text message authorising payment from her bank account or from her account with the mobile phone company to the merchant's phone.

A POS device is not a banking channel on its own. A human attendant must be available to count and store cash and to use the device to identify the customer,

---

[12] LaFraniere, "For Africa, a Godsend in Cellphones," *The New York Times*, August 25, 2005.

[13] Vodafone, "Africa: The Impact of Mobile Phones," Vodafone Policy Paper Series, No. 2, March 2005.

[14] Interview with Santanu Mukherjee, Visa International Country Director (South Asia), January 2005.

such as by having the customer swipe a debit card and input a personal identification number (PIN). The bank also relies on this person to answer customer queries, explain product features, and do other tasks. Supermarkets, drugstores, post offices, and other retail outlets are ideal locations for a POS device because they have cash on hand and staff to operate the device.[15] In return for "hosting" the POS device and offering banking services, the retail outlet expects to increase sales by attracting more customers and to earn a share of bank fees.

Table 3. Using POS devices for banking

Strategy	Business Operations	Services Offered	Examples
Retail Fee-based POS	• Issuing bankcards • Placing card readers with merchants	• Purchases • Cash back*	• Corporation Bank (India) • AgroInvest Bank (Tajikistan)
Deliver basic banking	• Issuing bankcards • Placing card readers with merchants	• Purchases • Balance inquiry • Withdrawals/ disbursals • Deposits/ repayments • Account opening* • Money transfers*	• CERUDEB (Uganda) • Lemon Bank (Brazil) • WIZZIT (South Africa) • Teba Bank (South Africa) • CARD (Philippines) • RBAP (Philippines) • Botswana Savings Bank • Fundacion Social (Colombia)
Expand market coverage	• Issuing bankcards • Placing card readers with merchants • Partnering with MFI "service agents" for loan appraisal and monitoring	• Purchases • Balance inquiry • Withdrawals/ disbursals • Deposits/ repayments • Account opening • Money transfers • Insurance products* • Loan appraisals	• Caixa Economica Federal (Brazil) • Banco Popular (Brazil) • Banco Postal (Brazil)

* not always available

[15] For simplicity, the term "retail outlet" is used to describe merchants, petrol stations, post offices, and other commercial operations in rural and low-income areas that can host a POS device and provide a staff person to help process the transaction.

What Financial Services Can a POS Channel Offer?

Mobile phones and other types of POS devices may be used to deliver a wide range of financial services when paired with a human attendant, for example, at a retail or postal outlet. Table 3 outlines three models banks can use to deliver these services.

In the first model, banks or payment processing companies lease POS devices to retail outlets (or "acquire merchants") to generate fees from processing electronic payments only, such as when a customer purchases groceries with a debit or credit card. This is how most banks around the world, and probably a majority of survey respondents, use POS devices. (Indeed, within most banks, the merchant acquiring unit and, in many cases, the division responsible for debit and credit cards has little interaction with the retail banking team.) The retail outlet usually pays the bank a percentage of the sale to process the payment. Some banks permit customers to make small withdrawals from the retail outlet's cash till along with their purchase (known as "cash back").

In the second model, banks offer a wider set of financial services through the POS device or mobile phone. Customers can use their bankcard and the POS device to deposit and withdraw cash and possibly to transfer money to other account holders. Faulu, an MFI in Kenya, recently began a pilot project, called M-Pesa, that allows customers to receive or repay loans through a mobile phone. In partnership with Safaricom, an affiliate of Vodafone, the MFI credits loans to the borrower's mobile M-Pesa bank account; the borrower can then exchange the credit for cash at a Safaricom dealer. Similarly, the client can repay a loan by giving cash to a dealer, who sends instructions to Faulu via a mobile phone text message to credit the customer's loan account. In this second model of delivering service through a POS channel, clients usually visit a branch to open an account or fill out applications available at the retail outlet. In some cases, a new account can be opened using the POS device itself. Customers of Banco Popular (a division of Banco do Brasil) in Brazil can open an account simply by keying their tax identification number and postal code into the terminal.

In the third model, banks use the POS channel to effectively replace a bank branch by providing nearly all the products and services, including loans, that a bank branch would provide. However, banks are still figuring out how, without the services of a loan officer, to deliver credit to borrowers who may not have a credit history.

How Are Banks Benefiting from These Technologies?

Most respondents to CGAP's survey use technology channels to automate basic transactions, reduce processing costs, and give customers added convenience. (See Table 4.) For example, of the seven respondents who answered questions about their use of POS devices, only two report offering services beyond payments and withdrawals through this technology channel.

Table 4. Reasons financial institutions use technology channels

Reason	% of respondents
Improve customer convenience	92
Lower processing costs	76
Reach areas having no branches	69
Generate more revenue	69
Collect more savings	69

A few banks are probably gaining more dramatic benefits by creating new channels with ICTs that allow them to gain new customers in areas where setting up a bank branch is too costly. Mobile phone operators, such as Vodafone's Safaricom in Kenya, MTN in South Africa, and Globe Telecom in the Philippines, are also beginning to offer banking services, usually in partnership with banks or MFIs. Operators are providing these services primarily to increase the volume of their text message traffic and to reduce customer turnover. In countries with underdeveloped payment systems, mobile phone payments may help leapfrog traditional, paper-based ways of making payments.

Improving Customer Convenience

Financial institutions such as Banco Ademi in the Dominican Republic and Pro-Credit Bank in Kosovo typically place ATMs in or near branches, where they can process routine deposit, withdrawal, and balance inquiry transactions at a far lower cost than the cost of using a teller, freeing staff to sell products or give customers personalised attention. ATMs also save customers from having to queue to get to a teller.[16]

Corporation Bank in India uses ATMs to serve urban and semi-urban customers who live far from a branch or who cannot visit banks during normal business hours because they are at work. The bank offers payroll deposit services to factories, allowing workers to withdraw cash from their accounts any time using an ATM at the factory. Most workers prefer this to carrying a lot of cash home on payday. Delivering banking services through retail and postal outlets equipped with POS devices offers similar client benefits. Many poor people are unfamiliar with bank branch procedures or feel uncomfortable dealing with tellers and other branch staff. In contrast, retail and postal outlets often enjoy substantial brand value and are trusted by community members; many retail and postal outlets have a long history of operating in the community. Instead of branch banking, customers may use POS devices located at a nearby post office or retail outlet that has longer hours than the bank branch. Uganda Microfinance Union trains merchants who host its

---

[16] See CGAP's IT Innovation Series at www.cgap.org/technology for more on ATMs.

POS devices to help poor, illiterate clients use the devices. Over time, customers learn to use the devices unassisted.[17]

Lowering Processing Costs

Bank branches are expensive because they require considerable investment in staffing, infrastructure, equipment, and security for storing and transporting cash and valuables. In the United States, the costs associated with opening a new bank branch are about $2 million, and costs can be as high as several hundred thousand dollars in developing countries.[18] The ATM channel is generally less expensive than the use of branch tellers because ATMs fully automate cash disbursements and collections, but cash still has to be transported to and from the machine. The use of POS devices is probably the least expensive of these channels, because the devices are placed at retail or other outlets that already maintain cash on hand.

In general, banks worldwide are trying to move customers toward low-cost technology delivery channels. From June 2000 to January 2002, ICICI Bank in India reduced the number of transactions at branches from 78 percent of all transactions to 35 percent. The remaining 65 percent were processed online, at ATMs, or over the phone.[19] In 2002, the cost of a transaction at ICICI Bank was estimated to be Rs 34 ($0.68) at a branch, Rs 28 ($0.56) through a call center (e.g., phone banking), and Rs 20 ($0.40) at an ATM. (See Figure 1.)

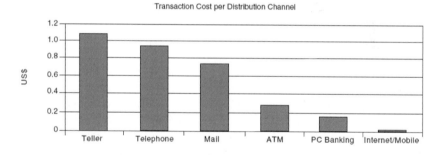

Fig. 1. Channel transaction costs for U.S. banks
Note: PC banking refers to a proprietary software programme that banks distribute to customers, through which they can connect to their accounts and conduct transactions. Internet/mobile banking refers to using the bank's Website, from any location, to do banking.

---

[17] Interview with Michael Kasibante, assistant director, Research and Development, Uganda Microfinance Union, July 2005.

[18] See *Bank Branch Growth Has Been Steady – Will It Continue?* Federal Deposit Insurance Corporation, August 2004.

[19] Singhal and Bikram, *Extending Banking to the Poor in India*, ICICI Bank, March 2002, p. 3.

Reaching Unserved Areas Through Technology Channels

Private and state-owned banks in Brazil pioneered the use of POS devices at retail outlets to deliver banking services to previously unbanked low-income and rural people. Since about 2000, two private-sector banks (Banco Bradesco and Lemon Bank) and two state-owned banks (Banco do Brasil and Caixa Economica Federal) have developed about 27,000 "banking correspondents." These correspondents are lottery outlets, post offices, supermarkets, grocery stores, petrol stations, and other retail outlets that are present in every municipality in the country, including very rural areas where bank branches would probably be too costly to set up. In small shops, the shopkeeper handles banking services for customers, and in larger stores, a store employee is designated for this purpose.

The banks equip each banking correspondent with a POS device, such as a card reader or PC. POS devices and mobile phones are less costly to install than ATMs, and running costs are limited to charges for telecommunications and transaction fees for the retail outlet. In addition, many POS devices can work without an always-on communication and electrical connection, making them ideal for rural locations.

At banking correspondents, customers can open current accounts and use a variety of services, including savings, credit, insurance, money transfers, pensions, government benefits, and bill payments. Since banking correspondents first emerged in Brazil in 2000, private and public banks have opened an estimated 8 million new current accounts through this channel. (See Box 1 for a brief look at Caixa Economica Federal's use of banking correspondents.)

Leapfrogging Traditional Banking Models

In countries where debit and credit cards, POS devices, ATMs, and even bank branches are virtually nonexistent, mobile phone networks may be a lower-cost way to expand access to financial services. Celpay, a mobile payments company that operates in Zambia and the Democratic Republic of Congo (DRC), issues special subscriber identity modules (SIM) cards through mobile phone companies. Customers can use SIM cards to make bill payments, store value, and transfer money. For DRC banks, which have only about 35,000[20] account holders (out of a population of 56 million),[21] tapping into the 1 million mobile phone subscribers[22] holds great potential. Because mobile phones work even in rural parts of DRC, they may be an ideal tool to quickly develop a national network for retail payments. Such an approach could leapfrog the check and card-based retail payment systems that are used in most countries.

---

[20] World Bank project appraisal document, 2003.

[21] United Nations estimate, 2005.

[22] International Telecommunications Union, 2003.

Box 1: Caixa Economica Federal: Brazil's Leading Operator of Correspondents

Caixa Economica, the state-owned bank that manages the country's lottery network and distributes government benefits, manages about 14,000 banking correspondents. It uses POS devices (a card reader, barcode scanner, and/or PC) with dialup or high-speed connectivity to process transactions at lottery houses and other retail outlets. Caixa has banking correspondents in all of the country's approximately 5,500 municipalities. The bank estimates that nearly 40 percent of its banking transactions are handled through this channel. It expects to operate 20,000 to 23,000 banking correspondents by 2007 and reach customers in virtually every district of the country, reducing the maximum distance between a customer and a correspondent to two to three kilometres. The most expensive POS devices cost R$ 7,000 (US$ 2,800), and connectivity charges are R$ 400 (US$ 160) per month. On the other hand, it costs up to R$ 1 million (US$ 400,000) to open a bank branch.

Through its correspondents, Caixa offers a full range of banking and payments services, including a simplified current account called Caixa Aqui. This account can be opened at any Caixa branch or correspondent using only an identification card, tax file number (CPF), and either a proof of residence or a declaration of current address. Caixa Aqui clients have access to Caixa's entire branch and correspondent network. Clients are allowed four withdrawals and four account statements per month; additional transactions are R$ 0.50 each. Deposits and balance inquiries are free. Between May 2003 and March 2005, Caixa opened about 2.8 million new Caixa Aqui accounts. Because monthly transaction volume (debits and credits) cannot exceed R$ 1,000 (US$ 400), account balances are relatively small.

Although Caixa has not released data on customer satisfaction, a study commissioned in 2003–04 found that banking correspondents are very pleased with the opportunity to offer banking services for Caixa. According to the study, business owners working as correspondents reported a 96 percent satisfaction rate. More than 88 percent of correspondents reported an increase in sales of 20 percent on average and an average increase in spending per client of about 16 percent.

Sources: Interview with Flavio Antonio Camargo Barros, National Channel Strategy Manager, and Luiz Felipe Pinheiro Junior, Special Advisor of Caixa Economica Federal.

Will Technology Make Microfinance Profitable for Banks?

It is too early to know whether technology channels will be profitable enough to encourage banks to target low-income customers. No thorough profitability analysis of replacing bank branches with mobile phones or POS devices at retail outlets is available. Although using ATMs or POS withdrawals to move transactions outside the branch for existing customers reduces costs, this approach probably does not help banks acquire customers who live far from bank branches.

In general terms, a technology channel that replaces a bank branch will be profitable only if it serves a critical mass of customers at each outlet and delivers a wide range of services to those customers. Building strong relationships with clients through the channel will help build customers' confidence in the bank, make it less likely for customers to switch to another provider, and encourage customers to purchase a wider range of financial services.[23]

Will staff of a retail outlet or a postal clerk be able to build this relationship on behalf of the bank or sell a wide range of banking services to customers? Recent information from Brazil suggests that this may be difficult. Thirty percent of the accounts opened at banking correspondents of Banco Popular do Brasil (a division of Banco do Brasil) never become active. After opening for business in June 2004 and attracting 1.05 million customers after six months, the division now maintains only about 771,000 active accounts and is closing unprofitable banking correspondents.[24]

Recognising the difficulties of cross-selling outside the branch, a handful of banks in developed countries have begun luring customers back into branches with coffee bars and children's play areas. This increases the cost of processing basic transactions, but improves the bank's ability to generate greater revenue from each client through contact with sales staff.

Challenges to Lending

The profitability of technology channels hinges on banks' ability to make loans to customers who use these channels exclusively. Traditionally, banks use credit reference checks through credit bureaus or information such as proof of income to assess the risk of making unsecured personal loans. But banks cannot rely on this approach for customers in previously unbanked areas who may have been outside the formal banking system. These customers are unlikely to have a credit history on record at a credit bureau, and poor customers who are self-employed or work in the informal sector are unlikely to have proof of income.

---

[23] von Pischke, *Finance at the Frontier*, World Bank, 1991.

[24] "Brazil: Banco Popular do Brasil hit by high levels of debt default and high cost," *ValorEconomica*, November 11, 2005.

How will banks handle loan appraisals for customers without established credit histories, or for those who have repaid loans fully in the past but are not listed by bureaus that record only negative information? Banks in Brazil are taking two approaches.

First, to make unsecured personal loans, banks are adjusting their in-house credit scoring models to evaluate demographic information, account activity, and bill payment history available for new customers. Demographic information is captured when the account is opened, and behavioural information such as account activity and bill payments is captured on an on-going basis. Emerging scoring methods may be able to assess individual repayment capability based on these data, but it is unclear whether this approach can work for micro-enterprise loans that may be larger than personal loans.

Banco Popular is also attempting to partner with specialised microfinance lenders to originate, appraise, and monitor loans to microentrepreneurs. During the past 30 years, MFIs have developed specialised techniques to identify potential customers in the informal sector, appraise small unsecured loans, and monitor the use and repayment of these loans.

A third approach attempted by Banco Popular is innovative but costly. Each new accountholder is automatically eligible for a R$ 50 (US$ 15) loan from the bank. If the customer repays this loan according to the terms, he or she is recorded as a good borrower and may be eligible for a larger loan, up to R$ 600 (or US$ 240). Defaulters are recorded as poor borrowers and may be reported to the national credit bureau. Although this approach gives the bank an individual credit history it can use for further lending, defaults have been high. In August 2005, provisions for debt reached nearly R$ 19 million (US$ 7.6 million), or about 29 percent of the total credit volume of R$ 65 million (US$ 26 million), up from 24 percent in July.

Low-cost delivery is not the only factor involved in whether banks can make money using technology channels to serve low-income areas. Banks must figure out how to maximise the number of services they can sell to these customers, what to charge for those services, and how to keep customers active over the long term.

Are Poor People Gaining Access to Financial Services Through Technology?

With technology channels such as POS devices and mobile phones banks in South Africa and Brazil are rapidly opening basic accounts for customers who previously were outside the formal financial system. Although many of these new account holders are likely to be poor, we do not know this for sure. We also do not know the characteristics of low-income people who have chosen not to use these delivery channels.

In October 2004, with government encouragement, the four largest South African banks and the postal bank began offering a low-cost transaction account intended for low-income customers. A May 2005 study of this Mzansi "national bank account" found that over 90 percent of new accountholders were previously unknown to the bank at which they opened their account. Given the thin branch coverage in the provinces where most customers opened accounts, it is likely that many of these new customers had not previously maintained accounts at any bank.[25] Absa Bank claims to have opened roughly 3.4 million new bank accounts (including Mzansi accounts) for people who were previously unbanked, operating through portable bank branches that are set up and run on generators, mobile bank branches, and cellular network phone booths.[26] (See Box 2 for a discussion of mobile banking in South Africa.)

Information from Brazil's banking correspondents which use POS devices at retail outlets also indicates early success at reaching rural and remote areas that had no banking infrastructure. In 2000, 1,628 municipalities in Brazil did not have bank branches or banking correspondents. However, by the end of 2003, banking services were available in all of Brazil's more than 5,600 municipalities, largely because of the increase in correspondents. In the country's poorest region, the Northeast, many municipalities are served *only* by banking correspondents. In the states of Rio Grande do Norte and Piauí, these municipalities comprise 72 and 71 percent of all municipalities, respectively. The Northeast has the second largest number of banking correspondents in Brazil (by region) and has the lowest regional gross domestic product per capita (R$ 3,010 or about US$ 1,204).[27]

In addition, a large portion of banking correspondent customers appear to be poor. Forty-eight percent of correspondent clients of Caixa Economica earn less than R$ 200 (or US$ 75) per month, less than the country's minimum wage. Similarly, 58 percent of Banco Bradesco's clients earn less than this amount per month.[28]

Still, one should not conclude that poor people will use formal financial services just because a technology channel is available. Witness the high proportion of inactive accounts opened at Banco Popular described earlier. More research should be done to understand why some poor people do not use these technology delivery channels. Is it because they are not comfortable using technology, do not trust the operator, are illiterate, or do not feel the financial products offered are suitable for them? Once these questions are answered, banks will be in a better position to tailor their channels and products to serve different types of poor people.

---

[25] The Banking Association of South Africa, www.banking.org.zs/documents/2005/MAY/ PresReleaseonemillionaccount.pdf.

[26] "Reaching the unbanked: Learning from South Africa's FIs," *ATM Marketplace News*, April 25, 2005.

[27] Kumar, Parsons, and Urdapilleta, Banking Correspondents and Financial Access: The Experience of Brazil and Potential for Other Countries, World Bank, 2006.

[28] Ibid.

Box 2: Mobile Banking in South Africa

In South Africa an estimated 16 million people, or 48 percent of the adult population, are unbanked or underbanked and lack access to formal financial services. There are also 20 million mobile phone subscribers, nearly 80 percent of whom are prepaid customers. Many of these subscribers have low-incomes. Mobile phone operators and banks are aggressively seeking ways to deliver financial services using the rapidly growing mobile phone network.

WIZZIT, a startup mobile banking provider, targets low-income customers with an interest-bearing bank account that customers access with their mobile phone. Customers can use their phones to make person-to-person payments, transfer money, and buy airtime for a prepaid mobile phone subscription. WIZZIT also gives customers a "Maestro" branded debit card with which they can make purchases at retail outlets and deposit or withdraw money at ATMs. WIZZIT is organised as a division of the South African Bank of Athens.

Competing with WIZZIT are the mobile banking initiatives of Standard Bank and First National Bank (FNB). Standard Bank has entered into a joint venture with MTN, a leading mobile operator in South Africa, to offer a service called MTN Banking. For Standard Bank the joint venture is a separately branded channel targeting low-income customers who use mobile phones but may not have access to, or comfort in, using a bank branch. MTN Banking uses MTN's dealers to distribute the special mobile phone SIM cards that are required to operate the mobile banking service. Customers who open accounts with MTN Banking in effect have a bank account at Standard Bank and are limited in the total monthly transaction volume and account balance they can maintain in the account. FNB offers mobile banking simply as an alternative channel for its existing customers, much as it offers customers the use of ATMs.

Each organisation is optimistic about using mobile phones to increase penetration of financial services among the unbanked, but creating a profitable business will be challenging. Because transaction fees are currently the main revenue stream, providers are seeking high volumes by looking to markets elsewhere in southern Africa, as well as trying to capture popular person-to-person transfers of airtime and money. At the same time, mobile banking providers must find ways to move customers from basic payment and transfer transactions to higher-value products, such as credit and savings. To achieve this, they need to build a network of service points, where customers can deposit and withdraw cash, and develop a methodology for assessing credit risk.

Sources: Interviews with Brian Richardson, CEO, WIZZIT; Jenny Hoffmann, CEO, MTN Banking; and Len Pienaar, CEO, FNB Mobile and Transit Solutions.

What Lessons Emerge from Early Experiments with Technology Channels?

The most powerful lesson learned from these initiatives is that government encouragement and supportive policy are important determinants of success. In addition, certain aspects of the financial sector infrastructure can improve the chances that banks will be able to use technology profitably to reach unserved areas. Finally, key operational challenges remain to be solved.

Supportive Regulation

Governments have considerable power in creating an environment that enables financial institutions to use technology delivery channels.[29] The precondition for this type of channel is a broad regulatory environment that supports the use of electronic payments. Financial contracts should be enforceable, telecommunications policy should foster widespread access, and privacy and data security must be ensured.[30] In addition, rules in three areas can thwart or promote the extension of electronic payments:

Rules Governing Electronic Payments

In some countries, regulations that govern electronic payment systems constrict the use of technology to deliver a wide set of services. In India, for example, POS machines are not permitted to deliver cash-back services (a form of cash withdrawal), and only security guards, and not bank employees, are permitted to manage ATMs.[31] The latter makes it difficult for banks to use ATMs to serve poor customers, because these customers need help from attendants to operate the machine. To overcome the obstacle, some banks train security officers to assist customers.

---

[29] See Porteous, *Making Financial Markets Work for the Poor*, for a thorough discussion of the ways in which policymakers can expand access to financial services – directly and indirectly.

[30] Claessens, Glaessner, and Klingebiel, Electronic Finance in Emerging Markets: Is Leapfrogging Possible? World Bank, 2002.

[31] Singhal and Duggal, *Extending Banking to the Poor in India*, ICICI Bank, March 2002, p. 9.

Rules Determining Account Opening Requirements[32]

To help banks attract low-income customers, regulators in South Africa and Brazil relaxed the identification requirements to open bank accounts with limited maximum balances. In South Africa, regulators waived provisions of the Financial Intelligence Centre Act, which requires proof of identification and addresses for all account holders. Customers opening a new Mzansi account require identification only. Brazil's banks can open basic transaction accounts for poor people with no proof of address or income.

Regulation Governing Agency Relationships

Banks that deliver financial services through retail outlets must have agents who are allowed to conduct a wide range of services for customers using POS devices or other technology, while mitigating risks of fraud, theft, and money laundering.[33] Brazil's legislation governing the use of banking correspondents has evolved since the early 1970s, and today banking correspondents can perform many of the same functions as tellers at bank branches.[34] In contrast, the Reserve Bank of India permits only bank employees or ATMs to handle savings deposit and withdrawal transactions.

Governments can also create a conducive environment for technology delivery channels by instituting national identification systems. When each citizen has a government-issued identification, it is relatively easy for banks to open savings accounts for customers, identify individual borrowers, and build a payment history based on transactions with a variety of payors and lenders. Opportunity Bank in Malawi accepts fingerprint biometrics stored on a smart card in lieu of the driver's license or passport that must be presented when opening a bank account. For the poor or illiterate, these documents are difficult and often costly to obtain.[35] National identification also lays the foundation for a credit bureau, which reduces banks' costs of appraising borrowers and increases incentives to repay.

---

[32] For more information on account-opening requirements as they pertain to international efforts on anti-money laundering (AML) and combating the financing of terrorism (CFT), see CGAP's Focus Note No. 29, "AML/CFT Regulation: Implications for Financial Service Providers That Serve Low-Income People," available at www.cgap.org.

[33] In-depth research on the various policy and supervisory approaches to the use of agents remains to be done.

[34] Kumar, Parsons, and Urdapilleta, Banking Correspondents and Financial Access: The Experience of Brazil and Potential for Other Countries, World Bank, 2006.

[35] Interview with Larry Reed, CEO, Opportunity International Network, August 2005.

Ensuring Widespread Usage by Poor People[36]

As banks have begun to create new technology delivery channels that serve low-income people, they have begun to realise that understanding this new client segment is essential for success. As one central banker explained, „[T]he foundation for creating such delivery channels is superior insights into customer behaviour. These can come in many forms, but at their most basic they entail understanding customer needs for the delivery of different products, how these needs vary by customer types […], current customer behaviour […], and customer profitability."[37]

The following issues are particularly important:[38]

- *Perceived value addition.* How do clients perceive the incremental value of using a technology-enabled network rather than a teller or other alternatives? Some clients in the Philippines prefer to travel to the bank or MFI branch and stand in line rather than pay a nominal fee to make a loan repayment through a mobile phone.[39]

- *Consumer education.* Experiments in which debit cards are offered to the employed poor in India have shown that, unless clients are specifically told not to reveal their PINs to others, they often will write these numbers on the debit card itself, rendering account security useless.

- *Usability.* Depending on the type of clients targeted, the technology device, customer interface, and usage process should be designed to make the system easy to use. To reach indigenous and illiterate customers, Prodem in Bolivia designed ATMs with colour-coded touch screens and audio instructions available in Spanish, Quechua, and Aymara.[40]

- *Cultural fit.* Cultural issues of gender, caste or class, technology, money, privacy, and so on must be addressed for the system to be successful. Vision S.A., an MFI in Paraguay, views the upbeat style of its Visa-branded debit cards as a key factor in its rapid uptake among poor customers.[41]

- *Trust.* MFI field staff who use hand-held computers to record transactions have found that customers learn to trust the system by gradually recognising the beeps the device makes when it is used correctly and when it prints a receipt.

---

[36] For information on the adoption of electronic banking technologies by consumers in developed countries, see Kolodinsky and Hogarth, "The adoption of electronic banking technologies by American consumers," *Consumer Interests Annual*, vol. 47, 2001.

[37] Address by Shri Vepa Kamesam, deputy governor of the Reserve Bank of India, at the Twenty-Fifth Bank Economists' Conference, Mumbai, 12 December 2003.

[38] Ivatury, "Harnessing the Power of Technology to Deliver Financial Services to the Poor," *Small Enterprise Development*, December 2004.

[39] Interview with Edwin Soriano, researcher, June 2005.

[40] CGAP's IT Innovation Series article on ATMs (www.cgap.org/technology).

[41] Interview with Beltran Macchi, CEO, Vision S.A., August 2004.

Mitigating the Risk of Fraud or Theft

Using third parties to handle cash on behalf of a bank creates risk of fraud and theft. In India, ICICI Bank appoints individual agents or franchisees to collect loan repayments. So that agents do not steal this money, the bank requires each agent to maintain a balance in an ICICI Bank account that the bank can tap. The agent is not permitted to collect more cash in a day than the balance in the account.

Banco Popular in Brazil uses intermediaries such as Netcash, a private banking correspondent management company, to identify and contract banking correspondents, to equip and train them, and to monitor their activities. The intermediaries are liable for all the cash correspondents handle on behalf of the bank. Using intermediaries also keeps overhead low: after six months of operations, Banco Popular had only about 80 employees, all in Brasilia, although it had acquired more than 1.05 million clients through 5,500 POS devices at retail outlets across Brazil.

Banco Bradesco, Brazil's largest private bank, gives incentives to its branch managers to help supervise its 7,900 banking correspondents in 4,732 of Brazil's roughly 5,500 municipalities.[42] The bank consolidates the financial results for each correspondent into the balance sheet of the nearest branch, explicitly making the performance of correspondents the responsibility of branch managers.

Ensuring Adequate Liquidity at the Retail Outlet[43]

Because Banco Postal works through post offices in remote parts of Brazil, including some reachable only by boat or airplane, it must serve communities where it is difficult and costly to transport cash. One solution has been to work with local businesses and government to ensure that their cash is deposited by the end of each month. This strategy allows them to provide cash withdrawals to pension and government welfare recipients at the beginning of each month. Banco Postal also uses simple strategies to manage intra-day cashflows. On the days pensions are paid, long lines begin forming at the banking counter at 7 a.m. To reduce these lines, post office employees offer free coffee to customers who arrive after 10 a.m. and give small gifts to those who withdraw money after lunch, rather than in the morning.[44]

Strategic Implications for Microfinance

The profitability of technology delivery channels, and the extent to which they can serve a wide range of poor people, is not yet known. Still, banks and microfinance practitioners have much to learn from the early experience of Brazil's private- and

---

[42] This banking correspondent operation has a separate brand called Banco Postal.

[43] For more information on the challenges of using agents to process cash transactions, see Ivatury, "Cash-In/Cash-Out: The Number One Problem," at www.cgap.org/technology.

[44] Interview with Andre Cano, director of Banco Postal, May 2005.

public-sector banks in reaching remote areas and from mobile banking initiatives underway in South Africa and the Philippines.

Three aspects of the use of technology for microfinance deserve more attention.

If governments want to harness technology to increase access to financial services for poor people, they must think more broadly about policy.

Many MFI advocates see a lack of specific microfinance legislation as the main regulatory obstacle to giving poor people greater access to financial services. In fact, a wide range of regulatory frameworks determine whether formal financial institutions, and even mobile phone operators, will develop innovative ways of delivering financial services to poor and excluded people.

Further study is needed to understand the extent to which poor people are excluded by technology delivery channels and the effect this has on channel profitability.

By making it technologically possible to distribute pieces of the financial services delivery chain among a number of actors – banks, retail outlets, payments companies such as Visa International or perhaps Vodafone, and MFIs – the ultimate point of contact for poor customers may be a grocery store or post office clerk and a POS device. How comfortable, convenient, and trustworthy poor customers find technology service channels will determine whether some customer segments will continue to be excluded from using formal financial services and whether a channel will be profitable for the bank.

Technology channels raise questions about the role of MFIs in providing financial services to poor people.

Today, MFIs' core strength is the ability to identify creditworthy low-income borrowers, appraise loans, and manage delinquencies. MFIs are also able to conduct market research, educate and train customers, and provide specialised customer support. However, as banks try to make technology delivery channels profitable, they will attempt to develop credit scoring and other techniques to replace MFI risk appraisal methods. As this evolution takes place in at least a handful of markets, MFIs will have to clarify their role in delivering financial services to poor people.

Annex 1. Financial Institutions That Use E-Payments to Serve the Poor

Region	Country	Financial Institution	Type	Technology	Description
AFR	Botswana	Botswana Savings Bank	Bank	ATM	Deposits, withdrawals, bill payments, money transfer, account opening, government contributions
AFR	Cameroon	Afrilandfirstbank	Bank	Internet	Deposits, withdrawals, bill payments, money transfers
AFR	Kenya	Faulu Kenya (Safaricom)	NBFI	Cell phone	Deposits, withdrawals, bill payments, money transfers, loan disbursement, account opening
AFR	Kenya	Kenya Cooperative Bank	Co-op	POS, ATM	Deposits
AFR	Kenya	K-Rep Bank	Bank	ATM	N/A
AFR	Malawi	Opportunity International Bank	Bank	ATM, POS	Deposits, withdrawals, bill payments, money transfers, loan disbursement, loan repayment, collecting insurance premiums
AFR	Malawi	First Merchant Bank/ FINCA	Bank/MFI	ATM	Deposits
AFR	Malawi	New Building Society	Building Society	ATM	Smartcards and biometrics for deposits, payments, credit management, and utility settlements
AFR	Namibia	Bank Windhoek	Bank	ATM, Internet	Mobile banking units in remote areas, international e-transfers
AFR	Senegal	ACEP PAMECAS PAME-AGETIP	Co-op Co-op Co-op	ATM, POS	Deposits, withdrawals, bill payments, money transfers
AFR	South Africa	Teba Bank	Bank	POS, ATM, Internet, Cell phone	Deposits, withdrawals, bill payments, money transfers, account opening, government grant distribution
AFR	South Africa	WIZZIT	Bank	POS, ATM, Internet, Cell phone	Bill payments, account opening, cash back
AFR	South Africa	SAPO	NBFI	POS, ATM	Biometric registration, deposits, withdrawals, bill payments, money transfers, account opening, collecting insurance premiums
AFR	South Africa	Standard Bank	Bank	POS, ATM	Withdrawals, money transfers, loan repayment, account opening
AFR	South Africa	ABSA	Bank	ATM	ATMS for pensions
AFR	South Africa	First National Bank	Bank	POS, ATM	Withdrawals, payments, biometrics
AFR	South Africa	Standard Bank	Bank	POS, ATM	Withdrawals, money transfers, loan repayment, account opening
AFR	South Africa	Peoples Bank Limited Sub: PEP Bank Part of Nedcor Banking Group	Bank	ATM	Savings, loans, and funeral insurance
AFR	Tanzania	Tanzania Postal Bank	Bank	ATM	Withdrawals, bill payments
AFR	Tanzania	CRDB	Bank	POS	Deposits, withdrawals, bill payments, money transfers, loan repayment

Region	Country	Financial Institution	Type	Technology	Description
AFR	Uganda	Uganda Microfinance Union	NBFI	POS	Deposits, money transfers, loan repayment
AFR	Uganda	FINCA Uganda	NBFI	POS	Withdrawals, loan disbursement, loan repayment
AFR	Uganda	Centenary Bank	Bank	POS, ATM, Internet, Cell phone	Deposits, withdrawals, bill payments, money transfers, loan repayment
AFR	Zimbabwe	Jewel Bank	Bank	POS, ATM	Withdrawals
AFR	Zimbabwe	Central Africa Building	Building Society	POS, ATM, Cell phone	Deposits/withdrawals
EAP	Indonesia	The International Visitor Programme, Bank Rakyat Indonesia	Bank	POS	Withdrawals, bill payments, money transfers
EAP	Malaysia	Agricultural Bank of Malaysia Bank Pertanian	Bank	ATM	N/A
EAP	Philippines	Rural Banks Association of the Philipines	Bank	Cell phone	Payments
ECA	Albania	Tirana Bank	Bank	POS, ATM	N/A
ECA	Czech Republic	Czech Savings Bank	Bank	ATM	Loan management
ECA	Kosovo	Procredit Bank (previously MEB Bank)	Bank	ATM	N/A
ECA	Moldova	Victoria Bank	Bank	POS, ATM, Internet, Cell phone	Withdrawals, bill payments, money transfers
ECA	Poland	National Association of Cooperative Savings and Credit Unions, Poland	NBFI	ATM, Internet	N/A
ECA	Tajikistan	AgroInvest Bank	Bank	POS, ATM	Withdrawals, bill payments
LAC	Bolivia	FFP Prodem S.A.	NBFI	POS, ATM, Internet	Withdrawals, money transfers, loan disbursements
LAC	Brazil	Unibanco	Bank	POS, ATM, Internet, Cell phone	Withdrawals, deposits, bill payments, money transfers, loan disbursements, account opening, remittances, collecting insurance premiums
LAC	Brazil	Banco do Brasil (Banco Popular)	Bank	POS, ATM, Internet	Online national and international transfers, bill and insurance payments, withdrawals, deposits, loan disbursements, account opening, remittances
LAC	Brazil	Caixa Economica Federal	Bank	POS, ATM, Internet	Government contribution, bill payment, deposit/withdrawals, money transfers, loan disbursements, account opening, remittances, insurance payments
LAC	Brazil	Lemon Bank	Bank	POS, ATM, Internet	Deposits, withdrawals, bill payments, money transfers, loan disbursements, account opening, remittances, insurance payments
LAC	Brazil	Banco Postal (Banco Bradesco)	Bank	POS, ATM, Internet	Savings, loans, transfers, checking, credit cards, withdrawals, deposits, bill payments, loan disbursements, account opening, remittances, insurance payments
LAC	Chile	Banco Estado	Bank	ATM, Internet	Deposits, withdrawals, money transfers, bill payments, loan repayment, IVR
LAC	Chile	Bandesarrollo	Bank	POS, ATM, Internet, Cell phone	Deposits, withdrawals, money transfers, bill payments, loan repayment, account opening
LAC	Chile	Banefe Banco Santander	Bank	Internet	N/A

Region	Country	Financial Institution	Type	Technology	Description
LAC	Colombia	Fundacion Social	NBFI	Cell phone	Deposits, withdrawals, money transfers, bill payments, loan repayment, account opening, collecting insurance premiums
LAC	Cuba	Banco Popular de Ahorro	Bank	POS, ATM	Deposits, bill payments, money transfers, loan repayment
LAC	Dominican Republic	Grupo BHD	Bank	POS	Remittance delivery
LAC	Ecuador	Banco Solidario	Bank	ATM	Remittance delivery
LAC	Guatemala	Banrural	Bank	POS, ATM, Internet	Withdrawals, deposits, bill payments, money transfers, loan disbursements, account opening, remittances, collecting insurance premiums
LAC	Guatemala	Bancafe	Bank	POS, ATM, Internet	Withdrawals, bill payments, money transfers
LAC	Haiti	Sogebank Subsidiary: Sogesol	Bank	ATM	N/A
LAC	Mexico	Banamex	Bank	Internet	Payroll consumer lending
LAC	Paraguay	El Comercio	MFI	POS, ATM, Internet	Consumer credit, savings, credit cards, and credit cooperatives
LAC	Paraguay	Vision	MFI	POS, ATM	Deposits, withdrawals, payments
LAC	Peru	Banco de Trabajo	Bank	ATM	N/A
LAC	Peru	Mibanco	Bank	ATM	N/A
SA	Bangladesh	Janata Bank	Bank	ATM, Internet	Withdrawals
SA	India	BASIX	NBFI	Internet	Loan disbursement
SA	India	Canara Bank	Bank	POS, ATM	Deposits/withdrawals
SA	India	Corporation Bank	Bank	POS, ATM	Deposits/withdrawals
SA	India	ICICI Bank	Bank	Internet	Remittance delivery, collecting insurance premiums
SA	Sri Lanka	National Savings Bank	Bank	ATM	N/A

Annex 2. Financial Institutions That Participated in CGAP's E-Payments Survey

Region	Country	Institution	Technology
AFR	Cameroon	Afrilandfirstbank	Internet
AFR	Kenya	Vodafone (Faulu Kenya)	Cell phone
AFR	Malawi	Opportunity International Bank	ATM, POS
AFR	South Africa	Teba Bank	POS, ATM, Internet, Cell phone
AFR	South Africa	WIZZIT	POS, ATM, Internet, Cell phone
AFR	South Africa	SAPO	POS, ATM
AFR	South Africa	Standard Bank	POS, ATM
AFR	South Africa	Standard Bank	POS, ATM
AFR	Tanzania	Tanzania Postal Bank	ATM
AFR	Tanzania	CRDB	POS
AFR	Uganda	Uganda Microfinance Union	POS
AFR	Uganda	FINCA Uganda	POS
AFR	Uganda	Centenary Bank	POS, ATM, Internet, Cell phone
AFR	Zimbabwe	Jewel Bank	POS, ATM
ECA	Tajikistan	AgroInvest Bank	POS, ATM
LAC	Bolivia	FFP Prodem S.A.	POS, ATM, Internet
LAC	Brazil	Unibanco	POS, ATM, Internet, Cell phone
LAC	Chile	BancoEstado	ATM, Internet
LAC	Chile	Bandesarrollo	POS, ATM, Internet, Cell phone
LAC	Colombia	Fundacion Social	Cell phone
LAC	Cuba	Banco Popular de Ahorro	POS, ATM
LAC	Guatemala	Banrural	POS, ATM, Internet
LAC	Guatemala	Bancafe	POS, ATM, Internet
LAC	Paraguay	El Comercio	POS, ATM, Internet
SA	Bangladesh	Janata Bank	ATM, INTERNET
EAP	Indonesia	The International Visitor Program, Bank Rakyat Indonesia (BRI)	POS

Bibliography

"Brazil: Banco Popular do Brasil Hit by High Levels of Debt Default and High Cost." *Valor Economica*, November 11, 2005.

"Reaching the Unbanked: Learning from South Africa's FIs," *ATM Marketplace News*, April 25, 2005.

Banking Association of South Africa.

www.banking.org.za/documents/2005/MAY/PresReleaseonemillionaccount.pdf.

Basu, Priya. "A Financial System for India's Poor." *Economic and Political Weekly*. September 10, 2005.

Cano, Andre, director of Banco Postal, interview in May 2005.

Center for Financial Services Innovation. Poll conducted at BAI's Retail Delivery Conference and Expo, Las Vegas, November 2004. www.cfsi.org.

CGAP IT Innovation Series article on ATMs. www.cgap.org/technology.

Christen, Robert P., Richard Rosenberg, and Veena Jayadeva. "Financial Institutions with a 'Double BottomLine': Implications for the Future of Microfinance." CGAP Occasional Paper No. 8. Washington, D.C.: CGAP, 2004.

Claessens, Stijn, Thomas Glaessner, and Daniela Klingebiel. *Electronic Finance in Emerging Markets: Is Leapfrogging Possible?* Washington, D.C.: World Bank, 2002.

Cracknell, David. *Electronic Banking for the Poor: Panacea, Potential and Pitfalls*. MicroSave, September 2004.

Federal Deposit Insurance Corporation (FDIC). *Bank Branch Growth Has Been Steady—Will It Continue?* FDIC, August 2004.

Hoffmann, Jenny, CEO MTN Banking, interview.

Isern, Jennifer, David Porteous, Raul Hernandez-Cross, and Chinyere Egwuagu. "AML/CFT Regulation: Implications for Financial Service Providers That Serve Low-Income People." CGAP Focus Note No. 29. Washington, D.C.: CGAP. www.cgap.org.

Ivatury, G. "Harnessing the Power of Technology to Deliver Financial Services to the Poor." *Small Enterprise Development*, December 2004.

"Cash-In/Cash-Out: The Number One Problem." www.cgap.org/technology.

Kamesam, Shri Vepa. Address by the deputy governor of the Reserve Bank of India at the Twenty-Fifth Bank Economists' Conference, Mumbai, December 12, 2003.

Kasibante, Michael, assistant director, Research and Development, Uganda Microfinance Union, interview in July 2005.

Kolodinsky, Jane, and Jeanne M. Hogarth. "The Adoption of Electronic Banking Technologies by American Consumers." *Consumer Interests Annual*, vol. 47, 2001.

Kumar, Anjali, Adam Parsons, and Eduardo Urdapilleta. *Banking Correspondents and Financial Access: The Experience of Brazil and Potential for Other Countries*. Washington, D.C.: World Bank, 2006.

LaFraniere, Sharon. "For Africa, a Godsend in Cellphones." *The New York Times*, August 25, 2005.

Macchi, Beltran, chief executive officer of Vision S.A., interview in August 2004.

The MIX. *MicroBanking Bulletin,* Issue 11. Washington, D.C.: The MIX, 2004.

Mukherjee, Santanu, VISA International country director (South Asia), interview in January 2005.

Pienaar, Len, CEO, FNB Mobile and Transit Solutions, interview.

Porteous, David. *Making Financial Markets Work for the Poor*. FinMark Trust, 2004.

Reed, Larry, CEO, Opportunity International Network, interview in August 2005.

Richardson, Brian, CEO, WIZZIT, interview.

Singhal, Amit, and Bikram Duggal. *Extending Banking to the Poor in India*. ICICI Bank, March 2002.

Soriano, Edwin, researcher, interview in June 2005.

Vodafone. "Africa: The Impact of Mobile Phones." Vodafone Policy Paper Series. No. 2, March 2005.

von Pischke, J. D. *Finance at the Frontier*. Washington, D.C.: World Bank, 1991.

World Bank. Project appraisal document. Washington, D.C.: World Bank, 2003.

CHAPTER 10:

Information Technology Innovations That Extend Rural Microfinance Outreach

Laura I. Frederick

President, echange, LLC

Introduction

Creating a breakthrough in delivering microfinance services to marginalised rural populations is one of the greatest challenges facing the microfinance industry. Best estimates indicate that 5,000 microfinance institutions worldwide—and thousands more counting credit unions and other cooperatives—serve approximately 50 million low-income individuals and their families.

While the success of microfinance is well documented, there is still room for improvement to meet existing demand, especially in rural areas. Possibly 20 institutions world wide have a client base of a million or more low-income customers, yet the majority of microfinance institutions (MFIs) serve fewer than 50,000. The reasons for differences in scale vary from country to country, but there remain a number of common problems in the industry worldwide, including:

- Many MFIs operate in an inefficient manner because centralised information processing has not been possible.

- Loan decisions are generated by time-intensive processes for gathering data, performing qualitative analysis and in efforts to form groups.

- Risk-based product pricing has recently become available with automated information systems, but many MFIs still offer only a single, generic product for all clients.

- Customers' transaction costs, such as for journeys to town, are often high in proportion to the amounts of money they transact.

- In some rural areas customers' access to financial services is limited to once a week or every other week when a field officer or mobile unit comes to the village.

- Much information is still recorded on paper though the number of institutions that have automated management information systems (MIS) has increased significantly.

- Very few institutions link their internal systems with external systems, either directly or through data protocols.

The primary approach of the microfinance industry in addressing these issues has been to increase the capacity of individual institutions so that each might serve more customers, collectively inching beyond the Microcredit Summit Campaign goal of serving 100 million[1] people at the bottom of the economic pyramid.

Looking ahead to 2015, imagine a financial services industry that serves 500 million or even a billion customers living on only a few dollars a day. Realisation of this scenario will require hundreds of thousands of outlets and locations from which to access services, massive information systems that process billions of transactions per month, and more than a million people involved in providing these services. This industry will require common data standards, more flexible structures and systems and a strong, customer-driven culture to create the necessary framework. Dramatically increasing the volume of microfinance service delivery to this level will require significant investments in product and process innovations, guided by strong management committed to change and creating business value, and building staff capacity. Information technology will simply facilitate or enable the growth; the pillars will be innovative business models and strategic partnerships. However, business processes often require revision in order to accommodate and reap the rewards of information communication technology (ICT).

This chapter focuses on the emerging role of ICT in the microfinance industry, and how new partnerships and collaboration models can enable microfinance service delivery systems to support an ever-growing demand. Different models that use ICT to improve and expand the capacity of microfinance providers are examined in detail and compared, concrete examples are described, and challenges facing implementation are identified. Microfinance (MF) providers are defined here as financial institutions that range from formal banks to semi-formal cooperatives, NGOs, and village savings banks, to informal savings and credit groups – institutions that provide financial services,[2] including insurance. The ideas and recommendations advanced here focus on the role of ICT in expanding rural microfinance outreach, although they could be adapted to urban and peri-urban areas.

---

[1] Microcredit Summit Campaign: Working to ensure that 100 million people of the world's poorest families, especially the women of those families, receive credit for self-employment and other financial and business services by 2005.

[2] CGAP, Building Inclusive Financial Systems, Donor Guidelines on Good Practice in MF, Dec. 2004 ('DG'), p. 2, fn 5.

How Can New Partnerships and Collaboration Expand Microfinance Outreach in Rural Areas?

Innovations that can scale up rural microfinance delivery systems arise as new business models—as new ways of doing business through collaboration that creates access to information communication technologies. Three types of combinations can expand rural outreach:

- partnerships that *leverage* technology,

- partnerships that *create* technology, and

- partnerships that *enable access* to technology.

All three categories will play important roles in creating the capacities to serve the 500 million or more customers at the bottom of the economic pyramid.

Financial service providers, particularly those serving rural areas, should examine the benefits that ICT can bring to their businesses and how these advantages can be exploited. In some cases MF providers cannot afford information technology because of its initial upfront costs and the costs of its continued operation. Nonetheless, many MF providers choose to own the technology – a costly decision covering software, hardware, internal information technology teams, and external technical support. At the other extreme, too many MF providers have only paper-based operations. An alternative strategy that is more appropriate and affordable for many is a shared approach that can take many forms, leveraging existing investments in technology. There are currently several possibilities for collaboration, such as:

- shared networks of point-of-sale (PoS) and automated teller machines (ATM)

- outsourced application and database management

- communal development—either private or open source

- aggregated purchasing of capital goods, such as PoS devices, smart cards and chips

- aggregated purchasing of services, such as telecommunication and switching

Many examples of shared approaches can be found: a few are reviewed here. A more comprehensive description of information communication technology is in the Appendix.

Models of Collaboration

Three distinct models of collaboration hold significant promise for rural microfinance. These models can be clustered into three types: leveraging, creating, or providing access to technology. The first model consists of financial institutions that develop alternative delivery channels by building relationships with companies that have networks of physical outlets. These institutions are leveraging technology, such as wireless infrastructures, electronic data chips, mobile phones, and PoS devices to provide financial services on behalf of microfinance institutions (MFIs). Customers complete their transaction with the merchant, not a teller, or through an ATM. This business model is referred to as the *delivery channel or network model*. This partnership is being adopted in emerging markets.

The second is the *consortium model*, which brings members together around the design, development and implementation of technology standards and solutions in a way that benefits all parties. The third model is an *aggregated outsourced service model* that makes access to information technology and the required support more affordable. Aggregating the demand for a particular ICT expertise or service creates an opportunity for a sustainable business that is more reliable and efficient than an efficient internal department of an existing institution.

Delivery Channel Model

By partnering with third party merchants with delivery channels such as airtime shops, petrol stations, grocery stores, or similar service outlets, MF providers can lower costs per transaction, expand hours and flexibility of customer service, and bring points of service closer to the customer. These automated transactions also provide the volume that enables institutions to create data repositories for improved risk management, product development, market segmentation and faster, safer growth. Customers benefit from more convenient, secure, and cheaper access.

Alternatively, non-regulated, rural microfinance institutions that lack the capacity to create and manage such a merchant network, but which have a network of offices, could partner with a commercial provider and become its rural delivery channel. This creates opportunities for expanding the services offered, co-branding with financial institutions in different market niches, sharing infrastructure to leverage investments in technology, and generating additional shared revenues. For example, in Bolivia FIE partnered with ProMujer, an NGO with offices in rural areas that collect savings on behalf of FIE.

In addition, co-branding via a delivery channel partnership helps raise the value of individual brands and leverages investment in physical infrastructure to create additional transaction revenues. By viewing their business as a delivery channel for their rural customers, MFIs can market their relationship with customers, their trust and brand in the community, and their physical location to gain a return that benefits customers as well as the provider. The last untapped market in the world is the rural areas. Many different entities, including government agencies, consumer product companies, and development organisations are trying to reach rural people.

Organisations that collaborate to build this "last mile" channel will be able to recoup costs and generate returns if they diversify the range of products and services they offer. This type of symbiotic relationship leverages existing investments in branch networks, can turn offices from a cost centre into outlets that generate profit. Additionally, the data that is collected through these electronic transactions can then be used to lower the cost of capital through improved portfolio reporting, faster capital turnover, market segmentation, investments, and securitisation.

Consortium Model

The consortium approach enables members to contribute resources such as time, money, expertise, and credibility in a way that no individual member could achieve alone. This approach has had tremendous success in creating industry standards, protocols, and shared software solutions in both the technology and formal financial sectors. Visa International, Bluetooth, Apache, and the Fair Isaac[3] data consortium are private sector examples of successful collaboration among competitors that has expanded markets and services for all consortium members. The primary example in the microfinance industry today is the Hewlett Packard (HP) led MFT[4] initiative that resulted in the remote transaction system (RTS), a front-end delivery solution available under an open source license.

This is a major step forward for the industry, eliminating duplication in developing delivery channel systems, sharing lessons from implementing last mile solutions, and gaining the momentum necessary to serve as a catalyst. Other collaborative open source initiatives are underway to develop a core management information system and standard credit bureau management system, both being led by the Grameen Technology Center. The anticipated results of these efforts is a common public good—open source software licences[5] that can create new business opportunities by using the technology or providing support services.

The consortium model lends itself to sharing credit and transaction histories that can be used to assess risk and build scoring models for underserved customer profiles. Although a common practice in formal finance, there has been little or no sharing of customer data for building scoring models in microfinance. Supporting an industry serving a billion customers will require a significant shift from time-intensive customer screening processes towards high-volume decision making processes, which is achievable only with automated scoring. Electronic transac-

---

[3]   The Bluetooth consortium created the Bluetooth standard for hardware devices to transfer data over a short range wireless connection. Apache is an open source web server application created by the Apache Group, which later became the Apache Software Foundation. Fair, Isaac and Company, Inc. is a leading developer and producer of credit scoring tables and associated products. They created a consortium of banks in the US to provide their data to help build and test these products, which the members can then use in their credit businesses.

[4]   Microfinance Development Team.

[5]   Open source software in essence is free to anyone that wants to use it as long as they adhere to the restrictions outlined in the licence.

tions increasingly provide the data that makes scoring models possible. The next step requires a willingness and commitment among microfinance institutions to share data sets and develop mutually useful scoring based on country, regional or customer profiles.

Aggregated Outsourced Services Model

An institution that can afford only one information technology (IT) staff member, or even a small team, assumes a great deal of risk. This person or persons will not always be available due to sickness, vacation, outside obligations, and other priorities. In addition, information technology has become complex and broad, often requiring considerable specialisation, making it difficult to be a generalist in the field. It is unrealistic to rely on one person or a small team to help an institution analyse all ICT options available, or to expect a team to remain up-to-date on the technology of greatest value to the business. IT staff in an organisation are usually so focused on day-to-day operations that they have little time to think strategically.

By outsourcing certain IT activities such as application or database management, network support, end of day processing, or backing-up and archiving tasks, internal IT departments do not require deep or broad skill sets. Also, outsourcing enables the internal team to focus on optimising business value and on the strategic thinking that the institution requires from those who are familiar with operations as well as technology. Outsourcing discreet activities can lower overall expenses while simultaneously allowing the microfinance institution to apply its limited resources to its core business, such as improving product portfolios and providing higher quality customer service.

Strengths and Weakness of Collaboration

Although these models of collaboration have proved successful for microfinance institutions, they are not without risks. The key is managing risks effectively, which requires commitment and attention. Collaboration will expand opportunities for everyone involved: to make them work successfully they must be well-managed with incentives properly aligned from the start.

Building a delivery channel network requires time and resources to determine the criteria or profile for the channel partner, conduct due diligence, build relationships and establish working agreements with good partners. Policies and their enforcement must be established regarding liability, liquidity management, security of handling cash, customer service levels, reconciliation, settlement, compensation, training, support, and quality control. Cultural differences in customer bases can be a problem, making market research on client behaviour essential throughout. The regulatory requirements of working with third-party agents must be understood, adhered to and in some cases changed. Institutions should follow international standards and precedents to make sure all risks are properly addressed. In countries lacking laws regarding third-party agents, such guidelines can help establish standards.

Creation and management of a consortium is time-consuming, especially in the early stages when commitments are made regarding working principles, overall objectives, and exit strategies for all participants. To be successful, the potential impact and value of the final results must be aligned with the objectives of all members of the consortium. A common vision and guiding principles for working together are an essential starting point, but relationships are truly built by promoting the principles and dedicating time and attention to them.

Outsourced service models also require due diligence to identify the partner with the right technology and the highest possible quality of service. If the technology provider is not committed to the results of the MF providers, the relationship is unlikely to be viable. Outsourced ICT services create dependency on external partners if the business is to survive as it grows in complexity. This position may be uncomfortable for institutions that are accustomed to operating independently. This makes due diligence on vendors critical. Clear contracts defining the responsibilities and commitments of each entity are essential.

All these partnership models contain the potential risk of falling apart before gains are realised. The most effective means of managing this risk is to require, from the start, a clear understanding of the intended purpose or benefits of the collaboration, authentic commitment to the process, and agreements or covenants to guide the work. Given this risk, the most common driver of collaboration is cost savings. Many microfinance providers cannot afford to create new IT solutions or to pay for the infrastructure required to expand operations, especially into rural areas. This key resource driver provides the essential rationale for overcoming the challenges and risks of collaboration. Collaboration provides a higher likelihood that institutions can obtain access to the most appropriate technologies without commitments to on-going development and investment in specialised expertise. Additionally, collaboration makes it possible for institutions to leverage fully their investment in information communication technology. In summary, collaboration enables MF providers to use technology creatively to expand operations without incurring the full cost of ownership.

Examples of the Potential of Information Technology Partnerships in Rural Microfinance Outreach

Operating in rural areas is difficult and expensive given low population density, long distances and travel time that lower staff productivity and raise costs or risks associated with moving cash, limited market access, and lower savings and borrowing capacities. Historically, telecommunication and power infrastructure is underdeveloped in rural areas. Each of these factors increases costs. Furthermore, the traditional space-based model of growth by expansion, by establishing more branch offices, is capital intensive and expensive to maintain, requiring higher transaction volumes to be sustainable. This cost structure limits the areas into which microfinance providers can expand, making it very difficult to reach rural populations. This section provides examples of the three models that are overcoming these barriers.

Model 1: Delivery Channel Networks

Several emerging IT solutions to support alternative delivery models demonstrate the potential to contribute to the scaling-up of microfinance. Most noteworthy is the creation of merchant networks using PoS and mobile solutions or ATM networks to expand access to cash transactions, payment and other financial services. Additionally short messaging systems (SMS), interactive voice response (IVR), and internet banking options make it easier and more convenient for customers to access account information, apply for new products or services, and perform financial transactions. All of these options offer different benefits and cost structures must be analysed to determine the strategic value of each in the local context.

A growing number of businesses are working to build solutions that support use of third party delivery channels. FERLO, a technology company in Senegal, has established separate private merchant networks for three cooperatives using PoS devices for prepaid services. Teba Bank in South Africa has pilot-tested a PoS solution enabling salaried workers and pensioners to purchase items, top-up airtime and make cash withdrawals through a merchant network. SMART Communications in the Philippines began in 2004 to offer remittance services – Smart Money and Smart Padala—using SMS messaging. MABS, a USAID project in the Philippines, is working with four rural banks, members of the rural bankers association, and two telecommunications companies, including SMART Communications and also GLOBE, which offers G-Cash, that have developed a chain of outlets to pilot test loan payment and remittance services using SMS messaging via mobile phones. In a recent study of microenterprise borrowers in the Philippines, 93%[6] had a mobile phone or a family member with one, making this approach viable.

In Latin America, a growing number of cyber centre networks offer services to microfinance service providers, small and medium sized enterprises or other businesses interested in delivering products and services to customers in urban slums ('barrios') and rural villages, creating yet another type of channel. Major banks in Brazil have developed nearly 30,000 points of service in every municipality in the country, making it possible to open accounts and access savings, credit, money transfers, insurance, government benefits, bill payment and other services. By combining technology (in this case PoS devices and PCs) at postal and lottery outlets and retail shops such as groceries stores, drug stores and butchers, the

---

[6] Of these, 68% had a mobile phone and the other 25% had a family member with a mobile phone.

banks now serve every town in Brazil, some of which can be reached only by plane or boat.

Vodafone is working with its African subsidiaries, Safaricom in Kenya and Vodacom in Tanzania, to transmit financial transactions through cellular networks. Safaricom and Vodacom airtime shop dealers will use either a mobile phone or a point of sale device in the store to complete transactions. Vodafone's subsidiaries leverage a bank partner for clearinghouse services and work with FAULU, an MFI, to pilot test the solution with their customers. Using their chain of airtime shops as outlets, Vodafone affiliates will offer loan payments to pilot test the initiative, which will be extended to include bill payments, checking credit information, and transmission of loan requests. The technology leverages Vodafone's SMS platform as well as mobile phone and PoS technology.

HP, in conjunction with the MFT consortium, has been working with three MFIs in Uganda to pilot-test a remote transaction system (RTS) that leverages web services, smart cards, and PoS devices. The technology supports loan payments, savings deposits, transfers, and withdrawals offline and online. An MF partner, Uganda Microfinance Union (MFO), has used the solution to build a network of independent third-party merchants in operation since January 2005.[7]

ICICI Bank in India has built a network of 1500 village kiosk operators who resell ICICI's insurance products. Operators were selected who had an existing business with a physical location, demonstrated an entrepreneurial attitude, and were respected and trusted in the community. The kiosk consists of a personal computer with an internet connection, a printer and a web camera. ICICI Bank built a web-based application for entering insurance requests as well as an online banking interface. The operator network is also a disbursement location for money orders paying out insurance claims. ICICI plans to offer other types of financial transactions through this network. The operators are free to use the equipment and connection to offer, and charge for, other services important to the community.

In all these scenarios an agent takes or gives cash, making these outlets cash input or output points. The agent model relies on liquidity management by the agent as well as the capacity to manage cash surpluses or shortages. In essence, the third-party merchant model rotates cash in rural areas and electronically in the capital city, limiting the movement of cash between urban and rural areas. Through these points of access customers can put cash in, take cash out, or conduct cashless transactions, which helps the rural poor to manage their liquidity.

An alternative example of a delivery channel is the strategic partnership of echange, LLC and Centro AFIN.[8] Centro AFIN is a private institution that contributes to the development and consolidation of the financial industry in Latin

---

[7] See Janine Firpo, "Banking the Unbanked: Issues in Designing Technology to Deliver Financial Services to the Poor" in this volume.

[8] Centro AFIN was founded in 2002 and is comprised of ACCION International, FINRURAL, BANCOSOL, CAF, DGRV, ECOLF Peru, FONDESIF, AGROCAPITAL and FUNDA-PRO, all of which are involved in microfinance.

America and the Caribbean, primarily by providing professional development services. Through an Inter-American Development Bank (IADB) grant, echange developed two e-learning courses. One is CD-ROM-based, coupled with facilitated discussions designed for loan officers dealing with delinquency management. The second is an on-line customer service course for branch managers, which incorporates facilitated chat sessions and web-based tools for launching a customer service initiative.

Through this partnership, AFIN can offer MF providers affordable, high quality, results-based training without having to develop the courses themselves. In addition, the MF employees do not have to leave their places of work, can incorporate their learning into their workflow, and apply course content immediately. Through this training method, MF providers can ensure the quality of the content and course delivery, have direct knowledge of participant progress, and measure performance improvements quickly. In an institution trying to expand rapidly, services that ensure staff are well equipped to perform their jobs is very important. Distance learning, especially through a strategic partnership such as this, provides that possibility.

Model 2: Consortium

In August 2002 HP convened a group of eight public and private organisations[9] interested in scaling up the delivery of microfinance services. The group's form and process was influenced by the approach Dee Hock used to launch the Visa International model in the 1960s. Early conversations led the consortium to a breakthrough that could be shared with the entire microfinance industry, acknowledging that a cross-industry approach would be required. This group envisaged a next generation transaction processing infrastructure that could connect individual customer transactions with global financial systems, creating a true last mile link. The key requirements were that it adhere to existing data standards, be affordable, scalable and ultimately accessible to all interested parties.

The consortium worked for nearly three years following a methodical process of business analysis, identification of requirements and technology specification, followed by development and testing. RTS is now available under an open source license issued by Sevak Solutions, a non-profit corporation created by the MFT consortium to hold the technology as intellectual property and provide coordination and leadership for its development. In addition, Sevak is working on national transacting systems to support stronger and deeper rural financial systems to serve the poor.

Grameen Foundation, through Grameen Technology Center, a member of the MFT consortium, is leading two further efforts to develop open source applica-

---

[9] Microfinance Development Team – ACCION International, Bizcredit, echange, FINCA International, Freedom from Hunger, Grameen Technology Center, Hewlett Packard, and Pride Africa.

tions that scale up microfinance service delivery. One is building a core management information system that will facilitate easy localisation, flexible configuration and still connect with the larger financial system. Mifos, as it is called, will be available for local installation, client-server, or web based usage. They have organised a product development group of MFIs to help define requirements and pilot-test the technology.

The second application, developed in collaboration with PlaNet Finance, will help create dedicated microfinance credit bureaus. The pilot country is Morocco, where nearly two dozen MFIs are testing the service and the technology. Both of these initiatives adhere to and propagate industry standard data protocols. Broader collaborations being defined will include alignment with a number of large microfinance institutions or networks as well as local vendors for localisation and implementation.

A key advantage of open source solutions is that they move companies away from making money on software licences towards business models that deliver technology. Open source development holds out the promise of creating shared knowledge for the key players in automating microfinance operations[10] that can create a common framework to support new models of access. Investments in development of software solutions are still required, but at a lower cost that excludes marketing and intellectual property protection costs. This benefits the entire industry, not just one institution.

Companies that have built their business strategy around open source solutions will also be motivated to support on-going development. The overall social return on investment for the main sponsors of an open source solution is generated by its broader use. A primary goal of the open source work that the MFT and the Grameen Technology Center have undertaken is to help the industry establish a set of low-cost, adaptable solutions that will eventually produce a shared, integrated, and flourishing network of financial institutions serving the poor.

Model 3: Aggregated Outsourced Services

A broad range of technologies is available to improve microfinance operations and services. Consequently, an MF provider could not afford to have all the required expertise in-house, especially where IT skills command a premium. While generic skills such as network administration are readily available locally, others, such as financial MIS expertise, require specialised skills that are harder to find. MF providers that plan to scale-up operations in a sustainable manner will need alternative means to support their information technology. If only a few institutions in one area outsource these services, the aggregate effect could be sufficient to build a viable local support business. Such a firm can provide more sophisticated and reliable services at a lower price than each institution could previously sustain on its own.

---

[10] Dailey, James and McKiernan, Lynn, "The Case for Automating Microfinance With An Open Source Architecture," The Grameen Technology Center, 2003, p. 25.

The types of aggregated services well suited for outsourcing include: hosting services, application or database management, and local area network (LAN) support, as well as external telecommunication services to create a wide area network (WAN) for sharing information across an organisation. Through reliable connectivity, the location of the servers – in the offices of the MFI, the application support team, or a hosting provider – becomes less relevant as long as users and the technical team can access the system, offering more flexibility and better data management. MF providers that can reliably access IT solutions through an aggregated model will have lower capital and recurring costs, the opportunity to upgrade software more seamlessly, and more management time to build the business.

The power of an electronically connected organisation is measured best through improved risk management, efficient information sharing, employee coordination, greater productivity, lower communication costs, and lower IT management costs. For organisations that are regulated, a connectivity strategy is imperative in order to determine accurately and easily their financial condition on a daily basis and for on-time reporting. Being fully connected through a wide area network is a requirement for any institution that wants to leverage front-end delivery technologies, such as PoS devices, ATMs, SMS messaging or interactive voice response systems.

Telecommunication companies such as Bushnet in Africa are working to extend wireless infrastructure deep into rural areas by using appropriate, leading-edge technology that is accessible and affordable for any size of microfinance provider. In 2004, Bushnet helped four microfinance providers in Uganda to implement wide area networks, connecting more than 50 branches across the country. Some of these institutions are NGOs that are becoming regulated, which is the primary rationale for their investment in technology. In addition, Bushnet offers local area networking services, reliable hosting or backup services, and some application support for its RTS partners in Uganda. Established local technology firms with reliable services are usually a better investment of limited IT resources than MF providers that try to maintain the skills and necessary environment in-house.

Opportunity International Bank of Malawi (OIBM) uses the Temenos eMerge management information system. In-house IT staff support and manage new initiatives, but they outsource end-of-day processing and application management support services to Bastion. Using a remote connection, Temenos eMerge experts in South Africa oversee processing and back-up activities of the servers in Malawi. The OIBM IT staff can leave the office at a reasonable hour assured that the system will be ready to go in the morning. Bastion support is quickly available if problems arise that the in-house team cannot handle or if new functionality is accessed. Bastion also trains new OIBM IT personnel. This arrangement is cheaper and more reliable than maintaining the expertise in-house.

A final example, Microbanx, offers an MIS application—COBIS—to customers off site. Pricing is based on the number of active client accounts rather than the user license fees traditionally charged by software vendors. Microbanx offers a full range of services including application hosting, management, data security, reliable power, data back-ups, mirroring[11] and connectivity for all branches for a monthly fee with no upfront capital investment. Microbanx's offices (and servers) in Ecuador serve customers throughout Latin America and the US. This application service provider (ASP) model significantly reduces internal IT skill requirements, especially at branches, and provides a flexible information infrastructure that can easily be scaled up.

Beyond this handful of examples, an informal mapping exercise by CGAP counted at least 63 financial institutions in 33 countries using ATMs, PoS, mobile phones or PC banking to serve poor people. Of these, 46 are universal banks. While there is still much to be learned and proved, especially regarding sustainability, a trend has been established. Considerable effort is required to scale up and replicate these pilot efforts.

Challenges and Opportunities for IT to Improve Rural Microfinance Outreach

The promise of technology to make breakthroughs in delivering microfinance is quite encouraging in spite of near-term obstacles. The greatest barrier to information technology is generally its cost. A key element of models described here is the leverage of existing and emerging infrastructures, such as chain outlets, telecommunications or even electric power. Sharing infrastructure reduces costs, facilitating delivery of financial products and services to rural areas. Sharing these services incurs minimal risks compared to the dependence on similar services such as roads and water. Our collective challenge remains reducing the cost of transactions so that institutions can process small transactions profitably in remote areas.

While many IT pilot projects have been conducted over the last 10 years in the microfinance industry, adoption and adaptation of these models has been limited. The cause is simply a lack of awareness about the initiatives and the technology. Those institutions that are aware do not have the expertise to explore or apply the ideas. In some cases a lack of understanding about technologies coupled with a fear of exposing this knowledge gap restrains progress. In other cases, a lack of resources to fund research or a pilot initiative is the excuse. As is typical to all industries, there are early adopters and innovators followed by far greater numbers that are risk averse and doing "business as usual", even when indicators show that the market is changing. Funds for researching and developing new business models, products and partnerships, additional advocacy and education are required to overcome these barriers and facilitate more rapid adoption of these three models of collaboration.

---

[11] Mirroring is the replication of a server for faster recovery in the event that information or applications on the main server are lost or damaged.

To date, no regulatory body has completely blocked the use of third-party merchant networks to deliver financial services. Each institution should examine local regulations to determine whether this type of partnership model can be used. Generally, if the formal financial sector is leveraging these types of partnerships and IT solutions, it should be possible for a microfinance provider to make a plausible case to do likewise. This regulatory due diligence should be part of the exploratory and design phase of the initiative. In addition, if an institution follows the risk management principles for e-banking and related resources provided by the Basel Committee[12] on Banking Supervision (2003) as a framework for their delivery services model, the auditors, investors and regulators are likely to be comfortable.

Products and Transaction Volume

Transaction volumes are low and outreach-per-customer is relatively expensive in rural areas. Reaching "the last mile" requires a diversity of new products and a range of services that can be delivered through a single access point online and offline. A limited range of financial transactions, such as loan payments and savings deposits alone, will not cover the capital and recurring costs of the delivery channel. Additional transactions, such as utility or pension payments, purchasing of airtime, or even health care or e-government services, can be added to cover the costs of the delivery channel in remote areas. The more points of access and diversity of products an institution can create to increase frequency of usage raises the overall value of a shared network, justifying the initial capital investments.

To be truly competitive, MF providers must shift their thinking from being a provider of products to being a provider of services for an array of activities that people at the bottom of the pyramid engage in nearly every day. These services must be provided when and where people want them, not where it is most convenient for the provider. These services may include purchasing raw material or agricultural inputs, paying for health services or insurance, educational and communication services, e-government or business development services, pension or retirement opportunities, household goods, and home improvements.

Technology

Cellular and wireless infrastructures are opening wide possibilities for alternative service delivery models. However, there are still a number of challenges such as poor fixed telecommunication lines outside capital cities, limited reach of wireless networks, low bandwidth, and high usage fees. In 2001, the number of mobile phones surpassed the number of fixed lines globally, and there are more mobile phones in developing countries than in industrialised countries. The growth of internet access is somewhat slower but steady, demonstrating exponential growth

---

[12] www.bis.org/publ/bcbs98.htm, www.bis.org/publ/cpss68.htm.

since 2000. Growth has been concentrated in industrialised countries, but is gaining momentum elsewhere. In South Asia, Latin America, the Caribbean, the Middle East and in North Africa internet access is surpassing mobile phone access.[13]

Growth has been primarily in urban areas, widening the communication gap between rural and urban. Mobiles are expensive to buy and use.[14] Thus, rural areas in the developing world are the last frontier of the information technology revolution.[15] Microfinance providers in countries with poor rural communications should collaborate, using their aggregated demand as a lever to attract resources and firms that will bring technology to the areas where they operate. This will also help ensure the reliability of the service provider and lower costs for the local industry, which should translate into affordable pricing for microentrepreneurs.

Where connectivity is available but not always operating, fall-back strategies should be devised. Options could include local data repositories, device memory, smart cards, or restricted policies and procedures to operate securely offline. Amounts invested in these alternatives should be related to the amount of time they are actually used.

Shared infrastructure and services strategies lower per unit costs, build value, and leverage economies of scale for expansion of microfinance delivery, even among competitors. Risks associated with using hosted or outsourced services can be mitigated by ensuring that the technology provider uses certified technologies, follows proper security and network procedures, and uses encryption to transfer data. In addition, microfinance providers must protect their networks against viruses, follow policies and procedures for assigning system access and passwords, and properly manage internal systems. Clients using a shared merchant PoS network or a MIS application that is hosted on a shared server must ensure that data cannot be mixed or accessed, except when a breech of security authorisation occurs.

Regardless of the solution, customers will always have to provide identification to authorise financial transactions using an encrypted code, personal identification number, password or biometric means. Creating electronic profiles of customers will help rural areas join the digital economy. Enabling customers to exist digitally and access their accounts remotely can transform service delivery, increasing electronic data repositories and additional product development, and offering access to new services. In nations where citizens inherently mistrust government, extra care is required if this type of information is to be shared with legitimate credit bureaus and data consortia outside the domain of the financial institution.

---

[13] "Wireless Internet Opportunity for Developing Countries," InfoDev Program of the World Bank, Wireless Internet Institute, United Nations ICT Task Force, 2003.

[14] "Completing the Revolution: the Challenge of Rural Telephony in Africa," Pandos Report, 2004, p. 1.

[15] Caspary, George and O'Connor, David, "Providing Low-Cost Information Technology Access to Rural Communities in Developing Countries: What Works? What Pays?" Abstract, p. 1.

Management Issues

In addition to external factors, serious consideration must be given to managing changes in the organisation adopting technology. Technology affects everyone: failing to acknowledge, communicate and prepare employees for new ways of doing business may result in complete rejection or sabotage of the IT strategy. An important aspect of managing expectations around change is to define new roles and responsibilities clearly, to train and empower staff to accept responsibilities, and to align incentives to motivate them. Committed and adequate staff is essential to expanding the sector to new heights. Results-based development and training should be required: investments in training create business value, as do investments in information technology. If management is not willing to commit time and resources to organisational change, it is useless to spend money on technology.

Second, thought, attention and leadership by senior management are absolutely critical to successfully implement an IT solution. Every IT approach or solution has technological, financial, operational, and business strategy advantages and disadvantages, requiring that critical IT choices not be left to the IT department. The top manager responsible for business strategy and performance must make the ultimate IT decision with input from the finance manager, the operations manager and the IT manager. It is the collective responsibility of the management team to understand and determine the financial, operational and technical risks and impacts of the solutions to be pilot-tested. It is the responsibility of managers, not the IT department, to extract value from IT investments.[16] Institutional investments in partnerships and IT solutions affect everyone in the organisation. Unless projects are well managed across the institution, they will fail to produce the required benefits.

Third, think beyond a pilot test. The design phase should include ways to scale up and ensure sufficient analysis to justify the long-term investment. Determining the break-even point is important, so that funding can be triggered when it is reached. Small investments in technology without planning and management ownership often result in increased costs with little return despite anticipated business value. Only by rigorously evaluating the solution periodically—such as on a six-monthly schedule—always making necessary adjustments, is it possible to ensure that business value is gained. Implementing new IT solutions is iterative, requiring multiple phases and adjustments to the deployment strategy, the use of the solution, and processes to expand continually that will leverage and increase the value of the investment.

Finally, managing pilot tests requires business leadership, rigour and discipline to ensure problems are overcome and business models are adjusted until the expected economic value is delivered. The importance of expertise in IT design, planning and project management skills must not be underestimated. Implement-

---

[16] Ross, Jeanne W. and Weill, Peter, "Six IT Decisions your IT People Shouldn't Make", Harvard Business Review, November 2002.

ing an IT solution is not like managing any other project because technical and organisational risks must be managed aggressively to stay on time and within budget. Paying for this expertise from the outset saves money in the long run; not having expertise in place causes problems, delays, budget increases and puts institutional credibility at risk. The importance of high quality project management cannot be overstated.

Conclusion

The large size of rural markets, coupled with technological improvements, provides much of the impetus for IT innovations. However, the true power to scale up lies not in the technology, but in the new business models and partnerships that technology enables. Reaching significant scale and increasing outreach to rural areas occurs only through collaboration to resolve issues, thinking differently about them, and making innovations in the way financial products and services are delivered. Through creative partnerships, information technology can help achieve broader impact, conserve limited resources and drive down transactions costs.

Of the three models of collaboration, the one with the greatest power to transform microfinance is technology-enabled partnerships that make processing small transactions in rural areas possible and profitable. Such partnerships could be those that bring large financial service providers and their capabilities into this market, partnerships that increase course offerings and quality of local training providers to increase human resource capacities, or technology companies with the capability to quickly roll-out or adapt technology for the unique challenges of rural markets. All forms of technology-enabled partnership are essential to expand the outreach of rural microfinance services.

The major lessons from these models of collaboration—shared delivery channels, consortia and aggregated outsourced services—are profound, providing a road map to move from thousands of isolated entities to financial systems for the poor that are linked to global financial networks. Collaboration is the key factor for reaching scale. In sum, collaboration:

(1) Allows responsible sharing and lowers cost structures of IT solutions that make it possible to reach rural markets.

(2) Paves the way for the standardisation required to expand the industry and build integrated financial systems.

(3) Enables organisations to achieve together what they cannot achieve alone.

For collaborative efforts to be successful, all partners—MF providers, technology companies, support agencies, and project sponsors—must invest time and create incentives to build relationships and work towards desired outcomes. This ensures that all parties benefit in an equitable and sustainable way, deriving value for their own institution and for the industry.

The general challenges of emerging market environments, such as limited or unknown return on investment across large populations, makes public sponsorship of collaborative and innovation partnerships essential. Sponsors, whether donors or investors, have an opportunity to insist that funding for these initiatives requires collaboration and sharing infrastructure to help managers shift their thinking from ownership of technology to access of information communication technology. This requires managers to give up some control and to trust that business and technology partners will deliver as promised.

Focused advocacy and additional resources are required to encourage institutions to operate differently and to partner with other large entities such as financial services companies, technology companies or training providers. Competition is usually the factor that drives this change, but in microfinance it may well be the diminishing amount of donor dollars and the push towards sustainability that changes thinking. Reaching rural markets is difficult and the economic benefits are limited or unknown. Consequently, it will take the voices and dollars of those truly committed to transforming rural markets to encourage institutions and the microfinance industry to try new ways of collaborating to access the information technology necessary to build tomorrow's integrated, rural financial systems that serve the poor.

Appendix

Table 1. Summary of access points and their enabling technologies[17]

Technology	Description	Requirements	Pros	Cons
Automated Teller Machine (ATM)	A machine that can furnish account information, accept deposits, effect balance transfers, and disburse cash	• Reliable and affordable communications and power infrastructure • Central database • Ability to transfer currency to machines securely	For clients: • Convenient service • Flexible account access • More hours of operation For MFIs: • Reduced transaction volumes/costs • No staff needed to complete transaction • Can attract savings deposits	• Expensive to own and operate • Requires integrated systems • Maintenance and replenishing cash is costly • Security issues (including transport of cash)

---

[17] Seminar Summary Report, "Information Technology as a strategic tool for microfinance in Africa," AfriCap, November 2004, p.47-48.

Table 1 (continued)

Technology	Description	Requirements	Pros	Cons
Mobile Branches	An ATM on a truck or a branch in a bus that goes from one village to another in rural areas which is served infrequently (e.g. once a week). Combines ATM functionality with operational staff.	▪ Should be combined with smart cards and point of sale devices ▪ MFI staff capable of providing range of services	▪ Full range of financial services ▪ Expands branch network to low density rural areas ▪ Much lower cost than setting up a branch ▪ More secure than a permanent ATM ▪ Not dependent on telecommunication infrastructure	▪ Clients can transact only when the mobile branch is in the village ▪ Higher per unit cost than ATMs ▪ Need a staff of 2-3 to drive and service the mobile branch ▪ Higher operating costs (travel distances, maintenance, security)
Point of Sale Device (POS)	Small machine located at a point of sale that can be used to authenticate the transfer of funds from customer to the retailer	▪ Retailer buy-in and support ▪ Solid communications infrastructure ▪ Centralised database ▪ Coordination between institutions	▪ Significant reduction of paperwork ▪ No need for data entry personnel ▪ Immediate reconciliation of transactions	▪ Expensive to implement and operate ▪ Need for inter-institutional coordination and shared infrastructure
Mobile Phones	Permit client to request information from, or conduct business with, an automated system through their mobile phones (SMS)	▪ Solid MIS ▪ Centrally stored, real time data ▪ Network availability at affordable rates	▪ Not reliant on poor land-line phone infrastructure ▪ Permits access to rural clients ▪ Frees staff time ▪ 24/7 accessibility	▪ Lack of mobile network in rural areas ▪ High cost of operation ▪ Expensive to install and maintain ▪ Need for centralised database
Smart Cards	Wallet-sized plastic cards with embedded computer chips that can process information or simply store data	▪ Reliable electrical and communications networks ▪ Dial-up facility for updates ▪ Software integration between cards, readers, central MIS ▪ Presence of associated technologies	▪ Store information ▪ No need for real-time connection ▪ Automated transactions ▪ More secure ▪ Quicker administrative functions ▪ Increased transaction accuracy	▪ Must purchase associated technologies ▪ High upfront development costs ▪ Security issues with stored information

Table 1 (continued)

Technology	Description	Requirements	Pros	Cons
Interactive Voice Response (IVR) Technology	IVR technology allows callers to request information from, or conduct business with, an automated system by speaking into a telephone or inputting information through its keypad	• Easy, affordable telephone access for clients • Centrally stored, up-to-date data • Secure databases	• Can serve many clients at once • 24/7 service • Frees staff time for more personalised tasks (business counseling, collection calls)	• Requires access to telephone services • Initial costs: US$10,000 to $50,000 for in-house system • Needs central system to control personal identification numbers (PIN)
Personal Digital Assistants (PDAs)	Small, handheld digital computers that can run specialised programmes to manage MFI and client data and perform financial calculations	• Well functioning MIS • High speed access to MIS data from branch offices • Capable technical support • Solid institution and good products	• Increased productivity of field staff • Applicable to wide range of tasks • Can run various software programmes • Can standardise procedures • Reduced volume of paper records • Reduced labour costs	• High initial and maintenance costs • Long development process (9 months to 2 years) • Requires custom-designed database applications
Internet Banking	Internet technology enables users to perform a variety of banking activities, including fund transfers, bill payments, securities trading	• Solid MIS infrastructure • Centralised database • Reliable and affordable communications and power infrastructure	• Flexible account access • No staff needed to complete transaction • Increased hours of operation • No data entry personnel required	• Requires internet access – connectivity • Requires integrated systems • High initial costs • Typically requires higher income and higher literacy rate
Biometrics Technology	Measures an individual's unique physical characteristics to recognise and confirm identity	• Reliable electrical power for card or biometric readers • Solid processes and adequate staff • Software integration between cards, readers and central MIS	• Greater security • Convenience for clients • Local verification • Speedy verification which does not require staff • User identity is stored safely and is tamper-free	• Time, money and energy required for setup and maintenance • Training users • Slow user acceptance or user refusal • System integration may require changes in other hardware

Table 2. Forms of telecommunication connectivity services[18]

Connectivity Technology	Definition	Speed (Bandwidth)	Average Monthly Cost (US$)
Dial-up	Any connection to the Internet or network connection made by a modem and a standard telephone line.	28 to 64 kbps	$20-$100 based on bandwidth.
DSL – (Digital Subscriber Line)	High speed digital connection using copper wires and modems.	16 kbps – 1.5 mbps	$20-$100 based on bandwidth
Dedicated leased line	Dedicated copper or fiber optic cables and modem or router provides network or internet connection.	128 kbps – 2 mbps	$100-$1000 based on bandwidth. Private leased lines: $2000-$4000.
ISDN – (Integrated Services Digital Network)	Special standards for digital transmission over ordinary telephone copper wire as well as over other media.	<2 mbps	$100-$1000 based on bandwidth
GSM – (Global System for Mobile Communications) 900 – 1800 Mhz	Mobile telephone system digitises and compresses data, used in Europe and 85 countries. Related wireless mobile data transmission technologies include High-Speed Circuit-Switched Data (HCSD), General Packet Radio System (GPRS), Enhanced Data GSM Environment (EDGE), Universal Mobile Telecommunications Service (UMTS).	9.6 kbps – 2 mbps	$100-$1000 based on bandwidth
Microwave 2 – 60 Ghz	Microwave signals (electromagnetic energy) perform wireless transmission of all data types, generally using the 802.11b standard (also called WiFi for broadband access).	<155 mbps	$100-$1000 based on bandwidth.
VSAT (Very Small Aperture Terminal) 6 – 14 Ghz	A small satellite antenna (1.5 – 3.0 meters) used for point-to-point or multi-point data communications applications. Microwave is the frequency for communicating to and from satellites.	56 kbps – 1.5 mbps	Based on usage, approx. $10 per MB. Fixed costs of routers and site equipment: $1000-$2000. Cost depends on no. of connected sites.
BGAN and R-BGAN (Broadband Global Area Network/Regional BGAN) 2 – 60 Ghz	A wireless, satellite-borne packet data service based on standard Internet Protocol (IP). Offers mobile high-speed Internet and network connections.	<144 kbps	Based on usage, approx. $10/MB. Fixed costs of routers and site equipment $1000 – $2000. Cost depends on no. of connected sites.

---

[18]   Frederick, Laura, "Connectivity," CGAP IT Innovation Series, 2005 p. 1.

CHAPTER 11:

Banking the Unbanked: Issues in Designing Technology to Deliver Financial Services to the Poor

Janine Firpo[*]

SEMBA Consulting

Introduction

The goals of economic development in many countries are unlikely to be realised while 1.7 billion working adults make less than US$2 a day[1] and have little or no access to basic financial services. The history of financial systems such as in the United States shows that citizens' access to capital and convenient savings services are key underpinnings of economic growth. Yet between 70 and 80% of the world's population has no access to even the most basic financial services.

Over the last 30 years, the microfinance industry has proved that the extreme poor are bankable. Not only do they repay loans, but they do so with very low defaults and relatively high interest rates. Microfinance institutions (MFIs) have become commercially viable enterprises. Yet the microfinance industry as a whole has not been able to grow fast enough to meet demand. At the same time, banks and entrepreneurs in developing countries are beginning to realise that there is a viable market for financial products among the world's vast unbanked masses.

How can microfinance have macro impact such that billions of today's urban and rural poor gain access to financial services? This is the question that a consortium of public and private sector partners convened by the Hewlett-Packard Company (HP) asked themselves. With financial support from the United States Agency for International Development (USAID) and HP, this consortium engaged in three pilot projects in Uganda to determine the role technology could play in increasing the reach of microfinance.

---

[*] Janine Firpo (jfirpo@semba.com) is the founder of SEMBA Consulting and chair of Sevak. She led the activity described in this paper while she was the Director of Global Multisector Initiatives at Hewlett-Packard.

[1] McKinsey & Company, 2005.

The outcome of the consortium's work was unexpected. Results came from a combination of multi-sector inquiry, research into other global initiatives, and findings on the ground in Uganda. The financial analysis conducted at the conclusion of the pilots pointed to a new direction that microfinance could take to achieve a dramatic increase in scale – the kind of scale that will make the industry grow from the 120 million people who are currently served to the 1.7 billion that could be served.

The three overarching lessons of the pilots were:

1. Technology combined with business process change yields the greatest return

2. Emerging markets require innovative, appropriate technologies that are designed for scale

3. The costs of building the infrastructure to support this enabling technology is beyond the capacity of individual MFIs

A growing number of microfinance practitioners and leaders are beginning to embrace concepts supported by these lessons – namely, that reaching significant scale in microfinance is likely to require changes in existing business operations and procedures, in standardising the collection and management of customer data, and in sharing the cost of infrastructure.

How could the reach of financial services to the world's poor be dramatically improved? What would it take to reduce transaction costs and help MFIs achieve greater business viability? What role, if any, might technology play? These were the questions that a diverse group of professionals calling themselves the Microdevelopment Finance Team (MFT)[2] rallied to respond to in July 2002.

The MFT has assembled a roadmap that provides direction toward a world-changing scale in the delivery of financial services to the rural and urban poor. The map reflects a number of pilot projects, the intellectual leadership of those working in microfinance, and the early experiences of the credit card industry in the United States which helped revolutionise the delivery of financial services in industrialised countries. It is an answer that focuses on the role of technology in achieving scale in microfinance.

Defining the Problem, Identifying a Potential Solution

The MFT started their weekly conference calls in August 2002 by exploring the state of the microfinance industry. What obstacles kept the industry from achiev-

---

[2] The Microdevelopment Finance Team (MFT) included participants from Accion International, Bizcredit, FINCA International, Grameen Foundation USA, Freedom from Hunger, Global echange, PRIDE AFRICA, and Hewlett-Packard Company.

ing greater scale? When the team had a working definition of the problem components, they shared their thinking with a wider audience of industry leaders. Together the team and its partners assembled the following list of obstacles to scale:

- An over-dependence on donor funds for wholesale finance and operating costs, and the importance of developing more sustainable, commercial sources of finance (such as local banks and global capital markets)

- The absence of consistent, sector-wide operating standards and business practices that are sustainable enough to stand up to external scrutiny by potential commercial investors and partners

- Fragmentation within the sector, and a lack of strong relationships with organisations outside the sector

- Technical challenges and high transaction costs that make it too expensive to reach, in a sustainable manner, poor people in urban, peri-urban or rural areas who are not yet served by microfinance

- The flexibility to offer diverse financial services that are appropriate for local conditions and priorities

After much research and discussion, the MFT decided that technology could help alleviate some of these problems by providing a secure, low-cost, and reliable means of capturing transaction data and then transferring these data to MFIs in a consistent, standardised manner. Such a system, they reasoned, could improve operating efficiency, decrease transaction costs, and provide sustainable outreach. The team also believed that, if more reliable data could then be shared in a standardised way with other financial service providers, the issues related to capital investment, fragmentation, and the potential for more diversified portfolios could to some degree be addressed.

In essence, the team envisaged a "data transaction backbone" that would link microfinance clients to their financial institutions and beyond. Efficient, reliable data capture – even in remote and rural areas – was the most critical and the most challenging element of the backbone. The team responded by developing the first module – the Remote Transaction System or RTS.

Technology Development and Deployment in Uganda

The RTS was designed to process loan payments, savings deposits, withdrawals and transfers activated through smart cards, point-of-sale (PoS) terminals, a transaction server and connectors that send data directly to the MFIs' accounting and general ledger systems. Clients are given smart cards that indicate their savings and loan account balances. To make a payment, the client inserts her smart card into a PoS terminal, which captures the transaction data, updates account balances on the card, and prints a receipt. Cash is exchanged between the client and the person responsible for the PoS terminal. All transactions saved on the PoS terminal are uploaded daily via the cellular network to the MFI's accounting systems where the transactions are reconciled.[3]

Following their decision to build the RTS, the MFT selected a country where they could test the solution. Uganda was chosen because it had many of the ingredients essential for scale – a large number of microentrepreneurs, a friendly legal and regulatory environment, and several microfinance institutions with long and successful track records. Uganda also posed many of the infrastructure challenges that confront any provider of technology services in developing economies: frequent power outages, unreliable telecommunication services, limited technical support, and illiteracy.

Three Ugandan MFIs agreed to participate in the pilot. Two provided loans through group lending or village banking methodology. The third offered individual loans. The RTS was used differently in each institution, testing three distinct business models. At the conclusion of the pilot, all three models were analysed in detail. Two of the models produced positive value for the MFIs.

Three Overarching Conclusions

Detailed results from the pilot study are available in articles and technical documents on the web and are not discussed in detail here.[4] What is most significant for the purposes of this chapter are the lessons from a combination of results generated by the pilot in Uganda, similar initiatives conducted in other countries, and analysis of both the microfinance and finance industries. Conclusions based on these lessons pushed the team to think in new ways.

Technology Combined with Business Process Change Yields the Greatest Return

A powerful lesson that emerged from the three pilot projects is that overlaying a new technology solution on existing business processes, without first rethinking those procedures, can increase rather than diminish the cost and complexity of doing business. Information technology provides the opportunity to update and introduce innovative business processes. Through such innovation, technology can be a lever that creates the potential for an industry to achieve dramatic increases in scale.

---

[3]   Complete details of the RTS technology can be found at www.sevaksolutions.org, including operational guides, technical documentation and other material about the RTS. Executable and source code are available at www.rts.dev.java.net.

[4]   Refer to www.sevaksolutions.org for a case study and the complete financial analysis of all three models tested in Uganda.

The value that technology delivers as a catalyst for change and as an enabler of new business models has been seen repeatedly. Within the financial sector there is a striking example of this principle. When credit cards were first introduced in the United States, merchants phoned a toll-free number to verify funds before accepting a credit card payment – a process that could take 5 minutes or more. It is not surprising that this innovation did not take off. It was only when technology reduced the card authentication and authorisation processes to less than a minute that credit cards became a widespread phenomenon. And as credit card usage began to soar, the business models for financial services began to change. The technology enabled dramatic scale, data mining and improved the industry's ability to manage risk. In essence, the business models and the underlying technology evolved together to create an industry that now transacts more than a US$2 trillion per year.

Three business models were used in the trials in Uganda. Each was based on modern technology, but with different modes of physical access:

- Remote Branch Model. The remote transaction system (RTS) was placed at a remote sub-branch built by the microfinance institution to reach their rural clients more effectively. After the group leader collected funds from a group meeting, she would travel to the remote branch to deposit the group's money. At this point, she transacted over an RTS that was managed by the branch teller.

- Field Officer Model. The field officers carried the RTS to group meetings to capture individual client data electronically rather than manually. Once optimised for the meeting, the manual processes were replaced by RTS data capture.

- Third-Party Agent Model. The RTS was given to a merchant who lived close to the microfinance clients. Clients went to the agent to perform their banking services. Transactions were captured by the RTS and cash was exchanged between the clients and agent.

The striking differences between the return on investment (ROI) for each of the three business models in the pilot also support the conclusion that business process change and implementation of new technology should proceed in tandem. When this was not done, the quantitative and qualitative benefits of the RTS were severely compromised. One pilot institution automated – and altered – only one portion of its data acquisition process. Clients were completely unaffected by the introduction of the RTS and their group meetings proceeded exactly as they had before. The scale of transactions captured by the RTS device was not sufficient to justify replacing manual data entry with electronic data capture. Financial analysis of this approach showed that the introduction of the RTS generated no return to customers, limited value for internal staff, and an actual cost increase for the MFI.

Part way through the pilot, a second MFI realised that if it did not re-engineer its business processes the RTS would increase rather than reduce its operating expenses. The technology would also prolong group meetings. On the other hand, if the institution did re-engineer some key business processes, the RTS would provide significant value to all members of the value chain – clients, staff, and the MFI. This institution reconciled its accounts on a monthly basis. With the RTS, the management could have daily updates on activities in the field and track their loan portfolios on an individual client basis. Previously the institution tracked loans on a group basis, and had virtually no information about client savings.

Based on this information, this institution attempted to proceed with process change. A consultant was hired to assist them. Subsequent financial analysis, which included expenses only, showed that the RTS lowered costs relative to manual data capture. The pilot did not proceed long enough to determine the qualitative benefits from improved business processes such as collection of in-dividual data, more efficient group meetings, and more timely information. At the conclusion of the pilot, this institution decided not to track loans on an indi-vidual basis. The institution stopped using RTS technology and reverted to its prior practices.

The third MFI engineered a new business approach to leverage the RTS, which achieved the greatest return for all constituents – customers, agents, and the MFI. In this model, PoS terminals were given to merchants, such as petrol station fran-chisees, making these merchants third-party "agents" of the MFI. Clients who visited a local agent to make loan payments or to deposit cash benefited from re-duced travel time and costs. The client transacted directly with the local agent, who acted as a virtual extension of the MFI.

It was expected that clients would benefit from the model used by the third MFI, due to the increased flexibility and reduced costs associated with banking transactions. A surprising result was that clients are actually the greatest benefici-aries. Experience and surveys consistently reported that women are very likely to have their earnings taken from them by family members at the end of the day, or they find that their funds are spent in unplanned ways. The convenience of stop-ping at a virtual bank on a frequent basis can dramatically increase the amount of savings for clients who seize this opportunity, producing dramatic impacts on their financial stability and on the funds that the MFI has to make additional loans.

The third-party agents receive a fee for providing a transaction service, making them beneficiaries of this model. The analysis indicates that an agent in Uganda can have an attractive side business with between 400 – 500 regular clients who transact twice a month. And the MFI shows a positive ROI on its investment after the scale is increased to more than 20,000 clients. Analysis indicates that extend-ing the reach of microfinance into rural areas through these virtual agents will be much less expensive than the current branch or bricks-and-mortar model.

Only the agent model, which pushed beyond existing business practices, showed a positive return for all participants.

Emerging Markets Require Innovative, Appropriate Technologies Designed for Scale

Emerging markets require creative technology solutions that are tailored to their unique and often challenging circumstances – environments where telephone connectivity is erratic, electricity sources unreliable, technical support limited or non-existent, and much of the customer base illiterate. Innovation should find a balance between the best that technology has to offer and the constraints of the local context. It also should find a balance between simply adhering to existing business practices and driving toward business model innovation, as discussed earlier. Taken together these conflicting forces provide a serious challenge which must be considered throughout the design, implementation, and redesign processes.

One lesson that continually surfaced in the Uganda pilots was the importance of making smart decisions in distinguishing between technology solutions that were "appropriate," and state of the art technology solutions that were of limited practical use. While technology innovation is necessary, it is equally important to shape solutions that are informed by the users' local environment. It is far better to provide a solution that can be used, rather than one that is optimised for flexibility and dependent on always-online infrastructures, which are the criteria often used for mature market products. The total cost of the solution and the capabilities of the local markets must be part of any design criteria. The team that developed the RTS thought they understood these issues as they began to develop their solution, which was designed and developed specifically for conditions in Uganda.

Since most MFIs cannot afford expensive solutions, the RTS was designed to keep costs low. Clearly, the total cost of a solution includes all the hardware required for its operation, the technical support team that maintains it, and the costs of infrastructure. All of these costs were considered in the RTS design. That is why the transaction server runs on a standard PC and requires limited technical support. While the solution was being designed for use in Uganda, the development team also ensured that the software met technology and financial industry standards so that it could be scaled up, enabling MFIs to share data with other financial service providers or capital markets. The RTS traded end-user flexibility for reliability, speed, and minimal training requirements, all of which are more important in Uganda. Thus the RTS is a true blend of core elements that would be expected in any enterprise software solution, with alterations that maximise its effectiveness in less robust environments.

With all these considerations integrated into the design of the RTS, the team expected their solution to work well when introduced in the three pilot institutions. They were wrong. They did not understand the depth of their mature market bias or their lack of awareness of how things really work in Uganda. The information the team received during their assessment visits did not match the realities they uncovered as they tested their solution at the local level. The MFIs' management were often just as surprised by unfolding events as were the RTS team. As a result, several disconnects occurred between what the RTS developers and management of the pilot MFIs initially expected the RTS to achieve, relative to what the pilot institutions actually were able to use.

Uganda, like many developing countries, is experiencing rapid growth of cellular and wireless telephone networks. The RTS developers originally assumed that there was enough cellular connectivity to allow an always-online solution that would transmit data to and from the field. When the RTS was first implemented the developers learned that, in Uganda, voice traffic takes priority over data traffic. Although the cellular network had a large footprint, it could be very unreliable. To respond to these concerns, the RTS developers engineered an offline mode for the RTS. This change accelerated data collection and lowered the transaction costs of the calls, alterations that dramatically improved the financial sustainability of the solution. Although the final solution was an improvement in many ways, the realities that drove the change were unexpected and required a tremendous amount of redesign.

Prior to designing the RTS solution, the RTS team and microfinance management and staff had explored each institution's operational procedures in excruciating detail. All the elements of the group payment process were discussed and documented. Flow charts were transformed into product specifications, and ultimately into product design. It was not until the RTS was in the field that a number of inconsistencies emerged between what the team had been told and what was actually occurring. In one case, a payment that was collected during each group meeting was not included in the design because the MFI did not track it on their books. The group tracked this payment, but without a way to account for those collections electronically. Both the old processes and the new electronic processes would have to co-exist, leading to a solution that would add complexity rather than reduce it. To overcome this obstacle, a combination of technical and business re-engineering was required.

The initial goal of the RTS developers was to enable the pilot institutions to conduct "real time reconciliations" that update accounts as soon as transactions occur. As noted, the business practices of the cellular provider made this impractical, so the RTS was switched to an offline mode that updated the MFIs' MIS once a day. Even this frequency was too much for one of the MFIs to handle at first. Its accounting staff requested that all transactions be held on the RTS server until the end of the month when they would be ready to reconcile their accounts. As staff and management of the pilot institution realised that the capability of the RTS exceeded their existing practices, they faced a dilemma. Would they change their business practices to make more frequent reconciliations, taking full advantage of the benefits of the RTS, or would they change the RTS, eliminating many of the gains the technology offered?

These examples demonstrate the importance of finding a balance between product innovation, local realities, and business process change.

The Cost of Technology Infrastructure Is Beyond the Capacity of Individual MFIs

The highest capital costs in the implementation of the RTS solution are those of the PoS terminals (US$700 each) and smart cards (US$3.00 to US$5.00 each). The Uganda pilot used blank cards procured in India for approximately US$1.15 each, which were shipped to Uganda and printed locally. Printing costs ran as high as US$4.00 per card. To minimise printing costs, a local IT company was encouraged to provide card printing services, reducing the total cost per card to less than US$3.00. If the local company could print greater quantities the price would drop: if the cards were purchased consistently in batches of 10,000, the total price per card could drop below US$2.00. These seemingly small differences have a tremendous impact on the break-even point at which the total solution returns a positive ROI for participating MFIs. The same effect applies to the PoS devices, which can cost less than US$500 when purchased in volume.

The local IT company that provided card printing and procurement services also handled server management and technical support for the participating microfinance partners. Each participating MFI pays service fees that enable this application service provider (ASP) to profit from the RTS. These fees would be a fraction of the cost that an MFI would incur if it built these capacities internally. If three or more MFIs used the ASP to manage the technical support and card related aspects of their RTS deployment, a sustainable, self-perpetuating model could be established in Uganda. The ASP would then have sufficient volume to sustain its RTS-related operations and to expand its RTS business in Uganda and the surrounding region. But if only one institution in Uganda participated, the sustainability model could no longer be supported until that institution has a very high volume of smart cards in circulation.

The model that showed the greatest potential and return in Uganda was the agent model in which merchants were designated as virtual bankers. The acquisition, training and support of agents creates a significant cost centre, particularly as the agent network grows. However, the model becomes more attractive to clients when there are more points of access for their financial transactions. This puts an MFI in a difficult position: they benefit from building the network, but as the network grows their cost savings decline overall. In industrialised countries, this 'Catch-22' was overcome when banks recognised that it was in their interest to share the cost of these infrastructure elements. Today, credit card clients in most countries can use their cards in any bank's ATM or PoS machines. This type of cooperation is probably required at the microfinance level if institutions want to build sustainable ways to extend their presence in remote and rural areas.

History and economics suggest that collaboration is critical for the sustainable deployment of the type of solution piloted in Uganda. However, cooperation is often resisted. The MFIs and local banks fear that their competitive advantage will be lost. This attitude surfaced in Uganda at the start of the pilot. The RTS was designed for cost reduction and it was anticipated by the designers that the participating MFIs would share one RTS server, connect their back-end systems through one generic connector, and adapt their business process to a common PoS interface. This approach would dramatically reduce costs associated with the design, deployment, enhancement and maintenance of the solution by a factor of more than three. However, when this approach was discussed with the three participating MFIs, they balked. Each institution wanted the RTS designed to meet their individual, and unique, business and MIS requirements. There was insufficient time or proof to convince them otherwise. The RTS team capitulated and created three distinct RTS servers, three separate connectors, and two PoS interfaces, which significantly increased the complexity and cost of the project. The results of the pilot clearly demonstrate that the original objective of a standardised core solution will be essential if the microfinance industry is to reach scale through this type of technology innovation. Creating separate solutions for each institution is neither sustainable nor scalable.

Shared Infrastructure: A Requirement for Scale

The conclusions generated by the pilot led several of the participants to realise that the possibility and opportunity to integrate technologies that will help microfinance achieve scale will become sustainable only when large numbers of participants use the system. Only through shared infrastructure and common standards can the costs of providing financial assistance to a dramatically larger client base be achieved. Sharing is required to increase the number and reduce the costs of access points at which clients obtain financial services. Sharing is necessary if MFIs are to obtain the consistent, high-integrity data that is required by investors or credit reference bureaus. The advent and growth of VISA is a prime example of the level of collaboration and technical sophistication that is required to achieve dramatic scale and commercial value throughout the entire value chain.

A recent survey conducted by ACCION International indicates that for many microfinance players, such as those participating in the pilot project, technology is viewed primarily as a means to control costs and increase efficiency. Whether these MFIs also view technology as a path towards significant scale is less obvious, particularly if reaching that scale requires changing business operations and procedures, standardising the collection of customer data, building networks of non-exclusive external agents, and sharing technology infrastructures. The pilot project suggests that without such steps, it is unlikely that small, customised investments in technology will produce greater scale for the microfinance industry.

Self-contained organisations that are not interested in sharing information, standards or solutions do not and, more importantly, cannot achieve scale. The walls they have built, literally and metaphorically, around their business operations are unlikely to permit the evolution of a fluid financial system that expands across and links a multitude of players. Very few MFIs reach one million customers. Serving hundreds of millions or billions of customers is unlikely while those walls still stand, separating MFI from MFI.

In the developed world, the financial sector reached significant scale and outreach only when its financial institutions agreed to adopt a number of shared standards that allow information to pass uniformly from one system to another. In the 1950s, the consumer finance market in the United States in many ways resembled the microfinance industry today. Average loan sizes were around US$300, repayment rates were as high as 96%, credit decisions and processing involved significant person-to-person interaction, market penetration was rather shallow, and transaction costs were high.[5]

In many ways, today's microfinance industry seems eerily reminiscent of the early stages of the credit card market in the United States when each bank issued its own cards, developed its own exclusive network of internal and external agents, and invested in its own technologies to serve this new market. Like those banks of yesteryear, it is not unusual to see today's microfinance institutions resist collaboration or sharing of systems, even when the cost savings of doing so are likely to be significant. In the Uganda project this was manifested in the participating institutions' resistance to sharing RTS servers, their demand for customised connectors to link to their in-house MIS, their desire for uniquely designed and printed smart cards, and their apparent disinterest in developing a network of shared external agents within the Ugandan microfinance community.

What spurred the dramatic growth of financial services in the United States? The simple answer is a combination of new customer-focused products, new business models, and new enabling technologies. Term loans were replaced with credit lines that gave customers more power to decide why, when and how much to borrow. Face-to-face credit decisions gave way to massive credit card "drops". Banks developed strategies for managing and evaluating the risks of these "impersonal" credit decisions. Business models changed to allow cooperation and competition to co-exist as institutions built shared infrastructure to reach a growing customer base.[6] Banks shared infrastructure costs, including technology investments that were too expensive for any single player, while continuing to compete on differentiated services. Breaking down the walls between the banks in turn permitted the

---

[5]   Nocera, Joseph. A Piece of the Action New York: Simon & Schuster, 1994.

[6]   Initially, banks issued their own credit cards for use within exclusive merchant agent networks. This exclusive strategy, however, dampened any chance to get to scale as it was becoming unsustainable for the issuing banks. Bank of America finally broke this logjam when, under the leadership of Dee Hock, it developed the VISA model – a shared network owned now by more than 20,000 member banks from around the world. Within the VISA model, member banks agreed to establish a common architecture with standards adhered to by all members that would permit shared technologies to be developed that could settle financial transactions among a large number of merchants and banks.

building of shared technologies that enabled the industry to scale up while improving the services delivered to a rapidly growing customer base.[7]

To some extent the preference revealed in the pilot for customised rather than standardised solutions can be directly traced to the donors' doorsteps. A possible unintended consequence of some donors' strategy of funding "microfinance champions" and "innovation leaders" has been to foster a mindset among MFIs to go their own way, to value customised solutions over standardised solutions. Yet, the opportunities for standardisation continue to surface – be it to standardise financial and accounting practices, social impact measurements, or business processes and operations for capturing individual customer data.

As noted by others, individual rural finance projects should be pursued with a financial systems perspective. This implies that horizontal and vertical integration should be fostered within a decentralised rural financial system.[8] This kind of up, down, and sideways integration goes beyond standardisation to create cross-sector relationships under which the system will operate. In short, it means building an ecosystem, much like that in the natural sciences, where a web of interconnecting relationships exists. Implementing this vision is complex and costly. That is why industry and sector solutions, at least at the national level, are necessary, rather than institution-by-institution solutions.

Those who have a stake in the growth of microfinance should develop incentives that encourage integration and sharing, directing support into research and development of innovative technology solutions that encourage cooperation and collaboration rather than customisation. Other investments worthy of donor support are shared infrastructures that decrease per unit costs for all participants, start-up capital for entrepreneurial businesses that are willing to provide technology services, and grants for MFIs willing to participate in such ventures.

There is also a growing imperative to identify and remove legal and regulatory roadblocks that impede the expansion of telecommunication services into rural areas. These frustrate the capture of microfinance transactional information (including the credit histories of microentrepreneurs) and limit the sharing of financial information among central switches, credit reference bureaus and bank regulatory authorities.

---

[7] When credit cards first were issued, it was not unusual for bank authorisations to take as long as 5 minutes. With advances in technology, most credit card authorisations in the United States rarely exceed 7 seconds.

[8] Zeller, Manfred, Paving The Way Forward For Rural Finance: An International Conference On Best Practices, June 2003, "Models of Rural Finance Institutions," p. 29.

CHAPTER 12:

Can Credit Scoring Help Attract Profit-Minded Investors to Microcredit?[*]

Mark Schreiner

Director, Microfinance Risk Management
Senior Scholar, Center for Social Development, Washington University in St Louis, USA

Introduction

Microcredit is uncollateralised cash lending to the self-employed poor.[1] The central challenge of microcredit is to manage the risk that a client will behave "badly", whether by defaulting, paying late, or not returning for repeat loans. Indeed, microcredit was founded on two innovations that reduce the cost of managing these risks: joint-liability groups and skilled loan officers' careful evaluations of an individual applicant's business, chattel, and character.

Outside microcredit, wealthy countries developed a third risk-management innovation. Scoring relates the risk of behaving "badly" with indicators associated with the borrower (for example, type of business and debt/equity ratio) and the loan (for example, amount disbursed and number of installments). With sufficient data and care, scoring predicts risk more accurately and less expensively than non-automated methods. Moreover, scoring explicitly quantifies risk as a probability (for example, a 17 percent risk of reaching 30 days of arrears). Research shows that scoring increases not only profits but also the number of clients and the number of poor people who become clients.[2] In general, scoring improves risk management, leading to a cascade of benefits.[3]

---

[*] Acknowledgements: I am grateful for funding from KfW Entwicklungsbank and for comments from J.D. von Pischke, Valerie Karplus, and Hanns Martin Hagen.

[1] This Excludes collateralised housing loans, uncollateralised consumer loans to salaried employees, and loans tied to the purchase of specific goods or services.

[2] Fishelson-Holstine (2004); Berger, Frame, and Miller (2002); Gates, Perry, and Zorn (2002); Longhofer (2002); Frame, Padhi, and Woosley (2001); Frame, Srinivasan, and Woosley (2001); Martel et al. (1999).

[3] Schreiner (2002a); McCorkell (1999); Lewis (1990).

Unlike scoring in wealthy countries, microcredit scoring has a short track record. Pilots and proof-of-concept tests using historical data exist, but without documented long-term use in practice. This is unfortunate because the development of microcredit on a global scale has been limited by dependence on the scarce funding available from socially-minded donors. For two reasons, profit-minded investors have been biding their time. First, microcredit returns are too low to compensate for the risk of investing in a new industry. Second, there is uncertainty about exactly what the risks are in investing in microcredit.

Can scoring help attract profit-minded investors to microcredit? It can, by addressing the two barriers just mentioned. First, scoring can increase profits, especially for large microlenders who, because of competition, seek to grow and improve efficiency. Second, scoring can decrease uncertainty about the risk of microcredit as an investment because "traditional" bankers and investors understand lending based on scoring better than they understand lending based on joint-liability groups or detailed evaluations of individual applicants at the lower end of the market. Thus, if a microlender uses scoring, investors without special expertise in microcredit can more confidently evaluate investment risk. This is partly due to investors' familiarity with the scoring process and partly because scoring quantifies the risk of the microlender's main asset, which is its loan portfolio. Scoring also reduces uncertainty about investment risk by helping centralise decision-making, giving non-specialist investors more confidence that they can maintain effective control.

How Does Scoring Work in Microcredit?

Introductory questions are: how does scoring in general as well as scoring for microcredit differ from scoring for credit cards, home loans, and car loans in wealthy countries?

How Scoring Works

Scoring assigns points to indicators associated with a loan, adds up the points, and then links the points with a probability of going "bad". Figure 1 is a simple hypothetical scorecard for the risk that a loan, if approved, will at some point be 30 days in arrears. Here, more points mean more risk. For the indicator "sector of business", retail or wholesale trade receives 0 points, while services or manufacturing receive 3 points. Likewise, repeat applicants get 0 points, and first-time or new applicants get 2 points. Repeat applicants also get one point (up to 7) for each day in the longest spell of arrears in their previous loan. (New applicants and repeat clients with no previous arrears get 0 points.) Finally, applicants with a savings account get 0 points, while others get 4 points. For example, a new applicant in retail trade without a savings account would score $0 + 2 + 0 + 4 = 6$ points. A repeat applicant in manufacturing who had 4 days of arrears in the previous loan and who has a savings account would score $3 + 0 + 4 + 0 = 7$ points.

Indicator	Indicator values		Points
A. Sector of business	Retail or wholesale trade	Service or manufacturing	
	0	3	
B. Experience of applicant	Repeat	New	
	0	2	
C. Days in longest period of arrears in previous loan	New applicant or no arrears	Repeat applicant with arrears	
	0	1 per day, up to 7	
D. Savings account holder	Yes	No	
	0	4	
Total:			

Fig. 1. Simple scorecard for the risk of being 30 days in arrears at some point

The score itself is not the probability of going "bad", but it may be associated with such a probability. Using the sample scorecard calculation, Figure 2 associates a score of 6 points with a risk (that is, a probability of going "bad") of 9 percent. Likewise, a score of 7 points is associated with a risk of 12 percent.

Score	0	1	2	3	4	5	6	7	8	9	10	11	12	13	14	15	16	17
Risk (%)	2	3	3	4	5	7	9	12	14	17	22	24	27	31	35	40	45	52

Fig. 2. Association between scores and the risk of at some point being 30 days in arrears

Of course, risk describes uncertain future events. Like weather forecasts, scoring is accurate to the extent that the average realised risk for a group of similar loans is "close" to predicted risk. For the sample scorecard, about one in two loans with a score of 17 (risk 52 percent) should go "bad". Likewise, about one in 50 loans with a score of 0 (risk 2 percent) should go "bad".

How Are Scorecards Constructed?

Indicators and points are selected so that the score is highly correlated with "bad" behaviour and have "face validity" for users.

Scorecards vary in scope and source of information (Figure 3). In terms of scope, scorecards can be generic (made for multiple lenders) or tailor-made (custom-built for a specific lender). In terms of source of information, indicators and points can be derived based on judgment (expert opinion) or data (statistics).

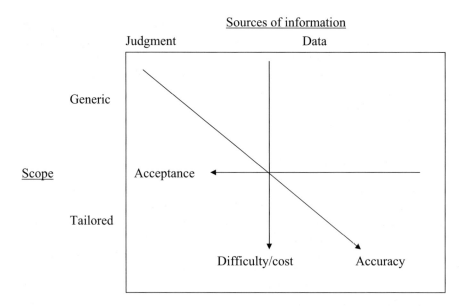

Fig. 3. Trade-offs among accuracy, acceptance, and cost/difficulty according to a scorecard's scope and sources of information

Tailor-made, data-based scorecards are the most accurate (Figure 3), but they are also the most difficult to construct.[4] Generic and/or judgmental scorecards are less accurate, but they require little (or no) data, are easier to build, may have a sufficient degree of accuracy,[5] and are more readily accepted by users, especially if the users help choose the indicators and points.

Only the largest microlenders who make loans to individuals[6] are in a position to benefit from tailor-made, data-based scorecards. Smaller microlenders could start with generic, data-based scorecards or even tailor-made, judgmental scorecards. At the same time, smaller microlenders can prepare for the future by initiating policies and processes to improve data quantity and quality. Appendix 1 presents guidelines in this regard.

Predictive accuracy matters, but it is not the only thing that matters. For example, many scoring projects in wealthy countries fail, not because the scorecard is

---

[4] There is no statistical law that dictates how many historical cases are needed, but a common (probably too liberal) rule-of-thumb is at least 500 "bads" and 500 "goods".

[5] Lovie and Lovie (1986); Kolesar and Showers (1985); Stillwell, Barron, and Edwards (1983); Dawes (1979); Wainer (1976).

[6] Scoring probably will not work for joint-liability groups or village banks. Groups are less "score-able" because they are like a diversified portfolio. Their indicators are difficult to collect and their arrears are more likely to arise from unpredictable social dynamics.

inaccurate, but because front-line workers did not embrace scoring, either because they did not know how to use it, because they feared it would change the status quo, or because they believed it would increase their workload or threaten their jobs.[7] Thus, scoring must be embedded seamlessly in processes, policies, and information systems that are easy-to-use and immediately and transparently beneficial to front-line workers. Success in scoring requires continuous training of and follow-up with those who use scoring.

How Do Microlenders Use Scoring?

The most common type of scoring in microcredit is pre-disbursement, using available information to predict repayment problems after disbursement. A loan officer gathers information on an individual borrower as usual, applying all customary screens (Figure 4). If the loan officer believes the application merits review by the credit committee, these data– along with any credit-bureau data and savings history – are entered into the information system to determine the risk of going "bad". If the credit committee rejects the case using traditional criteria, it is rejected, regardless of the score. If the credit committee conditionally approves the

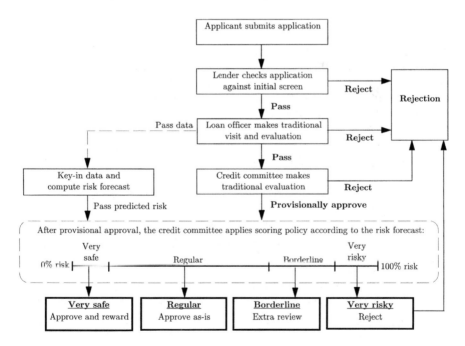

Fig. 4. Process of pre-disbursement scoring in microcredit

---

[7]   This fits the social theory of diffusion of technological innovation in Rogers (1983).

case using traditional criteria, it then makes a decision according to the value of the score. For example, it might reject "very risky" cases with a risk of 40 percent or more, send back for extra review "borderline" cases with a risk of 21–39 percent, waive fees to encourage loyalty for "very safe" cases with a risk of less than 5 percent and proceed to disbursement as usual for "regular" cases with a risk of 5–20 percent.

This approach to scoring for microcredit, in contrast to models commonly used in wealthy countries, does not save time by eliminating the loan officer's traditional, individualised evaluation (Schreiner, 2002a). Instead, scoring at this level adds a final hurdle, detecting some high-risk cases that slipped through standard screens. Such scoring cannot approve applications, but it can reject those that would otherwise have been approved, or flag applications for additional analysis and possible modifications to the loan contract. (Until further notice, the reader should assume the discussion is based on this approach.)

For three reasons, scoring does not replace loan officers and the "traditional" screening process. First, scoring for microcredit is less powerful than scoring for credit cards, home loans, and car loans in wealthy countries because there is less information about micro borrowers. For example, some countries lack credit bureaux, and if there are bureaux, many microcredit borrowers are not on the rolls. Furthermore, borrowers are subject to more risk from more varied sources: they are self-employed, poor, and live in a poor country. In many cases microcredit cannot fall back on collateral when loans go sour. Microenterprises cannot provide audited financial statements, nor can they be expected to fill out written applications without assistance. While scoring in wealthy countries can be used to approve applications based on 10–15 indicators from credit bureau reports and a few responses supplied by an applicant, scoring for microcredit must use 30–50 indicators gathered by a loan officer to attain a similar level of confidence.

Second, loan officers are thought to be needed to sniff out applicants with qualitative characteristics such as dishonesty that scoring might overlook. In wealthy countries, scoring detects such qualitative characteristics indirectly via previous arrears recorded in comprehensive credit bureau reports, but this is not yet feasible for microcredit. As information improves, scoring will receive more weight, and loan officers may become less judges-of-character and more enumerators-of-surveys. (This will reduce costs by allowing microlenders to hire less-qualified loan officers, shorten their apprenticeships, and keep them on-board longer before burning out.) It may turn out that qualitative factors are highly correlated with quantitative factors in scorecards, further simplifying the role of loan officers. However, no one currently knows how to quantify loan officers' "sixth sense", so the conservative course is to keep them.

Third, few microlenders store data on rejected applicants, which means that data-based scorecards can be derived only from approved applicants. But approved applicants differ from rejected applicants, partly in qualitative ways (such as dishonesty) that scoring cannot detect directly. Applying such a scorecard to applicants who have not passed the same qualitative screens will understate risk to some unknown extent, possibly leading to disaster. As noted above, if quantitative indicators turn out to be good proxies for qualitative indicators, the issue is moot. Therefore, the safe choice currently is to score only those applicants conditionally approved by traditional standards. Later, scoring can be experimentally walked back earlier in the evaluation process. Obviously, microlenders who want to do this should start storing data on rejected borrowers.

The approach advocated here is admittedly conservative and sometimes un-popular; many lenders (especially banks downscaling into microcredit) want to avoid costly individualised, qualitative evaluations by loan officers. Wishing that scoring could do all the work, however, does not make it so.

There is one documented case in which scoring—and only scoring—was used to downscale into microcredit (Rhyne 2001); it was a disaster. Backed by private investors, a consumer-finance company entered the Bolivian microcredit market in 1995 with an evaluation process based on a scorecard derived from experience with salaried employees in Chile. Scoring allowed low-cost, rapid evaluation, and initial growth was explosive. By 1998, however, inaccurate evaluations had led to high arrears and default and then bankruptcy, a textbook case of ignoring qualita-tive factors and blindly applying a scorecard in a context unlike the experience that generated the data it was based on.

What Are the Benefits and Costs of Scoring?

If scoring pre-disbursement does not replace traditional evaluation, what does it do? This section discusses benefits, costs, and how back-testing can estimate scor-ing's impacts even before roll-out.

Back-Testing

A strength of scoring is its "trialability" (Rogers 1983); it can be tried out in a low-cost, reversible way. Back-testing builds a scorecard using cases up to a cer-tain point in time and then applies it to later cases. Predicted risk is then compared with actual outcomes in the test period, showing how well scoring would have performed if it had been used.

Figure 5 shows results from a back-test for a Latin American microlender. Here, "bad" is defined as being in arrears on the last day of the month (the day when the lender reported to banking regulators). In the test period (January to August 2002), 36 percent of 8,549 cases were "bad" at some point.

Rejecting cases with risk in excess of the "very risky" threshold of 80 percent would lead to rejecting 1,259 "bads" and 295 "goods" (4.3 "bads" avoided per "good" lost). It also implies approving 5,137 "goods" and 1,858 "bads" (2.8 "goods" per "bad") with risk below the "very risky" threshold of 80 percent. All in all for the 8-month test period, scoring would have rejected 40 percent of "bads" (or 18% of all cases), and approved 95 percent of "goods".

| | | 'Very risky' threshold | | | | | |
Criteria	Formula	0	20	40	60	80	100
'Bads' avoided	A	3,117	2,967	2,591	2,020	1,259	0
'Goods' lost	B	5,432	3,904	2,223	1,056	295	0
'Bads' avoided per 'good' lost	A/B	0.6	0.8	1.2	1.9	4.3	#N/A
'Goods' approved	C	0	1,528	3,209	4,376	5,137	5,432
'Bads' approved	D	0	150	526	1,097	1,858	3,117
% 'bads' avoided	100*A/(A+D)	100	95	83	65	40	0
% 'goods' approved	100*C/(C+B)	0	28	59	81	95	100
% cases rejected	100*(A+B)/(C+A+D+B)	100	80	56	36	18	0

Note: 8549 cases, with 5432 (64%) observed 'goods' and 3117 (36%) observed 'bads'.

Fig. 5. Back-test for Latin American microlender, scorecard made with cases from 1993 up to December 2001, applied to cases from January to August 2002

The back-test also shows trade-offs for other "very risky" thresholds (such as 40 percent or 60 percent), showing managers the likely consequences of potential scoring policies before they are implemented. The back-test also provides the basic data required to estimate the impacts of scoring on profits and deal flow.

Given a "very risky" threshold of 80 percent, Figure 6 shows back-test estimates of changes in 30-day portfolio-at-risk. On average, scoring would have reduced portfolio-at-risk from 6.7 percent to 4.9 percent, a 27 percent reduction.

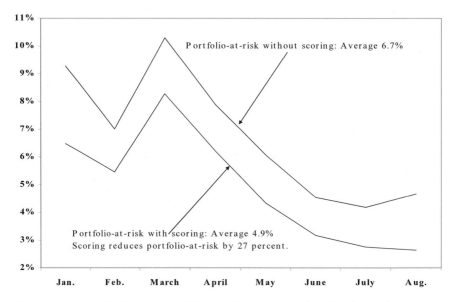

Fig. 6. Back-test of effects on portfolio-at-risk due to scoring with an 80-percent "very risky" threshold for a Latin American microlender; scorecard constructed with cases from 1993 to December 2001 and applied January to August 2002

Benefits of Adopting Scoring

Profits and Volume

As in the back-test example, the most immediate benefit of pre-disbursement scoring is better risk management: fewer high-risk loans are approved.[8] While this does not save time up-front in evaluation, it does save time for loan officers in collections after disbursement, as well as reducing write-offs and loan-loss provisions. With less time spent on collections, loan officers have more time to search for and evaluate new clients.

These gains from the pre-disbursement-scoring can increase profits and volume significantly. In the back-test in Figure 5, rejecting cases with risk above 80 percent would reduce "bads" by 40 percent. If loan officers spent two days per week on collections before scoring, they would save 6.4 hours per week (40 percent of two days). If loan officers also spent two days per week before scoring on marketing and evaluation, and if they used their new-found 6.4 hours as productively as before, they could increase evaluations by 40 percent. Netting out the 18 percent of cases rejected due to scoring (81 percent of them "bad") leaves a 40 percent decrease in "bads" and about a 22 percent increase in disbursements, a win-win for profits and outreach.

Scoring's quantitative impact on profit consists of decreased costs from approving fewer "bads" as well as increased costs from approving fewer "goods":

Change in profit = (Cost per "bad" x Number of "bads" avoided) –
(Benefit per "good" x Number of "goods" lost).

For the Latin American microlender in the back-test, the assumed cost of a "bad" is $100, and the assumed benefit of a "good" is $100.[9] Figure 5 shows that an 80 percent "very risky" threshold would successfully reject 1,259 "bads" and mistakenly reject 295 "goods", for a net impact of scoring on profit in 8 months of:

Change in profit = ($100 x 1,259) – ($100 x 295) = $96,400.

This gives scoring a pay-back period of less than half a year. Back-tests such as this one (and in Schreiner 2002a) are currently the best estimates available of scoring's impact on profit and volume. There appear to be no publicly available data on scoring impacts in practice, mostly because the first projects are still in their pilot stages.

---

[8]   The microlender can also give better service/lower prices to low-risk borrowers.

[9]   This is conservative; the cost of "bads" probably exceeds twice the benefit of "goods".

Scoring as a Teaching Tool

Especially for downscaling banks, scoring can be a teaching tool (Caire and Kossman 2003). Collecting data and tracking the resulting scores can help novice loan officers focus on key factors when analysing applications.

Furthermore, scoring policy is determined centrally, promoting consistency and reducing the effects of discrimination and prejudice by individual loan officers (Schreiner 2002a). Scoring also gives new investors greater control. Microcredit loan officers are known for their autonomy, acting like mobile mini-branches with implicit—and often widely varying—credit policies. By making corporate policy more explicit, scoring helps owners monitor loan officers and detect portfolios about to deteriorate. It is also possible to detect branches or loan officers who ignore scoring policy or forge data, approving a high proportion of high-risk loans and/or obtaining much worse results than their borrowers' scores would indicate.

Quantified Risk and a Culture of Rational Decision-Making

Scoring quantifies risk explicitly as a probability, improving decision-making rather than simply automating it. For example, back-testing lets managers set scoring policy bands based on actual trade-offs among profits and deal flow. After tasting rational decision-making, managers are more likely to resist seat-of-the-pants judgments for other decisions, seeking instead new ways to get more information. In short, scoring entices managers into a culture of explicit, data-based decision-making.

Microlenders' data bases are useful not only for predicting repayment risk but also for promoting "mass customisation" of products and services (segmentation) and strengthening client loyalty (drop-out analysis).[10] As rational decision-making takes hold, large microlenders will purposely gather data (rather than accumulating it only as a by-product of loan evaluations) and set up in-house data-analysis departments to inform decisions on a continuous basis. In-house analysis need not be complex, and quick turn-around between hypotheses and results will let managers go beyond the bounds of the reports that the information system currently produces, encouraging them to design reports that provide information to address specific business questions.

Costs of Adopting Scoring

Beyond human resources, the most obvious cost/risk is that scoring might not predict accurately. After all, scoring for microcredit has plenty of skeptics, no documented successes, and one documented failure. Not all scorecards work, and scoring—even if used conservatively as recommended here—may still overstate

---

[10] Schreiner and Sherraden (2005); Schreiner (2003, 2002c, and 2002d); Berry and Linoff (2000).

risk and reject many "good" applicants. This risk can be eliminated by back-testing, and no scorecard should be used without thorough back-testing.

Scoring quantifies how a microlender performs its central business task, which is evaluating risk. As with any large-scale, long-term change, it must be managed carefully and intentionally. Adopting scoring is not a project but a process, requiring commitment as well as funding and a high-level champion. The key challenge is not predictive accuracy but rather commitment to training and follow-up.

Training helps break down employee resistance to change. To get commitment from branch managers, loan officers, and data-input operators require training so that they know how scoring works, how to use it, and its immediate benefits. After years as the stars, loan officers in particular cannot be expected to believe that a computer can improve on—and sometimes reverse—their judgments. They require repeated demonstrations of predictive power in back-tests and in live tests with their own loans. A useful exercise is to show how scoring would have affected their previous month's bonus.

At first, loan officers and branch managers will seize any excuse to avoid using scoring. There are several ways to address this. First, upper management must establish a simple scoring policy, document it in a "Scoring Policy Manual", and teach it to front-line workers. Second, the scoring software must be impeccable, without clunky interfaces, misspelled words, or mysterious error messages. Any visible mistake or inconvenience—however trivial—will allow users to tell themselves that the invisible inner workings cannot be trusted. Third, users will want to tinker with scoring by adding indicators, adjusting points, or making (usually cosmetic) modifications to the software. Making these changes helps users take ownership and regain a feeling of control. Fourth, upper management must closely monitor overrides and track, by branch and loan officer, deviations between predicted and realised risk, which probably reflect careless (or deliberately false) data collection. Fifth, management must minimise the impression that scoring creates extra work. For example, do not ask loan officers to collect indicators that they do not already collect until after scoring is accepted. Also, integrate scoring seamlessly in the existing evaluation process and information system so that the same data are not entered twice or that scoring reports are compiled manually.

On a technical level, scoring is intensely mathematical: data processing requires software and adjustments to the information system. Furthermore, the scoring software draws on the microlender's computerised data base. All this tends to give the impression, at least initially, that scoring is about information technology when in fact it is about evaluating risk. Technology makes it easier for users to accept scoring and use it properly. The trick is not to get lost in the technology and not to forget the people and the process (Rogers, 1983).

Scoring has potential public relations costs. On the surface, scoring looks inhuman, consciously trading off one person's cost versus another's benefit, statistically judging a particular individual based on his or her similarity with others, and explicitly revealing (via back-testing) that some "good" applicants are mistakenly rejected. However, all lenders make these trade-offs, all evaluation methods compare individuals, and some "goods" are always mistakenly rejected. Scoring brings these facts into the open and thus makes them more susceptible to improvement, whereas traditional approaches may easily ignore them.

Scoring may raise legal issues. Using indicators such as age, gender, race/ethnicity, language, or marital status may be illegal. Microlenders must keep some data on their clients confidential in accordance with local consumer-protection laws—with or without scoring.

All in all, adopting scoring is a complex and costly process. Success hinges not on software or on statistics but on careful change management, persistent training, and consistent follow-up over the long-term. While the technical tools can be tested and tuned until they work perfectly, the human aspects are more delicate: mistakes the first time around make front-line workers even more skeptical about the merits of scoring.

Microlenders adopting scoring must view it as somehow different from other change processes. Scoring improves risk management, but it is not magic. No lender should bet the bank on any scorecard without careful back-testing and without a plan for training front-line staff.

Beyond Pre-disbursement Scoring

As described above, individual microlenders usually adopt pre-disbursement scoring first. Microlenders can also benefit from other types of scoring that predict the risk of other uncertain future events.

Pre-visit Scoring

Before the loan officer visits a new applicant in the field, data from the written application can be used to predict the risk of eventual rejection. Visits to clients who are almost certain to be rejected might be cancelled (saving the loan officer's time), or loan officers could be alerted to specific "risky" characteristics based on pre-disbursement scoring data already on hand that could be double-checked during the visit. Pre-visit scoring requires storing data on rejected applicants, recording precise reasons for rejections, and making sure that written applications collect as much information as is feasible and reliable before the visit.

Loyalty Scoring

Before a borrower pays off a current loan, information gathered up to that point can be used to predict the risk of the borrower's not returning for a repeat loan (drop-out). Figure 7 is a policy matrix combining loyalty scoring with traditional rules and pre-disbursement scoring to target (costly) loyalty incentives where they

		Disqualified under traditional rules	Qualified under traditional rules	
			High pre-disbursement risk	Low pre-disbursement risk
Drop-out risk	Low	"Kick-outs" No incentives	"Loyalists" No incentives	
	High		"Unsafe waverers" No incentives	"Safe waverers" Incentives offered

Fig. 7. Sample policy matrix for loyalty incentives

matter most by retaining desirable clients who are at-risk of dropping out. Examples of incentives include a field visit to encourage taking another loan, reduced application fees, access to a line of credit, or explicit recognition as a valued client. No incentives are offered to "kick-outs", that is, clients whose current repayment problems preclude a repeat loan. Among clients who qualify to for repeat loans, "loyalists" have low drop-out risk and regardless of pre-disbursement risk do not warrant loyalty incentives. Nor are incentives offered to "unsafe waverers" who are high risk as both drop-outs and problematic payers. Loyalty incentives are targeted only at desirable "safe waverers" who have a low risk of repayment problems but a high risk of drop-out.

Collections Scoring

Given a loan x days in arrears, information up to that point can be used to predict the risk of reaching y days. Together with value-at-risk (amount outstanding), collections scoring can guide collections efforts. Figure 8 shows a simple example. Cases with high risk and high value-at-risk receive immediate visits with strong messages. Cases with low risk and low value-at-risk are left alone for a few days in the hope that they cure themselves. All other cases receive immediate visits with gentle persuasion.

Collections scoring is a simple extension of pre-disbursement scoring. The only new information available after disbursement is arrears on the loan. If arrears have not yet been a problem, the collections score will be highly correlated with the pre-disbursement score. If arrears have occurred, scoring is hardly needed to indicate that the current spell of arrears has a high risk of becoming problematic. A pre-disbursement scorecard can easily serve double-duty as a collections scorecard, making a separate collections scorecard unnecessary.

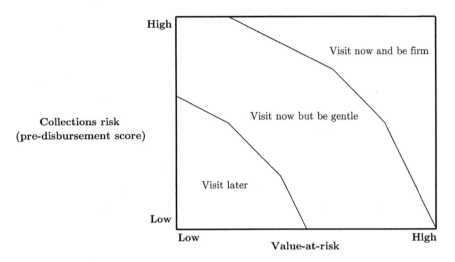

Fig. 8. Policy matrix for collections efforts

Loan-Size or Loan-Term Scoring

Some microlenders have bought scorecards that claim not to predict what loan size or term-to-maturity will be but rather what they should be. The promise of avoiding the work of setting size and term is tantalising, but such scorecards are problematic and cannot be back-tested. They can work only if the scorecard builder knows more than the microlender does about setting size and term, because such scorecards cannot be based on the microlender's data.[11] This is because size and term in the past were determined by the microlender's qualitative assessment of risk (low-risk applications were approved for larger amounts and longer terms) and by the size and term requested by the applicant. Setting size and term with scoring extrapolates from that context to a different one. If large, long loans in the past went to clients with exceptionally low-risk qualitative characteristics, then scoring could mistakenly approve larger and longer loans to borrowers whose quantified characteristics appear equivalent but who are riskier in qualitative terms. (If scoring sets a maximum cap on size and term—rather than increasing it—then all that is needed is a simple policy matrix applied to pre-disbursement scores.) Scoring to set size and term is like applying a scorecard derived from data on approved applicants who passed a qualitative screen to applicants who have not passed through a qualitative screen: it may or may not work, and cannot be back-tested.

---

[11]   That is, unless the lender ran an experiment to generate data for this type of scoring.

Net-Present-Value Scoring

Available information is used to predict, for a given client from now on, dollar-years borrowed, number of loans, number and length of periods in arrears, risk of default, dollar-years of savings, and the use of other services from the microlender. Then detailed data are collected from the microlender on revenue per dollar-year borrowed and the costs of evaluating and disbursing loans, collecting from clients in arrears, and provisioning for loan losses. Measuring the client's predicted usage against the microlender's revenues and costs produces an estimate of the client's net present value to the microlender. This enables microlenders to consider explicitly the long-term bottom line in every decision related to a client. While this type of scoring is complex and has not yet been tried in microcredit, it is used routinely by banks in wealthy countries. Schreiner (2002e) takes a first step in this direction.

Who Adopts Scoring for Microcredit and Why?

Scoring in microcredit has been driven by networks, in particular ACCION (in Bolivia, Ecuador, and Peru) and Women's World Banking (in Colombia and the Dominican Republic). Some competitors of these networks in Bolivia, Colombia, and Peru have also started to use scoring. Finally, scoring is being adopted by some Central and Eastern European banks that are downscaling into small-business lending (Caire 2004).

Microcredit scoring is still in its infancy. Progress is slow, perhaps because it seems so different from the two qualitative risk-management innovations that spawned microcredit. As explained by Everett Rogers in his 1983 *Diffusion of Innovations* (p. 4), "An important factor affecting the adoption rate of any innovation is its compatibility with the values, beliefs, and past experiences of a social system." While scoring has little compatibility with microcredit experience, it is highly compatible with traditional banking. This is why downscaling banks make scoring a central part of their approach while only a handful of microlenders are testing scoring, and that only on a small scale. Lacking the sunk investment that characterises traditional microcredit innovations, downscaling banks are more open to scoring.

Furthermore, while a strength of scoring is its "trialability" via back-testing and its ability to quantify its impact on profit and outreach, an innovation is rarely evaluated "on the basis of scientific studies of its consequences, although such objective evaluations are not entirely irrelevant, especially to the very first individuals who adopt....The heart of the diffusion process is modeling and imitation by potential adopters or their network partners who have adopted previously" (Rogers 1983, p. 18).

Experience indicates that the networks driving scoring in microcredit fit the theory; they are imitating banks that adopted earlier in wealthy countries after they perfect scoring with their initial adopters. They plan to replicate the process throughout their networks.

The networks have several features that encouraged them to launch pilot efforts. First, networks offer economies of scale; they can spread the costs of research and development over many affiliates and multiply the benefits when scoring has proved it value. Second, the networks have a reputation for successful innovation, increasing the likelihood that their affiliates would agree to be test cases. Third, the networks have the time and resources to plan strategically, and they are plugged into the wider microcredit community that has been debating scoring. They also have the financial resources to set up scoring systems. Fourth, the networks have to make themselves valuable to their affiliates, a perhaps surprisingly difficult goal that scoring serves well. Fifth, the networks compete for status in the larger microfinance community, pushing them to stay one step ahead.

Competition motivated early-adopting affiliates, which were all large, profitable microlenders in Latin America with effective traditional systems. They were motivated to produce greater profits and volume, to capture new markets, to preempt competitors, and to increase loan officer productivity.

The first few second-generation adopters were also driven by competition. These lenders in Bolivia, Colombia, and Peru are not affiliates of international networks. They adopted scoring largely because they did not want to fall behind their competitors, which are the affiliates of ACCION or of Women's World Banking that use scoring. Competition among banks forced to downscale, among networks seeking prestige, and among microlenders in national markets has spurred adoption.

Prime candidates for adopting scoring include the German firm IPC and the affiliates of its sister ProCredit Network, and the international credit union movements such as WOCCU and Desjardins. These networks have many affiliates who lend to individuals, a reputation for high quality technical assistance, and a focus on growth and profitability. Countries with large public banks that make microloans (such as India or China) may also test scoring. And finally, of course, most commercial banks trying to downscale into microcredit are likely to include scoring as part of their strategy.

Conclusion: Scoring, Investors, and Donor Opportunities

As a type of finance, microcredit must manage risk. To a given degree of accuracy, scoring quantifies the risk that clients will behave "badly". Lenders in wealthy countries routinely use scoring to reduce arrears and default, to target collections, to attract and keep "good" clients, and to increase profit and deal flow.

Can scoring help attract profit-minded investors to microcredit? Yes, and not only by increasing profits. By quantifying portfolio risk and rationalising decision-making, scoring reduces uncertainty about the risk of microcredit as an investment. Furthermore, scoring is simpler, easier to learn, and more familiar for traditional bankers and investors than microcredit's joint-liability groups or detailed evaluations of individuals. Scoring also gives top management greater control over branches and loan officers, increasing investors' confidence in their ability to control a microlender. Likewise, covenants that benchmark current and future portfolio performance to scoring-based measures can assure investors that a microcredit portfolio will not suddenly sour without a chance for a pre-emptive response. By quantifying risk in different segments of the loan portfolio, scoring may also eventually open the door to securitisation, facilitating liquidity management and thus investment. In sum, scoring makes microcredit less an art and more a science, or at least moves the art from the loan officers in the field to top management. This increases profits and volume while also reducing some of the institutional and governance barriers to investment.

Who Will Adopt Scoring?

Scoring is most attractive to large, profitable microlenders who can spread the costs and reap the benefits of adoption over many clients and many years. Growth requires simplification and specialisation until lower grade staff can do most tasks routinely: scoring allows microlenders to hire less-qualified loan officers trained in shorter apprenticeships. Thus, scoring helps large microlenders and feeds their growth. Large microlenders—especially if they face competition or want to pre-empt it—have the strongest incentives to adopt scoring and to use tailor-made, data-based scorecards. And investors are likely to engage large microlenders first.

Banks downscaling into microcredit or small-business lending may also combine scoring with qualitative, microcredit-specific techniques. This is especially the case for banks that already use scoring. Banks will still need loan officers and qualitative methods for some time, and their lack of historical data will force them to start with generic and/or judgmental scorecards. Basel II requires regulated microlenders to grade loans by risk, which also creates an incentive to use scoring.

Mid-size microlenders (5,000 to 15,000 borrowers) that lend to individuals and that seek to grow, become regulated, and attract private capital may adopt scoring as a major innovation. This means improving current lending processes and information systems, as well as data quality, and incorporating credit histories into their information systems. Successful adoption of scoring and graduation to tailor-made, data-based scorecards might help propel some microlenders from goodness to greatness.

Finally, scoring is less attractive to small, not-for-profit microlenders that work with joint-liability groups, that provide non-financial services, and/or that lack an impetus to grow and become profitable.[12] Most of these microlenders already have processes that are satisfactory for them. They also tend to resist making explicit trade-offs between risk and outreach in the short term that scoring can mitigate in the long term.

---

[12] They may, however, use scorecards to identify poor clients (Schreiner et al. 2004).

What Can Donors Do?

Scoring is a profitable proposition for large, established microlenders. Lenders in wealthy countries have adopted scoring on their own initiative and microlenders will do the same without help from donors or government. But if this were the whole story this donor-funded paper would be redundant, except to tell donors to focus elsewhere.

However, there are three possible short-term roles for donors. The first is to sponsor a few "proof-of-concept" projects, information about what scoring is and training about how it works. While education and demonstration would speed diffusion, they are not strictly necessary; scoring works, so microlenders will eventually adopt it on their own.

A second role is to sponsor the design of a standardised software "scoring module". With adjustments to parameters and other minimal customisation, this scoring module could be linked to microlenders' information systems to implement generic, tailor-made, judgmental, and/or data-based scorecards (Data Mining Group 2004; Schreiner 2002b). This would accelerate adoption by reducing start-up costs and improving user-friendliness.

The third possible role for donors is support for credit bureaux. Accurate scoring rests on good data; without credit bureaux, data are limited to what a microlender can collect from new borrowers or accumulate from repeat borrowers. Furthermore, credit bureaux produce a public good, so each lender wants others to contribute their data and pay for set-up costs without contributing themselves. Donors might pay initial costs and support governments in developing laws to require participation. Setting up a credit bureau is more a matter of replication than of innovation. There are many examples around the world that address the challenges of uniquely identifying people, safeguarding privacy, and managing information.[13]

Conclusion

Scoring helps attract profit-minded investors to microcredit by increasing profits and by decreasing uncertainty about the risk of investing in microcredit. Scoring is a proven technique, and microlenders need not invent, only adapt. At the same time, scoring is less powerful in microcredit in poor countries than it is in retail lending in wealthy countries. It will not single-handedly open the floodgates of private investment, nor will it replace loan officers or joint-liability groups. For large, established microlenders, however, scoring will become routine.

---

[13] Luoto, McIntosh, and Wydick (2004); Miller (2003); Staten (2001); Guillamón, Murphy, and Luna (2000); Jappelli and Pagano (1999).

References

Berger, Allen N.; W. Scott Frame; and Nathan H. Miller. (2002) "Credit Scoring and the Availability, Price, and Risk of Small-Business Credit", Federal Reserve Bank of Atlanta Working Paper No. 2002–06, http://www.frbatlanta. org/filelegacydocs/wp0206.pdf

Berry, Michael J.A.; and Gordon Linoff. (2000) *Mastering Data Mining: The Art and Science of Customer Relationship Management*, New York: John Wiley and Sons, ISBN 0–471–33123–6.

Caire, Dean. (2004) "Building Credit Scorecards for Small Business Lending in Developing Markets", Bannock Consulting, http://www.microfinance.com/ English/Papers/Scoring_SMEs_Hybrid.pdf

Caire, Dean; and Robert S. Kossman. (2002) "Credit Scoring: Is It Right for Your Bank?", Bannock Consulting, http://www.microfinance.com/English/Papers/ Scoring_For_Your_Bank.pdf

Data Mining Group. (2004) "Predictive Model Markup Language", http://source-forge.net/projects/pmml

Dawes, Robyn M. (1979) "The Robust Beauty of Improper Linear Models in Decision Making", *American Psychologist*, Vol. 34, No. 7, pp. 571–582.

Fishelson-Holstine, Hollis (2004) "The Role of Credit Scoring in Increasing Homeownership for Underserved Populations", paper for "Building Assets, Building Credit: A Symposium on Improving Financial Services in Low-Income Communities", Joint Center for Housing Studies, Harvard University, http://www.jchs.harvard.edu/publications/finance/babc/babc_04-12.pdf

Frame, W. Scott; Michael Padhi; and Lynn Woosley. (2001) "The Effect of Credit Scoring on Small Business Lending in Low- and Moderate-Income Areas", Federal Reserve Bank of Atlanta Working Paper No. 2001–6, http://www. frbatlanta.org/filelegacydocs/wp0106.pdf

Frame, W. Scott; Aruna Srinivasan; and Lynn Woosley. (2001) "The Effect of Credit Scoring on Small-Business Lending", *Journal of Money, Credit, and Banking*, Vol. 33, No. 3, pp. 813–825.

Gates, Susan Wharton; Vanessa Gail Perry; and Peter M. Zorn. (2002) "Automated Underwriting in Mortgage Lending: Good News for the Underserved?" *Housing Policy Debate*, Vol. 13, No. 2, pp. 369–391.

Guillamón, Bernardo; Kevin X. Murphy; and Saúl Abréu Luna. (2000) "Risk mitigation as a cost-effective microfinance strategy: A Case Study of the IDB-Peru Global Microenterprise Credit Program", Inter-American Development Bank, www.iadb.org/mif/v2/files/RiskMitigation.doc

Jappelli, Tullio; and Marco Pagano. (1999) "Information Sharing in Credit Markets: International Evidence", Inter-American Development Bank Working Paper No. R–371, http://www.iadb.org/res/publications/pubfiles/pubR-371.pdf

Kolesar, Peter; and Janet L. Showers. (1985) "A Robust Credit Screening Model Using Categorical Data", *Management Science*, Vol. 31, No. 2, pp. 123–133.

Lewis, Edward M. (1990) *An Introduction to Credit Scoring*, San Rafael, CA: Athena Press, LIC# 90–92258, ISBN 99–956–4223–9.

Longhofer, Stanley D. (2002) "Statement of Stanley D. Longhofer", Perspectives on Credit Scoring and Fair Mortgage Lending, Final Installment, Federal Reserve Bank of Saint Louis, http://www.stlouisfed.org/community/assets/pdf/installment5.pdf

Lovie, A.D.; and P. Lovie. (1986) "The Flat Maximum Effect and Linear Scoring Models for Prediction", *Journal of Forecasting*, Vol. 5, pp. 159–168.

Luoto, Jill; Craig McIntosh; and Bruce Wydick. (2004) "Credit-Information Systems in Less-Developed Countries: Recent History and a Test", University of California at Berkeley, http://are.berkeley.edu/courses/DEVELWORK/papers/Luoto.pdf

Martell, Javier; Paul Panichelli; Rich Strauch; and Sally Taylor-Shoff. (1999) "The Effectiveness of Scoring on Low-to-Moderate-Income and High-Minority Area Populations", San Rafael, CA: Fair, Isaac Company.

McCorkell, Peter. (1999) "Credit Scoring 101", Presentation at a Federal Trade Commission Public Forum on "The Consumer and Credit Scoring", www.ftc.gov/bcp/creditscoring

Miller, Margaret. (2003) *Credit Reporting Systems and the International Economy*, Cambridge, MA: MIT Press, ISBN 0–262–13422–5.

Rhyne, Elisabeth. (2001) *Mainstreaming Microfinance: How Lending to the Poor Began, Grew, and Came of Age in Bolivia*, Bloomfield, CT: Kumarian, ISBN 1–56549–127–0.

Rogers, Everett M. (1983) *Diffusion of Innovations, Third Edition*, New York: Free Press, ISBN 0–02–926650–5.

Schreiner, Mark. (2002a) "Scoring: The Next Breakthrough in Microfinance?" Consultative Group to Assist the Poorest Occasional Paper No. 7, Washington, D.C., http://www.cgap.org/html/p-occasional-papers07.html

Schreiner, Mark. (2002b) "Guía Técnica del Sistema de Scoring del Riesgo de Créditos", Saint Louis, MO: Microfinance Risk Management.

Schreiner, Mark. (2002c) "Who Drops Out of Microfinance Programs? A Segmentation Analysis for WWB/Cali", report to Women's World Banking.

Schreiner, Mark. (2002d) "Sales Growth Among Clients of WWB/Cali", report to Women's World Banking.

Schreiner, Mark. (2002e) "What Clients are Profitable at WWB/Cali?", report to Women's World Banking.

Schreiner, Mark. (2003) "Scoring Drop-Out at a Microlender in Bolivia", *Savings and Development*, Vol. 27, No. 2, pp. 101–118.

Schreiner, Mark; Michal Matul; Ewa Pawlak; and Sean Kline. (2004) "The Power of Prizma's Poverty Scorecard: Lessons for Microfinance", http://www. microfinance.com/English/Abstracts/Scoring_Poverty_in_BiH.htm

Schreiner, Mark; and Michael Sherraden. (2005) "Drop-out from Individual Development Accounts: Prediction and Prevention", Center for Social Development, Washington University in Saint Louis, http://www.microfinance. com/English/Papers/IDAs_Drop_Out.pdf

Staten, Michael E. (2001) "The Value of Comprehensive Credit Reports: Lessons from the U.S. Experience", paper presented at the World Bank conference on "Profiting from Small Business Lending", April 2–3, Washington, D.C., www.worldbank.org/wbi/banking/creditscoring/

Stillwell, William G.; F. Hutton Barron; and Ward Edwards. (1983) "Evaluating Credit Applications: A Validation of Multi-attribute Utility Weight Elicitation Techniques", *Organizational Behavior and Human Performance*, Vol. 32, pp. 87–108.

Wainer, Howard. (1976) "Estimating Coefficients in Linear Models: It Don't Make No Nevermind", *Psychological Bulletin*, Vol. 83, pp. 213–217.

Appendix 1: Collecting Data for Scoring in the Future

Most microlenders do not yet have adequate data to support tailor-made, data-based scorecards. With growth and planning, they can accumulate the necessary data, perhaps using judgmental, tailor-made scorecards. Improving data quality and quantity is unglamorous work, but successful scoring depends on it. This appendix offers some guidelines drawn from Schreiner (2002a).

Most microlenders who make individual loans already collect data on most of the indicators listed below. If the indicators are recorded accurately for a sufficient number of cases, it should be possible to construct a tailor-made, data-based scorecard.

In general, the more indicators collected, the greater the accuracy. Microlenders that plan to use scoring should start to record in electronic form at least credit bureau data, quantified measures of loan officers' subjective judgments, and indicators of household demographics and assets.

Credit Bureau Data

- Arrears in current and paid-off loans
- Amounts owed to current creditors
- Number of inquiries in past year
- Identity of current and former creditors

- Disbursement dates of current loans and dates paid off of paid-off loans

- Amounts disbursed for current and paid-off loans

- Amount of monthly installments for current and paid-off loans

- Maximum line of credit with current and former creditors

Quantification of Loan Officers' Subjective Judgments

Loan officers record their subjective impressions of applicants on a five-point scale (far below-average, below-average, average, above-average, or far above-average).

- Overall credit risk

- Honesty and transparency of responses

- Quality of references

- Entrepreneurial skill and determination to succeed

- Prospects for line/type of business

- Variability and seasonality of cash flows

- Extent of recent investment in the home and business

- Grasp of the rules in the loan contract

- Quality of family relationships and informal support networks

Applicant Demographics

- Year of birth

- Gender

- Marital status (married, cohabiting, single/never-married/never-cohabited, divorced/separated/no-longer-cohabiting, widowed)

- Year of most recent change in marital status

- Last grade completed in school

- Number of household members (including applicant) age 18 or older

- Number of household members age 17 or younger

- Number of household members with salaried employment

- Number of enterprises run by household members

Contact Information

- Phone number to contact at home
  - Is it a neighbour's phone?
  - Is it a cell phone?
- Phone number to contact at the business
  - Is it a neighbour's phone?
  - Is it a cell phone?
  - Is it different from the phone number to contact at home?
- E-mail address

Household Assets

- Home tenure (owner, renter, other)
- Year took up current residence
- Number of rooms (excluding bathroom and kitchen)
- Hectares of non-homestead land owned
- Housing materials (context-specific)
  - Roof
  - Floor
- Household services
  - Electricity connection
  - Source of drinking water (pipe/well/other)
  - Fuel used for cooking (gas/electricity/wood)
  - Toilet (latrine/indoor with piped water/indoor with bucketed water/other)
- Vehicles (working)
  - Automobile, tractor, truck, or bus
  - Motorcycle
  - Bicycle
- Appliances (working, context-specific)
  - Refrigerator
  - Colour television
  - Washing machine (clothes)

- Formal savings account
  - ○ Date opened
  - ○ Passbook and/or time deposit
- Frequency of receipt of remittances

Business "Demographics"

- Sector (manufacturing, services, trade, agriculture, other)
- Specific type of business (construct a list of 30–50 context-specific)
- Year started
- Formalisation
- Tenure status of place of business (owned, rented, other)
- Person-months of full-time-equivalent workers per year
  - ○ Applicant
  - ○ Family members (excluding applicant)
  - ○ Non-family members

Business Financial Flows (Monthly)

- Sales
- Expenses
- Installments on other debts (business and household)

Business Financial Stocks

- Cash and savings-account balances
- Inventory
- Fixed assets
- Debts
  - ○ Formal
  - ○ Informal

Repayment Record for Each Scheduled Installment

- Date due
- Date paid-off

Aspects of the Loan Contract

- Date application submitted
- Date loan disbursed
- Date paid-off
- Amount disbursed
- Amount of average installment
- Number of installments
- Frequency of installments
- Refinanced status
- Type of guarantee
- Value of guarantee
- Identity of cosigner

Identity of the Lender

- Branch
- Loan officer

CHAPTER 13:

Credit Scoring: Why Scepticism Is Justified

Christoph Freytag

Managing Director, IPC GmbH

Providing loans to micro and small businesses has been at the heart of IPC's activities for more than 20 years. In 2005, ProCredit Banks in Eastern Europe, Africa and Latin America disbursed more than 60,000 business loans per month. The ProCredit Banks achieved a return on equity of 15% in 2005.

IPC also advises private commercial partner banks on behalf of international financial institutions (IFIs) in "downscaling" projects, which are designed to build capacity in MSE (micro and small enterprise) lending. These banks disburse 75,000 MSE loans per month. An indicator of the profitability of the partner banks in the downscaling projects is that only about 15% of their combined MSE loan portfolio is being funded by IFIs. The remaining 85% is financed with resources these banks have mobilised in their domestic markets.

The levels of profitability implied by these figures are being achieved because the lending methodology – or "credit technology" – which the banks use is efficient and keeps credit risk under control. A recent in-depth vintage analysis of bad loans within the ProCredit Group revealed that only 0.5% of all loans disbursed were not recovered. From this analysis, we also learned – once again – that in the vast majority of cases, loan defaults are triggered not by the borrower's "individual" inability to repay the amount outstanding, but rather by an unwillingness to repay or by an inability to fulfil payment obligations brought about by events such as crises, natural catastrophes, civil unrest or fraud. Another type of risk – "operational risk" – that can contribute to loan delinquency is a lack of institutional discipline, which in most cases is a result of insufficient management attention, specifically on the part of middle management staff.

Credit scoring will not protect lenders against these risks. That is something that only conscientious, well-qualified employees can do. Accordingly, IPC and the ProCredit Group are investing on an increasing scale in staff and management training at all levels – as evidenced by the creation of training centres in the individual banks, regional middle management academies and a central academy for senior management training. We strongly believe that investments in people are of paramount importance in identifying and managing risk. Trying to "revolutionise" microfinance through credit scoring is an attempt to shift attention away from people and focus instead on systems and procedures.

It is easy to understand why, at first glance, credit scoring is appealing to microlenders. Scoring is generally applicable to mass-market lending products with a high degree of standardisation, including rather uniform terms and conditions, which are sold to clients whose incomes and financial behaviour patterns are usually stable and predictable. Scoring requires the lender to compile large databases containing information on "good" and "bad" borrowers as well as applicants whose loans have been rejected. Ideally, if scoring is to be effective in assessing risk, credit information should be easily obtainable and simple to verify. If these conditions with regard to the availability and quality of the underlying information have been met, scoring can result in higher efficiency, faster loan processing, less dependence on staff and consistent, explicit risk assessment, which in turn makes risk-based pricing feasible.

All of this makes scoring even more attractive for banks: They usually have large databases and strong IT support. Banks that serve corporate and retail customers are usually very centralised and, as a rule, their procedures are highly standardised. A traditional microfinance approach, however, requires decentralisation, which conventional bankers are afraid of. Credit scoring, a radically centralised and standardised loan approval system, therefore fits perfectly into the kind of corporate culture that is characteristic of large, mainstream banks.

A thorough analysis of the borrower's repayment capacity and his or her willingness to pay are at the heart of IPC's credit technology. This is due not only to reduce risk-related costs, but also to a fundamental desire to implement socially responsible lending practices. We must not forget that credit – a loan from the banker's point of view – is a debt for the borrower. Lending that leads to the over-indebtedness of clients must be avoided: especially for those who might have limited skills in financial planning and tend to overestimate their repayment capacity.

Credit scoring creates a temptation for the lender to take a different approach: By replacing the well-trained, expensive loan officer with a machine, costs amounting to at least 3-4% of the portfolio can easily be saved. The temptation is to allow higher losses in order to gain a larger market share and lending volume. Nobody today would deny that over-indebtedness of households due to aggressive credit card, consumer, car and mortgage lending is a social problem in Western markets. In most cases, the rapid expansion of these types of lending has been based on the use of scoring techniques, often in conjunction with nontransparent pricing practices and aggressive marketing. This has caused traditional lenders to be crowded out of traditional credit markets. In certain emerging and transition economies, similar trends can already be observed. In Turkey, for example, credit card and consumer debt increased by 800% between 2001 and 2004 and the NPL (nonperforming loan) level reached 9%. As Schreiner rightly notes in the preceding chapter, such practices can have – and indeed have had – a disastrous impact on microfinance markets, as is shown by the example of Bolivia.

It is clear that the aggressive use of credit scoring will have severe negative impacts in the long run and hinder the development of a healthy credit culture. One could argue that the answer is simply to fine-tune the scoring system by applying more rigid criteria. But even if this is done, the temptation inherent in credit scoring, as described above, will continue to exist as long as advocates of shareholder value continue to seek to maximise profits regardless of the social costs involved. It is interesting to note that a conservative lender, a major Austrian bank, has recently adopted a policy designed to facilitate micro-lending using a rather rigid scoring system. This system requires data from tax declarations and information on bank transactions, and automatically rejects businesses that have existed for less than two years.[1]

We do not believe that such approaches are in any way compatible with the development goals which microfinance pursues. Almost invariably, the more rigid the criteria and rules which are applied, the sooner a microfinance provider will end up lending in the "comfort zone", where lending staff can rely primarily on narrowly defined systems to assess creditworthiness, without having to assume responsibility for analysing borderline cases. As a consequence, a large number of low-income clients that would be able to repay loans tailored to their personal repayment capacity will be denied access to credit. In essence, microfinance is about building relationships between finance providers and clients among the low-income target group. Abandoning this type of relationship banking for the sake of potentially more efficient banking transactions will neither be beneficial for individual microfinance providers nor in terms of the sound development of microfinance markets. For all of these reasons, we cannot see why credit scoring would be a worthwhile activity for donors to support.

Schreiner and others do not advocate a complete shift from the traditional microfinance credit technology to credit scoring. Rather, credit scoring is seen as a tool which would supplement and refine the traditional credit technology by adding a "third voice" to the credit committee and making credit risk management more explicit and consistent. In principle, we agree. Learning from statistical evidence, drawing lessons from practical lending experience and implementing gradual improvements to the credit technology must be an ongoing process. Thus, credit scoring offers very little that is really new, given that the truly useful aspects of this approach are already being applied by a substantial number of microfinance providers in various parts of the world. A new buzzword is certainly not necessary in order to drive institutional development in microlending.

---

[1] This is in line with the bank's strategy, as expressed by its CEO, who wants to "select the cream of the cream of customers". See: "Expansionist where others fear to tread", interview with Raiffeisen International's Chairman Herbert Stepic, The Banker, Feb. 5, 2006.

Partnerships to Mobilise Savings and Manage Risk

Introduction to Part III

Two topics are presented in part III. While they may seem quite different, they have in common the management of risk where risks are relatively high and where transaction costs are also high, at least at early stages of development. Microinsurance and micropensions, at the bottom end of the market, is one member of this odd couple. At the top end of the market is structured finance and securitisation, the other part of this odd couple. In each case the motivation is to increase access at the bottom end of the pyramid. In each case the initiatives are innovative and complex, involve coordination by many different parties for successful execution, have the potential to serve very large numbers of clients, and create new structures with the capacity to achieve far-reaching developmental effects.

Stuart Rutherford in Chapter 14 explores the challenges of security in old age among the poor, and the ameliorating role that microfinance can play. His insights rely in part on "financial diaries" of poor people that he and his team have recorded over years of research in South Asia. This empirical basis makes it clear that poor people do want to save, but that facilitating formal institutions are not yet sufficiently in place to meet demand. A tremendous market for micropensions could be built, but many challenges must first be overcome. Rutherford describes these issues and lessons from attempts at institutional development, and suggests what might be done to create a market.

In Chapter 15 a team of authors describe the ins and outs of finance and old age in Sub-Saharan Africa. Demographic and other changes add a sense of urgency to the challenges of maintaining or improving safety nets as populations age. Unfortunately, low-income Africans rarely plan for old age. Very few attractive formal financial practices, instruments and institutions are close at hand for the majority, whether urban or rural, who live on a dollar or two a day. However, informal and non-financial activities provide support in emergencies, more young people are becoming aware of problems they are likely to face as they grow older, and incentives are strong.

In Chapter 16 Michael McCord explores risk management possibilities in low income insurance markets. He foresees a large potential market that will enable people of modest means to manage the risks they and their families face, offering greater security and protection against catastrophic risks. His scope includes health, accident and life coverage. His structure is based on coverage, premiums, delivery channels, terms and benefits. Examples from Ghana, Georgia, India, Mexico, the Philippines, Uganda and elsewhere are provided, offering lessons for further development and opportunities for development assistance.

Two chapters by KfW authors round out this book. Each deals with structured finance and securitisation as innovative means of overcoming barriers or features that constrain access to global capital markets. Harald Hüttenrauch and Claudia Schneider provide a road map for securitisation in Chapter 17, specifically targeting its application to microfinance. The mechanics of this relatively new tool are explained, and its complexity is sorted out. These aspects include explanation of the roles of all parties concerned plus legal and data requirements. Pioneering deals are described.

In the final chapter, Klaus Glaubitt, Hanns Martin Hagen, Johannes Feist, and Monika Beck discuss structured finance as a means of promoting microfinance, specifically through mechanisms that attract more private funds. Diversifying, broadening and deepening the supply of funds can be achieved by reducing barriers and constraints in capital markets. Construction of an enabling framework for securitisation and structured investment funds in emerging markets is essential for massive outreach. Regulatory issues are a critical factor in facilitating securitisation, while potential benefits reach far beyond specific deals because they create new structures with longer time horizons. The mechanics and advantages of structured investment funds are illustrated by the example of the European Fund for Southeast Europe, in which KfW has an important role.

CHAPTER 14:

Micropensions: Old Age Security for the Poor?

Stuart Rutherford

Chairman, *Safe*Save, and Senior Visiting Fellow, Institute for Development Policy and Management, University of Manchester, UK

How can microfinance be expanded to include approaches to the problems facing poor and very poor people in developing countries when they become too old to support themselves? Microfinance clients have long been signalling their demand for such services by doing their best to use current microfinance products, such as microcredit, in ways that create assets that can help protect them in old age. However, "micropensions" will not, at least at first, look like miniature versions of developed-country private pensions, because most would-be clients are not formally employed and do not "retire." The most promising platform for developing suitable products can be found in medium term "commitment savings" plans for the poor that are now growing in popularity and scale in a number of countries. This chapter describes the challenges that face the microfinance industry as it strives to scale up these financial instruments and to make them ever more appropriate for their users and potential users.

A Framework for Micropensions

Pensions are generally understood as a regular flow of receipts from retirement to death. They became common in the rich world as industrialisation advanced and formal employment replaced casual or self-employment as the main source of income for most people. Pensions are therefore coupled with the notion of "retirement." Rich-world pensions answer the question "what happens after I retire and stop earning?"

To the extent that formal employment has grown in the developing world – where microfinance has its main focus – employment-based and private pensions resemble those in advanced economies. Government and private sector formal employees are usually enrolled in retirement pension schemes, and some workers buy private annuities.

But in many developing countries formal employment is not the norm. Most poor people in villages and slums patch their livelihoods together from a mix of self-employment, casual employment, or low-grade formal employment – full-time, part-time or intermittent. To them, the idea of "retirement" is foreign. The question they raise about their old age is "what happens when I can no longer support myself?"

Two forms of pension provision can help them answer that question. The first is the public or "social" pension, where the state raises revenue (sometimes from general taxation, sometimes through dedicated contributions) and redistributes it to citizens when they reach a stipulated age in order to guarantee them a dignified life. Such schemes command huge public support from taxpayers (and pensioners), are virtually universal in the developed world, and are spreading to developing countries. And, the debate on how to fund them is fierce in both the developed and developing worlds.

The Case for Social Pensions ...

Some of what we know about pension use and impact on poor people comes from groups that lobby for social pensions. The NGO HelpAge International, for example, estimates that 80% of the old people in developing countries have no regular income and that 100 million old people live on less than a dollar a day. By 2050 the number of over-60s in the developing world may jump to 1.5 billion from 375 million today. As life expectancy rises, the accumulation of funds that will be needed to deal with pensions grows steadily greater. HelpAge has studied the impact of social pensions on health, longevity and child-care (many old people live in multi-generational households where grandparents care for the young). These surveys and case studies have been conducted in poor countries that have advanced social pensions provision, such as Brazil and South Africa. Research results make a good case that even low-value pensions can make a big difference to household welfare (Gorman 2004).

But these figures point in two directions. While they make a strong case for extending and improving social pensions, they raise doubt about whether state revenues will be able to manage such a massive task.

... and for Micropensions

So it looks as if there is plenty of room for *micropensions* – pensions for poor and very poor people. But formal employment and formal retirement are rare among this group. This requires a search for a broad understanding of the purpose of micropensions: to help poor and very poor people answer the question – "what happens when I can no longer support myself?"

Microfinance clients have long been signalling their demand for micropensions. Early microfinance was almost exclusively microcredit. Loans could be invested in microenterprises (as most lenders insisted) and some of the resulting businesses have contributed to income and asset growth and thus to improved security in old age. But many microcredit clients have sought more direct ways to invest in their futures. Todd (1996), for example, describes the lengths to which some women clients go to retain the capital value of successive yearly loans – repaying them from any available source while storing them in cash at home or with a money guard, or as livestock or as on-lending – until they had accumulated enough capital to buy a small piece of land that would offer them some security in their widowhood. Rutherford (2000) points out that saving and borrowing are simply alternative ways of converting saving capacity into usefully large lump sums, and that when poor people have restricted access to safe ways of "saving up" they will find ingenious ways of "saving down" (borrowing) to satisfy their most pressing money-management goals. As Todd's example shows, these cases include security in old age.

Micropension products will enable the poor to focus on managing money for old age. These products will consist principally of medium- to long-term saving schemes that produce capital for reinvestment in real, human, social or financial assets that can create a flow of income to support the non-working elderly. In some cases the reinvestment will be in real property for rental, or in the businesses or education of family members in exchange for future income or subsistence support. But, crucially, micropension products will also offer the option of rein-vestment in a financial asset that produces a flow of income: either interest in-come, or perhaps by the purchase of an annuity, which is the financial product that specialises in maximising income streams.

Microfinance and Micropensions

How far has microfinance travelled on the road to micropensions? At first glance not far – if in early 2005 you had typed "micropensions" into the search engines of microfinance initiatives such as CGAP or *MicroSave*, you would have found no answers.

Nevertheless, microfinance products are becoming more diverse and more widely available, and each improvement makes it easier for clients to use microfinance for old-age security. But as each new opportunity opens up, new challenges appear. The opportunities and challenges created by a small selection of microfinance products are summarised in Table 1.

Growing Old Poor

In Bangladesh, wives are customarily younger than their husbands, and women tend to live longer than men. Women must anticipate a long widowhood, a cause of much anxiety. When a panel of near-poor, poor and very poor men and women were asked how they thought they'd survive in old age and widowhood, answers came out in hesitant stages (Rutherford 2002). Many women felt obliged, first, to acknowledge that the matter lies in the hands of Allah. They would then say that their children (especially their sons) would care for them. But their faces showed

Table 1. Managing money for old age: the opportunities and challenges of a selection of current and future microfinance products (the products are listed in ascending order of their direct relevance to pension provision)

Products	Opportunities	Challenges

Microcredit	Clients can store loans and convert them to larger assets (like land) that can produce 'unearned' income for the aged.
	
	    Business investments strengthen household economies and create assets, and like social investments (e.g. in health, education, social links) they strengthen a household's capacity to care for its elderly.
	
	    Compulsory savings (which often accompany microloans) can build up to valuable 'terminal' sums that can help retiring clients.
		Relatively few. Microcredit is well established and profitably practised by both specialist microfinance institutions (MFIs) and, more recently, formal banks; and outreach is growing quickly if erratically.

Basic microsavings	Reliable current accounts and passbook savings help poor people to save more (in both senses: they can deposit more, and can build up larger balances) than in most other savings vehicles available to them: for many poor people, saving is a better way of building capital sums for reinvestment than microborrowing.	*Safety of deposits:* Savings (in situations where clients hold savings balances that exceed their loan balances) require that MFIs develop new management skills. In many countries only *licensed, regulated and supervised* providers can take deposits, though in some cases MFIs with good track records have been found to be safe savings mobilisers.

Medium-term commitment savings plans	Huge potential, now rapidly growing.
	
	    These plans allow clients to amass financial assets over time in rhythm with their own savings capacity.
	
	    Matured sums can be reinvested in real or social assets, or can be retained as financial assets producing income streams for the elderly in the form of interest income (or even as fixed-term annuities).
		Fund management: where these plans achieve scale, MFIs will need to master advanced fund management skills – using these funds purely as loan capital may be risky. In addition, *governance, training and information management* need upgrading.
		
		Inflation losses, currency collapse, and product pricing: as savings terms lengthen, risks to providers and consumers grow.
		
		Privacy and client identity: MFIs may have to recognise a greater demand for privacy, which may

Table 1 (continued)

		be hard to reconcile with the poor or uncertain legal identities of many poor and very poor people. These challenges have led observers to recommend *partnerships* between MFIs skilled at working with the poor and formal providers with advanced management capacity.

Endowments	Endowments attach life insurance policies to commitment savings plans and therefore add further security, especially where the life insured is that of a main bread-winner.
	    Experiments in endowments for the poor are becoming more numerous: this is a promising development.
		Formal insurance skills are essential to handle endowments properly – another reason for advocating *partnership*.
		    As products become more complex and sophisticated, the risk of *overselling or fraudulent selling* grows.

Annuities	Could help some formally-employed low-paid workers, but may not yet be of immediate relevance to the mass of self-employed or irregularly employed poor.	*Formal actuarial skills* are required: the challenges of developing them for the illiterate self-employed or irregularly-employed poor are formidable.

they doubted this, and this sorrow often led them to express bitter feelings: "I hope to die before my husband," or "before I'm unable to care for myself," and even "an old woman without wealth is kicked like a dog." They spoke of their envy of women with solid assets like land or housing. When they recovered their spirits more than half the women – perhaps because they remembered that we has asked them questions about money – told how nice it would be to save up money against old age, but they said it in a tone of voice that showed that they doubted that would ever be possible. This was true even though the sums of money that women thought would be sufficient were often surprisingly small – as little as $300, thought one slum-dweller in Dhaka.

This story illustrates how difficult it can be for poor people, especially women, to plan for a secure old age. As many researchers have found:

- traditional systems of inter-generational care are either breaking down or are no longer perceived as reliable

- assets, especially land and property, are seen as the best way to guarantee old-age security, but seem out-of-reach for many poor people. As one near-poor villager with some land put it, "if the children turn out good, they'll get the land, work it, and look after me; if they turn out bad I'll keep the land and rent or sell it."

- poor people usually have a low estimate of and little experience with their capacity to use savings as a route to old-age security

Scepticism about building up savings for old age is expressed by men, too. Here is a transcript of another Dhaka slum dweller, Rahman, a low-paid transport worker:

"On the one hand there are my own parents, on the other my wife and children. I can't manage so many things. How can I save? Here is two taka: what shall I do with it, eh? Shall I take care of my family, or of my parents, or educate my kids, or marry off my daughter? Or you think I will save it for when I'm old? Which?" (Recorded in Dhaka, March 2005).

But Rahman does save: minutes later he was showing me his piggy bank: it takes about 6 months to fill up with coins, and yields about $40 each time. Then I saw the up-to-date passbooks for the two ten-year term commitment savings accounts he and his wife have in local banks where they save a total of $13 each month. Then the passbook for his wife's membership of a well-known microfinance institution, ASA, where she has $28 of savings stored and pays in another $1 each week and also has a loan.

Such situations are not uncommon, and from them we learn that:

- poor people have surprisingly active and complex financial lives

- when appropriate instruments are available, poor people may choose to make regular savings that are large relative to their incomes

- poor people do not reject the idea of saving for old age, it is merely that current demands for cash tend to push pension-savings to the bottom of the priority list

In southern India children may be enrolled soon after birth in 'marriage funds' managed by institutions which are permanent but whose main function is not financial services – institutions like churches, temples, and workers' clubs. Their parents (including many poor people) then pay in small regular deposits at convenient intervals – each Sunday as they come out of church, for example. The rules are simple and uniform across whole areas: savers take out double what they put in, but only after a minimum of fifteen years of regular deposits and only if the child has reached the legal age for marriage and is betrothed or reaches age 25 unmarried. Meanwhile, the fund is lent out in small loans to savers, short-term, at 4% a month. This way of investing the fund not only provides short-term liquidity to savers, but has the happy effect of reassuring them that the fund is still there and well-managed.

Although this story is not about saving for old age, it does illustrate some important aspects of poor peoples' propensity to save over the long term:

- they may be willing to save continuously for long periods – of up to 20 years

- small, local, convenient and frequent pay-ins make it easier to save

- a well-established local institution can be trusted with long-term savings

- savings accounts in the names of children can be popular

- if the rules are clear, simple, and uniform in the community, they will be understood and followed

- very strong illiquidity safeguards (you can't get your money back until you are 17 and betrothed) may be actively welcomed by many savers

- savings for a specific purpose (such as marriage) may spur a greater effort to save

- being able to tap the savings – even if through relatively expensive borrowing – helps foster confidence, and helps to avoid conflicts between long-term savings goals and current liquidity needs as well as financing the interest paid on the savings

In the Philippines, Dean S Karlan and his team from Princeton University (Karlan 2004) ran a unique experiment that studied how commitment savings devices are used by people in developing countries. As part of it, they designed, in association with a reputable local bank, a commitment savings product that permits users to choose the term and the goal of their savings and to make choices about illiquidity by selecting from a set of product controls on depositing and withdrawing. Their behaviour was compared to a control group of similar bank clients. The results of the experiment include the findings that:

- use of these accounts had a strong positive effect on the overall level of savings: that is, people enrolled in commitment savings devices tend to save more rather than simply shifting their savings from other products into the commitment product

- interviews with savers showed that they were able to identify those aspects of the product that most encouraged them to save (in this particular case, the naming of specific savings goals, the use of "lock boxes" and the ways that illiquidity was safeguarded), and to suggest other features that would have encouraged even greater savings (in this particular case, the use of deposit collectors)

Bangladesh has experienced a rapid growth in the outreach of commitment savings plans for members of many of its NGO-MFI schemes, nearly all of which have adopted the general approach pioneered by the Grameen Bank. Typically, the commitment savings products are five or ten year schemes with fixed monthly pay-ins and a lump sum payout at maturity. Recent research (Rutherford 2004) shows that, asked what they intend to do with the matured sum, savers most often say, "marriage of daughters," then "a business or job for a son or husband," then "purchasing land or property or other asset" and then some unspecified "major work."

Subsistence in old age is not often mentioned. Yet is it clear that these products are especially popular among older women – who may have been group members for 20 years or more, with children whose education and careers may have been boosted by past loans. At their stage of life they see saving long-term as a better use of their spare cash than repaying loans short-term. Much of their thinking is directed at protecting their own old age, by settling children who will care for them or by acquiring assets. Further, the mere existence of the savings hoard in the MFI's safe hands is a source of comfort. Ramisa, for example, a poor villager in her 40s from southern Bangladesh, holds a commitment account that she highly values. She told us she was expecting to take a lump sum, but when she heard from us that it could be taken as a flow of monthly interest income she immediately said that she would prefer that option. However, her preference was not so much that she valued the flow of income but rather that keeping the savings in the bank would give her security of mind. This demonstrates that:

- as people age, their financial service priorities change: within multi-generation households it can make sense for the middle-aged to start saving long-term while younger members borrow short-term to invest

- savings can be used to secure future income (asset purchases in this example), to enhance future income (businesses and careers for sons, in this example), or to reduce expenditure (marrying out daughters, in this example): all of which improve prospects for security in old age

- the very poorest may have difficulty with fixed, equal periodic instalments and may need especially flexible, or extremely frequent, payment schedules

In late March 2005, Joyce Mulama filed a story from Kenya for the IPS press service:

> In 1998 Rispah Anyanga's husband retired after working twenty years as a clerk in a Nairobi office and received the equivalent of $1,600 as his lump-sum pension payout. But Rispah says, "He put it all in a hardware business. The business didn't do well and after three months it closed down. We had no other source of income and had to pay bills like house rent, electricity, school fees, transport and food. My husband couldn't take it any more. He just lost hope and committed suicide three months later, leaving me to take care of our three children who were then all in high school."

The lessons here are clear:

- a pension does not solve every problem for a retiree, and

- lump sum payouts are not always wisely invested

Finally for this section, the popularity of saving for funerals requires elaboration. Although funeral-savings are unrelated to old-age security except in so far as both events occur at life's end, the worldwide concern for putting enough cash together for a decent funeral is an important driver of savings, and may explain some of the popularity of endowment savings (which incorporate life insurance into a savings plan). In southern India research found that of all informal savings devices, local "burial funds" attracted the biggest proportion of the very poorest (Rutherford and Arora 1997). In northern India and Bangladesh desperately poor people are sometimes found, after death, to have tied surprisingly large sums of money into their saris and loincloths to secure a proper funeral. In northern Philippines the number of savings accounts in a rural credit union rose dramatically when funeral costs were included as a benefit for good savers (Rutherford 1998). And in South Africa, University of Cape Town researchers found in their study of a panel of near-poor, poor and very poor households, that informal burial societies are the single most common financial instrument in use (among 23 different instruments identified in the households), with an average of 1.6 memberships per household in a panel of 61 households (Collins 2005).

The Annexes report comments from a panel of poor people in Bangladesh and elsewhere that further illustrate these stories. The picture that emerges is clear and is consistent with other research on the money-management habits of the poor (Rutherford 2000) and with the Women's World Banking paper Asset Building for Old Age Security (WWB 2003):

> *Poor people well understand the purpose and value of saving. They sense that there may be a savings route to old-age security, and grab opportunities when they come their way. But they are beset by many difficulties, both in their own circumstances and in the financial services available to them, so that in practice success remains the exception rather than the rule.*

For microfinance organisations, the solution must be to imagine and test products and alliances that progressively improve our understanding of how to design and deliver the most appropriate services. The next section explores these challenges.

The Challenge of Developing Micropensions

Commitment Saving Plans: The Best Platform for Micropension Development

I first chanced upon commitment savings plans expressly designed for the poor in villages in Bangladesh in the early 1990s. I was surprised, because at that time there were no formal financial services for poor villagers, and the new semi-formals (NGO-MFIs) were concentrating on short-term credit. But here was a local NGO offering five and ten year savings plans to middle income and poor villagers, and they were very popular. The MFI understood the demand and designed well – a simple plan with fixed monthly pay-ins and a lump-sum payout, easy to understand, producing an attractive lump of capital that capital-starved villagers would have no trouble finding a good use for. They got the delivery right, too: door-step collection at weekly intervals, some scheduling flexibility if poorer users missed or underpaid a week or two, and simple passbooks that allowed savers to track their progress. They kept a close watch on costs, operating with low-paid local agents working out of cheaply rented branches, and spent almost nothing on marketing, relying on fieldworker contact and word-of-mouth recommendation from client to client.

Unfortunately they had an inadequate legal identity and got their investment planning badly wrong – failings that proved fatal. At first they ploughed much of the inflow of deposits into household durables – fans, bicycles, hot-irons and the like – that they sold to clients on deferred payment terms. Growing bolder, they went into the business of importing corrugated roof sheets, got into trouble, came to the notice of the authorities, were banned and then collapsed, taking thousands of poor people's savings down with them.

The story helps us to visualise the most obvious lessons and pitfalls of mobilising recurrent savings among poor people:

- know your clients, their conditions, and the transaction values that suit them

- design simple products that clients and low-wage staff can easily understand

- develop delivery systems that suit the environment, such as door-to-door collection or other forms of mobile banking, lock-boxes, and so on

- do not grow faster than you can learn

- do not do it at all unless you know what you are doing and have an appropriate legal identity (in most countries this will mean being a licensed, regulated entity, though in some a track record of reliable service and sufficient size might be enough)

These rules apply to all kinds of savings services, and have been thoroughly explored in several excellent texts (Robinson 2005; Hirschland 2005), so they will not be pursued here.

Scale

Instead, we pursue the Bangladesh story, since Bangladesh may now boast the world's widest outreach of commitment savings plans to poor and very poor people, and because learning how to scale-up commitment savings plans is an urgent task for micropension development.

For many years state-owned commercial banks in Bangladesh offered a Deposit Pension Scheme (DPS): a ten-year commitment savings plan much loved by the middle and wealthy classes. The genius of the failed rural NGO whose sad story heads this section was to recognise, earlier than others, that such schemes would be as popular among the poor and very poor as among the better-off. Soon, better-managed NGO-MFIs noticed: BURO Tangail, for example, was an early adopter of DPS type schemes for their group members. ASA, one of the Bangladesh giants, followed. But scale was given a significant boost when the scheme was finally adopted by Grameen Bank as part of the general overhaul of its offerings in 2001 known as "Grameen II." In 2005 Grameen reached about 2.5 million group members with its version of the DPS, known as "Grameen Pension Savings" or GPS.

GPS is a commitment savings product with a five or ten year term and low minimum monthly deposits – less than $1, and to accommodate really poor savers even that can be subdivided into smaller weekly payments. It pays a generous rate of interest relative to the similar DPS product of commercial banks. It is offered to the Bank's 4 million group "members," almost all of whom are women. Take-up has been very rapid and enthusiastic, even after controlling for the fact that a GPS is mandatory for members who borrow more than $130.

Grameen Bank membership ranges from the very poor to the middle-income near-poor, and attitudes to the GPS vary between these extremes. For many middle-income group members the GPS is the main reason to be a Grameen member. At the other extreme, there are very poor members who feel it is "not for them" because they believe they have "no capacity to save." But such members take loans that they service in weekly instalments, and now that the GPS scheme is five years old and better understood, many of them are beginning to see the GPS "saving up" route as a viable alternative to high-cost borrowing. Take-up also varies with household age and structure, with younger, growing households more likely to prioritise borrowing while older ones may favour saving.

Understanding Commitment Savings Plans

Unfortunately, Grameen's GPS initially failed to receive much notice. *MicroSave* fielded a team (Rutherford 2004) that looked carefully at the overall experience of Grameen II in the field over a three year period that ended in December 2005. Its results should shed further light on lessons that can be learned from the massive GPS outreach.

Dean Karlan's team (who conducted the commitment savings experiment in the Philippines) has carried out a recent review of commitment savings products in developing countries. Their paper has important implications for policy makers and MFIs. Chief among these is a call for proper pilot projects to test innovations in commitment savings, to hasten learning about the relative merits of different product features. Karlan suggests that selected MFIs might take a lead in piloting product features under close scrutiny from researchers in a "careful and scientific randomised launch." Others have suggested that a dedicated entity, perhaps on the lines of the Micro Insurance Centre could help to consolidate advances in learning – or that the Micro Insurance Centre broaden its remit to include work on micropensions.

Lessons about proper piloting also emerge from Wright et al (2001). This study examined the processes within ASA, an NGO-MFI, that led to the rapid scaling-up of a GPS-type scheme followed by an equally rapid retreat. Among the tricky questions that ASA faced was whether or not to set targets for their branch managers in opening DPS accounts, and whether or not to link the scheme with lending. Negotiating an understanding with the central bank was also an issue because ASA is not a registered bank.

Grameen's GPS experience also sheds light on the question of how to manage lending alongside commitment savings products. This is a particularly urgent question for the many Grameen or village bank style MFIs around the world in which continuous borrowing is almost a condition of membership.

If opening a commitment savings account is a condition for borrowing, problems may arise when the client finds it hard to service both sets of periodic payments – the loan repayments and the savings. Grameen Bank, for example, where members must hold a GPS in order to borrow $130 or more, soon found it necessary to break larger-denomination GPS accounts into a "red GPS" (a low-value one that satisfies the borrowing requirement) and a "green GPS" (the balance of large-denomination accounts, or additional accounts). SafeSave in Dhaka abandoned the mandatory link between borrowing and long-term savings after a three year trial. Bearing in mind what was said above about savers' preference for accessing their capital in some way during the saving term, the best advice may be: offering loans secured against commitment savings account balances is more workable than requiring a commitment savings account as a condition for borrowing.

Term Continuity and Payout Policy

Most commitment savings plans simply deliver a lump sum at maturity. Some observers believe, based on experience from microinsurance, that there may be a "natural" expectation for this to be the case and some reluctance to take the payout as an income stream or other form of staged payment. However, other evidence is beginning to emerge.

When Dr Yunus, Grameen's founder and managing director, first introduced the GPS (Yunus 2001) he wrote that the matured sum can be taken as a lump sum *or* as income (not an annuity – just monthly payments of interest). This message had not yet reached the field in 2005. My research indicates that staff and clients universally supposed that there will be a lump-sum payout. So I have been testing attitudes of GPS holders towards the income alternative, and many account holders favour it – as much for the mental satisfaction of retaining the sum as for the sake of the income itself. A strong well-trusted MFI may not find it difficult to attract clients to staged payments – a step closer to a "pension."

These days, annuities are seen by insurance professionals as income streams paid from a certain date (usually retirement) until an uncertain date – death: hence the difficulty of pricing them. But that was not always so. Annuities have also been paid for fixed terms. Matured sums from commitment savings plans such as the GPS could be paid out as "fixed term" annuities,[1] at least on an experimental and voluntary basis, as a further development towards micropensions. Monthly payments of interest plus returned capital over ten years would be relatively easy to calculate and price. The resulting increase in the size of the income may make such a product attractive to some poor people in certain situations – such as waiting for an offspring to finish her education and start earning, perhaps. We do not yet know. Testing is required.

The fact remains that most GPS holders do not associate it directly with old-age management. This may be because the time horizon is too short – GPSs have terms as short as five and ten years. However, Grameen already offers attractively priced fixed deposit products (CDs), especially its "seven year double" scheme which is already very popular with better-off non-members with spare cash to invest. Thus although not many younger people appear to be thinking about it yet, in theory they could start saving in their twenties and use the GPS in tandem with the fixed deposit scheme: over their working life they could build an attractively large "retirement fund" from very modest deposits – as little as $2 a month. Talking to women in Bangladesh recently about this arithmetic can have a strong effect: several mothers-in-law listened in and then wagged figures at their daughters-in-law and told them, "You be sure to open a GPS at the very next Grameen meeting!"

The arithmetic, in nominal terms, is as follows: assume the saver starts at age 20 and saves 100 taka a month (about $1.75) for life, in four successive ten-year GPS terms. Each will produce 23,000 taka at maturity. If the first three matured sums are invested in a series of "seven year double" fixed deposit accounts, the total sum at age 60 will be 598,000 taka, producing a monthly income of 3,987 taka. This is about $63 per month, equivalent to a lower-middle-class salary – at 2005 prices.

Inflation and Interest Rate Risk …

But some say that holding a high proportion of one's savings in a bank account is a mug's game: inflation makes losses inevitable. For those with the least to save –

---

[1]   Not to be confused with 'term life insurance,' which is a form of life insurance in which the policy holder pays a premium for a fixed term in return for a payout should she die during that term: there is no savings element – when the term expires the policy holder has no further claim on the insurer.

the poor and very poor – a high proportion of cash savings may be particularly risky. Are those Bangladeshi mothers-in-law wise to recommend continuous saving to the next generation? Maybe, since in South Asia inflation has not been rampant. Besides, inflation-caused losses in bank deposits, as work by *MicroSave* in Africa has shown (Wright et al 2001) may still be less severe than losses in other savings vehicles such as livestock, home-saving or on-lending.

Nevertheless, as the terms of savings plans lengthen, the savers' risk of losses from inflation rises, especially where interest rates are fixed. Also, as terms lengthen, the risk to providers of offering fixed-rate savings plans also rises, since market rates may fall during the term. If the provider then fails to adjust rates downward for new savers, it risks attracting too much savings, multiplying the problem.

In the principal current pro-poor savings plans, such as Grameen's GPS, rates are indeed fixed, and these risks are held in check in only one way – by limiting the term length (in Grameen's case to no more than ten years for commitment savings and seven years for fixed deposits). The rates paid on the GPS through 2005 were high relative to the market, attracting many non-poor savers to the bank. Grameen's deposits grew to be larger than its loan portfolio in December 2004, for the first time in the bank's 28 year history. The bank welcomes this liquidity, which has allowed it to expand its lending and experiment with new forms of (higher value) enterprise loans. But Grameen is also diversifying its fund management: in 2005 it announced the opening of its mutual fund scheme, under which some of the pool of members' savings will be placed in the Dhaka stock market.

Clearly, Grameen will face challenges as it continues to go it alone, developing its own in-house expertise as its business grows. Grameen is a large institution: most providers will find that to move beyond ten-year terms, and into experiments with income-streamed payouts, endowments and true annuities, partnerships with formal sector providers skilled in sophisticated fund management will have to be sought. This could lead to fewer of the deposits being recycled as loans and more of them invested in inflation-safe vehicles, held in hard currencies or otherwise hedged.

… and so, a Role for Donors?

As microfinance has matured, the role of official foreign assistance in promoting it has changed. Especially, and happily, the role of donors as suppliers of funds has diminished, as other sources become available. However, cash set aside by donors (and, perhaps, by the international insurance and pension industry) expressly to protect poor savers from currency crashes and inflation losses could be, as J D von Pischke in this volume has put it, "the final hurrah" for donor-driven microfinance funds. Carefully designed, it might be less prone than other forms of subsidies to the risk of distorting natural markets, and unlikely to do much damage through the moral hazard of undermining incentives for sound economic and financial policy.

Aside from that, there is scope for donors to spend a little money on encouraging MFIs to learn higher-level management skills and fostering their collaboration with formal providers.

Privacy

Many MFIs rely on carrying out all transactions in public meetings as an internal control mechanism, and by and large this has been successful. However some transactions need more privacy – even for poor people! This issue came up in relation to the GPS surprisingly often in my Grameen research – surprising because Bangladesh's is one of the least private of all cultures. Here is a typical extract from my notebook:

> *[in a poor rural household in central Bangladesh]* There is another young man here who's a visitor. His wife is in Grameen and he says that she doesn't have a GPS. She is present and we ask her why and she refuses to reply, pretending to be asleep. We stop pursuing the story when we realise from whispers that she is keeping her GPS secret from her husband. I hope we didn't spill the beans. The young man himself ostentatiously goes on to say that he approves of the idea of the GPS, but his wife keeps her eyes, and her mouth, firmly shut.

The privacy problem may not be an easy one for Grameen or village bank style MFIs to solve, but it requires attention.

Commitment Savings Plans Today

Karlan (2003) concludes that "savings products with commitment mechanisms are a valuable complement to flexible savings products....More suitable to meet long term goals..." and he notes that there is strong interest on the part of MFIs to develop new savings products (74 of the 80 MFIs that responded to his web-based survey reported an interest in new savings products and marketing strategies). The Women's World Banking paper notes that the four commitment savings products it reviewed enjoy "high profitability, efficiency, and client satisfaction." Grameen Bank alone has enrolled more than two million savers into its Pension Savings scheme in the last five years. Commitment savings plans for the poor are becoming well established and are growing in visibility, popularity and design. Nevertheless, Grameen's massive GPS roll-out has begun to demonstrate that large scale operation will require sophisticated management skills, above all in fund management and pricing.

Endowments and Annuities

Endowments expand the scope of commitment savings plans by linking them to life insurance policies, thereby giving added security to participating households. If the policy-holder survives the term, the matured sum is taken, but if he or she dies, the household can use the proceeds of the insurance to mitigate the loss, which is especially useful if the policy holder was also an important income earner.

Among the best known and probably the largest-scale endowment schemes deliberately designed for poor people are the "Grameen Bim' and „Gono Bima" (village, and peoples' insurance) schemes of Delta, a private sector insurance company in Bangladesh. The products featured medium-term (mainly 10-year) savings plans linked to a life insurance policy for which no medical checks were needed, and up-to-date savers were guaranteed access to loans repayable Grameen-style in small, frequent instalments. Sales of policies and collection of premiums and of loan repayment instalments were done door-to-door by local agents. Profits were redistributed to savers as bonuses: in this part of its business Delta's motives were social. The scheme, started in 1988, grew quickly – a decade later more than 400,000 policies were sold in a single year.

The Delta scheme convincingly demonstrated the popularity of the endowment idea among low-income groups. Although it is not absolutely clear to what extent the promise of a loan inflated the take-up of the scheme, research in the slums of Dhaka suggests that many users were as attracted by the savings and insurance elements as by the loans: some did not even ask for loans.

However, the schemes fared badly: and although they are now being rescued by new management at Delta, many clients lost their savings in the process. The story has been told in detail by Michael McCord (2005) and is not repeated here. Management's errors included inadequate internal controls, poor policy design, and massive failure in the part of the business with which it was least experienced – microlending. Ironically, Delta had at first sought an alliance with an MFI (I was present at some of the early meetings): an instinct that, in this case sadly, turned out to have been right. It would be an oversimplification to say that the story shows that formal institutions cannot easily go "down market" without access to the expertise in working with poor people that MFIs have built up over many years. However, it does strengthen the view that an alliance between formal and semi-formal (MFI) players is likely to be the best way of massifying the sale of the more complex financial instruments, such as insurance and pensions, to the poor.

Financial Literacy and Overselling

But even when endowment schemes are more professionally managed, and become common and popular among the poor, poor people may have difficulty using them effectively. This is shown in research by Jim Roth in South Africa (Roth 1999).

For at least three decades endowment policies have been sold in large numbers to low-income South Africans. The introduction of electronic debit orders, and the ease with which a client can commit to a monthly direct debit, have facilitated the rapid growth of these schemes.

The policies are sold to township residents with formal employment. In the study of financial services used by township residents in a small rural town in South Africa conducted by Roth, half of all respondents reported owning at least one privately bought endowment policy, and some respondents owned more than one. Although these policyholders were formally employed, many were not well-off, as they supported large households.

The policies were designed to coincide with the end of the policyholder's formal employment. However, many policies were sold that did not coincide with this period. As a result many policyholders cashed in their schemes and received only a low surrender value.

International experience has shown that where there is an abundance of such schemes and competition to attract deposits is great, fraudulent or unethical selling practices often emerge. Over the last two decades many Grahamstown Township residents who were unhappy with their endowment policies approached a community advice office run by Black Sash, a human rights organisation, for assistance. In the last six months of 1994 this office assisted 157 rural people with insurance policies (Roth 1995). In the vast majority of cases, agents had misrepresented the nature of the policy to their clients.

Agents frequently misled buyers into believing that they were purchasing a simple savings plan, when in fact they were being sold a hybrid of savings and insurance. In other cases, clients were insufficiently informed about surrender values. This has an especially significant impact on illiterate and semi-literate buyers who relied on the good faith of the insurance agent. The root problem is that the vast majority of insurance agents work on commission. This encourages poor selling practices as the agent's income becomes dependent on the volume of policies sold. In such a situation, rural people with little formal education become prime targets for unscrupulous agents.

But in spite of such practices endowment policies remain a popular financial instrument among poor South African households that have few alternative illiquid savings instruments.

An Example of a Formal/Semiformal Partnership

More recently, Roth has been looking at a new attempt in India to market endowments to the poor that feature a link between a major formal institution and a well-established civil-society body (rather than an MFI as such).

In India insurers are legally obliged to sell a percentage of their policies to low income clients. For the most part they have sold straight term insurance (see footnote 1). However they are increasingly requested to combine insurance with savings policies. Unlike the endowment policies in South Africa, the terms are typically quite short – 5 to 15 years at the moment. These policies are new and experimental (and not specifically aimed at providing old age security). TATA-AIG, an Indian insurance company, has such a policy called the *Jana Suraksha Yojana*, that has a small savings component and a large insurance benefit (up to $900) for a $1.60 per annum policy. The entire private insurance industry in India is relatively new (the market was denationalised early in the present decade), and it is difficult at this stage to see how these products will develop. But there are signs that insurers may develop more endowment policies for the poor in India.

Annuities

"True" annuities, as currently understood, are the purchase, for a fixed sum, of an unlimited flow of fixed periodic receipts until death. They require reliable information about clients, and highly sophisticated pricing technology combined with advanced fund management – matters familiar to formal institutions, which have few poor clients, but virtually unknown to MFIs, who have many. CARD's brave but doomed venture in the Philippines provides a vivid illustration (McCord 2004).

CARD offered an insurance/pension scheme to its members that offered a guaranteed monthly income flow from retirement to death. It was very popular but its pricing flaws threatened to bring the institution down. Happily, CARD acted in time to buy its way out of the problem, link up with a formal provider, and relaunch a more measured life-insurance scheme which is still running well with more than half a million subscribers.

Early participation in CARD's scheme by a formal pension institution using actuarial skills may have eliminated the more egregious pricing flaws. However, such collaboration may not have solved the many other technical problems that arise in marketing low-value annuities to large numbers of illiterate and informally-employed poor people with poorly defined identities and age, shifting addresses, and little or no experience with the insurance and pension industries. Micropension activity for the foreseeable future is unlikely to feature "true" annuities. Rather, it will focus on scaling up and improving commitment saving plans and learning how to offer endowment schemes to the poor.

Conclusions

It will be many years before developing world states are able to offer social pensions to low- income households, particularly those who lack formal sector employment. Meanwhile, the demand for financial solutions to the problems of the poor in old age is growing. It is time for the microfinance industry to start thinking about micropensions.

Precisely because members of most poor households in developing countries are not formally employed and do not look forward to retirement, micropensions are unlikely to be scaled-down versions of the typical pension scheme found in rich countries, in which savings made during the working life are swapped for an annuity at a defined retirement age. The best platform for developing micropensions is the medium-term commitment savings plan. Such plans are already available to the poor in some countries, and are growing in number. A key task is for more MFIs in more countries to experiment with, and then scale up, their commitment savings schemes.

Several challenges will emerge as this process takes place. When savings portfolios held by MFIs begin to outgrow their loan portfolios, the question of how to safeguard deposits arises. In most cases, this will require MFIs to become licensed, regulated and supervised deposit-takers, although in exceptional cases a good track record as a deposit taker may be sufficient.

When MFIs take commitment savings deposits as well as short-term (passbook) deposits they will need to improve their knowledge and practice of fund management. In many cases this will reveal the importance of improved governance, training and information systems. As the length of term offered to savers grows, the risk to the saver of losses through inflation or currency collapse increases – and the risk to providers of losses through poor fund management and pricing policy also increases. When MFIs proceed to the next level, and offer endowments (commitment saving schemes with attached insurance policies) or even begin to experiment with annuities, they will require advanced fund management and actuarial skills. The example of microinsurance has shown that a good way – perhaps the best way – of climbing this steep learning curve is to go into partnership with professional formal sector insurance and pension providers.

Much of the initiative in developing micropensions has been taken by MFIs themselves, and this will continue to be the case. However, outsiders can help. One intriguing suggestion is that donors and the international insurance and pension industries might work together to develop a global facility to insure the value of poor people's long-term savings in the face of hyperinflation or currency collapse – devastating events for which poor people cannot be blamed and over which they enjoy no control.

Annex 1: "How Are You Preparing for Your Old Age?" Responses from Poor People in Bangladesh

During the preparation of this chapter, Stuart Rutherford (assisted by Imran Matin, S K Sinha, Md Yakub and Rabeya Islam) asked a number of poor rural and urban respondents in Bangladesh about their attitude towards securing their livelihood in old age. In the summary which follows, a small number of typical responses are reported. The responses are ordered by the age, then by relative wealth and location (urban slums or rural villages) of the respondents. Monetary values have been converted to US dollars.

Young People

Rural very poor young woman: Ramisa said, "I didn't think anything about it [my old age]. However, I have my son. I am working very hard to raise my son. I hope that my son will look after me in future. And, if my son or my husband does not look after me, I will remain as Allah pleases to keep me." Later, she said that she deposits 16 cents every week in the NGO BRAC as savings. She said, "This savings will help me in future. Whether I take loans from BRAC or not, I will always deposit savings there." She said that at present she has $16 savings at BRAC, deposited from her earnings from bamboo and cane work.

Urban upper poor young woman: We asked Monoara about her old age: she says she isn't married yet but when she is married her husband and/or children will take care of her. She'd like to save if she could and would preferably do it in a bank.

Rural poor couple in their 30s: For their old age, they are saving money weekly in the NGOs World Vision and Caritas. They say that it is not possible to keep small sums like 8 or 16 cents at home as savings. Soon they will have to arrange her daughter's marriage, which will erode their life-savings this year. They assume that they will have to continue to earn from now on for their old age. They have no son, but two daughters. There is therefore likely to be no one to look after them in their old age.

Rural upper poor woman in her 30s: Sayed's wife Asma said, "I have not thought about my old age yet. However, I have planted several hundred trees, for the future." She added, "My husband hopes that in future, from the income of his timber business, he will buy cultivable land on which he will be able to depend in his old age." Later she said, "I do not intend to take an insurance policy. However, if we can earn a lot from the business, we will save in the bank."

Urban poor man in his 30s: Siraj said his old age is entirely up to Allah, but then added that his sons will look after him. Then he said, "If I could open an account in a reliable organisation I could save as a much as possible and buy a house at Savar, but that would require around $6,600." Then he confessed that he is not entirely sure whether his sons will look after them in their old age.

Urban upper poor man in his 30s: Karim says that his wife Asma is much cleverer with money than he is: she bullies him to save and not to smoke. He says that he likes to support his parents and expects that his sons will support him in old age, whereas Asma doesn't like him supporting his parents and advises him to save up for his own old age. So he tries to hide his support to his parents from his wife. But he says he is beginning to think about his old age.

Middle-Aged People

Rural poor women in her 40s, talking about Grameen Bank's "Grameen Pension Savings" scheme: Her group fell into severe problems and now it mainly consists of borrowers who do not attend the weekly meeting and are not repaying. Kohinoor has been in the group since the 1988 floods and says that the group is now more or less finished. However there are a few regular members that pay their loans and have a GPS and Kohinoor is one of them. Her GPS is for about $3 per month. She has two sons, both teenagers, both dropped out of school and now working, one in the brick field as a brick moulder ($1.36 per 1000 bricks, average monthly take home pay $41 – $50), and one as a mason. Her husband is sick and only works occasionally, collecting honey. She said the most common use that people have in mind for a GPS is marrying daughters but she has no daughters, so she hopes to buy some land for her sons. Part of the reason why she took a large GPS is to get a bigger loan: at present her loan is for $230, used to recover land that had been mortgaged out. But she also opened a large GPS in order to achieve a large lump sum. We explained to her that she could choose to take her mature GPS as income rather than as a lump sum, and we calculated roughly what that would be in her case. ($3.33 per month produces $400 capital or about $766 with accumulated interest after 10 years: at 8% a year that would produce $5.10 per month). She liked the monthly income scheme very much, especially after we told her that she could always take the lump sum if she wished at any time, and that on her death the lump sum would be inheritable by her sons.

Urban poor widow in her 40s: On old age, she says, "Allah will look after me" but then "my children will look after me" and then "but I don't really believe for sure the children will look after me." So we asked what she might do and she said she'd try to save – that's why she opened the insurance plan at $5 per month: "I'll continue as long as I get a wage. If I can save for 10 years I'll get more than $1,666, and I'll buy land in the village to build a room to rent out, or I'll send a son abroad (to work)."

Rural poor woman in her 50s: We asked her about ageing: she says she didn't think much when she was young, and her husband Hakim was lazy for a long time. When we asked what advice she'd give to younger people she started to cry, so we dropped it. Husband Hakim said, "Now I have become old. I do not have any other way except death. Thinking about anything is useless. The time of earning has passed. Now there is no time. Now there is no other way for me except going to the street and begging from people."

Urban poor woman in her 50s: On old age, she hopes she'll die before her husband does, so that she doesn't have to face the problem of surviving in old age – there's no chance of her son looking after her as he's married and has to look after his own family. If she had to, she'd go back to her village and take an NGO loan, trade rice and try to build a small hut on a piece of land. If more money came her way she'd buy farmland or invest in a bank.

Urban poor widow in her 50s: In old age "only Allah knows" what will come of her. "I'd like to die before I become inactive, before my son beats me: if I had money in a bank – say Janata – that would help: $830 would do. My son isn't a real man so I can't expect to live off his income. I'm very dependent on my daughter – she's my main resource."

Old People

Rural poor woman in her 60s: Jamila is saving at an NGO, thinking about the future. She said that in the end of their life, when they won't be able to go out to work because of being very old and sick, this savings would help them.

Rural poor man in his 60s: Saman Ali says that one year ago he gave $5 to one of his neighbours. In future, at any time if he becomes very sick he will use this money as a provision against funeral costs. He gave it to his neighbour for this reason only. He will not take any interest. But the neighbour will invest this money in a business and Saman hopes to get a share of any profit from the business. Saman said that his wife, sons and daughters do not know about this money. He asked us not to disclose the secret.

Rural elderly poor couple: When they married they imagined their children would care for them in old age, yet this has barely happened. So the advice they'd give to their own children is (after thought), "earn and save for the future with an NGO or bank, and buy assets." But he says his own son Zia isn't saving because his income is barely enough to support his family. In this village the children of wealthy families care for parents (especially if the parents have set them up with a home), but in poor families they don't or can't.

Urban poor elderly man: With regard to old age management, Hossen Ali said, "it is the will of Allah. I think when I'm much older, my sons will look after me." Later he said, "but my sons may not look after me. It would be better if I could have saved some money. If I would have some regular income, I could have saved at least $333 in any commercial bank and it would be possible to cover my daily expenses out of the interest. Then I would not need to depend upon my sons. Though my wife still has her garment factory job she can't make any savings out of her monthly salary."

Urban near poor couple: man in his 60s, wife in 30s: She says they're bringing up the children well, spending money on their education: they'll look after her and Sultan in old age. "And then I have the insurance policies as a back up. Then I have a bit of land, too."

Annex 2: "How Are You Preparing for Your Old Age?" Responses from Poor People in Africa

In a similar exercise, staff of *MicroSave*, a microfinance initiative working out of Nairobi, Kenya, recorded some interviews with rural and urban poor households. Here is a sample of responses.

Rural poor men, Kenya: You ask us, "what do we do when we are too old to work? I'll tell you what the answer is – we pray to die. Quarrymen like us have no savings or pension schemes." (Collected by *MicroSave*, 1999)

Urban poor man, Dar es Salaam, Tanzania: "If I had some kind of insurance or pension plan I could be saving for my old age. As it is, I give money to my brother in the village to buy goats and cows. Whether he'll look after them for me, and whether he'll pay me in the end, only God knows." (Collected by *MicroSave*, 1999)

Clients of Pride, an MFI in Tanzania: They said their preparations for old age include investing in children's education and future, for example by building a house so that they can live without much difficulty should they die "prematurely." They said they were happy that PRIDE was contemplating introducing savings as one of the products, because it would enable to them to save for old age. (Collected by Leonard Mutesasira for *MicroSave*,1999)

Rural elderly man, Uganda: Kyamala passed away in 1992. However at the beginning of 1999 one of the big trees in Kyamala's compound was cut down and inside one of the holes they found many torn old currency notes. When he died, nobody knew where old Kyamala was keeping his money – if they had known, the money would have been used to pay school fees for his grandson who dropped out of school soon after his death – for lack of money. (Collected by Graham Wright and Leonard Mutesasira for *MicroSave*, 2001)

In the slums of Kampala, Uganda: "The difference between comfortable and struggling old people is how they planned for the time of their old age," says an MFI client in Katwe slums of Kampala. "If you build rental houses while you are still young and energetic you are likely to have a relatively comfortable old age. If you do not you will be miserable, striving, working, and perhaps even begging until you die. You will have no money for food and medical care. Under those circumstances you cannot live for long." (from *Savings and Needs in East Africa: An Infinite Variety*, Leonard Mutesasira for MicroSave,1999

References

Collins, Daryl. Unpublished preliminary report, subject to final analysis. (2005) www.financialdiaries.com

Gorman, Mark. "Age and Security." London, HelpAge International. (2004)

Hirschland, Madeline (ed). "Savings Services for the Poor: An Operational Guide." Kumarian Press, USA. (2005)

Karlan, Dean 2003, Nava Ashraf, Wesley Yin and Nathalie Gons of Development Innovations. "A Review of Commitment Savings Products in Developing Countries." Princeton University. (June 2003)

Karlan, Dean 2004, Nava Ashraf and Wesley Yin: "SEED: A Commitment Savings Product in the Philippines." Princeton University. (2004)

McCord, Michael and Craig Churchill. "Good and Band Practices in Micro-insurance: Delta Life, Bangladesh." CGAP Case Study 7. (March 2005)

McCord, Michael and Grzegorz Buczkowski. "Good and Bad Practices in Micro-insurance: CARD MBA, The Philippines." CGAP Case Study 4. (December 2004)

Robinson, Marguerite. "Mobilizing Savings from the Public, Basic Principles and Practices." Speed, Women's World Banking and USAID, Kampala, Uganda. (2005)

Roth, Jim 1995, email to the author, June 2005

Roth, Jim 1999, email to the author, June 2005

Rutherford, Stuart 1998: "Mountain Money Managers." Unpublished report for CECAP, a European Union development project. (1998)

Rutherford, Stuart 2000. "The Poor and their Money." New Delhi: Oxford University Press. (2000)

Rutherford, Stuart 2002. "Money Talks: Conversations with Bangladeshi Households about Managing Money." Manchester UK, Institute for Development Policy and Management. (2002) (available on the cgap.org website)

Rutherford, Stuart 2004, with Maniruzzaman and Acnabin & Co. "Grameen II at the end of 2003." *MicroSave*. 2004 (available on the microsave.org web site)

Rutherford, Stuart and Arora, Sukhwinder. "City Savers: How the Poor, the DFID and its Partners Are Promoting Financial Services in Urban India." DFID New Delhi. (1997)

Todd, Helen. "Women at the Center: Grameen Bank Borrowers After One Decade." Westview Press. (1996)

Yunus, Muhammad. "Grameen II: Designed to Open New Possibilities." Dhaka, Grameen Bank. (2001)

Women's World Banking. "Asset Building for Old Age Security." WWB. (2003).

Wright, Graham, Imran Matin and Bob Christen. "Introducing Savings into a MicroCredit Institution – Lessons from ASA." Washington DC, CGAP. (2001)

Wright, Graham. "The Relative Risks to the Savings of Poor People." MicroSave Briefing Note 6. (2001)

CHAPTER 15:

Cash, Children or Kind? Developing Old Age Security for Low-Income People in Africa

Madhurantika Moulick[1], Angela Mutua[2], Moses Muwanguzi[3], Corrinne Ngurukie[2], Michael Onesimo[3], and Graham A.N. Wright[4]

[1] Financial Systems Specialist, *MicroSave* India
[2] Financial Systems Consultant, *MicroSave* Consulting
[3] Freelance consultant
[4] Programme Director, *MicroSave*

Introduction

Declining fertility rates and rising life expectancy are driving global demographic change. With an aging world population, both the number and proportion of the aged are increasing. Presently, two-thirds of the world's older people live in developing countries. By 2050, this will increase to 80%. The number of people aged over 60 in the developing world is predicted to rise from 375 million in 2000 to 1,500 million in 2050 (Gorman, 2004). In Sub-Saharan Africa the number of people aged 60 and over will more than double in the next 30 years, despite the impact of HIV/AIDS (Mark, 2004). Africa's older population will increase to 204 million by 2050, from the present 42 million (HelpAge, 2005a): more than one in ten Sub-Saharan Africas will be over 60 (Gorman, 2004).

This growth rate of the elderly population will bring economic and social problems, the effects of which will be seen at different levels – from the individual through the continent as a whole. The aged will increasingly face additional crises on two fronts: disintegrating social safety nets and the effects of HIV/AIDS.

While 50% of Africans live on less than a dollar a day, fewer than 10% of those in Sub-Saharan Africa are covered by social security (i.e. those who have been employed in the formal sector). Close to 90% are therefore without, while many who are covered receive benefits that fall short of their basic needs (HelpAge International, 2005).

Of the forty nations with the highest rates of HIV/AIDS prevalence in adults, thirty-seven are in Africa (CIA – The World Factbook). Around 60% of orphans in Sub-Saharan Africa live in households headed by grandparents (HelpAge International, May 2005). A WHO study of caregivers of orphans and other vulnerable children in Zimbabwe in 2002 found that 71.8% of caregivers were over 60 years old, 74.2% of them women. A major reason for this is the high prevalence of HIV/AIDS (HelpAge International, 2005a). Of Kenya's 1.7 million orphans, 650,000 have lost their parents due to AIDS (HelpAge International, 2005b).

This chapter focuses on security for low-income people in their old age. The most relevant question for this population is often – what happens when a person is no longer able to earn money due to old age or infirmity? Or how does one support oneself after retirement? So, 'old age', a relative concept, is used in this paper in relation to regular income earning capacities, regardless of age or source of income. The paper describes how low-income people prepare or cope with the changing situation as they age, and examines the potential role of microfinance in providing security for them during their old age. The data and findings of this paper are based on the experiences of more than 180 respondents who participated in focus groups in Kenya, Tanzania and Uganda. The focus groups were driven by a discussion guide and by ranking exercises specifically designed to examine how people prepare or save for old age and which financial services might assist them to do so.

Challenges of Old Age

People get used to a certain life style during their productive years, and then, with age, comes the time when they cannot support themselves any longer. People lose their direct source of income and have to depend on previous investments, if any, or on their social safety nets. This transition has both economic and social dimensions that are related to the financial realities of older citizens, as suggested by the focus groups.

Economic Dimensions

Participants' economic concerns consisted of three aspects:

Small regular source of cash: For most respondents food, shelter and clothing are the biggest challenges in old age. The issue is not the high cost of meeting these consumption needs but that of planning to ensure a small but regular source of cash during old age.

Perhaps unsurprisingly, food is the biggest expense – and old people are reported even to die of hunger. This is more common in urban areas where earning from *shambas*[1] is not possible, or in remote arid areas. In East Africa, most of the elderly population is rural, because those who worked in urban areas prefer to shift upcountry at retirement. This move often requires money to set up a new house or repair an existing one. Age brings physical weakness and illness, and thus medical bills also become substantial expenses, in part because rural areas have very poor

---

[1] Very small scale farming usually on land measuring two acres or less that acts as a source of supplementary income for rural households.

or no medical facilities. Prevalent diseases include cancer, psychiatric problems, TB, diabetes, stress, blindness or poor sight and heart related problems. Divon Kimondo, a taxi driver in Nairobi says, *"It is not that the poor living upcountry need a lot of money, but they do not save up for even a small amount. People do not worry about the future. Also our income is so less, we spend everything to meet our regular consumption needs."*

Mismanagement of funds: Those privileged enough to retire with a pension from a company or the government often receive a lump sum, which has its own dangers. In many cases, lack of knowledge of investments or of business acumen leads to the loss of the whole amount within a very short time. A respondent in Kangari, in the Central Province of Kenya said, *"Those who were employed suffer more than business people. The employed are unable to cope...business people are sharper and know how to look for money."*

Access to credit: People who retire at 55, or when they reach this age, feel that they are still capable of working and may merely want to shift to some work or business activity that demands less physical labour. As a result they may want credit to start a business but lack the necessary collateral in the form of assets or savings. Epainitus Mwigai, 48, a telephone operator in a small hotel in Nairobi says, *"I will be working for another 7 years. I would want to start a business after that. But from where will I get the money? I have no savings or assets to mortgage as security."*

Social Dimensions

Social aspects are often related to health, both physical and mental:

High social and financial costs: The HIV/AIDS pandemic is shifting much of the responsibility for taking care of children to their grandparents – who themselves are often old with meagre incomes.

> "Average life expectancy is 52 years in Sub-Saharan Africa, and efforts to increase it and make aging healthier are put at risk by the AIDS pandemic. The extended family has been a very resilient agent of support for the elderly, and studies show that most rural elderly have traditional tasks, such as caring for children, which are mutually beneficial. Extended family members, mainly the women, usually care for the elderly. However, AIDS threatens the viability of this system.

Grandparents are often left with few financial resources when their economically active sons and daughters die, but they are compelled to try and act as a complete substitute for the parents in caring for their orphaned grandchildren. Instead of reaching the time they had looked forward to, of being looked after by their children, they are faced with the arduous task all over again of raising children and finding money for clothes, food and school and clinic fees" (Hampson, 2005).

These practices leave many elderly people caring for school age children. Meeting educational expenses after retirement is a big challenge. Furthermore, the number of single mothers is high and on the rise, and this adds the financial burden of the grandchildren from unmarried, separated or divorced daughters. James Kijua Maliti working as a housekeeper/cleaner in a hotel in Nairobi says, *"We are ten siblings, my mother, a widow, has to take care of my younger siblings, four of whom are of school going age (but the elder two have dropped out) and now she also has to take care of my sister, 19, who came back home last month with two children."*

Social challenges: When people retire, their lack of engagement in work makes them feel unwanted, a problem exacerbated by the disintegration of extended family structures, which leave parents and grandparents uncared for. This results in a feeling of loneliness, neglect and depression. The old are often made to feel that they are a burden to society. As one respondent said, *"They* (old people) *die early due to stress."* Old people in rural areas are associated with witchcraft, which makes some old people social outcasts and further increases loneliness. *"As we grow old and young people start dying around the village, it's believed that we are the ones bewitching them,"* says Kiiza, 55, a retired teacher from Kawempe division a suburb of Kampala, Uganda. Lack of money for transport and communication, which would have allowed them to visit children and relatives, aggravates the issue.

Some African countries have special issues. Older people in Cameroon face a multiplicity of abuses of their rights and are often imprisoned for flimsy and sometimes trumped up charges. Elderly Cameroonians own almost 80% of the land both in towns and villages. With the rising value of and demand for land, rich and energetic younger people are keen to acquire the land and find ways to chase the old out. Any legal battle that follows is costly and almost always lands them in jail due to lack of sufficient knowledge of land tenure laws, inability to hire lawyers, inability to speak French or English, and no option of bail (HelpAge, 2005).

Preparing for Old Age

The focus groups revealed both economic and social issues in preparing for a secure old age. On the social front, respondents felt that Africans in general do not plan for their future – there is little or no culture of saving for the future. Daily consumption takes priority and is not always restricted to necessities. Money which could have been saved for the future is used up. *"A lot of people do not prepare for old age. They take life easy. They do not think about the future. They come to regret,"* says a respondent from the tea growing area of Kangari in Central Province, Kenya.

The common activities that are undertaken to provide income in old age resemble traditional practices more than a conscious preparation for old age. These include:

Investment in tangible assets: Savings in the form of a lump sum of cash is rare. Most people save up to invest in some asset, which is expected to reduce costs (for example, build a house and save on rent in old age) or to help earn cash (cows, to earn from selling milk and calves, or rent from previously constructed low cost houses).

In rural areas, the most common form of investment is buying farmland for subsistence or generating supplementary income by selling some part of the produce, such as vegetables or fruits. They exchange farm produce such as milk, beans, maize and bananas. Most households have livestock (cows, goats, chickens) which help earn money by selling milk and eggs, sale of calves (the animal is reared by a household, the owner gets the first two calves, the cattle rearer gets the next), or sale of an animal to meet an emergency, often big medical bills. Long-term investments are also made in cash crops such as coffee, tea and vanilla. In recent years planting trees has become a lucrative business because of the high demand for wood for charcoal, construction of houses, firewood for the tea factories as well as for domestic use, and for electricity poles.

In urban areas in particular, people build houses or other buildings to live in or to rent out. Others invest in equipment such as weighing scales, brick-making machines, workshop tools and similar items that can produce income later.

In simple terms, the common trends in investment may be categorised as:

- Those with small savings commonly invest in small-scale farming – growing crops and rearing animals.

- Those with medium-sized savings invest in small businesses, e.g. butcheries, trading or land to rent out for commercial farming.

- Those with larger savings invest in plots of land and build houses for rent, or buy a tractor to operate as a contractor on large wheat farms.

Investment in children: While school fees constitute a significant part of household expenditure, parents view this as an investment, assuming that children will take care of them in their old age. Depending on social background, some send their children to school or engage them in vocational education to acquire skills through apprenticeships, while others invest in their children by ensuring they get to university and find good jobs.

Education is expensive in East Africa. In Kenya, education is free in government primary schools. Ordinary private schools cost about Ksh (Kenyan shillings) 15,000 ($200) annually. Secondary school costs Ksh 45,000 to Ksh 60,000 ($600-800) per child per year. There are additional costs for books, uniforms, stationery, boarding and food. A common feeling among the respondents is, *"We parents try to give our best to our children – they are our biggest investment. But with the way things are changing, one can never be sure of returns on this investment."*

Invest in parallel businesses: Many employed people invest in small agricultural projects or small enterprises during the years they are employed, which are run by their children or other family members until they take over after retirement or in old age. Those who can accumulate a lump sum invest in long-term businesses such as starting schools or renting houses in the towns and cities.

Save cash in banks: Saving in banks is not the most common way to save. Most citizens of East Africa simply do not have enough faith in banks to entrust their long-term savings to them: *"Many banks have collapsed in the past...we do not trust banks anymore...."* In addition, banking charges are very high – particularly in Kenya. Market Intelligence's "Banking Survey of 2004" identified 129 types of charges levied by banks on their customers. With the small amounts that people manage to save, customers feel that banks deduct too much of their savings for too little service. Chris, a taxi driver in Nairobi says, *"I have withdrawn my savings and stopped operating my account in Kenya Post Office Savings Bank as they deduct Ksh 720 from my savings as ledger fee, they charge me a withdrawal fee for a service for which I have to stand two hours in a queue while I am also missing out on business opportunities."* James, a salary account holder in Akiba Bank, has the same lament: *"I am charged Ksh 100 for every withdrawal. That most often would be half or the total amount I would want to withdraw. So I withdraw a lump sum when my salary is credited, and retain it with me, though I know it makes me spend more and also my money is not safe in my house in Kibera (the biggest slum in Africa)."* Some respondents said that while people save in banks through savings accounts or fixed deposits, these were more for short-term purposes than very long-term requirements.

Informal groups: Most women respondents (from low- and middle-income groups) and men (from low-income groups) are members of informal financial groups – the "merry go-rounds" or rotating savings (and sometimes credit) associations. These help them save money that is eventually invested in an income-generating project or to buy small household items. Women attach a lot of importance to these groups for two reasons: first, the social benefit of being part of a local homogenous group, and second, the secrecy of the membership and/or the amount saved without their husbands' knowledge. Some people engage in a variety of menial jobs[2] such as gardening and lawn mowing, making charcoal, thatching houses, etc. The small amounts earned from such activities are saved in these informal groups, which accept small deposits at frequent intervals. Women find value in saving with microfinance institutions such as Faulu and savings and credit cooperatives so that they can borrow against these deposits. The money borrowed allows them to purchase livestock or plots of land, or to expand their small businesses. Only those people who are more informed and better off invest in shares, co-operatives and insurance policies.

---

[2]   This differs depending on whether it is rural or urban, and may also differ by community e.g. the Kikuyu are more likely to engage in farm employment while people from Western Kenya would engage in thatching houses.

Methods of Saving

All the above activities require funds big or small, short-term or long-term. Savings are acquired in various ways.

Specific schemes or savings plans: With the lack of strong savings habits and a reliable financial system for low-income people, cash savings come mostly through forced savings as government schemes (National Social Security Fund – NSSF) or welfare schemes in cooperatives. People also join cooperatives to save an amount that will make them eligible to obtain a loan which will help them buy an asset which in turn will produce income in their old age.

Cash savings: Savings in cash are mostly short-term, with an aim to pay for some planned or regular consumption purpose, or to use as security for a loan. People feel that income is disproportionate to their expenses and thus savings is not possible. People usually tend to consume all that is earned, even before the month end when salaries are paid. If they manage to save small amounts, it is saved in banks, through informal groups or with MFIs.

These small cash savings are not directly targeted for the long term. They are short-term savings that are used to buy assets that will help in the long run to earn income or to use as security to get a loan. As Makanga from Mukono in Kampala, Uganda says, *"This* [savings with an MFI] *is just a stage for this money to rest as I plan for it."* Talking to clients of *Jijenge,* a contractual savings/recurring account with Equity Bank in Kenya, reveals that people find contractual savings very helpful in saving small lump sums to use mainly for school fees or for buying household items such as electronics in urban areas and working tools or cattle in rural areas.

However, the clients also said that a special savings product like the *Jijenge* is not yet understood or popular in the region, and that the bank should conduct additional promotion to take the product into the market. The performance of the product reinforces this view: the *Jijenge* contributes no more than a very small portion of the bank's deposits. By contrast, at BURO, Tangail in Bangladesh, the contractual savings product accounts for two-thirds of the net savings mobilised (see Box 1 below). However, discussion with the respondents, including staff of Equity Bank and *Jijenge* account holders, reveals that more than 90% of the *Jijenge* clients renew their contract as soon as the account matures, rolling over the balance.

Save at home: Due to high banking charges, limited outreach in rural areas and poor past performance of banks in East Africa, much of the cash savings is found under the mattress. This kind of saving is often targeted, but for even smaller amounts, such as buying small Christmas gifts. When the target is met, the saving cycle is repeated for another purpose. This behaviour is common to all age groups, especially for the old.

Designing a Savings Scheme for Old Age

Focus group participants offered a broad range of recommendations that they thought would encourage people to save, citing information and user-friendly institutions as important motivations.

Awareness generation: The most important issue in the design of a savings scheme for old age, which was reinforced by the statements of many focus group participants, was that most people do not purposely save. Thus it is important first to educate people about why savings are so important before offering a savings scheme to assist them to develop the habit of saving for old age. Advisory services on investment and business planning were also requested, as many retired people lose their accumulated life savings in a few months as businesses fail due to lack of basic business management skills.

Savings product: An analysis of the challenges faced by respondents and their approaches to saving, as well as their recommendations, allows us to suggest the following product features. According to the respondents, the product *"should target the forties and fifties simply because at this age one starts thinking ahead – 'old-age'."* Eligibility age should be above 40 and up to 70 years.

Table 1. The "P's" and desired features of long-term savings products

The "P's"	Features
Product (design)	• Small opening balance and small minimum balance • Small deposit amounts at high frequency without charges • No or limited withdrawals (such as a lump sum every 5 or 10 years) • Long term recurrent, contract or disciplined savings • Free withdrawals (of limited partial amounts) for emergencies – especially medical bills • Use of savings to obtain loans (up to 90% of the amount saved) or up to 40% of the total investment • Fund diversion/withdrawal to cover unpaid loan arrears not permitted • Save up for a long period of time and at retirement permit the saver to choose to take out a lump sum of cash or to receive a specified amount of money per month until death, like a pension scheme
Price	• No or low transaction fees • High returns on investment • Interest rates paid on loans in proportion to interest rates earned on savings

Table 1 (continued)

The „P's"	Features

Promotion	• Most important, the product has to be actively promoted
	• All terms and conditions must be explained in detail
	• Should have excellent customer service for the elderly
	• Ensure long term security of saved amount:
	   o *"We prefer government involvement since what would happen if the NGO collapses"*
	   o *"We dislike government sole involvement in the proposed scheme due to bureaucracy in accessing savings"*
	   o *"We prefer NGOs due to easy decision making"*
	• Involvement of religious institutions may attract potential savers
	• Incentives and benefits: Should have support services such as medical treatment, funeral support, counselling and business (investment) advisory services, and medical insurance cover. Special staff should monitor the scheme, educate people, encourage savings. Respondents felt that financial institutions could also educate people about preparing for old age as well as how to run businesses
	• The name of the product should attract potential customers and communicate the target and purpose, such as: Savings for the Elderly, Long-term Savings Fund, Save for the Future.

Place	• Accessible in remote areas: *"services need to be convenient, since we'll definitely become so weak to walk long distances".*
Positioning	• Helps people to develop security • Helps plan a secured future • Cares for the client's welfare even when they are not most productive for the bank
Physical Evidence	• Documentation should be minimal and simple • Branches should have special arrangements for the elderly, especially those who are sick
People	• Good support from staff who deal with clients: time, patience and clarity • Staff specially trained to deal with the elderly
Process	• Should be minimal and simple • Access to amounts saved by the beneficiary should be simple • Additional support in counselling or training for business

A Pension-cum-Mortgage Scheme

Another scheme that sparked interest was based on long-term investment: Many participants felt that their savings should not remain as cash in the bank but should rather go into investments in order to generate a higher return. They referred to SACCOs (savings and credit cooperatives) that engage in property investments – although some of these are seen as unreliable. They suggested that:

- The saver should commit to regular and long-term saving.

- The bank should use these (long-term) funds to purchase property (land and/or buildings) on behalf of the savers.

- At or around retirement the land would be subdivided into small plots and distributed to the savers.

- If the investment were in building(s), the bank would continue managing the building(s) and the savers would receive their earnings on a monthly basis.

- The saver should be allowed to borrow against his or her long-term pension savings.

- The bank should also provide insurance services so that in case of death or disability the policy provides for basic subsistence.

Conclusion

Demand side: Currently, low-income people rarely plan for old age – either because they do not think they need to do so until it is too late, or because they are too busy living hand-to-mouth. However, many low-income customers seek access to emergency funds to respond to crises and opportunities. These emergency funds can take the form of loans against, or of limited withdrawals from, long-term contractual savings.

When low-income people start to provide for old age, they use a variety of informal and often insecure approaches to meet this goal. The most common way of saving is through small investments in land, housing, livestock, working tools, small business, etc. A key motive for saving through in-kind investment rather than saving in cash lies in the economic trends in East Africa (Kenya, Tanzania and Uganda). The inflation rate has ranged from 4% to 9% in the three countries and the currencies have mostly devalued over the past five years (CIA – The World FactBook). This increases the cost of living and has negative impact on long-term savings, especially for the poor who save small amounts. Furthermore, most banks in East Africa are highly liquid and the T-bill rates in the region are relatively low (as of March 2006 6.8% in Kenya, 7.5% in Uganda and around 9% in Tanzania). As a result banks do not provide attractive interest rates on deposits, particularly for accounts with low balances.

While in-kind investments can bring better returns than cash savings, these approaches often fail – investments are unsuccessful, children do not take care of their parents as hoped, livestock die, crops fail or people to whom they have rented land or housing do not pay (Wright and Mutesasira, 2001).

Savings in cash is preferred over investment when helpful conditions are attached. For example, for all the discussion of returns amongst the focus group participants, it is primarily the *discipline* of contractual savings arrangements that makes them attractive. Small but regular savings soon generate a relatively large lump sum. As noted above, at Equity Bank in Kenya, even though the interest rate paid was low, over 90% of those who completed one *Jijenge* contract, renewed and started another contract immediately.

Box 1: Contractual Savings at BURO, Tangail in Bangladesh

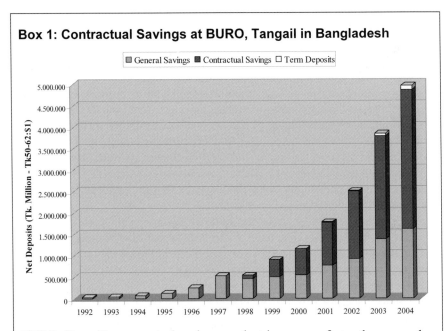

BURO, Tangail's contractual savings product has grown faster than any other and constitutes 65.5% of the total savings deposited with the institution. At the beginning of 2004 there were 135,091 Contractual Savings Accounts. 48,238 of these matured during the year and were withdrawn, and 89,541 accounts were opened, producing a total of 176,394 accounts (with an average balance of $18.45) as of December 31, 2004, amounting to $3,254,672. In the eight years since the contractual savings accounts were pilot-tested in 1997, a total of 305,860 accounts were opened and 129,466 matured. At the end of 2004 BURO, Tangail had 221,366 customers and (given that some members have multiple accounts) around 70% of customers owned a contractual savings account.

Source: BURO, Tangail Annual Report, 2004.

The potential market for long-term contractual savings services that provide security in old age is huge and growing over time. The two potential markets are:

- The middle aged who would want to use old age financial services in about 20 years; and

- Young people who are entering their income-earning years and who have shown a rising consciousness about the importance of saving for old age.

Clearly the earlier people start saving, the lower the amounts they will have to save weekly or monthly to generate a lump sum for their old age. When young people start saving from an early age, they will generate an asset against which they can borrow in times of need or opportunity – thus reducing their insecurity not just in old age but throughout their lives.

Supply side: As noted above, banks in East Africa are presently cash rich and most of them exceed the minimum liquidity requirements of their respective Central Banks by a significant margin. Hence a long-term high interest savings product may not be what many financial institutions would want to promote – and indeed in East Africa the vast majority of savings accounts offer negative real rates of return. Nonetheless, such long-term savings instruments for the low-income market may be attractive products for savings banks to offer. Alternatively, it may be more desirable, for both the banks and their customers, to offer short- and medium-term contractual savings products. Customers could then use the lump sums generated through these products to buy the land, housing, and other assets that they hope will provide security in old age.

While the potential for longer-term contractual savings instruments is significant, so are the potential pitfalls. The financial institutions that offer these products must be exceptionally stable so that they do not put precious life savings at risk. Longer-term savings instruments also necessitate excellent asset-liability management to ensure that returns are optimised without compromising risk or liquidity management. Finally, these products are complex and require careful selling – both to attract customers and, of particular importance, to ensure that the customers are aware of what they are buying. For example, in South Africa, low-income people are often sold multiple life insurance policies with premiums that they cannot afford – and thus they surrender the policies at heavily discounted values.

And of course, sadly, the lump-sum payout upon completion of the contractual savings agreement will not ensure a secure old age if it is inappropriately invested. In this case, it can rapidly disappear when the "pensioner" needs it most.

References

Aging in Africa, HelpAge International, Issue 23, 2005a

Aging in Africa, HelpAge International, Issue 25, 2005b

BURO, Tangail, Annual Report, 2004

CIA – The World Factbook,
    http://www.odci.gov/cia/publications/factbook/index.html

Ferreira, Monica and Karen Charlton, "Aging inequitably in South Africa,"
    http://www.islamset.com/healnews/aged/Monica.html

Gorman, Mark, "Age and Security," HelpAge International, 2004

Hampson, Joe, "Threats to Health and Well Being in Africa," n.d.,
    http://www.islamset.com/healnews/aged/Joe_hampson.html

Market Intelligence, "Banking Survey, 2004", *Economic Intelligence*, Nairobi,
    2005

Wright, Graham A.N. and Leonard K. Mutesasira, "The Relative Risks to the
    Savings of Poor People." *Journal of Small Enterprise Development*, Vol. 12,
    No. 3, ITDG, London, 2001

CHAPTER 16:

Microinsurance: Providing Profitable Risk Management Possibilities for the Low-Income Market

Michael J. McCord

President, The MicroInsurance Centre

Introduction

Insurers have hardly touched a massive potential demand for specialised insurance products in the developing world's low-income markets. The demand for appropriate risk management services offers insurance companies an opportunity to expand this market greatly by treating it as a specialised niche rather than as a development activity. This perspective can lead to profitable operations for insurers and can make a dramatic impact on the development of this low-income market.

What Is Microinsurance? Quick Definition: Products and Delivery Mechanisms

> "Microinsurance is the protection of low-income people against specific perils in exchange for regular premium payments proportionate to the likelihood and cost of the risk involved. Low-income people can use microinsurance, where it is available, as one of several tools to manage risks.[1] Together, these tools form a complex matrix through which low-income people manage their risks."[2]

---

[1] "The Preliminary Donor Guidelines for Supporting Microinsurance" define social protection as a set of policies and programmes designed to reduce poverty and vulnerability by promoting efficient labour markets, diminishing people's exposure to risks, and enhancing their capacity to protect themselves against hazards and interruption or loss of income. Social protection policies and procedures involve five activities: Labour market policies and programmes, social insurance programmes, social assistance, micro and area-based schemes, and child protection.

[2] CGAP Working Group on Microinsurance. "Preliminary Donor Guidelines for Supporting Microinsurance." October 2003. Available at: http://www.microinsurancecentre.org/index.cfm?fuseaction=resources.documents.

Table 1. Key differences between insurance and microinsurance

Characteristics of Insurance:	How Microinsurance Is Different:
Coverage	• Coverage is often more restricted. • Efforts made to cover only easily verifiable events. • Key exclusions (for example, chronic illness) are usually made to keep the premium as low as possible.
Premiums	• There are very limited data on which to base risk premiums. • Risk structures are different for low-income than for upper-income people. This requires special consideration (risk provisions). • Efficiency is required to keep premiums within the reach of this market.
Delivery Channels	• Must be able to obtain high policyholder volumes at a very low cost. • Insurers often pair with others who deliver financial products to the low-income market.
Terms	• Access is often granted only through membership in a group that is based on loans and other simple financial services. • Policy duration is frequently not annual, in order to match policyholder cash flows.
Benefits	• Life cover for outstanding debt, funeral expenses and/or transitional expenses. • Some policies provide in-kind benefits, such as payment of utilities for a defined period or a monthly credit at a super-market. • Health benefits may cover reasonable un-receipted expenses.

Microinsurance products are specifically designed for the low-income market in terms of coverage, premiums, delivery channels, terms, and benefits. Table 1 identifies key areas of divergence between microinsurance and insurance generally.

Several types of microinsurance are currently offered – mostly life and health care with some forays into property, livestock, and indexing of rainfall and commodity prices. By far the most common microinsurance product in the low-income market is credit life insurance covering a loan balance payable upon the death of a borrower. Some term life policies are offered to help families cover basic necessities, while others provide funeral and transition funds. La Equidad in Colombia has been particularly innovative with life plans that cover costs such as utilities and children's medical care for a period after the death of the insured person. A summary of their Basic Protection and Small Business Protection plans is presented in Appendix 1.

Why Is Microinsurance Important to Development?

Risks Facing Low-Income People

Low-income people are often on the edge of deep poverty, only a crisis away from falling back into it. Although they generally face the same financial crises as everyone else – loss of a breadwinner, health care costs, or property damage due to natural calamities, for example – low-income people have a limited ability to manage these risks. This is a principal reason why microinsurance is important for development.

Several microinsurance demand studies have identified (1) which risks low-income people face, (2) how they manage those risks, and (3) where there are gaps in risk management tools (Simkhada et al 2000; Matul 2004, Cohen and Sebstad 2005). These qualitative studies indicate that low-income people view events that adversely affect health, life and property as their most significant risks. Loan repayment coverage in the form of credit life insurance is not a major priority for low-income people.

Impact of These Risks

Serious financial stress may deplete the resources of low-income families. The reduction of their assets occurs as a result of the risk event and also because of the way they address the loss. Different risk events result in different responses and different impacts. A mild risk, such as an outpatient visit for a minor illness, typically causes only low stress on the household. The small reduction of available funds may be recouped through a few days of reduced consumption. The death of a breadwinner typically causes more serious financial stress because of the costs of the funeral and related events, which often require contributions from family and friends. This creates social obligations for the family, but it may also satisfy social obligations of others to the household of the deceased. After the funeral the family may have a significantly lower level of income, which may result in a shift to a cheaper residence, taking children out of school and putting older children to work. The family's ability to manage future shocks may be considerably reduced.

A very serious financial crisis such as a fire or road accident might cause a family to liquidate its assets in order to generate cash. Consequently, families affected by such an event often have nothing left to rebuild their financial security, and are left to struggle.

Fig. 1. Risk management choices

How People Respond to Risks

Everyone faces risk. Intentionally or subconsciously, people identify risks, consider their potential impacts, and develop strategies to manage them. Options for managing risk are illustrated in Figure 1.[3]

The effects of each of these strategies are varied. Risk avoidance minimises innovation: people do what they can to avoid risky situations. Reducing risk can be easily implemented by everyone, such as the market woman who brings all her inventory home at the end of the working day because there is no safe place to store it in or near the market. Sharing risk through local groups is very common, especially for funerals. Members of these groups pay into a fund through periodic contributions or when a covered event affects a member. These groups provide very important social benefits which often outstrip the financial advantages.

Retaining risk is often the principal risk management strategy of a low-income household. They may save money "for a rainy day", or join a microfinance provider (MFP)[4] or another group that provides emergency credit. However, such services are often unavailable to low-income and rural people. Thus, they generate funds from their own resources by reducing caloric consumption, liquidating consumer household goods or selling business inventory, discounting and selling the rice paddy as in Cambodia, or the cow in Kenya, or the gold in Ghana. The strategy of retaining risk can often lead to much suffering within the household. Finally, people may have access to the risk-pooling benefits of insurance. Insurance

---

[3]   Adapted from Charles van Oppen, 2001.

[4]   MFPs are defined here as banks, NGOs, cooperatives, credit unions, and others that conduct financial transactions with low-income members or clients.

allows them access to a much greater range of cover at values that are usually more appropriate to their situations.

In a number of countries the state provides some risk management options related to health care, retirement, disability, and even funerals. However, low-income people who do not have cash or "friends" in the appropriate institutions may find these benefits difficult to obtain.

Everyone manages risk using some combination of these options. The risk management strategies of the wealthy are skewed much more towards insurance, with limited use of the retention strategy through deductibles. Low-income people, especially in rural areas, are much more focused on retention and risk-sharing through groups. Low-income urban families often focus on retention, avoidance, and reduction, since groups do not feature as prominently in urban areas.

Adequacy of These Mechanisms

Qualitative research on microinsurance demand (Simkhada et al 2000; Matul 2004, Cohen and Sebstad 2005) typically begins with inquiries about the risks people face. Participants are queried on how they manage these risks, and then on the voids in or limits of these strategies. When many people decide to liquidate their productive assets and move into deeper poverty simply to recover from risky events, it becomes apparent that current risk management mechanisms are inadequate.

People try to avoid and reduce risk, but they cannot eliminate it. The local sharing of risk is often insufficient because it is intended to cover only a portion of the costs of an insurable event. Some funeral groups, for example, pay only for the coffin, or will meet their obligation by donating money to purchase food for the mourners. To reiterate, group risk management activities are often more social than financial.

The insufficiency of these risk management methods weakens a family's "protective armour". This leads to a demand for products and services that will strengthen this armour. However, several components must be considered when trying to understand the complex construct of demand and how it is generated. Insurance is particularly difficult for low-income people to obtain. They frequently do not know much about insurance or have negative impressions based on unsettled claims (often of old parastatal insurers). Developing demand requires a product that addresses the market's appetite, a market that understands insurance, and a structure for easy payment and claims settlement.

How Microinsurance Assists Development

Much has been done since the 1980s to provide basic financial services for micro and small businesses and their owners throughout the developing world. The credit and restricted savings facilities that were first offered are slowly being expanded to provide a variety of borrowing opportunities and more respect for customers' efforts to save. Credit and savings can and do assist people to manage risks, but these buffers rarely are sufficient to meet high-cost, low-predictability shocks. Throughout financial markets, credit, savings, and insurance go hand-in-hand. When these three products are not available, the market is inefficient because people use non-financial means to manage their financial lives.

Social Protection and Private Insurance: Competition or Partners?

Governments also have a role in allocating funds to protect the destitute and those without the ability to generate sufficient funds for their own risk management. Private insurance will never be able to cover this market fully. However, if private insurers could develop, manage, and sell microinsurance products that effectively mitigate the risks facing the working poor at a premium that provides reasonable profits, the burden on government would be reduced. A system in which those with incomes manage their own risks through microinsurance products offers an opportunity for the government to be more effective in providing social protection to those who have no other option. Social protection and private insurance, as well as informal insurance mechanisms, should not compete. They should collaborate to provide protection across the entire income spectrum.

Figure 2 clarifies the roles of those involved in microinsurance[5] by disaggregating the Indian consumer market into five levels of income: destitutes, aspirants,

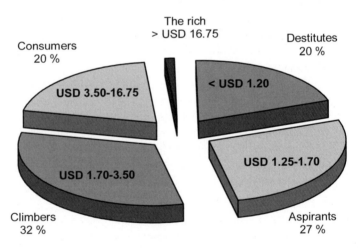

Fig. 2. Classification of the consumer market in India by income distribution (% of 165 million households, with income ranges in USD per day)

---

[5]   IndiaOneStop.com slightly modified from the National Council of Applied Economic Research (NCAER). Data from 1995/6.

climbers, consumers, and the rich. The destitutes, earning less than USD1.25 per day, comprise about thirty-three million households. Providing insurance for this segment should be the responsibility of the government, although in India there are microinsurance products available for those earning less than USD1 per day. The aspirants and the climbers earn between USD1.25 and USD3.50 per day. They are moving forward economically and if they have not already done so, are likely to become interested in commercial risk management products. Aspirants and climbers account for almost sixty percent of households in India, or about ninety-seven million households.

Consumers, at the fourth level of income, may already buy health and even life insurance through their employers and automobile insurance directly with insurers. The lower end of the consumer group is also likely to obtain microinsurance products because these may be better suited to their concerns and more easily accessible. The rich are either well insured or self-insuring. Insurers focus an inordinate amount of energy on the rich, often trying to undercut their competitors.

Hence in India, possibly thirty-three million households should be insured by the government. At least one hundred million could buy microinsurance if the products were appropriately designed and available. Finally, up to thirty-five million households might have access to traditional insurance.

Indigenous risk management tools are found everywhere. In many places – Georgia, Ghana, Indonesia, Mexico, Uganda, and many others – these tools continue to be used, primarily because they offer important social benefits and secondarily because they provide a financial benefit. Microinsurance products reduce reliance on these local risk management tools.

The government's social protection programmes, insurers offering traditional as well as microinsurance products, and indigenous groups all have a role in the management of risk. These parties can and should work together to provide effective and efficient cover.

The Role of Insurers in Microinsurance

Expertise, Risk Management, Systems, Reinsurance

Insurers' skills and infrastructure can be adapted to microinsurance. Insurers may offer products to the low-income market, but they are often neither particularly interested in this market nor well positioned to influence it. Even a good commission rate yields premiums that generate only relatively small returns for the agent. Accordingly, few insurers have been active in low-income markets. Even where insurers have seen potential, they lacked an efficient means of access.

Insurers are now finding infrastructure within the low-income markets that can provide access in much more efficient ways. Commercial insurers' new recognition of this market comes at a time when growth within the high-end market is limited, motivating many of them to look for new opportunities. To be effective, insurance companies have to develop or adapt new delivery mechanisms. Aldagi Insurance in Georgia, for example, offers health cover through the Constanta Foundation, a local MFP (microfinance provider). Delta Life in Bangladesh created a new division with an entirely different set of agents, rather than their traditional agents, to create an infrastructure that makes it possible to offer life insurance and long-term savings attractive to extremely poor people in a profitable manner.

Microfinance has helped insurance move into the low-income market in several ways.

- MFPs have effectively entered low-income markets and have created infrastructure to conduct financial transactions.

- MFPs have shown that low-income people save, pay bills on time, and can be financially responsible.

- MFPs have identified risk management opportunities among their clients.

- Some MFPs have begun bringing mainstream insurers into microinsurance through relatively simple products such as credit life and basic term-life insurance.

The health insurance market has hardly been touched by commercial insurers, although the potential demand is staggering. Their general lack of interest reflects the difficulty in calculating adequate premiums. Margins are very small because it is difficult, even for actuaries, to estimate the likely frequency of illnesses and accidents.[6] There is often no data available for their actuarial calculations. Compounding these deterrents is the cost of controls to manage fraud, moral hazard, and adverse selection. Typically, life insurance provides a greater return to insurers than health insurance, as reflected in the divergent levels of insurer interest and development. In fact, commercial insurers' interest in microinsurance has focused largely on life products, less so on personal accident and property coverage.

Although few, there are examples of health microinsurance products, including:

- Microcare Health Limited in Uganda offers comprehensive health cover.

- Constanta in Georgia is working with Aldagi Insurance.

- La Equidad in Colombia provides life insurance that covers the health of children.

---

[6] Utilisation data are collected mainly through hospitals. Whatever data are available are therefore more relevant to the experience of middle to upper income people, rather than on lower-income people who have limited access to hospitals. The risk profile of low-income people in developing countries is much different from that of middle and upper income people.

Box 1: The Case of Insurance Liberalisation in India

In 2000, India liberalised its insurance market. A new law prescribed quotas requiring insurers to maintain an annually increasing outreach to rural areas based on the number of policyholders for life insurers or percentage of premiums for other insurers. Unlike any other country, India, through its Insurance Regulatory Development Authority (IRDA) has actively promoted microinsurance in this way. The IRDA is also developing a separate microinsurance law.

How Microinsurance Can Be Delivered Efficiently

Simplistically, insurance premiums should be set using the following calculation:[7]

Table 2. The basic method of calculating premiums

	Premium Component[8]	Description
+	Risk Premium	(The benefit amount) times (the probability that the risk event will occur). This projected amount should approximate the actual value of claims when they occur.
+	Operating Costs	Include: marketing, administration, reinsurance, actuarial activities, commissions, and others.
+	Profit Margin	Value based on a percentage of premiums projected by the institution.
-	Investment Income	Most relevant for long-term products like endowments. Short-term products may generate some investment income.
=	The Premium	Initial operating subsidies from government or donors, or from public or private investors at any stage, could reduce the premium.

There are several ways to keep the cost of microinsurance low while maintaining profitability:

---

[7] Actuarial skills are required to compute the actual premium, but this calculation shows the cost components that are generally considered by actuaries.

[8] Churchill, C., D. Liber, M.J. McCord, and J. Roth. "Making Insurance Work for Microfinance." ILO,Geneva, 2003.

288   Michael J. McCord

- Reducing the value of the benefit or restricting the coverage can reduce the risk premium. AAR Health Services in Kenya reduced the value by limiting access to "C," "D" and some "B" level hospitals.[9] GRET Cambodia restricted coverage by specifying illnesses and covering certain diseases only and "surgery of the torso".[10] However, demand research clearly highlights that many low-income people would like more comprehensive protection. Thus, the objective for developing a health microinsurance product would include the widest possible range based on the demand in particular areas.

Box 2

AAR Health Services in Kenya had 220 policyholders in November 2003. 199, or 90%, chose comprehensive cover even though it cost about 2.5 times the cost of the product that provided only in-patient coverage.

(AAR Health Services data calculated by the author)

- Controls also reduce costs, as elaborated later. Having systems that simply confirm that the insured is the one receiving care, or who is the deceased, can reduce claims costs. Substitution of an uninsured for an insured is a classic loss for insurers, especially where doctors might not be very well paid. One health insurer claims to save between thirty and forty percent of premiums through their careful, yet efficient, management of controls.[11]

- Providing an inexpensive, popular, comprehensive, profitable product requires processes that ensure maximum efficiency in all areas of operation. Most community-based health microinsurers do this partly through volunteer management and the elimination of commissions. Some hospitals set up their own provider-based schemes that take the premiums right into their coffers, but this requires several types of insurance skills that are often lacking. Insurers are also developing more efficient networks with MFPs and others for the low-income market.

- Subsidies have been very important for institutions like SEWA in India that leverage donor subsidies to reduce the cost of premiums. However, subsidies can be dangerous, often promising too much, especially when the donor is not knowledgeable about efficient insurance operations.

---

[9]   The hospital quality scale ranks "A" as the highest quality facilities, "D" as the lowest.

[10] McCord, M.J., "Microinsurance: A Case Study of an Example of the Provider Model of Microinsurance Provision – GRET Cambodia", Nairobi, MicroSave, 2001. Available at www.microinsurancecentre.org.

[11] McCord, M.J. and S. Osinde, "Microcare Ltd. Health Plan (Uganda): Notes from a visit 17– 21 June 2002." MicroSave, Nairobi, 2002. Available at: www.microinsurancecentre.org.

Linkages between insurers and MFPs in the broad sense are being created in many countries.

Microinsurance is typically offered through a partnership of regulated insurers selling through intermediaries, or by a mutually-owned entity. These relationships create a synergy of skills when organisations that have access and capacity to work with low-income people are coupled with insurers who know the risks and how to manage them. In this case, each party shares its skills, without which neither could effectively serve this insurance market. For these relationships to be successful, transactions have to be efficient, and good communication is essential between insurers and the party representing the insureds.

Several areas of growth are soon likely to occur on parallel paths. Programmes and relationships will be upgraded and expanded as insurers become more interested in this market and experiment with new mechanisms for effective collaboration. Gemini Life is experimenting by placing an agent in rural bank branches in Ghana to sell life and endowment products. Many MFPs are making microinsurance mandatory for borrowers, which is more efficient but not an ideal response to client demands. A few new insurance companies may arise from MFP activities such as the CARD Mutual Benefit Association in the Philippines or from NGOs like Microcare. But this greenfield route is difficult.

Some insurers may be enthusiastic about downscaling into this market and may modify their operations to reach down-market clients. For example, Delta Life successfully built its own low-income market network. Others will downscale through intermediaries such as MFPs. AIG Uganda is a good example, with 1.6 million lives insured as of mid-2004 through nineteen group policies to MFPs. The success of either method will depend on costs. Though preliminary and not a perfect comparison, the operating cost ratio of Delta Life's proprietary delivery structure[12] was about ten percent greater than that of AIG Uganda's MFP network.[13]

Opportunities for Insurers in Microinsurance

Growth

A study conducted by Swiss Re sigma on the future market for insurance products in India and China states that, "emerging markets will be at the frontier of insurance in the 21st century. Non-life premiums collected in emerging markets are expected to double by 2014...at constant prices. Life premiums will increase even

[12] McCord, M.J., and Craig Churchill. "Delta Life Bangladesh: CGAP Working Group on Microinsurance – Good and Bad Practices in Microinsurance, Case Study No. 7", ILO, Geneva, 2005.

[13] McCord, M.J, Felipe Botero, and Janet S. McCord. "AIG Uganda: CGAP Working Group on Microinsurance – Good and Bad Practices in Microinsurance, Case Study No. 9", ILO, Geneva, 2005.

faster ... over the same period."[14] While China and India will provide a dispropor-tionate amount of this growth, dramatic expansion is also likely in many other developing countries and emerging markets. There are great opportunities for innovative and flexible insurers that seek profitable growth in the low-income market. Growth will come from expanding markets that will cover a much wider range of household incomes. Microinsurance will be a key instrument for insurers who want access to these markets.

Box 3

„[The low-income markets] were previously regarded as not worth spending any time developing products for. However, clearly they are a big emerging market. Any insurer would be well advised to give it focus, to study their needs, and get in there whilst there is still time."

Barrie Cambridge, Chief Executive, East Africa Underwriters

How Big Is This Market?

Nearly 3000 MFPs participated in the 2003 Microcredit Summit Campaign. They reported that they served a combined pool of 81 million borrowers of whom 55 million were amongst the "poorest",[15] and 45 million were women.[16] These num-bers typically represent one family member within an average household of possi-bly five people, which could translate into life, property and health cover for 400 million people. Many large MFPs are or will soon be able to offer savings prod-ucts, which is likely to produce client bases in which depositors typically far out-number borrowers. Finally, annual aggregate MFP growth in the numbers of cli-ents is between twenty-five and fifty percent in many countries. Although this growth rate will certainly decline, the opportunity for growth is phenomenal. If insurers develop appropriate products that can be managed efficiently, the micro-insurance premium potential could dwarf that of other insurance products. It is not unreasonable to expect that the total microinsurance market could consist of well over one hundred million policyholders before 2015.[17]

---

[14] Swiss Re sigma study: "High growth potential puts emerging markets at frontier of insurance – China and India in the spotlight". 7 October 2004.

[15] "Poorest" refers to the bottom half of the population living below the poverty line of any country.

[16] Daley-Harris, Sam. The State of the MicroCredit Summit Campaign Report 2004. http://www.microcreditsummit.org/pubs/reports/socr/2004/SOCR04.pdf.

[17] Growth will be relatively slow initially, building momentum as more insurers enter the markets and more people understand insurance.

The Microcredit Summit Campaign also points out that the upper fifty percent of the poor who live below the poverty line comprise 235 million families around the world. If efficient outreach mechanisms were available, these families could potentially be microinsured.

Profitability

Profitability in microinsurance is earned by offering appropriate products to masses of people in an efficient manner. Microinsurance products have very low margins. But if these products are sold to large numbers of people, the accumulated income could be quite substantial. A number of microinsurers have reported profits from microinsurance operations, especially with life products. Examples include La Equidad in Colombia, Tuw Skok in Poland, CARD MBA in the Philippines, AIG Uganda, and Delta Life in Bangladesh.

Creating profitability in health insurance is more difficult. Despite several attempts by regulated insurers, no sustained profitability has been recorded for health microinsurance. Some community-based groups show a surplus because they use local volunteers, keeping their operational costs low while permitting a higher loss ratio that benefits their members, but other factors may make it difficult for some to keep their loss ratios below 1.0.

What makes one programme or product more profitable than another? The key seems to lie in the quality of the risk premium calculation and operating efficiency. Too many "microinsurers" still base their premiums on what they think their customers can pay or at a level the customers say they will pay, often without any real understanding of the product they are asked to value. At the same time, such insurers usually want to offer as much coverage as they can, leading to diverging cash flows. Where actuaries carefully set premiums, there is a significantly better chance that the risk premium will be consistent with claims.

Controls

Microinsurance demands strong and innovative controls for adverse selection, moral hazard, and fraud. Lax controls in these areas commonly bankrupt even regulated insurers. While microinsurance requires strong controls, there must be a flexible approach to managing them. For example, a death certificate usually accompanies a death claim But in many countries it is almost impossible to obtain a death certificate in rural areas, making it inappropriate to require such a document from rural policyholders. To confirm the death, some organisations use a service with a wide network and may settle the claim immediately in cash or in kind. Others require letters of confirmation from religious and/or local political leaders. In this way, control is maintained using mechanisms that are manageable for rural policyholders.

Health insurance is prone to fraud and moral hazard. Doctors will submit claims for treatments and medications that they do not dispense, even splitting the proceeds with the policyholder. Another common ruse is to substitute an uninsured person for an insured. Both of these deceptions can be disastrous for the insurer. Microcare in Uganda counters these problems by having an insurance desk in the waiting rooms of the hospitals they work with, which allows them to confirm the identity and status of the covered person. Using these strategies hand in hand with software that they have developed has minimised these control issues. Microcare Management believes these processes save more than thirty percent on premiums after covering the costs of their personnel and equipment in the hospitals. These controls are examples of insurance risk management in a niche market.

Quality of Care

The quality of care and availability of facilities that provide it strongly limit the potential expansion of health microinsurance. In many areas care or facilities that an insurer can trust are simply not available. This problem led organisations like BRAC and Grameen Kalyan in Bangladesh, and GRET in Cambodia, to develop their own health care facilities. National policy issues such as these arise in many countries lacking good quality medical facilities.

Good quality care is important, but not just because an insurer should pay only for good treatment. The availability of good treatment, combined with microinsurance that helps people to pay for it, reduces losses for the household as well as for the insurer. In contrast to the uninsured, evidence from Uganda and South Africa shows that people who have health microinsurance are more likely to seek care earlier in the disease cycle. This leads to faster recovery, reduced business losses, and lower treatment costs charged to the insurer.[18]

A Role for Donors

Microinsurance is and should be a commercial venture. Donors should focus on research and product development when insurers are reluctant to invest. With such support, some of these products, like that of AIG Uganda, might have been launched in a form better suited to the market. For insurance to be successful, the insured must pay at least the cost of claims based on realistic projections.

The GLICO life policy with an endowment rider in Ghana had significant donor input through CARE in its research and development (R&D) phase. This collaboration produced a product that was well received, though marketing requires invigoration. Without donor input, GLICO would probably not have entered the low-income market. Other insurers, such as Tata AIG in India, have received lim-

---

[18] Blanchard-Horan, C. "Health Microinsurance Affects Health Behaviour and Malaria Treatment: A Multi-Site Case Comparison Study in Uganda," 2006, and "Health Microinsurance in Uganda," International Journal of Public Administration, 2007. Also see David Dror et al., forthcoming.

ited donor funds and/or donor-paid research. Donor funding that was promised was slow to come in these cases, prompting the insurers to use their own funds to invest in these products. Some microinsurance has been developed and offered without direct donor funding. These include Delta Life, CARD MBA, and AIG Uganda. Donors can have the greatest influence on microinsurance development by funding R&D in ways that are likely to lead to commercial sustainability.

Table 3. Examples of activities for investors in microinsurance markets

Investment option	Discussion
Insurance brokerages	Brokerage activities are weak in many developing countries. Brokers could serve the whole market with a special focus on microinsurance products. Brokers help develop products and ensure that communications and processes are efficient. Their activities might be manageable on a regional basis, increasing market potential and bridging the gap between insurers and potential delivery channels.
Licences for joint ventures in other countries for successful domestic companies with good microinsurance operations	Some domestic insurance companies are testing and proving systems and procedures that create successful microinsurance provision for insurers, intermediaries, and policyholders. Invest in these companies' expansion in other countries and in the adaptation of their "technology" to a new market.
Development of efficiency-enhancing infrastructure	Microinsurance success is predicated on efficient operations and huge numbers of policyholders. New technology will be necessary to manage the volume of small premium payments. In India, for example, ICICI is testing life insurance sales by computer from the villages.
Efficient claims settlement companies	With multitudes of insured, ways must be developed to settle claims efficiently. A company with a wide network of agents could confirm death, for example, and provide a cash settlement or the requirements for the funeral, as is done by at least one company in South Africa. This improves customer service and promotes better controls, which could lead to greater demand for insurance.
Long-term savings custodian	In Georgia and many other countries the private sector is or will be able to collect pensions and long-term savings. The limited confidence in these institutions could be enhanced by a credible custodial company that would expand the market by encouraging reluctant savers to invest.
New delivery channels	Partnership model delivery channels have tended to have limited success. Innovative delivery mechanisms should be identified and developed, such as through remittances, enhanced technology, or new linkages.

Assisting Greenfield Microinsurers

The extensive network of insurance companies throughout the world obviates the need to start specialised microinsurance companies. Exceptions consist of situations in which there are no insurers to provide the critical services that the low-income market requires. For example, the demand for health care financing was great, but no insurance company would offer coverage after the last one remaining in the market went bankrupt because of weak controls. This was one reason for the development and licensing of Microcare in Uganda. Private investment provided the capital for its insurance licence, and donors are funding some of its transition and scaling-up. In the Philippines CARD helped start a Mutual Benefit Association (MBA), which has CARD (an NGO) and CARD Bankas the MBA's only insured clients. Being an insurer would have created a great risk for CARD as an NGO with a small capital base. The MBA as an independent legal entity does not generate a financial risk for CARD.

There is a role for donor support in helping insurers expand into the low-end market. Initial R&D assistance could help more insurers better understand the low-end market as a viable risk.

Role for Investors

There are a number of opportunities for investors in microinsurance, some of which are suggested in Table 3.

Key Market Access Points – Efficiency Is the Key

Microfinance Providers

Organisations conducting financial transactions in the low-income market can produce efficient interventions for microinsurance. Typical institutional agents have been banks, credit unions, and other MFPs. These institutions that work intensively in the low-income market can process additional financial transactions such as microinsurance at little additional cost.

As microinsurance sold and serviced by "traditional" agents becomes better understood and managed, it should be expanded to include other potential agents. The prolific funeral societies might be able to provide better financial services to their members if they were linked to insurance companies. Community-based groups might also be able to improve their risk management services if they were linked to an insurer or overseen by a "social reinsurance" mechanism. Around the globe, many cooperatives and mutual benefit associations are moving towards specialised regulation, and some may be able to offer new products. For example, CARD Mutual Benefit Association manages life and long-term savings very well, and is negotiating for health cover with PhilHealth[19] through CARD MBA and its CARD partners. This type of relationship enables insurance organisations to provide additional products keyed to their own level of risk.

If microinsurance is to realise its potential, agents must be skilled and well-regarded, the importance of such non-traditional relationships must be recognised, and tools must be developed that make these relationships efficient and effective.

Remittances

The World Bank's Global Development Finance report for 2005 noted that remittances to developing countries approximated USD128 billion,[20] and that the volume was growing by an average rate of about twelve percent per year.[21] Linkages between remittances and microinsurance products might create efficiencies: migrants could have a more powerful effect on their home country households if they could designate part of their remittances to pay microinsurance premiums. For example, a life policy could cover the cost of their parents' funerals and the migrant's cost of going home to attend. And, the family could be covered for health care. By smoothing the expenses of the migrant and providing protection for the family, these types of arrangements could produce a very positive, valued impact.

Electronic Applications to Speed up Processes and Expand Cover

The objective of providing effective microinsurance products to as many low-income people as possible requires the development of efficient physical processes and technology-based infrastructure. Although this infrastructure is expensive to develop, test, and bring online, it could dramatically and efficiently expand the market. Some examples:

- A project to create employment and electronic access to people in rural India has led to the installation of computer kiosks in over three thousand villages. Beyond the benefit of access to information and potential participation in national, regional, and/or international markets, kiosks could be used to sell insurance products. In fact, they already are used to promote basic life insurance products, and it might be possible to expand their use to include in-patient health insurance.

---

[19] PhilHealth is the Philippine Government social health care programme.

[20] "Global Development Finance, 2005." The World Bank, Washington DC, 2005.

[21] C. Sander in "Capturing a market share", Bannock Consulting, 2003, reminds us that remittance data is notoriously difficult to quantify, partly because of the variety of formal and informal means of transmitting remittances. Thus, these data should be viewed as the minimum amount of remittances for these years.

- To speed premium collection, one church-based funeral insurance programme created a procedure so that its parishioners could pay their premiums after church services. This church developed bar coding for their policyholders' insurance cards, which speeded up transactions.

Conclusions

Insurance companies are searching for ways to expand their markets in developing countries. The microcredit and savings services offered by most MFPs do not provide sufficient risk management in the low-income market. Yet, there is substantial demand for effective risk management tools specifically designed and supplied for this market. The market potential is huge – possibly one hundred million covered lives within the next ten years. Regulated insurers should view the low-income masses as a market niche that can yield reasonable profits. Success will require extremely efficient delivery mechanisms that greatly reduce operating costs. Such innovation starts by using banks and other agents. It must also identify new and effective intermediaries, and make better use of technology to simplify all processes in ways that enhance efficiency for the insurer, agent, and policyholder. The roles and potential roles of the numerous parties involved in microinsurance are likely to become increasingly integrated, reducing transaction costs. Service should inevitably expand to cover more people and more risks.

Appendix 1: Summary of La Equidad Basic Protection and Small Business Protection Plan Coverage

Basic Protection[22]	Insured Benefits (USD)	
	USD1850 Plan	USD3700 Plan
Death by Any Cause	1,850	3,700
Total and Permanent Disability	1,850	3,700
Dread Disease	930	1,850
Monthly Children's School Fees (24 months)	17	33
Monthly Public Utilities	19	37
Monthly Grocery Costs	37	74
Medical Costs for Children	185	370
Death of a Child (1st child)	185	370
Assistance with household member Funeral Rites (1st only)	615	615

[22] Martha Bohórquez of La Equidad Seguros, in a presentation to the VII Inter-American Forum on Microenterprise, Cartagena, Colombia, September 2004.

Small Business Protection[23]	
Fire	Basic
Proven Theft	Basic
Civil Liability	Basic
Repair	Basic
Earthquake	Optional
Unemployment	Optional
Electrical Equipment and Electricity	Optional
Machine Damage	Optional
Transport of valuables except in war or strikes	Optional
Broken Glass	Optional
Group Life	Optional
Personal Accident	Optional

References

Blanchard-Horan, C. "Health Microinsurance Affects Health Behaviour and Malaria Treatment: A Multi-Site Case Comparison Study in Uganda." International Journal of Public Administration, forthcoming

Blanchard-Horan, C. "Health Microinsurance in Uganda." International Journal of Public Administration, 2007

Bohórquez, Martha. Presentation by La Equidad Seguros, VII Inter-American Forum on MIcroenterprise. Cartagena, Colombia, 2004

CGAP Working Group on Microinsurance. Preliminary Donor Guidelines for Supporting Microinsurance. ILO, Geneva, October 2003. Available at: http://www.microinsurancecentre.org/index.cfm?fuseaction=resources.documents

Churchill, Craig, Dominic Liber, Michael J. McCord, and James Roth. Making Insurance Work for Microfinance. ILO, Geneva, 2003

Cohen, Monique and Jennefer Sebstad. Reducing vulnerability: the demand for microinsurance. Journal of International Development. Volume 17, Issue 3, 2005. Pages 397-474. John Wiley & Sons, Ltd.

Daley-Harris, Sam. The State of the MicroCredit Summit Campaign Report 2004. Washington DC 2005

http://www.microcreditsummit.org/pubs/reports/socr/2004/SOCR04.pdf 23 Mar. 2005

Dror, David M., Elmer S. Soriano, F. Marilyn E. Lorenzo, Jesus N. Saron, Jr., Rosebelle S. Azcuna, and Ruth Koren. "Field based evidence of enhanced health

---

[23] Ibid.

care utilization among persons insured by Micro Health Insurance Units in the Philippines." International Journal of Public Administration. Forthcoming

"Global Development Finance, 2005." The World Bank, Washington DC, 2005

IndiaOneStop.com 25 February 2005

Matul, Michal. Understanding Demand for Microinsurance in Georgia. Memphis TN, The MicroInsurance Centre, February 2004

McCord, Michael J. Microinsurance: A Case Study of an Example of the Provider Model of Microinsurance Provision – GRET Cambodia. Nairobi, MicroSave, 2001. Available at www.microinsurancecentre.org

McCord, Michael J. and Craig Churchill. Delta Life Bangladesh: CGAP Working Group on Microinsurance – Good and Bad Practices in Microinsurance, Case Study No. 7. ILO, Geneva, 2005

McCord, Michael J., Felipe Botero, and Janet S. McCord. AIG Uganda: CGAP Working Group on Microinsurance – Good and Bad Practices in Microinsurance, Case Study No. 9. ILO, Geneva, 2005

McCord, Michael J., and Sylvia Osinde. Microcare Ltd. Health Plan (Uganda): Notes from a visit 17 – 21 June 2002. MicroSave, Nairobi, 2002. Available at: www.microinsurancecentre.org

Sander, Cerstin. "Capturing a market share." London, Bannock Consulting, 2003

Simkhada, Nav Raj, Sushila Gautam, Mira Mishra, Ishwori Acharya, and Namrata Sharma. Research on risk and vulnerability of rural women in Nepal. Kathmandu, December, 2000

"Swiss Re sigma study: high growth potential puts emerging markets at frontier of insurance – China and India in the spotlight." 7 October 2004

van Oppen, Charles. "Insurance: a tool for sustainable development." Insurance Research and Practice. Volume 16, Part I, pp. 47-60. London, Chartered Insurance Institute, 2001

CHAPTER 17:

Securitisation: A Funding Alternative for Microfinance Institutions

Harald Hüttenrauch[1] and Claudia Schneider[2]

[1] Vice President at KfW Bankengruppe, Securitisation, Eastern Europe and Emerging Markets
[2] Formerly KfW, now Country Manager Germany of PMI Mortgage Insurance Ltd.

Introduction

According to *The Banker*, approximately 2.5 billion people from low-income countries and many of the 2.7 billion people from middle-income countries have been and still remain widely underserved or even completely disregarded by the conventional financial services industry.[1] This is the potential customer base for microfinance. It ranges from the low end of the middle class to the poor and includes households, self-employed people, (owners of) microenterprises, (owners of) small businesses, and dependent workers. Similar to banking customers in high-income countries, the consumer base of microfinance demands not only on a broad range of high-quality retail financial services, but also choices among institutions. Furthermore, since the customers are willing and able to pay for the services, the financial products made available to them need to be readily usable, flexible and competitively priced.

Over the past two decades microfinance institutions (MFIs) around the globe have successfully accepted this challenge. Today, typical loan products in microfinance consist of short-term and medium-term loans, longer-term mortgages, leasing (hire purchase), and personal or consumer loans. In addition, MFIs also offer savings accounts and time deposits, contractual products for pensions, (micro-) insurance as well as transaction banking products such as payment transfers, remittances from abroad, etc. Experience also suggests that microfinance is a risk-manageable business. Moreover, provided that the microfinance operation is properly structured and run, and sufficient scale is achieved, there is mounting evidence that banking with low-income and even poor consumers of financial services can generate healthy returns on equity and assets. However, despite the fact

---

[1] Timewell, Stephen: "Microfinance gains momentum", in: The Banker, February 2, 2005, p. 82.

that MFIs have been successfully making inroads into their target markets for almost two decades, there is still an enormous gap between potential demand for and actual supply of microloans. Recent research estimates that MFIs already serve approximately 100 million clients, while about 1.5 billion of the working poor are potential clients.[2] A further indication of the enormous gap is the extremely low microloan penetration rates, which do not exceed 5% or even 1% of the poor in many developing countries and transition economies.[3]

Against this background, today's big challenge for the nascent microfinance industry is to deepen its integration with local and international capital markets. To sustain future growth and to further expand its outreach to the under-banked and unbanked customer base, MFIs have no choice other than to increasingly access more commercially priced private debt and equity funding. To this end, structured finance instruments such as securitisation seem to be a viable strategic option mainly for MFIs in the "top tier" of the microfinance pyramid. In 2004 such innovative financings appeared for the first time in the international capital market and since then more leading MFIs have successfully begun to seize such opportunities.

The purpose of this chapter is to explore to what extent securitisation is already a viable *funding strategy* for MFIs, its future potential and to what extent, under which conditions and at which speed securitisation of microfinance assets can further be developed. To this end, the *first* section introduces the basic concept of securitisation as a financing technique and true sale (or cash) securitisation as a funding concept. The *second* section presents a quick glance at the securitisation markets. In the *third* section, we discuss selected legal and technical requirements for securitisation, whilst the *fourth* section explores the extent to which MFIs and microfinance assets can meet these requirements. The *fifth* section discusses recent developments in the securitisation of microfinance assets and highlights prototypes of securitisation structures that have emerged so far in the international and local capital markets. The *conclusions* section contains general reflections on the topic and ends with suggestions as to the possible roles a bilateral financial institution such as KfW could play in furthering the development of microfinance securitisation.

---

[2] Tilman Ehrbeck: "Optimising Capital Supply in Support of Microfinance Industry Growth", a McKinsey & Co. presentation to the Microfinance Investor Roundtable in Washington DC on 24-25 October 2006, organised by Omidyar Network/The SEEP Network. We agree that a supply gap exists on a global scale regarding microloans, but cannot verify specific estimates.

[3] Patrick Honohan (2004). "Financial Sector Policy and the Poor. Selected Findings and Issues", World Bank Working Paper No. 43. The World Bank. Washington, p. 4. The penetration rate measures clients borrowing at MFIs as percentage of population in a particular country.

What Is Securitisation?

Overview

As one of the fastest growing forms of structured finance, "securitisation" is a financing technique increasingly used for risk management, balance sheet management, and to obtain funding.[4] It refers to a process in which a bank (or the originator) converts preferably stable and predictable cashflow streams in a segregated pool of rather illiquid financial assets (or the asset or collateral pool) into debt instruments (or securities or notes) tradable in the capital markets. Basically, the securitisation process consists of three key elements:

- The *pooling* of risky but relatively homogenous financial assets tends to achieve diversification and better predictability of default risk in the asset pool.

- The *tranching* of cashflow and undifferentiated credit risk of the overall asset pool into multiple parcels (or classes) of securities with *different* payout and risk-return profiles allows different investors with different interests and risk appetites to acquire exactly the security profile they like. Payments of interest and principle on these securities depend exclusively on the availability of cashflow from its collateral, i.e. the underlying pooled assets, which is why these instruments are known as asset-backed securities (ABS).

- The transfer of the asset pool to a *special purpose vehicle (SPV)* aims to protect the investor since it legally isolates the benefits of the assets from the insolvency risk of the originator.

Generally, any stream of preferably stable and predictable cashflows – which is almost always the case for financial contracts – can be securitised and it is not necessary for those assets or contracts to exist at the time of securitisation. Examples of commonly securitised asset classes include auto loans, consumer loans, credit card receivables, equipment leases, export receivables, mortgage loans, remittances, SME loans, student loans, tax revenues, toll road revenues, trade receivables, etc. Recently, microfinance receivables have supplemented the steadily broadening spectrum of asset classes.

---

[4] For comprehensive introductions refer to Mitchell, Janet: "Financial Intermediation Theory and the Sources of Value in Structured Finance Markets", mimeograph, National Bank of Belgium, December 2004; Basu, Sudipto: "Securitization and the Challenges Faced in Micro Finance". Institute for Financial Management and Research, Centre for Micro Finance Research, Working Paper Series, Mumbai (April 2005); Fender, Ingo and Janet Mitchell: "Structured Finance: complexity, risk and the use of ratings" in: BIS Quarterly Review, June 2005 p. 67-79; and Vinod Kothari: Securitization. The Financial Instrument of the Future. Second Edition, Wiley & Sons (Asia) Pte Limited, Singapore, 2006.

Normally, ABS are placed privately (i.e. with a defined group of investors who remain largely unknown to the public) or publicly in capital markets with institutional investors such as banks, insurance companies, pension funds, specialised investment funds, hedge funds, and more recently, also with microfinance investment vehicles (MIVs), or even with bilateral and multilateral financial institutions. ABS investors should have a thorough knowledge of these rather sophisticated financial instruments.

For a securitisation market to develop, investors must be able to compare the risks of the various tranches. Since securitisation attempts to provide buyers of risk with the risk they seek, how can investors know whether a certain tranche of ABS offered to them carries a level of risk with which they are comfortable? Therefore, mainstream ABS investors in developed structured finance markets rely on the services of rating agencies since these tend to provide an objective and independent assessment of a given securitisation structure and a universal scoring system that allows investors to compare credit risk.[5] Depending on the originator's specific objectives, ABS transactions are rated privately (i.e. the agency in charge issues a rating letter to a defined group of investors) or publicly (i.e. the rating reports are available to the general public). Privately placed transactions can also have a public rating, which is a very important source of information for potential originators and investors: they can learn about possible structures, new asset classes and their respective performance over time.

One of the advantages of ABS is that they permit investors to further diversify their fixed income portfolio and, at the same time, to improve the risk-return profile. For example, investors can freely choose the desired underlying asset class, the geographic region and the specific credit risk and payout characteristics of a certain class of securities. Another advantage is that the credit ratings of ABS are also often higher than that of the originator itself. Investors can buy into risk which is related to a specific part (e.g. SME lending) of the originator's overall business but do not have to rely on the bank's cashflow to achieve the necessary debt service or investment return. Furthermore, compared with traditional debt instruments such as corporate bonds, highly rated ABS provide investors with greater liquidity. This is very important for institutions that are restricted from investing in lower rated instruments. Finally, ABS ratings have shown a more stable rating history than corporate ratings. However, the flip side of these advantages is that, given its complexity, each ABS issue has to be analysed and valued individually, sometimes even extensively, which increases transaction costs for the investor.

From a financial system development perspective, by matching available risk and investor appetite, the structured finance markets allow the movement of investments from the less efficient debt markets to more efficient capital markets.

---

[5]   ABS investors should never base investment decisions exclusively on the rating report provided by rating agencies. Given the complexity of the instrument, third party information can only complement the own extensive assessment of credit and legal risk in a securitisation.

A greater symmetry between risk buyers and risk sellers provides the financial markets as a whole with better and cheaper pricing. Over time these efficiency gains are expected to be translated into cheaper pricing flowing to the ultimate consumers of debt (for example, mortgage loans to private households or investment financing to small businesses, etc.). Moreover, since selling a portfolio of undifferentiated risk may be difficult – if there is no buyer for such risk – structured finance enables a potential originator to transfer risk to investors. Finally, since this financing technique permits banks to manage their risks more efficiently, securitisation is expected to enhance the overall stability of financial markets.

Why Do Banks Securitise?

As an important source of financing and risk transfer, securitisation is gaining attractiveness as a part of a new business model for banks in Europe. This technique permits the banks to increase their risk-bearing capacity and, at the same time, to achieve the desired risk-return profile. Furthermore, changing risk management practices, improvements in risk modelling, adequate risk pricing together with financial innovations in the capital markets enable the banks to conceive credit risk as a 'tradable product' which can be sold to investors or bought from the capital market. Active portfolio management is incrementally replacing the traditional

Table 1. Motives for securitisation

	Banks use securitisation, among other things:
Overall profitability	• to increase return on equity (RoE)
Risk management / risk transfer	• to diversify and to re-balance, if necessary, the asset portfolio
	• to remove risky assets from the balance sheet and to expand dept capacity
	• to improve the risk profile and to achieve corporate rating upgrades
Funding / liquidity management	• to access funding at lower cost than available through alternative instruments
	• to better match maturities of assets and liabilities
	• to diversify funding sources and to expand investor base
Balance sheet management	• to increase efficiency in asset-liabilities management
	• to uncouple lending growth from the capital base
	• to bring capital adequacy in line with regulatory requirements (i.e. to free up regulatory capital)

but relatively costly principle of "buying and holding" the receivables to maturity (for example, long-term loans to SMEs). The forthcoming regulatory implications of Basel II, which call for a more differentiated treatment of risk, will further push banks to optimise the allocation of economic and regulatory capital. Banks use securitisation techniques for several reasons:

"Synthetic" securitisation and "true sale" (or "cash") securitisation are the two basic forms of securitisation. The originator's objective determines the securitisation type to be chosen.[6] Since this chapter explores a *funding* strategy for MFIs, we deal only with *true sale* securitisation, which changes the legal and/or economic ownership of the securitised assets. True sale securitisation permits the originator (or seller) of the assets to turn formerly immovable financial assets into proceeds available to *fund* the expansion of its lending operation. Note that, for the originator, selling a portfolio to another bank would have the same effect.

Basic Elements of a Securitisation Structure

Securitisation is "structured" finance. Arrangers are hired with the objective of achieving a solution tailored to the originator's specific problem. Specific features – for example credit enhancements such as cash reserve accounts, hedge arrangements, etc. – are often added solely for the purpose of designing a fixed income instrument that can find investors but still generate a positive economic return for the originator. In this way, each securitisation is "structured" and the transaction

---

[6]   In a *synthetic* securitisation, the originator seeks protection against default from a segregated asset pool. Using credit derivatives such as credit default swaps (CDS) and/or credit linked notes (CLN), only the credit risk of the asset pool is transferred to investors in capital markets. The originator retains the ownership of the assets which remain on the balance sheet. The benefits for the originator consist in risk reduction, risk diversification and capital. The originator can use the economic and regulatory capital freed up as a result of the risk transfer to provide additional loans, for example to the small and medium-sized enterprises (SMEs). In order to comply with the local regulator's capital adequacy requirements, for fast growing banks synthetic securitisation constitutes an additional option to access new capital – besides increasing the share capital and/or accessing hybrid tier-1 capital. Finally, synthetic securitisation also permits the originator to increase the return on equity for its shareholders, an important motive for banks to securitise continuously. *Synthetic* securitisation is increasingly used in the US and only a few other markets, while it has been very prominent in developing the German ABS market since 2000. For a detailed discussion of KfW's synthetic securitisation programmes PROMISE (for SME loans) and PROVIDE (for mortgage loans) in which KfW has transferred more than EUR 100 billion in default risk to capital markets refer to Jobst, Andreas: "Asset Securitisation as a risk management and funding tool. What small firms need to know", in: "Managerial Finance, Vol. 32 Issue 9, pp. 731-760, Research Paper, 2005 and Glüder, Dieter: "Regulatory impact of synthetic securitisation" in: Watson, Rick and Carter, Jeremy (Eds.): "Asset Securitisation and Synthetic Structures. Innovations in the European Credit Markets", pp. 51-66, Euromoney Books, London, 2005.

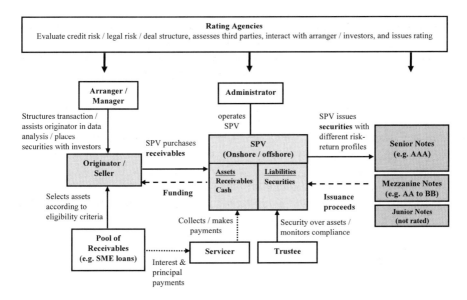

Fig. 1. Stylised overview of a "true sale" securitization

reflects the specific nature of the asset class being securitised, particularly the cashflow and the timing and consistency of such cashflow. The following figure presents a basic securitisation transaction model in a true sale securitisation.

At the centre of each true sale securitisation is a stand-alone legal entity, the SPV (or issuer), set up specifically for the transaction and usually operated by specialised administrative entities. Depending on local legislation, the SPV can be established in various forms such as trust, a limited liability company, or a foundation. The SPV should be structured to minimise, or ideally remove entirely, any tax liabilities. It is very common for the seller of the assets to be appointed to act on behalf of the SPV as the servicer of the pool.

The interposition of the SPV is necessary to achieve the *structural and legal separation* of the benefits of the asset pool from the insolvency risk of the originator itself. Hence, the economic return on an investment in ABS depends *exclusively* upon the availability of (sufficient) cash flow from the segregated asset pool. ABS investors have no recourse to the originator.[7] To improve the predictability of outcome for the investor, the legal structure must comply with two key conditions. First, the benefits of the assets have to be transferred to the SPV in such a way as to create legal independence from the originator of the assets and its creditors. Typically, only the *true sale* of assets permits the *insolvency proof* transfer of assets. Second, the SPV must be established in a manner which mitigates

---

[7] Any recourse to the originator would give the transaction the character of a secured loan rather than of a securitisation.

voluntary and involuntary insolvency or bankruptcy risks for the SPV itself, a status referred to as *bankruptcy remote*. Typical risk mitigants are, for example, contractual restrictions on the purpose of the SPV and the power of its management as well as limited enforcement rights of the transaction creditors over the asset pool and against the SPV (limited recourse and non-petition).[8]

The SPV transfers the proceeds from the ABS issuance to the seller as the purchase price for the assets acquired. This enables the originator to access funding at costs that are based on the quality of the asset pool– and not on its own institutional credit which would be the case if the originator opted to issue a corporate bond.

Tranching in ABS tends to optimise the cost of funding and other benefits of the securitisation (e.g. the extent of capital relief) for the originator and to match preferences in risk, return, maturity and liquidity for the investor. To this end, the cashflow and undifferentiated credit risk of the underlying asset pool is divided into several tranches (or classes of securities) with different degrees of seniority, each representing a different payout and risk-return profile.[9] For example, a relatively large tranche of investment grade debt (the senior tranche), one or more tranches of non-investment grade debt (the mezzanine tranche) and a relatively small tranche of a security representing equity (the junior tranche or first loss, which is normally not rated). In this way, subordination provides credit enhancement since it produces low risk, low return senior securities for less informed, more risk-averse investors. On the other hand, the creation of high-risk, high-return junior tranches of securities is targeted at well-informed, more risk-tolerant investors.[10]

To increase investor confidence in the quality of the pool, the originator – the best informed investor – often retains the first loss tranche on its own balance sheet, thus avoiding moral hazard. Retaining the first loss tranche may have a positive effect on the transaction when only a small number of well informed investors are available. In such a market environment, investors in junior tranches would charge the originator an unnecessarily high risk premium.[11] On the other hand, for the originator, insufficient risk transfer limits the extent to which existing

---

[8] For a more detailed discussion of legal implications in a true sale securitisation refer to the section "Requirements for securitisation in emerging markets" below.

[9] Credit enhancement for the most senior notes is provided by subordination of the mezzanine and junior notes.

[10] Byström, Hans: "The Microfinance Collateralized Debt Obligation: a Modern Robin Hood?", Department of Economics, Lund University, Working Paper 14-2006, 22 June, Lund.

[11] Depending on the overall market sentiment, investors in first loss or junior tranches may command spreads ranging from between 1,000 basis points (bps) per annum (p.a.) to 1,500 bps p.a. over the respective reference rate (e.g. 3-months-Euribor). One hundred basis points equal one per cent.

regulatory and economic capital is freed up, thus jeopardising another important strategic objective of the securitisation, which is to increase lending capacity.

During the lifetime of the transaction, the SPV distributes the collections due on the assets in the underlying pool according to the priority of payments (or cash waterfall) agreed in the legal documentation. For example, in a sequentially amortising structure the ABS investors receive interest and principal payments on the securities after senior expenses such as SPV administration, servicer, guarantee fees, etc. are deducted. Over time, defaults that turn out to be higher than expected reduce the collections from the asset pool available at the SPV, which can in turn cause a shortfall in interest and/or principal for investors. In such case, investors in the security class with the highest risk, i.e. junior tranche, will suffer losses first, followed by investors in the mezzanine and senior tranches in a reverse order of seniority.

Many mainstream investors in developed structured finance markets require a securitisation to carry at least two ratings from the three major internationally accepted rating agencies Fitch Ratings (Fitch), Moody's Investor Service (Moody's) or Standard & Poor's (S&P). The basic function of rating agencies is to avoid, as much as possible, asymmetric information between the originator of the asset pool and the investors. The factors that rating agencies take into consideration vary according to the type of asset class being securitised. In general, the ratings of the securities are based on:

- the quality of the collateral (i.e. the assets, claims or receivables), either assessed by historical loss experience or internal rating systems;

- the extent of credit enhancement in the form of subordination among the different tranches, the availability of excess spread[12] and of reserve funds (the latter is frequently funded via a subordinated loan from the originator to the SPV at the inception of a transaction);

- the scope of guarantees from third parties and the quality of guarantors, if available;

- the quality of policies and procedures for underwriting, managing and monitoring the securitised assets (i.e. the origination and servicing principles applied by the bank);

- the effectiveness of foreclosure procedures to resolve problem loans;

- the soundness of the financial and legal structure of the deal;

- the availability of interest rate and currency swaps and the quality of their providers;

---

[12] In general, the term "excess spread" refers to any surplus from interest collections remaining in the SPV after covering the senior expenses and paying out interest to investors. For example, excess spread can be held in a reserve account as a form of credit enhancement to protect the senior tranche investors against higher than expected losses.

- the general macroeconomic conditions;

- the soundness of the legal regime; and

- the likelihood and probability of sovereign interference (in cases of cross-border structures).

Due to the credit enhancement provided by tranching, the most senior tranche may carry an international or a national AAA rating, while the more risky mezzanine tranches may even fall below investment grade. First loss tranches are normally not rated. The ceiling of the country of the originator which can be different (e.g. higher) than the rating of the sovereign usually constitutes the rating ceiling for the senior tranche.[13]

The rating reflects the expected losses for the different tranches determined under both normal and stress scenarios, thus influencing the economics of the transaction. Furthermore, pricing depends on investors' risk perception regarding a specific asset class, the quality of the originator and/or servicer, the expectations regarding the overall economic development in the particular country and industry, and the interest rate environment.

While senior tranches are priced at quite narrow spreads above a reference rate such as three-month-Euribor, investors' risk premiums increase with the degree of subordination. The overall funding spread is equal to the weighted average of the spreads to be paid on the various tranches at time of closing.[14] Obviously, the smaller the portion of the junior and mezzanine tranches, the lower the originator's overall funding cost in the capital structure. The case study in the text box below provides an example of tranching and pricing in securitisations.

Case Study: FTPYME Santander 1 – A Spanish True Sale Securitisation

FTPYME Santander 1 closed in 2003 and is an example that illustrates tranching, subordination levels and pricing. Banco Santander Central Hispano S.A. was the originator. Initially, the pool consisted of about 23,000 loans to Spanish SMEs, mostly collateralised by mortgages.

---

[13] For a more detailed discussion of rating caps due to country risk refer to the section "Requirements for securitisation in emerging markets" below.

[14] The economics of the transaction decline from year to year. This is due to sequential amortisation of principal within the waterfall which causes the most senior tranches (i.e. those paying the lowest risk premiums) to amortise earlier than the more expensive junior tranches. Therefore, the average cost of funding increases considerably throughout the lifetime of the transaction.

Fitch rated the five classes of securities (Classes A to D) issued by FTPYME Santander 1, from AAA to BBB. Credit enhancement in the form of subordination for the Class A notes is provided by the mezzanine tranches (ranging from Classes B1 (G) to D) and the reserve fund. Senior note holders (i.e. the AAA rated class A notes) would suffer losses of principal only if accumulated losses exceeded 45.15% of the initial pool volume during the lifetime of the transaction. The credit enhancement in this transaction is unusually high for SME securitisations. Normally, credit enhancement levels of 10% to 15% would suffice to achieve an AAA rating for the most senior note. Within the mezzanine tranche, the AAA rated Class B1 (G) notes were backed by a guarantee from the Kingdom of Spain. However, it is very likely that Fitch would have assigned an AAA for most of this tranche even without such a guarantee.

The securitisation raised EUR 1.8 billon (Classes A to D) at an initial funding spread of around 27 bps over 3-months-Euribor. This calculation assumes that the originator obtained the guarantee from the Kingdom of Spain at a risk spread of zero.

FTPYME Santander 1 – Capital Structure

Security class	Volume (€)	Share of tranche	Rating	Credit enhancement	Coupon rate
A	1,014,300,000	56.35%	AAA	45.15%	Euribor + 25 bps
B1 (G)	537,100,000	29.84%	AAA	15.31%	Euribor + 0.0 bps
B2	134,300,000	7.46%	AA	7.85%	Euribor + 40 bps
C	27,000,000	1.50%	A	6.35%	Euribor + 90 bps
D	87,300,000	4.50%	BBB	1.50%	Euribor + 180 bps
Reserve Fund	27,000,000	1.50%	NR	n. a.	n. a.

Source: Fitch (2003), FTPYME and Fitch (2006), FTPYME

A Glance at Securitisation Markets

Since the 1970s, the securitisation market has grown exponentially and now constitutes an important segment of global fixed income and credit markets. During 2006 the global ABS issuance grew by about 6.8% to reach a total of approximately USD 4.03 trillion. For many years, the US has been by far the most important market. However, its market share has steadily decreased during the last three years from approximately 90% (2003) to about 79% (2006). Although the European

Table 2. Global securitisation issuance in 2005 and 2006 (in USD billions)

Country	Total volume of securitisations in 2005	Total volume of securitisations in 2006	Market growth	Market share
USA	3,139	3,187	1.5%	79.1%
Europe	407	577	41.8%	14.3%
Australia	74	102	37.8%	2.5%
Japan	81	86	6.2%	2.1%
Canada	25	24	-4.0%	0.6%
Emerging markets	50	55	10.0%	1.4%
Asia	32	30	-6.3%	0.7%
South Korea[a]	*28*	*24*	*-14.3%*	*0.6%*
Latin America	14	20	42.9%	0.5%
Brazil	*5*	*5*	*0.0%*	*0.1%*
Mexico	*4*	*7*	*75.0%*	*0.2%*
EEMEA[b]	4	5	25.0%	0.1%
Total	3,776	4,031	6.8%	100%

[a] Italicised items in the emerging market section are breakdowns of the most important countries within the respective sub-markets

[b] EEMEA (Eastern Europe, Middle East and Africa); securitisation there is concentrated on South Africa, Egypt, Russia and Turkey.

Source: International Financial Services (2006, 2007).

market has taken off impressively during the past decade, it surpassed 10% of the global market for the first time in 2005. Currently, with a total issuance of approximately USD 577 billon in 2006, the European market represents more than 14% of the global securitisation market. Residential mortgage backed securities (RMBS), which are collateralised by a pool consisting of private residential mortgage loans, continue to be the most important asset class in the US and Europe.

Securitisation is still at an early stage of development in emerging markets with a total issuance in 2006 of approximately USD 55 billion, slightly up from USD 53 billion in 2005, equivalent to a global market share of about 1.4%. South Korea, Brazil, Mexico, South Africa, Russia and Turkey were the most active markets in 2006.

Cross-border securitisation has dominated the development in emerging markets, with Russia being the most recent example to follow this pattern. In cross-border deals, the SPV is located offshore, i.e. outside the country of the originator, mainly in industrialised countries such as the US, the Netherlands, Ireland and

Luxemburg, or in offshore financial centres such as the Cayman Islands and the Channel Islands, with a legal, regulatory and tax environment conducive to achieving highly rated international ABS issuance. Typically, the underlying assets are *existing* receivables denominated in foreign currency, such as residential mortgage loans, auto loans, consumer loans or credit card receivables owned by domestic banks.

Other cross-border transactions are structured to securitise existing and *future* receivables and require the foreign debtors (e.g. international correspondent banks) to make their payments directly on the SPV's collection accounts outside the originator's country. For example, in a securitisation of "diversified payment rights" (DPRs), the off-shore SPV purchases from the originator (e.g. a bank in Turkey) the rights, title and interest in all existing and future payment orders in USD and Euro which the originator is expected to receive from its offshore correspondent banks between the closing of the securitisation transaction and the final maturity of the notes. Typically, such payment orders arise from capital inflows that are directed back into the country of the originator to pay for the export of goods and services from that country, from foreign direct investments in the country or from the repatriation of migrant workers' earnings into the country.[15] Structuring a deal in this way significantly reduces the transfer and convertibility risk for the investor, since the collections on the securitised assets are kept offshore during such collection period until the SPV has made the respective payments falling due to investors under the notes. In each period, the remaining collections are released to the originator. Usually, future flow securitisation appeals to highly rated banks located in countries with sub-investment grade rating (i.e. below BBB minus). Furthermore, in some cross-border securitisations the receivables never enter the balance sheet of an emerging market originator since legally the assets are originated directly on behalf of the offshore SPV.[16] For originators holding assets in foreign currency, cross-border securitisation can leverage such assets and achieve stable foreign currency refinancing at attractive rates and longer tenors.[17]

Cross-border securitisation can also constitute an interim solution for banks operating in countries in which the legal and regulatory framework does not yet support domestic securitisation. In addition, cross-border securitisation is also an option for originators located in countries with low convertibility and transfer risk.

---

[15] For example, these payment orders are usually made by a SWIFT message directed from the international correspondent bank to the originator as (electronic) MT102 or MT103 transmission.

[16] Such securitisations are known as "future flow transactions". Typical asset classes are export receivables, e.g. export of crude oil. The key feature is that the assets being transferred by the originator are not existing claims against existing obligors, but future claims against future obligors.

[17] S&P: "The Three Building Blocks of an Emerging Markets Future Flow Transaction Rating", November 16, 2004, p. 1.

Such a profile has characterised some Central and Eastern European countries that are now EU member states.[18]

On the other hand, cross-border securitisation is less appropriate for receivables denominated in local currency. By securitising local currency assets on a cross-border basis, the originator increases its dependence on international capital markets with all its risks of interest rate, maturity and currency mismatches. The same concern arises for institutions that originate assets in foreign currency, but whose domestic customers are exposed to transfer and convertibility risk. This profile applies to many economies in Latin America or Eastern Europe in which the US dollar or the Euro are the dominant currencies.

Onshore securitisations have dominated the development of the South African and several Asian markets. They are significantly increasing in Latin America (for example, in Argentina, Brazil, Colombia, Mexico, Peru, etc.) where in 2004 onshore issuance surpassed offshore securitisation for the first time, amounting to more than twice the cross-border volume.[19] The main reasons for the impressive take-off of local ABS issuance are supportive tax, legal and regulatory reforms, and the increasing liquidity and activity in local bond markets. Similar developments can be observed in China, and most structured finance experts expect the Chinese securitisation market to grow significantly.[20]

Experience of domestic securitisations in emerging markets is relevant when assessing the potential for the securitisation of microfinance assets. From an originator's perspective, onshore securitisation is appealing since the institution can access local currency funding at matching maturities. Assets denominated in local currency are transferred to a domestic SPV which, in turn, issues local currency denominated ABS placed with local investors. Typically, the development of local ABS markets takes off with the securitisation of highly standardised receivables, such as mortgage loans, consumer loans and auto loans.

Furthermore, onshore securitisations may, in most cases, be more economic and less risky than cross-border transactions. The cost of securitising in local markets will be influenced by various factors including transaction size, overhead cost of the deal, investor appetite for a specific asset class, and interest rates charged by the originator to the borrowers at the time of origination of the receivables. Due to the high overhead cost of international deals (with international rating agencies and international and local law firms involved), the average size of such offshore securitisations is possibly well above USD 100 million. In contrast, local securitisations can in some cases be worthwhile for the originator with deal sizes around USD 10 to 20 million.

---

[18] Ibid, p. 2. In 2004 cross-border securitisation of local currency denominated assets were completed in Poland and Romania.

[19] Fitch: "Structured Finance in Latin America's Local Markets, 2004 Year in Review and 2005 Outlook", March 1, 2005, p. 3.

[20] HSBC Global Research: "Asian Securitisation – A new ABS market ready to unfold", May 2005, p. 16.

Residential mortgage and consumer loan securitisations in developing countries offer good examples for MFIs contemplating a securitisation, as previously noted. Relevant cases include the mortgage loan securitisation programme of South African Home Loans Ltd. (The Thekwini Fund), residential mortgage loan securitisations in Mexico (e.g. Su Casita), and consumer loan securitisations in South Africa and Mexico (Nedbank's Synthesis programme and Fonacot).[21] Interesting examples include local securitisations without a guarantee and locally rated servicers as well as unrated servicers backed by a rated back-up servicer.

Requirements for Securitisation in Emerging Markets

Typically, loan portfolios of MFIs consist either of local currency receivables or foreign currency denominated assets owed by local debtors. Prerequisites for on-shore securitisations in emerging markets are defined here, along with an exploration of the extent to which MFIs can meet such criteria. The requirements for cross-border securitisation are also briefly discussed.

Country-Specific Aspects

Inter-related factors determine the extent to which securitisations can be conducted in different countries. These factors include the depth of local capital markets, the legal and regulatory framework, regulation of securities issued and regulation of securitisation itself.

Depth of Local Capital Markets

Securitisation will develop in a country only to the extent that local securities and debt markets have reached a certain level of diversification and maturity.[22] For instance, some securitisation structures require interest rate swaps, while others may lack sufficient investor demand for medium and long-term securities. Most domestic securitisation markets start with a demand from local pension funds, mutual funds and insurance companies for fixed-income instruments denominated in local currency with medium-term maturities of three to five years. Institutional investors can develop a meaningful appetite for such instruments only if they have liquidity in excess of that required by their local regulators.[23] Another consideration is that the formation of financial assets greatly depends on the stability of the domestic currency and the country's sovereign credit outlook. Furthermore,

---

[21] For more details on these projects refer to the respective rating reports from Moody's and Fitch.

[22] Moody's: "Securitisation in New Markets: Moody's Perspective", September 5, 2006, p. 2.

[23] Lee Maddin, International Finance Corporation (IFC): "Structured Finance in emerging markets", in: Global Securitisation Review 2004/05, Euromoney Yearbooks, p. 3.

a reasonable degree of overall macroeconomic and political stability is also supportive to the development of a local bond and ABS market.[24]

Most institutional investors prefer or are required to hold high quality assets. They first acquire mortgage bonds as an alternative to government and large corporate bonds. Given their collateralisation, mortgage bonds are considered low risk. In some cases, as in South Africa, institutional investors actively urged potential originators to issue mortgage bonds. In other cases, lobbying by investor groups led to legal changes that facilitated the issue of mortgage bonds.

Once an ABS market takes off with RMBS, it is only a question of time before investors will buy somewhat riskier asset classes. In addition to ensuring sufficient investor demand and a supportive tax, legal and regulatory framework, an adequate capital market infrastructure including arrangers, clearing agents and stock exchanges are required for the creation of a securitisation market.[25] In most cases the involvement of a local credit rating agency acceptable to investors is also essential. In structured finance transactions, the local affiliates of international rating agencies are likely to have a competitive edge over independent domestic rating agencies, at least initially.

Legal, Tax and Regulatory Framework

It is important to explore fully whether, and under which conditions, the legal, tax and regulatory environment of a jurisdiction permit onshore securitisation.[26] Many countries have promulgated securitisation laws, giving strong impetus for the development of domestic markets (e.g. Brazil, South Africa). In other countries, securitisation developed following amendments of existing capital market laws (e.g. Mexico). Unfortunately, some countries have introduced special securitisation laws but their scope has been too narrow for local markets to develop (e. g. Bulgaria, Poland, Romania, Ecuador).

To support true sale securitisation, the main aspects which need to be analysed to determine whether a country's legal, tax and regulatory framework is supportive to the development of securitisation are:[27]

---

[24] Gabriel DeSanctis: "Guaranteeing progress", in: International Financing Review, IMF/ Word Bank Special Report, September 2004; and Fitch: "Structured Finance in Latin America's Local Markets, 2004 Year in Review and 2005 Outlook", March 1, 2005, p. 3.

[25] Lee Maddin, International Finance Corporation (IFC): "Structured Finance in emerging markets", in: Global Securitisation Review 2004/05, Euromoney Yearbook, p. 4.

[26] Comprehensive information on the status of the legal and regulatory framework of securitisation is publicly available for many countries. For example, refer to Global Legal Group: "The International Comparative Legal Guide to: Securitisation 2006", London 2006 (the guide is updated yearly). Refer also to http://www.globalsecuritisation. com, a website on the state of global securitisation and structured finance, sponsored by Deutsche Bank AG, and to http://www.vinodkothari.com/seclaw.htm.

[27] Moody's: "Securitisation in New Markets: Moody's Perspective", September 5, 2006, p. 10, lists are series of legal and regulatory issues to be addressed for a (first time) securitisation in emerging markets.

- *Transferability of assets.* It must be legally possible to transfer the assets from the originator to a third party, the SPV, and that loan agreements must allow for such transfers. In addition, the transfer must be *insolvency proof.* The successor's ownership of the receivables must be immune to legal challenge if the originator becomes insolvent or bankrupt so as to assure investors that neither the assets, nor their proceeds on realisation, are available for distribution as part of the bankruptcy estate of the originator to parties other than the ABS investors.[28] Potential pitfalls in domestic legislation which could adversely affect an *insolvency proof* transfer include provisions that prohibit the transfer of assets or the assignment of the corresponding collateral or provide for burdensome and costly registration requirements, and those that require the borrower's (prior) consent to the transfer or that require the explicit notification of the borrower. Finally, banking regulations that permit only licensed banks to hold loans originated by a bank hamper the development of securitisation.

- *Bankruptcy remoteness of the SPV.* Local legislation must provide for the establishment of a *bankruptcy-remote entity* (i.e. one that is sufficiently protected against both voluntary and involuntary insolvency risks). To reduce voluntary bankruptcy risks (excluding fraud) for the SPV itself, legislation must make it possible, mainly by contract, to restrict the business purpose of the SPV and to limit the decision power of its management.[29] Moreover, to mitigate involuntary insolvency risks triggerable by third parties, transaction creditors agree to limit their enforcement rights over the asset pool and against the SPV by way of limited recourse and non-petition clauses in any agreement between the SPV and its creditors. It is crucial for these provisions to be enforceable under domestic legislation.

- *Taxes:* In order to minimise potential tax liabilities of the SPV, issues such as withholding tax on the transfer of the underlying asset and/or on the payments by the SPV to investors have to be evaluated. Furthermore, issues relating to value-added taxes may also arise in connection with payments by the SPV to the originator in its role as servicer of the asset pool. Most jurisdictions deem SPVs and securitisation transactions to be generally tax-neutral, since their sole purpose is to administer the ABS and to channel the cash flows related to the transaction on a non-profit basis.

---

[28] Fitch: "Securitisation in Emerging Markets: Preparing for the Rating Process", February 17, 2006, p. 3.

[29] Normally, the purpose of the SPV is restricted to the purchase of the asset, the holding of the assets for the benefit of investors (or other secured parties) and the issuance of *tranched* securities (debt instruments and equity) to investors in order to refinance the purchase.

- *Regulation of the securities issued:* The type of security that is most appropriate for a securitisation has to be determined. In most cases there is a choice – different securities are regulated differently. Some jurisdictions limit the ability of institutional investors to invest in certain types of securities. Accounting and tax regulations also have to be considered.[30]

- *Regulation of securitisation:* The extent to which domestic bank regulations require the local regulator to approve the securitisation transaction has to be clarified. Furthermore, the originator must determine, to the satisfaction of its auditors, whether a potential securitisation structure complies with national accounting rules and whether the particular transaction achieves the envisaged funding or equity targets. For example, accounting rules and bank regulations in many countries treat assets as truly sold only if transfer of the majority of risk and rewards has taken place and only if the originator does not retain too large a portion of the asset's risk.[31]

Country Risk and Country Ceiling

In cross-border securitisations, if the national government imposes a moratorium on all foreign currency debts, the SPV risks default on the payment of interest and principal to the ABS investors. Therefore, country risk in the form of convertibility, transferability and expropriation risk has to be assessed and mitigated. This may be achieved, for example, through a political risk insurance policy, an offshore liquidity facility or guarantees provided by highly rated financial institutions such as international banks, monoline insurance companies and multilateral or bilateral financial institutions such as KfW.[32]

In the past, without mitigation of country risk, the most senior ranking securities issued in cross-border structured finance transactions generally could not command a credit rating superior to the sovereign bond rating (or sovereign ceiling). However, in spring 2006, rating agencies adjusted their methodologies to decrease the influence of a sovereign's long-term foreign currency rating on the ratings of cross-border structured finance transactions.[33] Based on empirical observations from recent financial crises, the general rationale behind this development is that many governments appear to be significantly less likely than in the past to impose measures such as payment moratoria on issuers or capital and/or foreign-exchange

---

[30] Lambe, Geraldine: "Securitisation gives food for thought", in: The Banker, 4 August 2003, p. 30.

[31] Basel II stipulates many criteria for determining whether securitised assets are truly sold.

[32] Fitch: "The Role of Multilaterals in Structured Finance", March 16, 2006.

[33] Refer to Fitch: "Existing Asset Securitisation in Emerging Markets – Sovereign Constraints", May 12, 2006; Moody's: "Securitisation in New Markets: Moody's Perspective", September 5, 2006, and to S&P: "Weighing Country Risk In Our Criteria For Asset-Backed Securities", April 11, 2006.

controls, even in times of serious financial distress or upon default of the sovereign entity. Obviously, governments are expected to behave differently, since the future costs of such actions to be borne by the economy are considered increasingly high, especially for countries with liberalised trade and capital accounts. In the new approach, rating agencies are now trying to estimate the probability of the government to impose a moratorium or to establish capital controls during a financial crisis of the sovereign[34] – and no longer assume this to happen automatically. The agencies now take into consideration factors such as the overall political and macroeconomic situation, the soundness of the legal regime as well as the availability of structural elements to mitigate the consequences of sovereign interference. These elements include such as offshore liquidity facilities and frequent sweeps of collections from the servicer's onshore collection account to the SPV's offshore account.

Today, applying the revised approach, the maximum rating achievable for a senior note in cross-border structured finance transactions is capped at the "country ceiling for foreign-currency denominated bonds,"[35] which may be up to several notches above the respective sovereign rating of the country in question. Moreover, provided external credit enhancement is available to mitigate country risk (see above), it may be even possible to rate the senior note above the country ceiling.[36]

Originator and Servicer Requirements

Originator Motivation

From the perspective of the originator, a potential securitisation must offer a positive trade-off between costs and benefits. In emerging markets, the primary benefit consists of access to asset-based funding and equity. Depending on the profile of the originator's balance sheet, additional benefits could include improved risk management such as through risk transfer, as well as better asset liability management. Secondary benefits such as access to domestic capital markets and diversification of funding sources can also be important.

---

[34] This more differentiated view is commonly referred to as "joint-default approach".

[35] This is the terminology of Moody's. Fitch and S&P apply different terms for a similar concept.

[36] For example, as of June 2006, Moody's rated the Russian sovereign bond Baa2, whilst the "country ceiling for foreign-currency bonds" was at A2 (i.e. three notches above the sovereign). In June 2006, the first RMBS out of Russia (originator: JSC Vneshtorgbank) was closed and Moody's rated the most senior tranche A1 (i.e. one notch above the country ceiling). "Piercing" the country ceiling was possible due to external credit enhancement in the form of an International Payment Facility provided by JSC Vneshtorgbank but guaranteed by IFC. Refer to Moody's: "Russian Mortgage Backed Securities 2006-1 S.A.", International Structured Finance, Europe, Middle East, Africa, New Issue Report, July 19, 2006.

Whether the benefits of a securitisation exceed its costs will depend on factors such as the direct cost of securitisation, the availability of alternative and cost-efficient funding and/or equity sources, and on the costs the originator incurs from transaction-related reporting and disclosure requirements. Moreover, the quantification of regulatory and economic capital relief achieved by the originator is becoming an increasingly complex exercise due to Basel II regulations and – in some cases – the revision of national accounting rules. Although preparation and implementation of a securitisation may constitute a major challenge for an originator, especially a first time issuer, the effort will be well rewarded as long as the originator can offer a sufficiently large and well-diversified asset pool and is able to act as repeating issuer (i.e. to issue ABS on a continuing basis).

Originator and Servicer Issues

In any securitisation the rating agencies and investors involved will want to understand the objectives of the transaction. Furthermore, they will want to appraise the quality of both the originator and future servicer. Their main concern is that a situation might arise in which the servicer would no longer be able to administer the securitised receivables properly. In most cases, the originator and servicer are the same entity, since the originator is appointed to service the loans on behalf of the SPV. In a securitisation with a revolving asset pool, investors also evaluate the seller's capacity to originate new loans as the receivables in the asset pool amortise.

During due diligence, investors and rating agencies normally require the originator/servicer to demonstrate at least:[37]

- a convincing financial track record and governance/ownership structure;

- a clear definition of core markets and a good understanding of their competitiveness;

- a sound corporate strategy for sustaining a current market position and for achieving growth objectives;

- a qualified management team and skilled staff;

- a rational organisation structure;

- an appropriate and powerful management information system (MIS);

- appropriate policies and procedures for underwriting, managing and monitoring loans, as well as procedures for the resolution of problem loans; and

- a convincing purpose or motivation for the securitisation transaction.

---

[37] Fitch: "Securitisation in Emerging Markets: Preparing for the Rating Process", February 17, 2006, p. 3.

A technical requirement that servicers have to meet is the ability to separate each securitised loan from others within the asset pool and also from unsecuritised loans. This is important not only for transaction reporting but also for the originator's accounting. In essence, the originator has to qualify as a third party servicer. Although no longer part of the originator's balance sheet, the securitised loans still have to be administered with respect to risk and data integrity as if they were loans belonging to the originator's own account.

Rating agencies or investors may also consider it necessary for a back-up servicer to be appointed when the transaction is closed. The availability of qualified back-up servicers increases the investors' comfort to the effect that they are expected to step in if the rating of the servicer is downgraded below an acceptable level or if the servicer defaults.

Rating agencies or investors could also require both the originator and the back-up servicer to be rated, at least on a national level.[38] Although unrated emerging market originators, especially capital market debutants, might find it difficult to provide a sustained track record in some of the key areas mentioned above, securitisation is still possible. If servicer risk cannot be otherwise reduced, investors and rating agencies would simply factor more risk into the securitisation, resulting in additional credit enhancement. More subordination for the senior tranche can be accomplished by increasing the sizes of the mezzanine and junior tranches, raising the average weighted funding cost for the originator. In addition, back-up servicers and potential government support for a servicer in default could also mitigate servicer risk.[39] However, rating agencies would take account of this only if potential government support is highly likely, for instance, due to the systemic importance of the originator.

Loan Characteristics and Data Requirements

Diversification and Standardisation

The more homogeneous, diversified and granular a loan portfolio, the easier it is to securitise. Asset pools are homogeneous if their receivables have similar contractual terms and interest rates, probabilities of prepayment, default and recovery.[40] Therefore, standardised loans such as mortgage loans or even unsecured short-term microloans are much more suitable for securitisation than other loans. For example, the cash flow of a pool is easier to predict if loans are originated in accordance with standardised underwriting criteria and loan documentation. Diversi-

---

[38] ibid, p. 3

[39] Geraldine Lambe: "Securitisation gives food for thought", in: The Banker, 4 August 2003, p. 31.

[40] Fitch: "Securitisation in Emerging Markets: Preparing for the Rating Process", February 17, 2006, p. 6.

fication refers to the dispersion of the asset pool's exposure into many uncorrelated risk factors such as geographic region, economic sector or industry, etc. Finally, the asset pool is granular if every single asset contributes only a small amount of relative exposure (i.e. a large number of small components).

Data Requirements

In order to place ABS successfully with local or international investors, the originator has to provide rating agencies – and to a lesser extent investors – with data illustrating the characteristics of the underlying assets and demonstrating their performance under certain recession and stress scenarios. According to Fitch, provision of data constitutes the major challenge for risk assessment or rating of an emerging market transaction.[41] Often, the data format used by the originator to administer a loan portfolio differs from the data essential for securitisation. When data are available and formats have been adjusted, originators find repeated securitisation very efficient. Costs incurred in the collection of initial data are usually amortised across later transactions.

The objective of data analysis is to predict expected loss, consisting of future defaults and losses of the receivables in the asset pool. Data requirements usually comprise:

- *Historical data*: at least 3 to 5 years of default and delinquency ratios, recoveries and prepayments of the relevant portfolio;

- *Borrower data*: ideally some kind of credit score in addition to geographic location, industry type, payment history, and financial data;

- *Pool data*: original amount, outstanding balance, maturity, seasoning, interest rate, collateral, repayment schedule on a loan-by-loan basis.[42]

If an originator cannot provide sufficient data, securitisation may still be feasible. Again, the rating agencies – and the investors – will make conservative assumptions where limited or no data are available, requiring greater credit enhancement and a higher weighted average cost of funding to the originator. Additional efforts by the originator in data collection usually pay off in lower transaction costs.

Furthermore, the originator must continue to provide data on the securitised portfolio on a monthly or quarterly basis during the lifetime of the transaction. Investors and rating agencies require periodic standardised reporting that enables them to monitor the performance of the pool. Reporting provides a basis for calculating pool ratios that measure delinquencies or default rates against predefined benchmarks that trigger certain actions in the securitisation.

---

[41] ibid, p. 5

[42] ibid, p. 6

Can MFIs Securitise Their Assets?

Any MFI considering a securitisation must respond to the issues discussed above. In-depth analysis of country-specific issues has to be carried out at the local level in cooperation with lawyers, regulators and possibly accountants/auditors. In this section we explore criteria related to MFIs as originators and microloans as an asset class. Given the sophistication of securitisation instruments and the related data requirements, this section refers exclusively to leading MFIs.

MFIs as Originators and Servicers

Overall Characteristics

The development of microfinance has been anything but uniform, creating a highly fragmented market. The divide between a small group of leading MFIs (or the top-tier MFIs) and thousands of MFIs with limited growth potential may deepen even further. An estimated 10,000 or more MFIs operate worldwide in very different institutional settings: tiny microloan programmes, sophisticated non-governmental organisations (NGOs) specialising in microfinance, commercial banks created specifically to provide the customer base of microfinance with a broad range of high-quality retail financial service choices, and commercial banks delivering microfinance products along with their traditional products. The majority of MFIs can be characterised as institutionally weak and heavily donor-dependent with little chance of achieving the scale that could diminish their dependence on grant funding.[43]

The peer group of leading MFIs as defined here consists of about 150 to 300 MFIs considered economically viable.[44] These top-tier MFIs are professionally managed, have been operating in the market for more than five years, and originate microloans and administer their portfolios according to generally accepted underwriting and servicing principles. Furthermore, many of these MFIs consistently generate very healthy profits. Finally, many are rated by international rating agencies or their local affiliates, and are also evaluated by companies specialised in MFI evaluation and rating, such as MicroRate Inc. based in Washington D.C., Planet Rating SAS in Paris, Microfinanza Rating srl in Milan or M-Cril in Gurgaon, India.

---

[43] Elizabeth Littlefield and Richard Rosenberg: "Microfinance and the Poor. Breaking down walls between microfinance and formal finance." In: Finance & Development (2004): 38-40, p. 39.

[44] BlueOrchard Finance s. a., a Geneva-based Microfinance Investment Advisory firm, expects the number of economically viable MFIs to grow to approximately 500 over the next few years. Refer to this web document at http://www.blueorchard.ch/en/microfinance_institutions.asp.

MFIs' Motivation for Securitisation

Many leading MFIs operate in markets with demand by far exceeding supply. Various estimates suggest a total demand for microloans exceeding USD 300 billion worldwide, while current supply is below USD 4 billion.[45] There is still enormous potential for the top-tier MFIs despite their loan growth of roughly 10% to 30% annually, with variations according to conditions in their local markets.[46] Recent research on MFI funding suggests that microlending could grow at rates of between 15% and 30% annually, assuming a stable funding base. To achieve such growth an enormous volume of additional debt and equity financing is necessary. Recent estimates suggest the appetite ranges between USD 2.5 billion and USD 5 billion per year in new funding via liabilities and from USD 300 million to USD 400 million per year in new equity.[47]

For the leading MFIs, access to funding and the cost of debt and equity financing vary according to their legal form, financial strength and geographic location. Rapidly growing loan portfolios and increasing competition in local markets are pushing MFIs to reduce their funding costs. However, within the group of leading MFIs, many institutions still do not have banking licences. However, to overcome growth restrictions and to tap the market for local deposits, more and more MFIs are becoming licensed financial institutions.

For deposit-taking MFIs, the cheapest source of funding is generally their own deposit base. Some of these MFIs would consider a potential securitisation of microloans only if their deposit base became unstable, while others would do so to improve the match between the maturities of assets and their liabilities. However, non-deposit-taking MFIs might have a different view. They often face restrictions in obtaining commercial funding on a continuing basis. Frequently, non-deposit taking MFIs borrow from local commercial banks, often at expensive rates and with cumbersome collateral requirements established by their local banking regulator. Increasingly, they also borrow from the steadily increasing number of debt and equity funds, the so-called microfinance investment vehicles (MIVs). The terms and conditions of this liability funding compare favourably with those of local commercial lenders. Finally, we would not exclude the possibility that non-deposit-taking MFIs among the market leaders, under certain conditions such as strain on liquidity that hampers growth, might even return to the relatively cheap funding provided by development agencies and/or by apex programmes.

---

[45] Jennifer Meehan: "Tapping the Financial Markets for Microfinance: Grameen Foundation USA's Promotion of this Emerging Trend". Grameen Foundation USA Working Paper Series. (October 2004), p. 1.

[46] In some cases growth rates may even be higher, achieving levels over 40%.

[47] M. de Sousa-Shields, E. Miamidian, J. Steeren, B. King, and C. Frankiewicz. (2004): Financing Microfinance Institutions: The Context for Transitions to Private Capital. USAID (December 2004), p. 4 ff.

As an alternative to borrowing from local banks and/or from MIVs, several top-tier MFIs have successfully issued debt instruments in their local markets, initially supported by third party guarantees.[48] Partial guarantees from IFC, USAID or FMO enabled banks like Mibanco in Peru and Financiera Comparta-mos in Mexico to issue bonds with better ratings and at lower coupons. Furthermore, the availability of partial guarantees has been instrumental in attracting new local and possibly even international investors. Examples of access to local capital market on a stand-alone basis include the bonds issued by Pro-Credit Bank Bulgaria, Financiera Compartamos, and in Colombia, FinAmérica and the NGO affiliate of WWB in Cali.[49]

Furthermore, some top-tier MFIs have started to partner international commercial banks which are beginning to view microfinance as a business opportunity – no longer as charity. In parallel with the diversification of MFIs' funding sources, commercial equity investors are increasingly found beside the traditional shareholders of MFIs such as development agencies, development banks or foundations. For instance, ABN AMRO and Citibank have started to cooperate with MFIs through equity investments, guarantees and funding.[50] However, it remains to be seen whether this trend will be sustained when the international capital market environment changes. On the one hand, commercial equity investors are attracted by MFIs' healthy returns reported on equity and assets. However, on the other, the sustained global low interest rate environment, and hence the lack of high return investment opportunities in developed markets, has led many of these commercial investors to consider relatively risky emerging market investments.

Analysis of the growth potential of leading MFIs and their equity and funding structures suggests that a selected group of non-deposit-taking MFIs will have to tap alternative funding and equity sources to achieve their growth targets. A similar situation occurs when MFIs' credit lines from commercially oriented local and international investors or from development agencies are fully used. In principle, any MFI – be it a licensed bank or a non-deposit taking institution – facing such a challenge to its expansion should examine the possibility of securitising at least parts of its loan portfolio on a continuing basis.

---

[48] ibid., p. 6. The amount of loan guarantees outstanding to support MFIs is approximately USD 300 million to USD 500 million.

[49] ProCredit Bank AD, Bulgaria (rated BB plus by Fitch) repeatedly placed bonds in different currencies (EUR, Bulgarian Leva) in the local market.

[50] ABN AMRO has set up Real Microcrédito, a joint venture in Brazil. Citigroup has set up a microfinance unit within its global consumer banking business and provided investment banking services to Compartamos, MiBanco and others through their local affiliates.

MFIs' Origination and Servicing Quality

It is estimated that 150 to 300 MFIs have either local or international ratings.[51] The ratings were assigned by companies specialised in the evaluation and rating of MFIs, or to a lesser extent by international rating agencies such as Fitch, Moody's or S&P or their local affiliates. It is difficult to define the average rating or average credit quality of the top-tier MFIs because the various rating scales are not comparable. Furthermore, the few international ratings awarded to leading MFIs are meaningful only to a limited extent because of rating caps imposed by country ceilings. However, many of the ratings of large MFIs can be considered as local investment-grade ratings. In principle, these MFIs could qualify as servicer or originator of a securitisation.

Difficulties can still arise. Most of the specialised MFI rating agencies may not yet be in a position to rate structured finance transactions. Potential ABS investors may require ratings by international agencies or their local affiliates. Generally, international rating agencies are more expensive than local rating agencies. Furthermore, they do not accept originator or servicer ratings assigned by other agencies. Therefore, international agencies would consider many of the top-tier MFIs as unrated.

These "unrated" MFIs, as far as they regard securitisation, would have to decide whether to prepare an unrated securitisation, which is more difficult to market to mainstream investors from the banking community,[52] or to pursue a rated transaction. In such a case, the unrated MFI would either have to become a rated institution[53] or have to find a rated back-up servicer.

The basic role of back-up servicers is to step in when the servicer to the transactions is downgraded below a predetermined rating level, or when the servicer defaults. Theoretically, also a rated shareholder such as a local commercial bank or even the rated holding company of an MFI network (e.g. ProCredit Holding AG with an international Fitch rating of BBB minus) could step in, if necessary. In principle, qualified back-up servicers should be available. However, if the servicer declares bankruptcy or is liquidated, the underlying assets will be severely affected. This is due to servicer characteristics in microfinance such as the fact that

---

[51] For further information refer, for example, to the web site of the Rating Fund, a joint initiative of the Inter-American Development Bank (IADB), the European Union (EU) and the Consultative Group to Assist the Poor (CGAP) with the objective of increasing the availability of information on the risk and performance of MFIs (http://www.ratingfund.org/).

[52] The Basel II regulatory framework will penalise banks with a 1-for-1 deduction (a risk weighting of 1.250% equal to a 100% capital charge), if they invest in *unrated* ABS transactions. The same capital charge will apply to ABS rated B and below. Tranches rated BB will carry a risk weighting of 350% (equal to a 28% capital charge). The same applies to originators retaining similar rated tranches in a securitisation.

[53] Moody's: "Securitisation in New Markets: Moody's Perspective", September 5, 2006, p. 2.

the collection process is remote and labour intensive – and not automated as in many traditional securitisations - and the importance of the personal relationships between the debtor and the originator/servicer.[54]

Therefore, the natural candidates for taking over the role of back-up servicers are likely to be the main rated competitors in the same country. There may even be strong MFIs in neighbouring countries with the same business language and similar loan underwriting and servicing technologies. However, the originator would be very reluctant to provide the full set of required data to a local competitor. A possible solution could be to use a back-up servicer belonging to the same MFI network. This would presumably have the advantage of applying the same underwriting, portfolio administration and foreclosure standards during the remaining term of the securitisation.

But are the MFIs capable of performing the duties of a servicer in a securitisation? From a credit risk management perspective, most of the top-tier MFIs would qualify as servicers, since the operational results to date are convincing, based primarily on low reported loan default rates and even lower loan loss rates. These MFIs use credit techniques which combine the mundane but essential virtues of conventional banking with incentive structures for customers, such as gradual increases in loan amounts, more favourable loan terms, etc., and through performance-based remuneration for loan officers.

However, the technical capabilities of MFIs' information systems vary greatly. Frequent (i.e. daily or weekly) tracking of default and delinquency appears to be quite common among most MFIs.[55] However, the group of MFIs that would qualify to act as a third party servicer might be smaller than expected, given the basic requirement that a third party servicer has to meet, which is to ensure sophisticated transaction reporting while maintaining the quality of accounting standards. MFIs' information systems must be capable of separating each securitised loan from others within the asset pool, on a loan-by-loan basis tracking delinquencies, defaults, cash balances, prepayments and restructurings as well as managing information related to its own unsecuritised assets. Probably, even leading MFIs would have to improve their IT in order to meet the basic requirements of a securitisation.

---

[54] Fitch: "Rating Methodology for Bolivian Microfinance Credits", Criteria Report, April 19, 2007.

[55] Most MFIs do *not* report actual *loan loss* rates. The industry standard is limited to the report of a "portfolio-at-risk" ratio (i.e. the entire balances of any loans that have payments in arrears for more than 30 days). According to the Microfinance Information Exchange, known as The MIX, data on default and repayment rates can be hard to verify (Silverman, Rachel: "A New Way to Do Well by Doing Good - Microfinance Funds Earn Returns on Tiny Loans To Poor Entrepreneurs Abroad", The Wall Street Journal, January 5, 2006.

Characteristics of MFI Assets and Data Requirements

Diversification and Standardisation

From a capital market perspective and in principle, MFI loan portfolios have interesting features. They contain a large number of relatively small loans (i.e. the pool is highly granular) and the correlation between individual borrowers is relatively low because the pool is well diversified by regions and economic activity, particularly those portfolios of large MFIs that operate nationwide. However, a key question is whether the loan products offered by the MFI are sufficiently standardised (i.e. homogenous). In addition to traditional unsecured short-term loans, the microfinance products of top-tier MFIs also include medium-term loans, longer-term mortgage loans, leasing (hire purchase) and consumer loans.

The majority of loans originated by MFIs are traditional microloans: short-term, unsecured loans to individuals or very small, usually informal businesses. Maturities usually vary between 3 and 12 months and average loan size ranges from USD 50 to USD 5,000. Provided that a single set of underwriting criteria and collection policies is used, such an asset pool might be considered as standardised. The fact that microloans are unsecured does not constitute a barrier to selling ABS collateralised by cash flows from microloans to investors in traditional capital markets.

Multiple loan products originated by an MFI using different underwriting policies are less suitable for securitisation in the same pool unless sufficient loans of the same type constitute a sizable sub-pool that merits independent evaluation. Some MFIs might have mortgage loan sub-pools of significant size to qualify for a separate securitisation.

Data Requirements

Most rating agencies would view short-term, unsecured microloans as consumer loans. In some cases, where average loan sizes are higher, rating agencies might also apply risk assessment techniques used for analysing trade receivables transactions. Whatever the case, rating agencies and investors would model the predicted cash flow of the receivables pool under different stress scenarios. The modelling exercise requires the following data on a loan-by-loan basis: (i) the original loan amount, (ii) the current outstanding loan balance, (iii) the remaining maturity, (iv) the interest rate, (v) the collateral, (vi) the repayment record,[56] (vii) the seasoning of the loan and (viii) the repayment schedule. Normally, an experienced arranger would help the originator prepare the data for the rating agencies and investors.

Rating agencies try to determine the behaviour of the cash flow of the pool in a harsh recession or other stress scenarios such as a natural disaster. For this purpose they would ideally want to analyse data on the creditworthiness of the individual borrowers, using credit scoring or credit bureau information and on historical per-

---

[56] The borrower's payment record on previous loans would also be helpful for the risk assessment.

formance data, preferably over a business cycle. These data sets are rarely available,[57] so the agencies employ a much smaller data base. Usually, when rating an initial transaction of an originator or for a country, rating agencies' assumptions for the default models will be fairly conservative. Models are adjusted as more data become available from other securitisations of the same asset class and from the performance of securitised portfolios. In any case, the first loss or junior tranche of an initial securitisation of microloans can be expected to be based on a multiple of the originator's historical losses. Lack of data makes it very important to present many arguments to demonstrate the high quality of microloan portfolios. For instance, the limited empirical data suggest that when macroeconomic shocks and natural catastrophes occur, the relative strength of microloan portfolios is superior to that of SME or corporate loans,[58] at least as long as microfinance is not fully integrated into the financial markets.

Recent Developments in Securitising Microfinance Assets

As noted previously, securitisation opens up new opportunities for refinancing an ever-broader range of assets and to obtain equity finance. In spite of the complexity of the financing technique, the microfinance industry has successfully begun to seize such opportunities in 2004. The following section gives examples of typical securitisation structures created to date with the objective of linking top-tier MFIs to international and local capital markets.

Sale of a Portfolio to Another Bank – the Wholesale Models of ICICI Bank, India

Portfolio sales have many aspects that are relevant to securitisation. An interesting option for an MFI seeking access to local funding is the sale of a microloan portfolio to a local bank. The following case of a microloan portfolio sale in India is an excellent example for MFIs considering a securitisation.

---

[57] Despite having invested millions of USD – including grant funding from development agencies - to develop IT platforms, many leading MFIs still do not present historical time series performance data, including loss data.

[58] Anecdotal evidence suggests that during Indonesia's banking crisis in 1998 the default rates of Bank Rakyat Indonesia (BRI) microloans did not exceed 6%, whilst the overall banking system's nonperforming loans (NPL) averaged 60%. After Hurricane Mitch afflicted Central America in 1998, the quality of ProCredit Bank El Salvador's portfolio deteriorated significantly but nonperforming loans (NPL) were reduced to less than 5% within a short period. More research is required to determine whether these results are typical.

ICICI, India's second largest commercial bank, underwrites microloans origi-nated by Indian MFIs.[59] The MFI acts as a distribution agent. ICICI, through its distribution agent, concludes loan agreements with the MFI's borrowers and funds the microloans underwritten by the MFI on a portfolio basis. The MFI retains a percentage of the portfolio risk. Depending on its portfolio quality, the MFI is liable for first losses within a range of 5% and 20%, which is an example of tranching similar to those in securitisations.[60] These arrangements give MFIs a strong incentive to underwrite microloans according to prudent criteria and to maintain portfolio quality. Again, similar to a securitisation, the MFIs service the microloans for ICICI and receive a servicing fee. If an MFI defaults, ICICI can appoint another MFI or another entity as servicer. ICICI has used this wholesale approach since 2002. At the end of 2004 about USD 150 million in microloans originated by more than 30 Indian MFIs were outstanding. Their overall default rates were consistently below 5%. ICICI plans to extend this partnership model to about 200 Indian MFIs.[61]

From an MFI's perspective the partnership model offers attractive funding based on the quality of its portfolio rather than on its own (inferior) institutional credit standing, which is another feature similar to securitisation.[62] Furthermore, the MFI reduces its capital requirements. Normally, a financial institution has to hold Tier 1 (or core) capital to cover its retained first losses. In the partnership model ICICI provides an overdraft facility to the MFIs that is equivalent to the volume of retained first losses. As to capital requirements, ICICI has to put regulatory capital against the credit risk in its microloan portfolio – which is credit enhanced via the first loss retention of the MFI up to a local AAA quality – and also against the overdraft facility provided to the MFI. In this way both the MFI and ICICI achieve higher leverage on their capital.[63] Many Indian MFIs have significant lending activities in rural areas, in part because of Reserve Bank of India requirements that favour branching in rural areas. The partnership model helps ICICI meet these requirements.[64] Other banks, mainly driven by regulatory incentives, can be expected to follow the ICICI model to gain experi-ence in lending in poor rural areas.

ICICI developed this model further in 2003 when it bought a complete microloan portfolio from Share, a leading Indian MFI with a good track record, growth rate

---

[59]   ICICI Bank, "ICICI Bank's microfinance strategy: A big bank thinks small", September 2003.

[60]   Ananth, Bindu: "Financing microfinance – the ICICI Bank partnership model", in: Small Enterprise Development, Vol. 16 No. 1, March 2005, p. 61.

[61]   ibid, p. 61

[62]   ibid, p. 62

[63]   ibid, p. 61

[64]   Basic information on partnerships between commercial banks and MFIs is found in CGAP: "Commercial Banks and Microfinance. Banks Outsource Retail Operations".

and scale of operation.[65] In two transactions ICICI purchased microloan receivables from Share having a net present value of USD 5.3 million.[66] As credit enhancement for the receivables sold, Share provided ICICI a first loss guarantee equal to 8% of the portfolio. Share acts as servicer and collection agent, remitting payments to ICICI Bank monthly. From the MFI's perspective, the results of the portfolio sale are similar to those of the partnership model: the MFI can overcome capital and funding constraints, scale up its business and expand outreach more rapidly. Furthermore, rating arbitrage lowers the MFI's cost of funding,[67] which enables it to negotiate more favourable terms with borrowers in the future.

This transaction pioneered a secondary market for microloans in India. ICICI not only purchased the microloan portfolio from Share but also sold the portfolio to another private sector bank in India.[68] As noted, the portfolio sale involves many elements required for a securitisation, such as tranching, reporting, and third party servicing. Small additional steps complete the basis for a rated ABS issue. However, sufficiently strong demand from banks and other financial institutions as buyers for microloan portfolios could make further steps unnecessary because funds would be readily available for lending to MFI customers. In addition, ICICI and the Grameen Foundation are establishing an entity that would provide credit enhancement for microfinance portfolios. This can be very helpful for further portfolio sales from MFIs to banks and also for securitisations of microloan portfolios.

Cross-Border Securitisation of Loans to MFIs (the "MF CDO")

To our knowledge, the world's first securitisation of microfinance assets in the capital markets was BlueOrchard Microfinance Securities I (BOMFS I), LLC[69] that was closed in August 2004. The deal was structured as collateral debt obligations (CDOs), a securitisation structure with a collateral pool that consists of a *limited* number of debt obligations such as loans (to MFIs). In two closings, the Delaware-based issuer BOMFS I raised approximately USD 86 million and used the issuance proceeds to disburse long-term loans to 14 MFIs located in 7 countries, mainly in Latin America.[70] Developing World Markets LLC (DWM), an invest-

---

[65] Ananth, Bindu: "Financing microfinance – the ICICI Bank partnership model", in: Small Enterprise Development, Vol. 16 No. 1, March 2005, p. 64.

[66] The portfolio used in the second transaction did not originate with Share, but was acquired from Basix, another Indian MFI. See: http://www.businessweek.com/magazine/content/04_39/b3901146_mz035.htm.

[67] Ananth, Bindu: "Financing microfinance – the ICICI Bank partnership model", in: Small Enterprise Development, Vol. 16 No. 1, March 2005, p. 63.

[68] ibid, p. 64

[69] Typically, securitisation transactions are labelled with the corporate name of the SPV.

[70] Basic information on the first and second closing of this privately placed securitisation is available at the Website of Developing World Markets, LLC (http://www.dwmarkets.

ment advisory group with a focus on emerging economies, structured and arranged the deal and placed the notes with US investors. The asset manager was BlueOrchard Finance S.A., a Geneva-based microfinance investment advisory company which selected the borrowing MFIs and acted as servicer for the receivables pool. After almost three years, we are not aware of any MFI having defaulted on its payment obligations to the SPV.

Over time, MF CDO transactions structures have become more sophisticated. To date, the most advanced securitisation was BOLD 2006-1 (see case study in the text box below) which closed in April 2006.[71]

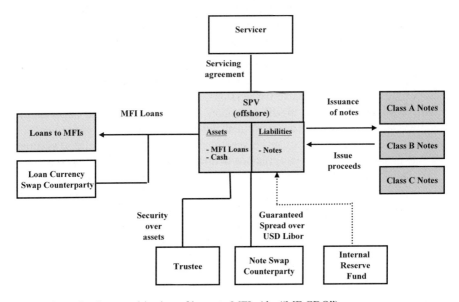

Fig. 2. Cross-border securitisation of loans to MFIs (the "MF CDO")

---

com). For more details refer to Developing World Markets, LLC: "BlueOrchard MicroFinance Securities I. Helping MicroFinance Institutions Alleviate Poverty. An Introduction & Overview", MFS Pitchbook, distributed at the 2004 Financial Sector Development Symposium organised by KfW on 11th and 12th November 2004 in Berlin. Mimeo

[71] The Website of BlueOrchard Finance S.A. (http://www.blueorchard.org/jahia/Jahia/op/ edit/pid/86) presents basic information on this transaction. Refer also to Morgan Stanley: BOLD 2006-1 Investor Presentation, February 2006, mimeo; and to: Callahan Ian, Henry Gonzalez, Diane Maurice, and Christian Novak: "Microfinance-On the Road to Capital Markets", in: "Journal of Applied Corporate Finance, Volume 19, Number 1, Winter 2007, A Morgan Stanley Publication by Blackwell Publishing, Malden, MA and Oxford.

To expand the investor base, structural features of MFI CDOs vary from offering to offering. However, the typical MF CDO appears to have many of the following noteworthy features:

- *Asset pool, terms of MFI loans, asset manager, servicer.* The pool consists of 7 to 30 unsecured senior loans. The borrowing MFIs mainly belong to the "top-tier." Asset managers specialised in microfinance select the MFIs and act as servicer for the pool. [72] The MFI loans are disbursed at closing by the SPV and have medium to long-term maturities (from 3 to 7 years). Loans start to amortise after a grace period (e.g. 2 years) or are redeemed in a single final (or bullet) payment. Usually, the interest rate is fixed. The MFI loans are denominated in USD and/or Euro. Though still the exception, a portion of MFI loans is sometimes denominated in their respective local currencies.

- *Liability structure, credit enhancement, rating.* The capital structure of MF CDOs has at least two tranches. The SPV issues debt and/or equity notes in a single or multi-currency offering (USD, EUR, GBP, etc.). Furthermore, the notes issued consist of fixed-rate and/or floating rate notes, varying in yield and subordination levels. Usually, the notes mirror the amortisation profile of the underlying asset pool. Internal credit enhancement for the senior notes is available in the form of (i) subordination of the mezzanine and junior (or equity) notes, and (ii) a reserve account to be funded from the issue proceeds at closing and/or by retaining cashflow from the junior note holders during a certain period. External credit enhancement, for example in the form of a guarantee provided by highly rated bilateral (e.g. OPIC) or multilateral financial institutions (e.g. European Investment Fund, EIF), has been available in earlier MF CDOs with the objective of guaranteeing full and timely payment of interest and principal on the senior notes.[73] So far, none of the MF CDOs has obtained an external rating.[74]

---

[72] In addition to BlueOrchard S.A., the microfinance advisory firm Symbiotics S.A. also acts as asset manager and has participated in several MF CDOs. Together with the European Investment Fund (EIF), it selected and arranged the OPPORTUNITY EASTERN EUROPE 2005-1 transaction, which raised approximately EUR 29.5 million for seven MFIs in Opportunity International's network in Eastern and Southeastern Europe. Furthermore, together with the Seattle-based NGO Global Partnerships, Symbiotics S.A. also selected the assets and services the pool in another MF CDO, which was closed in June 2006. For information on that deal refer to Developing World Markets: "Microfinance Securities XXEB (MFS)", Press Release, June 29, 2006. For information on those deals refer to the respective websites of Symbiotics S.A., EIF and Developing World Markets, LLC.

[73] Note that without these guarantees, the groundbreaking transaction BOMFS I (first closing) and OPPORTUNITY EASTERN EUROPE 2005-1 would not have closed at all.

[74] However, at the time of the final review of this chapter, it became evident that Standard & Poor's was about to rate the BOLD 2007-1 transaction which was expected to be forthcoming in late spring 2007.

- *Mitigation of country risk and currency risk.* Usually, there is no mitigation of country risk (transfer and convertibility risk) in the structure. Thus, the SPV may default on its payments to investors if one of the countries in which the MFIs are operating imposes restrictions such as capital controls or foreign-exchange controls.[75] So far, internal credit enhancement plus the priority of payments (i.e. the cash waterfall) appear to have provided sufficient comfort to investors. These provisions include directing all of the cashflows to senior note holders if an MFI defaults under the loan contract.. Furthermore, currency swaps permit local currency funding to MFIs, reducing their currency risk exposure and also mitigating the SPV's exposure to currency mismatches.

- *Investors.* Investors in MF CDOs have ranged from socially oriented individual investors and foundations to the broad universe of microfinance investment vehicles (MIVs) and purely commercially-oriented institutional investors. The latter include banks, pension funds and mutual funds.

Case Study: BlueOrchard Loans for Development (BOLD 2006-1)

The BOLD 2006-1 transaction was closed in April 2006. As the largest MF CDO to date, the transaction raised the equivalent of approximately USD 100 million. The asset pool contained 21 senior unsecured medium-term loans (all but two had five year maturities) to MFIs located in 13 countries, mainly in Latin America. Investors gained exposure to three different institutional MFI structures namely commercial banks, non-bank financial intermediaries and NGOs. Some of the top-tier MFIs have already participated in BOMFS I. On average, the size of MFI loans was equivalent to approximately USD 4.7 million. BlueOrchard Finance S.A., Geneva, selected the MFIs and is the servicer of the asset pool. Several innovative features will further pave the way for microfinance en route to mainstream capital markets: Whilst the notes consisted of a multi-currency offering (EUR, GBP, USD), approximately 30% of the volume of receivables was denominated in local currencies such as Colombian pesos, Mexican pesos and Russian roubles. Thus, the participating MFIs could reduce their exposure to hard currency financing. All of the non-USD currencies were swapped back to USD to avoid currency mismatches at the SPV. Though the transaction was not rated, the securities were listed on the Dublin Exchange.

---

[75] If an external guaranty is available, and depending on the scope of its coverage, senior note investors may not be exposed to country risk.

It was the first microfinance securitisation transaction arranged by a major international investment bank (Morgan Stanley), and also the first truly commercial placement of senior notes backed by exposure to microfinance institutions. Credit enhancement for the Class A notes in the form of the subordinated Class B notes equalled 28%. FMO, the "anchor" investor, fully underwrote the Class B notes with the intention to subsequently sell portions of this allotment to similar organisations in Europe. Both the unusual thickness of the junior tranche and FMO's early commitment created sufficient comfort to senior investors. Additional credit enhancement came from a cash reserve account amounting to 2% of the outstanding notes, funded by retaining cash flow from Class B investors during the first 18 months of the transaction. The SPV can draw on this cash reserve to cover any shortfall in the payment of interest and principal to senior Class A note holders. The SPV raised funding on the three tranches of the senior Class A at a weighted average cost of 78 bps p.a. over the USD five-year swap rate of 5.41% prevailing at the time of closing. KfW purchased a portion from FMO's Class B note.

BOLD 2006-1 - Capital Structure

Class	Volume	% of Notes	Credit Enhance-ment	Scheduled Maturity	Coupon
A1	EUR 32,900,000	40%	28%	March 2011	3-month-Euribor +75 bps
A2	GBP 14,000,000	25%	28%	March 2011	5.586%
A3	USD 7,000,000	7%	28%	March 2011	6.017%
B	USD 28,000,000	28%	n.a.	March 2011	Residual cashflow
	USD Eq. 99,211,000			Avg. USD	5 year swaps + 78 bps

Source: Morgan Stanley BOLD 2007-1 Investor Presentations, transactions documents; Callahan, Ian et al (2007)

Preliminary Assessment of MF CDOs

For top-tier MFIs, the MF CDO – the currently prevailing instrument – is a viable means of diversifying funding sources and raising capital in the international capital markets at longer tenors and at more attractive costs. It can also be useful for those MFIs whose borrowing limits with traditional creditors such as donors and/or bilateral and multilateral financial institutions or microfinance investment vehicles (MIVs) are fully utilised. On the other hand, for investors in the capital markets the creation of ABS collateralised by microfinance assets such as loans to MFIs is a way to gain exposure to the risk of MFIs, at least indirectly. Since MFIs have not issued corporate bonds in international capital markets yet, to our knowledge, it is still impossible to directly access corporate risk related to MFIs. Finally, with each new MF CDO coming to the market, the liquidity and investors' knowledge of this new asset class are expected to increase. Going forward, the underlying asset class is expected to become more differentiated and it is certainly only a question of time until subordinated loans to MFIs will be securitised.

To date, arrangers have created MF CDOs exclusively for investor accounts in the international markets. Therefore, from a capital market developmental perspective one of the remaining challenges is to create MF CDOs to target domestic markets. For MFIs, possible benefits would include first and foremost raising local currency funding, thus reducing their structural exposure to foreign exchange risk. Furthermore, leading MFIs could increasingly replace their participation in traditional apex programmes. On the other hand, more rated transactions and more frequent local issuances would further spark interest from institutional investors, provided that local regulations permit them to invest in microfinance assets. MF CDOs are useful instruments to raise additional funding for MFIs while acquainting private investors to microfinance risk.

MF CDOs represent debt funding, which appears to be the inherent "shortcoming" of this instrument. To support lending growth, gearing up the debt to equity ratio is a feasible strategy as long as the respective MFI is not yet fully leveraged. As capital adequacy ratios of fast growing MFIs decline to a level just exceeding local regulators' requirements, and instruments to increase equity are not available on time, the instrument's usefulness declines since it does not transfer risk-weighted assets from the balance sheet to the capital markets.

Cross-Border Securitisation of Microloan Portfolios (the "MF CLO")

In addition to helping investors obtain exposure to the credit risk of different types of MFIs, as highlighted in the previous section, the creation of collateralised loan obligations (CLOs) permits investors to gain exposure to the credit risk of the customer base of microfinance itself. This is possible because CLOs are securitisation structures having a collateral pool that consists of a *large* number of debt obligations such as loans.

ProCredit Company B.V. was the world's first securitisation of a portfolio that included loans to microenterprises. It was also the world's first securitisation involving microfinance assets rated by an internationally accepted rating agency (Fitch). The transaction launched the entry of the ProCredit network into the international ABS market and was structured and arranged by Deutsche Bank AG. KfW supported the transaction from the very beginning, assuming the role of a structuring investor ensuring that the final setup was compatible with its capital markets development objectives.[76]

---

[76] The fact that ProCredit Company B.V. obtained a public rating was instrumental in providing the credibility to promote the project. Potential investors interested in microfinance assets can obtain information and learn from this experience.

The originator, ProCredit Bank Bulgaria AD (PCB) is a subsidiary of ProCredit Holding AG in Frankfurt whose operations commenced in October 2001. This originator initially raised EUR 47.8 million in long-term funding, securitising an Euro-denominated portfolio consisting of loans to SMEs and microenterprises in Bulgaria.[77] Figure 3 below provides an overview of the transaction which closed in May 2006, after only four months of preparation. The securitisation constituted a benchmark, not only for microfinance but also for cross-border securitisation in new markets in the European Union.[78]

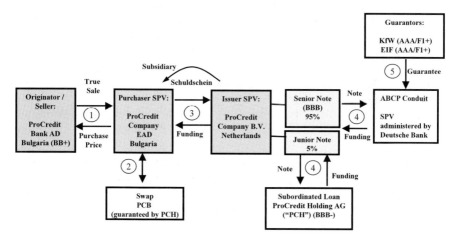

Fig. 3. Cross-border securitisation of a microloan portfolio (the "MF CLO")

The securitisation was structured as a two-tired multi-issuance platform: one SPV was established in Bulgaria to purchase the loans from PCB, the other SPV was set up in The Netherlands to issue the notes. The securitisation mechanics can be summarised as follows:

1. The originator, PCB, sells and transfers a pool of eligible assets to ProCredit Company EAD, a Bulgarian bankruptcy remote SPV (or purchaser). At the closing, the Euro-denominated asset pool consisted of 1,286 loans to SMEs and microenterprises. Assets had a maturity of up to seven years with a weighted average life remaining to maturity of three years. Each month during a 12-month-period the Bulgarian SPV will purchase additional eli-

---

[77] For detailed information refer to Fitch: "ProCredit Company B.V.", Credit Products / Bulgaria, New Issue, May 15, 2006, and to press releases on the websites of PCB and Deutsche Bank AG.

[78] Bulgaria joined the EU on January 1, 2007, with 10 other mainly former socialist countries.

gible assets from PCB to draw further amounts under the initial funding facility that reached EUR 80 million at closing. This revolving facility, subject to uninterrupted annual renewal, can be increased up to a maximum of EUR 120 million.

2. To avoid mismatches, the purchaser swapped the cashflows of fixed paying assets into variable rates through a swap arrangement with PCB. Given PCB's international rating of BB plus,[79] its parent company, ProCredit Holding AG (or PCH) rated BBB minus, guaranteed the swap.

3. To finance the acquisition of microloans from PCB, the purchaser issued certificates of indebtedness (Schuldscheine) under the Loan Note Facility entered into with its parent company, which is the insolvency remote Dutch SPV (or issuer).

4. At the same time, to finance the purchase of the Schuldschein, the Dutch SPV issued two classes of notes, each with a different risk-return profile: The Senior Note in the initial amount of EUR 45.4 million and the Subordinated Loan Note in the initial amount of EUR 2.41 million.

5. The funding provider, i.e. the investor in the Senior Note was a bankruptcy remote Asset-Backed Commercial Paper (ABCP) vehicle, administered by Deutsche Bank.[80] In buying the Subordinated Loan Note, PCH assumed the first-loss in this securitisation, set by Fitch at approximately 5.05% of the securitised asset pool. Therefore, PCH had to consolidate the assets on its balance sheet.

6. Fitch rated the Senior Notes at BBB, which is in line with Fitch's "country ceiling" for structured finance transactions out of Bulgaria.[81] In order to allow the ABCP conduit to purchase the Senior Note, the EIF and KfW guaranteed the full payments under the Senior Note on a pari passu basis.

---

[79] At the time of closing, Fitch's country ceiling for Bulgaria was BBB.

[80] In a nutshell, an ABCP programme is a way of using short-term money to finance longer-dated assets. Banks use an SPV (or conduit) that buys short-dated trade receivables, longer-dated structured finance securities, outright mortgage loans or SME loans and funds them via issuing short-term ABCP. Maturities can span anywhere from one day to 364 days. As the short-dated CP matures, banks place new CP to repay it (also known as "to roll the CP"). There are varying levels of protection for ABCP investors all targeted at repaying ABCP investors in full. Among other things, to ensure the high rating of the CP can be maintained, the conduit can only purchase assets that exceed a certain minimum rating.

[81] Since PCH's own rating was below the country ceiling and as there was no other element built into the structure to mitigate country risk, the credit rating of the Senior Note could not "pierce" the country ceiling, despite the fact that the pool consisted of high quality assets.

For PCB the key benefits of the transaction were manifold: The securitisation allowed the originator to tap a new source of medium to long-term funding at attractive costs. PCB transferred substantially all risks and rewards of the assets to a bankruptcy remote SPV in Bulgaria and, as a result obtained off-balance sheet treatment under IFRS. Thus, PCB has significantly freed-up its existing regulatory and economic capital, which can be used to support additional lending. Even more importantly, the revolving structure has allowed PCB to refinance newly origi-nated eligible loans on an ongoing basis by selling them to the Bulgarian SPV. In other words, during the lifetime of the securitisation transaction, the originator will be able to uncouple lending growth from its capital base; this constitutes an extremely supportive benefit for fast growing smaller banks. The structure also has a benefit for the ProCredit network, since the Dutch SPV could also be used to refinance assets from ProCredit entities in other jurisdictions.

Domestic Securitisation of Microloan Portfolios (the "MF CLO")

The world's first ever *domestic* securitisation of a microloan portfolio is the BRAC Micro Credit Securitisation Series I, which to our knowledge is the only transaction of this type to date as we go to press. It was closed in September 2006.[82] BRAC has the legal status of an NGO and serves more than 5 million mostly women members in rural areas of Bangladesh. It is possibly the largest MFI in the world. Since it was set up in 1972, the institution reached scale and diversity in its operations. On aver-age, the microloan balance per borrower is equivalent to approximately USD 165 in local currency, the Bangladesh Taka (BDT).

The key objective of this securitisation for BRAC consisted of establishing a term funding platform through the securitisation of microloan portfolios, enabling it to diversify its sources of funding at lower interest rates. Selling risky assets from its balance sheet improves BRAC's overall risk profile, strengthening its balance sheet. Moreover, tapping the domestic capital market has permitted BRAC to broaden its investor base. For the originator, this transaction marks an important step from donor based to unsecured commercially priced funding sources. The securitisation is expected to foster the development of the capital market in Bang-ladesh.

Over a period of six and a half years, this landmark securitisation will give BRAC access to the equivalent of USD 180 million in local currency funding. Under the programme, BRAC assigns microloan receivables to BRAC Micro Credit Securitisation Series 1, a Bangladesh SPV established as a trust, which issues certificates to investors representing undivided beneficial interest in the underlying assets. At the closing, and thereafter every six months, the SPV issues

---

[82] For a brief description of the transaction refer to Zaman, Shams and Kairy, S.N.: "Building Domestic Capital Markets: BRAC's AAA Securitization", in: MicroBanking Bulletin, Issue 14, Spring 2007, Microfinance Information Exchange, Inc. p.13-15.

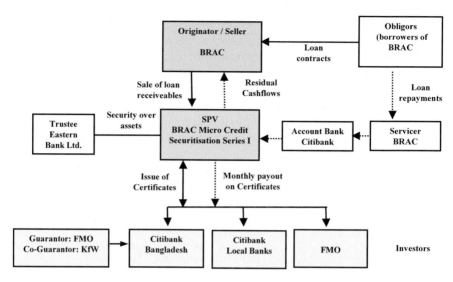

Fig. 4. Domestic securitisation of a microloan portfolio (the "MFI CLO")

securities amounting to BDT 1 billion (about USD 15 million). Each tranche of securities is collateralised by a pool of eligible unsecured microloans that will be purchased by the SPV from the originator at each issuance. The scheduled maturity of each series of securities is one year. The securities are floating rate notes and tranche-specific pricing will be referenced to the Bangladesh government six-month Treasury Bill rate at the time of a new issuance.

The Bangladesh central bank required the structure to be rated. The Credit Rating Agency of Bangladesh rated this first ever securitisation transaction launched in Bangladesh. The certificates in this first local ABS issue obtained an AAA rating on a national scale.[83] There is no subordination among the notes. However, there is credit enhancement to sustain their high rating. In addition to several risk mitigating features built into the structure, BRAC as the servicer is required on each issuance date to assign additional receivables to the SPV equal to 50% of the purchased asset pool.

The structure includes the creation of a dynamic pool of receivables. Each tranche will be based on tens of thousands of microloans, and it is estimated that over the lifetime of the transaction approximately 3.3 million microloans will be assigned to the SPV. The original selection of the pool, its proper administration and subsequent replenishment constituted a big challenge for the execution of the transaction. In order to handle such huge numbers of receivables, the Boston-based company MF Analytics, with partial grant financing from KfW, developed a software package to

---

[83] Refer to Credit Rating Agency of Bangladesh, BRAC Micro Credit Securitisation Series I, Preliminary Rating Report, February 28, 2006.

enable BRAC to generate pools that have similar characteristics, ensuring asset diversification across product type and geographic region.

RSA Capital, a small financial advisory firm based in Dhaka and Boston, arranged this complex and challenging securitisation structure. As structuring investors, KfW, through its Regional Asian, Securitisation and Legal Departments, and FMO provided substantial input to the financial and legal structure of the transaction. Citibank acted as co-arranger. Clifford Chance (Hong Kong branch) and the local law firm Lee, Khan and Partners acted as legal advisors and generated the documentation.[84]

Investors in the initial tranche of this securitisation included FMO, which purchased one-third of the securities which were the equivalent to USD 15 million in BDT. Citibank N.A. Bangladesh funded the equivalent of USD 5 million against a guarantee provided by FMO (with a counter-guarantee from KfW), covering timely payment of interest and principal. Finally, Citibank N.A. together with two other local banks purchased the remaining USD 5 million of certificates, without a guarantee.

In early 2007, BRAC Micro Credit Securitisation Series I was selected "Securitisation Deal of the Year 2006" by the International Financing Review Asia (IFR Asia). This award will certainly increase the acceptance of microfinance in the capital markets and of microfinance risk as a commercially viable asset class.

Preliminary Assessment of MF CLOs

The securitisation of granular pools of microloans is expected to have a positive impact on the balance sheet of the originator, including:

- In exchange for the assets sold and transferred to the onshore or offshore SPV, the MFI receives a cash payment in local or hard currency from the SPV which leads to an accounting exchange on the asset side of the balance sheet.

- The funding obtained from the capital markets neither constitute new liabilities for the MFI nor create a strain on the MFI's borrowing limits with existing creditors and/or investors. Selling assets from the balance sheet also reduces total assets, since the funds raised will be used to (partially) reduce liabilities.

- The sale of pools with risky assets improves the risk profile of the MFI, which in turn increases the financial standing of the institution in the market.

- The more that risks and rewards of the segregated asset pool are transferred from the balance sheet to the SPV (and to investors), the larger the extent to which regulatory and economic capital formerly tied-up with the securitised pool can be freed-up. Securitising microloan portfolios is a time-saving and

---

[84] The original closing planned for August 2005 was postponed for more than a year due to a cumbersome approval process inside Bangladesh's regulatory bureaucracy.

cost-efficient alternative strategy for MFIs to obtain equity, in addition to a traditional capital increase via shareholders or Tier-1 hybrid capital.

- Finally, provided that a revolving (or dynamic) pool is structured, the MFI can immediately refinance its newly originated assets, thus de-linking lending growth from its capital base.

Though the securitisation of microloan portfolios is more advantageous for the originator, the arrangers have focused on creating MF CDOs. This may reflect the fact that a true sale of assets across the border or into the domestic markets is far more complex to achieve given issues such as availability of good quality pool data and legal requirements. As with MF CDOs, the big challenges for the future are to structure more domestic deals and, to increase their volumes to achieve economies of scale and to consider multi-seller securitisations, especially for MFIs operating in highly competitive local markets such as Peru and Bolivia. Preferably, multi-seller structures would have to focus on domestic markets and could possibly become a viable funding strategy for MFIs with smaller portfolios and a continuous capacity to originate new loans.

To conclude, the securitisation of pools of microloans permitted the originators to raise additional funds in the European ABS market (the case of PCB) as well as in the Bangladesh capital market (the case of BRAC), and to free-up regulatory and economic capital (though this was not relevant to BRAC as an NGO). At the same time, the transactions permitted private investors to gain direct exposure to the borrowing base of microfinance.

Conclusions

Earlier, we presented estimates that the microfinance sector requires new debt financing in the magnitude of USD 2.5 billion to USD 5 billon per year, and new equity financing from USD 300 million to USD 400 million to maintain growth rates of between 15% and 30% annually.

As the examples suggest, securitisation structures such as the MF CDO and the MF CLO have mainly allowed top-tier MFIs to enter international capital markets. Furthermore, the BRAC securitisation in Bangladesh marked the first microfinance deal to transfer the credit risk of a pool of microloans to investors in a domestic market. The wholesale models of ICICI in India, though not a securitisation in the narrow sense, permit qualified MFIs in the rural areas to scale up their operations. Altogether, these recent developments are promising signs of the expansion and increasing maturity of the microfinance industry. Using standardised securitisation techniques has also allowed microfinance to create opportunities for private investors in the capital markets.

As the shift to capital market based lending leads to a close link between primary markets (lending) and secondary markets (where receivables are traded), securitisation is expected to have a beneficial impact on MFI funding as well as on the flow of loans to the customer base of microfinance. Securitisation is now a funding *alternative* for MFIs. However, securitisation can become an *important* funding technique for MFIs. To date, liquidity of microfinance assets in the capital markets is still very low and secondary trading of microfinance risk has yet to happen. The more deals that come to the capital markets, the more local and international investors learn about the characteristics of this new asset class and the performance of microfinance assets and the related ABS.

Securitisation can help non-deposit taking MFIs as well as those with a banking license to gain access to alternative funding sources and to grow on the basis of their existing capital. In addition, securitisation can help these MFIs to reduce their cost of funding and to manage their capital base more effectively.[85] Given the complexity involved in the preparation of a true sale of microloans, it is clear that any MFI considering a securitisation should do so with the strategic long-term objective of becoming a repeat issuer. This is because of upfront costs involving data, legal expenses, rating agencies, high risk premiums on initial ABS issuances, reputation building, etc. A one-time transaction is likely not to be cost-efficient. An MFI considering a first-time securitisation has to have a sizable loan portfolio that can generate periodic ABS issuances, permitting the MFI to amortise these costs quickly.

If local investor demand is sufficient, a local securitisation is usually most efficient because it avoids issues related to currency risk. Where local investor demand requires expansion, MFIs should pursue an intensive dialogue with potential local institutional investors, with other financial institutions and with the relevant authorities in order to learn more about investors' risk appetite and to introduce them to the emerging asset class of microloans or, more generally, microfinance risk.

In principle and from the point of view of a potential ABS investor, a microloan portfolio serviced by a leading MFI appears to have a very appealing risk profile. Granularity, diversification, standardisation, low prepayment risk and relatively low default and even lower historical loss rates constitute a plus for potential ABS investors. The operational challenge for the MFI is to deliver data and to construct and maintain a historical data base to quantify these loan characteristics. For first time issuers, data management normally requires an extraordinary effort that pays off slowly.

From a financial system development perspective, the securitisation of microfinance assets appears promising: First, the creation of a domestic secondary market dedicated to pricing and trading microfinance risk will deepen and broaden the local financial system. Second, development of a more liquid secondary market for microfinance risk contributes to poverty alleviation as more poor people gain access to financial services at lower interest rates. As investors learn more about microfinance, the capital markets will reduce the risk premiums for this asset

---

[85] The Financial Express: "Crisil Study: Securitisation of Microfinance assets: a winning position", December 2004

class. Assuming a competitive environment and aggressive growth targets, MFIs will pass on to their clients at least in part of the funding advantages gained through securitisation. Third, securitising loan portfolios of rural MFIs may help offset the negative effects on rural economies caused by the drain of rural savings into urban centres. Provided that domestic institutional investors such as local insurance companies or pension funds are permitted to invest in structured micro-finance assets, rural-based MFIs could diversify their funding sources and become more independent from government programmes and donor funding. Moreover, creating high quality ABS collateralised with microloans originated by rural-based MFIs would provide institutional investors an opportunity to channel commercially priced funding back into rural areas.[86]

As the shift to more capital-market based lending leads to a close link between primary markets (lending) and secondary markets (where receivables are traded), securitisation is expected to have a beneficial impact on SME financing and microfinance.

What can a financial institution such as KfW do to support securitisation of microfinance assets in new markets? In general, KfW supports the development of structured finance in new markets with the *objectives* of creating a secondary market, enabling the securitisation of challenging asset classes such as microfinance, supporting MFIs in their efforts to securitise microloan portfolios, and deepening secondary markets through increasing the liquidity of microfinance risk. In doing so, MFIs are expected to increase the origination of new loans to KfW's target groups, i.e. the customer base of microfinance.

As a public-law institution, *KfW's approach* is centred on the principles of promoting securitisation of microfinance assets through risk taking. However, such risks need to be properly gauged. Structured finance implies that KfW's involvement in a project is tailored to best respond to the demand of the client, the specific requirements of the structure and the respective market situation. Against this background, KfW's possible involvement can be manifold:

- As a *structuring enhancer or investor* KfW becomes involved at an early stage in the structuring process together with the arranger to provide a tailor-made credit enhancement in order to achieve the target rating for most senior notes. Typical instruments include partial guarantees which are a very powerful and cost-effective instrument, especially to promote domestic securitisation. They assist the originator in establishing the capital market's view of the credit risk of the microloan portfolio. Over time, more informed investors and rating agencies will move further down the credit curve, no longer requiring guarantors to bring these transactions to market.

---

[86] It might be worth exploring potential links between insurance companies writing policies for their microfinance customer base and their opportunities for investing in ABS backed by microfinance assets.

As an *"anchor" investor*, the role of KfW is to commit its participation to the originator at an early stage, especially in transactions with new and innovative features. KfW's participation in such transactions builds confidence in the capital market and facilitates the placement of the transaction with investors. It is the actual market environment that determines the strategic focus of a KfW investment. In this context, the concept of anchor investor can also include participation at senior tranche level, for example to avoid crowding out private investors seeking opportunities in more risky tranches and to make the closing of transactions feasible. As recent experience with securitisations in new markets has shown, private investors can be attracted as long as adequate compensation for risk is offered for first-losses and risky positions of the mezzanine tranche – the absence of which has been a major shortcoming in the microfinance securitisations seen so far. On the other hand, typical senior investors are often restricted to purchasing AAA or at least AA-rated tranches. Since it is impossible to achieve such ratings in cross-border deals from emerging markets due to country cciling issues – unless an AAA rated institutions provided a full wrap of the senior tranche – KfW's participation might be required to successfully place the senior tranche.

- As *provider of a liquidity facility,* KfW aims at reducing specific risks such as market interruptions, especially in cross-border transactions (e.g. mitigation of transfer and convertibility risks. etc.).

To promote the securitisation of pools of microloans, development agencies can target further investments to *partially* finance: (i) brief legal and regulatory feasibility studies;[87] (ii) technical assistance to MFIs, strictly limited to improving areas such as data generation, warehouse management and control of data quality; and (iii) public ratings of ABS structures, preferably through internationally accepted rating agencies or their local affiliates.[88]

To take the microfinance industry a step further, a joint effort is required. Leading MFIs, local investors, international rating agencies or their local affiliates, local regulators, major investment banks and specialised microfinance investment boutiques, and, possibly, the collaboration of like-minded development finance institutions should be assembled for this purpose.

---

[87] According to KfW's experience, such legal and regulatory studies can normally be conducted within a very short time, and at moderate cost, since the relevant questionnaires are highly standardised. Furthermore, international law firms tend to have local partners so that, under normal scenarios, the presence of an international expert in the field is not required.

[88] Public ratings from the major agencies are instrumental in educating mainstream investors and promoting the securitisation of microfinance risk. As noted earlier, the Basel II regulatory implications will make it quite unattractive for banks to invest in unrated ABS.

KfW, a leading investor supporting microfinance-related ABS transactions, is ready to support such processes. Its unique institutional profile combines outstanding expertise in financial sector development, in-depth knowledge of local financial markets, its reputation in international capital markets and its broad expertise in securitisation.

References

Ananth, Bindu: "Financing microfinance – the ICICI Bank partnership model", in: Small Enterprise Development, Vol. 16, No. 1, March 2005 http://www2.gsb.columbia.edu/socialenterprise/academics/research/papers/ICICI_Bank_Partnership_Model_Bindu_Ananth_SED_2005.pdf

Basu, Sudipto: "Securitisation and the Challenges Faced in Micro Finance". Institute for Financial Management and Research, Centre for Micro Finance Research, Working Paper Series, Mumbai, April 2005 (http://ifmr.ac.in/pdf/workingpapers/2/Securitization.pdf)

BlueOrchard Finance S.A.; Microfinance: Microfinance Institutions. 2006 (http://www.blueorchard.ch/en/microfinance_institutions.asp)

BlueOrchard Finance S.A.: "BlueOrchard Loans for Development 2006-1", 2006 (http://www.blueorchard.org/jahia/Jahia/op/edit/pid/86)

Byträm, Hans: "The Microfinance Collateralized Debt Obligation: a Modern Robin Hood?" Department of Economics, Lund University, Working Paper 14, June 22, 2006 (http://www.nek.lu.se/publications/workpap/Papers/WP06_14. pdf)

Callahan Ian, Henry Gonzalez, Diane Maurice, and Christian Novak: "Microfinance-On the Road to Capital Markets", in: "Journal of Applied Corporate Finance, Vol. 19, No. 1, Winter 2007, A Morgan Stanley Publication by Blackwell Publishing, Malden MA and Oxford

CGAP: "Commercial Banks and Microfinance. Banks Outsource Retail Operations. n.d. (http://www.cgap.org/docs/bank_profiles_retail.pdf)

Credit Rating Agency of Bangladesh: BRAC Micro Credit Securitisation Series I, Preliminary Rating Report, February 28, 2006

DeSanctis, Gabriel: "Guaranteeing progress", in: International Financing Review, IMF/Word Bank Special Report, September 2004. Also available at (http://www.ifc.org/ifcext/treasury.nsf/AttachmentsByTitle/MH_IFCGuaranteeingProgress/$FILE/IFR.pdf)

de Sousa-Shields, M., E. Miamidian, J. Steeren, B. King and C. Frankiewicz. 2004: Financing Microfinance Institutions: The Context for Transitions to Private Capital. USAID, December 2004 (http://www.esglobal.com/pdf/Financing%20Microfinance%20Institutions.pdf)

Deutsche Bank AG and ProCredit Bank Bulgaria: Press Release. May 15, 2006 (http://www.deutsche-bank.de/presse/pdfs/PCB_Bulgaria_15.5._engl.pdf)

Developing World Markets, LLC: "BlueOrchard MicroFinance Securities I. Helping MicroFinance Institutions Alleviate Poverty. An Introduction & Overview", MFS Pitchbook, Distributed at the 2004 Financial Sector Development Symposium organised by KfW on 11th and 12th November 2004 in Berlin. Mimeo

Developing World Markets, LLC: "BlueOrchard Microfinance Securities I, 2nd Closing" (http://www.dwmarkets.com/transactions2.htm)

Developing World Markets, LLC: MicroFinance Securities XXEB (MFS), Press Release, June 29, 2006 (http://www.dwmarkets.com/News/DWM%20Press %20Release_MFS_06-29-2006.pdf)

Ehrbeck, Tilman: "Optimising Capital Supply in Support of Microfinance Industry Growth", a presentation to the Microfinance Investor Roundtable in Washington DC on 24-25 October 2006, organised by Omidyar Network / The SEEP Network

European Investment Fund: "EIF signs innovative deal to assist Micro Finance Institutions in Eastern Europe", Press Release, December 18, 2005 (http://www.eif.europa.eu/news/press/press.asp?press=110)

Fender, Ingo and Janet Mitchell: "Structured Finance: complexity, risk and the use of ratings" in: BIS Quarterly Review, June 2005 p. 67-79 (http://www.bis.org/publ/qtrpdf/r_qt0506f.pdf)

Fitch Rating: "Rating Methodology for Bolivian Microfinance Credits", Criteria Report, April 19, 2007

Fitch Ratings: "Special-Purpose Vehicles in Structured Finance Transactions", Derivative Fitch, Structured Finance Criteria Report, June 13, 2006

Fitch Ratings: "ProCredit Company B.V.", Credit Products/Bulgaria, New Issue, May 15, 2006

Fitch Ratings: "Existing Asset Securitisation in Emerging Markets – Sovereign Constraints", May 12, 2006

Fitch Ratings: "The Role of Multilaterals in Structured Finance", March 16, 2006

Fitch Ratings: "Securitisation in Emerging Markets: Preparing for the Rating Process", February 17, 2006

Fitch Ratings: "Structured Finance in Latin America's Local Markets: 2004 Year in Review and 2005 Outlook", March 1, 2005

Fitch Ratings: "FTPYME Santander 1 FTA – Deal Summery" Issuer Report Grade Date 02-May-2006

Fitch Ratings: "FTPYME Santander 1, Fondo De Titulización de Activos", New Issue Report, September 30, 2003

Global Legal Group: "The International Comparative Legal Guide to: Securitisation 2006", London 2006 (http://www.iclg.co.uk/)

Glüder, Dieter: "Regulatory impact of synthetic securitisation" in: Watson, Rick and Carter, Jeremy (eds.): "Asset Securitisation and Synthetic Structures. Innovations in the European Credit Markets", pp. 51-66, Euromoney Books, London, 2005

Honohan, Patrick: *Financial Sector Policy and the Poor. Selected Findings and Issues.* World Bank Working Paper No. 43. The World Bank, Washington, 2004 (http://www1.worldbank.org/finance/assets/images/0821359673_Financial_ Sector_Policy_and_the_Poor.pdf)

HSBC Global Research: "Asian Securitisation – A new ABS market ready to unfold", May 2005

ICICI Bank: "ICICI Bank's microfinance strategy: A big bank thinks small", September 2003 (http://www.microfinancegateway.org/content/article/detail/ 13446)

International Financial Services: Securitisation, City Business Series, London, March 2007 (http://www.ifsl.org.uk/uploads/CBS_Securitisation_2007.pdf)

International Financial Services: Securitisation, City Business Series, London, May 2006 (http://www.ifsl.org.uk/uploads/CBS_Securitisation_2006.pdf)

Jobst, Andreas: "Asset securitisation as a risk management and funding tool. What small firms need to know" in: Managerial Finance, Vol. 32, Issue 9, pp. 731-760, Research Paper, 2006 (http://www.emeraldinsight.com/Insight/viewPDF.jsp? Filename=html/Output/Published/EmeraldFullTextArticle/Pdf/0090320903.pdf)

Kothari, Vinod: Securitization. The Financial Instrument of the Future, Wiley & Sons (Asia) Pte Ltd, Singapore, 2006

Lambe, Geraldine: "Securitisation gives food for thought", in: The Banker, 04 August, 2003

Littlefield, Elizabeth, and Richard Rosenberg: "Microfinance and the Poor. Breaking down walls between microfinance and formal finance." In: Finance & Development (June 2004). 38-40 (http://www.imf.org/external/pubs/ft/fandd/ 2004/06/pdf/littlefi.pdf)

Maddin, Lee: International Finance Corporation (IFC), "Structured Finance in emerging markets", in: Global Securitisation Review 2004/05, Euromoney Yearbooks

Meehan, Jennifer: Tapping the Financial Markets for Microfinance. Grameen Foundation USA's Promotion of this Emerging Trend. Grameen Foundation USA Working Paper Series. October 2004 (http://www.microfinancenetwork. org/images/GFUSA-CapitalMarketsWhitePaper.pdf)

Mitchell, Janett: "Financial Intermediation Theory and the Sources of Value in Structured Finance Markets", mimeograph, National Bank of Belgium, December 2004 (http://www.bis.org/publ/cgfs23mitchell.pdf)

Moody's Investor Service: "Securitisation in New Markets: Moody's Perspective Europe, Africa and the Middle East", September 5, 2006

Moody's: "Russian Mortgage Backed Securities 2006-1 S.A.", International Structured Finance, Europe, Middle East, Africa, New Issue Report, July 19, 2006

Morgan Stanley: BOLD 2007-1. Blue Orchard Loans for Development. Investor Presentation, Mimeo, May 2007

Morgan Stanley: BOLD 2006-1. Blue Orchard Loans for Development. Investor Presentation, Mimeo, February 2006

Standard & Poor's: "Weighing Country Risk In Our Criteria For Asset-Backed Securities", April 11, 2006

Standard & Poor's: "The Three Building Blocks of an Emerging Markets Future Flow Transaction Rating", November 16, 2004

Silverman, Rachel: "A New Way to Do Well by Doing Good – Microfinance Funds Earn Returns on Tiny Loans to Poor Entrepreneurs Abroad", The Wall Street Journal, January 5, 2006

Symbiotics S.A.: "Symbiotics structures collateralized loan obligation with the European Investment Fund to support Opportunity International microfinance institutions in Eastern Europe", symbiotics newsletter, No. 2, February 2006 (http://www.symbiotics.ch/medialibrary/site1/newsletter_february06.pdf)

Telpner, Joel: "A securitisation primer for first time issuers", in: Global Securitisation and Structured Finance 2003, Global White Page, London, pp. 85-91 (http://www.gtlaw.com/pub/articles/2003/telpner03a.pdf)

The Financial Express: "Crisil Study: Securitisation of Microfinance assets: a winning position", December 2004 (http://www.finanicalexpress.com/fe_full_story.php?content_id=76655)

Timewell, Stephen: "Microfinance gains momentum", in: The Banker, February 2, 2005, p. 82 (http://www.thebanker.com)

Zaman, Shams and S.N. Kairy: "Building Domestic Capital Markets: BRAC's AAA Securitization", in: MicroBanking Bulletin, Issue 14, Spring 2007, Microfinance Information Exchange, Inc., pp. 13-15 (http://www.mixmbb.org/en/assets/MIX_2007_Spring_MBB14_Inside.pdf)

CHAPTER 18:

Reducing Barriers to Microfinance Investments: The Role of Structured Finance

Klaus Glaubitt[1], Hanns Martin Hagen[2], Johannes Feist[1], and Monika Beck[3,]*

[1] Vice Presidents, KfW Entwicklungsbank
[2] Principal Sector Economist
[3] Principal Project Manager

Introduction

The microfinance industry has experienced dynamic development. Microfinance now reaches close to 100 million clients worldwide and is growing fast.[1] It has played and will continue to play a key role in contributing to the UN Millennium Development Goals (MDG).[2]

Yet it is estimated that close to half a billion potential microfinance clients, mainly from low income households, still lack access to formal financial services.[3] While the reasons for this gap are multifarious, lack of funding for microfinance institutions (MFIs) has been cited as an important barrier to achieving growth and massive outreach.[4]

Many young and small MFIs still rely on grant funding, but the number of financially sustainable MFIs is increasing. More and more MFIs finance their growth by systematic mobilisation of local savings, commercial refinancing loans and retained earnings. Yet equity and long-term funding by development finance institutions (DFIs) and grants for technical assistance still play a key role, even for commercially viable MFIs. However, DFIs are not capable of meeting the huge demand of microfinance providers that results from the growing demand for microcredit. According to a recent analysis by Morgan Stanley, the outstanding global microloan portfolio is estimated to grow from USD 17 billion at present to

---

[*] The authors are grateful to Ms. Jana Aberle for her support in coordinating and revising their drafts.

[1] Byström (2006), p. 1.

[2] Littlefield and Latortue (2004).

[3] Callaghan, Gonzalez, Maurice and Novak (2007), p. 118.

[4] CGAP/Mix Study on "MFI Demand for Funding" (CGAP 2004a).

USD 250 to 300 billion within the next decade.[5] If MFIs are to reach their full potential, new and innovative ways must be sought to upscale sustainable microfinance and to integrate microfinance institutions fully into local and international financial markets.

Financial markets in the developed world have recently generated a rapid development of structured finance instruments such as securitisations and structured investment funds that enable investors to tailor their risk and returns.[6] Structured finance may have the potential to change the microfinance landscape. Initial structured microfinance transactions have opened the gates of private commercial capital to MFIs, often for the first time. Yet many MFIs face barriers to capital market access, and institutional investors continue to view the asset class with trepidation. Innovative and creative deal structuring, combining the strengths of private and public financiers, may help surmount these barriers by altering risk/return profiles in ways that could attract private capital to microfinance.

This chapter focuses on the two areas of structured finance most relevant for microfinance: securitisation and structured investment funds. First, we discuss the potential of private capital markets as a funding source for MFIs and address their challenges. Next, we define securitisation as it applies to microfinance. This is followed by a description of a basic framework for microfinance securitisation. Using the example of a recent microfinance securitisation transaction, we specify deal characteristics and depict the ambit of current microfinance securitisation transactions. Next, we describe the application of structured finance techniques to microfinance investment funds (MFIFs), and illustrate their potential, using as an example the European Fund for Southeast Europe (EFSE).

On the basis of the projects described here, we attempt to evaluate the appropriateness of various structured finance components for MFIs and their impact on financial sectors in transition and developing countries. In addition, we discuss the role of donors and DFIs, and outline how instruments at their command can be structured to "crowd in" private capital. We conclude by reaffirming the potential and underscoring the challenges of structured finance as a mechanism that can reduce barriers to investments in MFIs.

Accessing Private Capital Markets

Typical MFI Funding Strategies

The largest financing sources of commercially viable MFIs include deposits (by institutions with banking licences), retained earnings and long-term loans at near

---

[5] Callaghan, Gonzalez, Maurice and Novak (2007), p. 115.

[6] See recent definitions of structured finance suggested by staff of the Bank of International Settlements, Basel, Fender and Mitchell (2005), pp. 69-71.

market conditions from DFIs and commercial banks.[7] In rare cases, local capital markets are tapped through local bond issues.[8] Yet many MFIs have reached the limits of the funding potential of domestic savings in low- and middle-income countries. Additionally, deposit-taking MFIs (with a banking licence) have to meet the minimum liquidity requirements prescribed by their respective financial regulatory agencies. These requirements limit the use of short-term and sight deposits to fund longer-term loans. Furthermore, MFIs in rural regions often decline when economically active members of the labour force move to urban centres, taking their deposits and deposit relationships with them.[9] Even financially sustainable MFIs have difficulties raising funds through commercial loans,[10] and funding through retained earnings is confined to highly profitable MFIs.

Donors' funding and support for MFIs through grants, loans with favourable conditions and technical assistance have played the role of venture capitalists in the microfinance industry. Donor financing has provided the risk capital, particularly for young MFIs, to promote early-stage growth and catalyse additional investment from other sources. The availability of these funds is by no means certain, nor is their pricing.[11] In view of overall budget constraints and changing political priorities, donor funds cannot be regarded as a stable funding solution in the long term. The same may be true for private foundations and non-governmental organisations that have played key roles in bringing microfinance to its current status.

Continued funding of mature MFIs on concessional terms does not benefit resource allocation overall, nor does it serve the cause of development. As private finance is beginning to identify MFIs as an asset class eligible for investment, especially through the instruments of structured finance, this new opening should not be crowded out by highly subsidised donor funding.

As we demonstrate here, the tools of structured finance provide appropriate means for donors and DFIs to continue their support for successful and financially sustainable MFIs without crowding out private investors' interest, but rather "crowding it in." Mobilising additional capital for the 150 to 300 financially

---

[7] CGAP Focus Note No. 25. Foreign Investment in Microfinance (CGAP 2004b).

[8] One example is Compartamos, one of the largest Latin American MFIs, which in 2004 and 2005 issued bonds in Mexican pesos.

[9] Transferring remittances to the families remaining in rural regions can become an additional market for MFIs, but this is a fee and not an asset-based business line.

[10] CGAP/Mix Study on MFI Demand for Funding. Report of Survey Results. 2004. Online at http://www.microfinancegateway.org/content/article/detail/14588. The Study finds that among the financially sustainable MFIs sampled, only 42% forecasted that they would be able to raise funding from commercial banks equivalent to 30% of their assets over the next year.

[11] Jennifer Meehan. "Tapping the Financial Markets for Microfinance: Grameen Foundation USA's Promotion of this Emerging Trend." Grameen Foundation USA. Working Paper Series. October 2004. Available online at http://www.haas.berkeley.edu/HaasGlobal/docs/gfusacapitalmarketswp1004.pdf.

strong MFIs[12] through donor/DFI-supported structured finance can continue, while plain vanilla donor and charity funding can increasingly be freed to finance new MFI ventures. These new activities can be targeted on remote rural areas or in countries with relatively weak or nascent microfinance industries. With demand growing across the whole spectrum of microfinance, more can be done with every funding dollar available – while at the same time other financing can be mobilised. Two key questions arise: First, which innovative refinancing instruments are appropriate to complement the funding sources of MFIs? Second, how can donors and development finance institutions like KfW support the professionalisation of MFI funding strategies while diversifying and broadening funding sources?

Hurdles to Tapping Private Capital Markets

Private capital holds the greatest quantitative potential for MFI funding, especially for the upper echelon of financially successful MFIs. Given their sheer size and rapid growth over the past two decades, private capital markets are the only source deep enough to meet MFI financing demand in the future. Yet many MFIs face challenges which preclude their access to capital markets or which make their funding prohibitively expensive. These obstacles include the following:

- The **average size of an MFI** tends to be quite small, especially in comparison to the average commercial bank. Thus the volume of demand tends to be small, making transaction costs high relative to the funding volume, which usually rules out capital market funding for a single MFI.

- The size of an average MFI makes it prohibitively expensive to acquire a rating from an internationally recognised rating agency. Despite ratings by specialised microfinance rating agencies, the **lack of rating from international agencies** – Fitch, Moody's or Standard & Poor's – may discourage or even preclude private commercial capital investments.

- **Low MFI transparency** may impede due diligence efforts and discourage private investors, perpetuating a view among institutional investors that microfinance is a "risky" asset class. Moreover, the dearth of regulation governing MFIs in many countries impedes transparency and the standardisation of reporting.

- **Location within developing or transition countries** may create additional hurdles for MFIs. Although many MFIs lend to those living at a subsistence level, non-performing loan (NPL) rates have proved to be low and MFIs

---

[12] BlueOrchard Finance s.a., a Geneva-based Microfinance Investment Advisory firm, expects the number of economically viable MFIs to grow to approximately 500 over the next few years. Refer to http://www.blueorchard.ch/en/microfinance_institutions.asp.

tend to be resilient to regional risk factors.[13] Capital markets have yet to recognise these seemingly counter-intuitive advantages. Country risk factors and MFIs' inability to pierce the sovereign rating ceiling may also contribute to high capital costs relative to the stand-alone credit risk, ceteris paribus.

In sum, these limitations usually restrict MFIs to their traditional but constrained funding sources: limited grants provided by private charities and public donors, customer deposits and retained earnings, and long-term loans from DFIs and commercial banks.[14] International capital markets, although highly liquid and hence interested in diversification, usually remain closed to MFIs. Several hurdles that hinder their access to capital markets must first be overcome.

Structured Finance and MFIs

Among the potential financing alternatives available to MFIs, structured finance may be the most appropriate vehicle for improving access to local and international capital markets. In comparison with traditional methods of financing, such as plain vanilla debt or equity, structured finance can be designed to mitigate the challenges that are faced by young financial institutions from developing and transition countries that seek to tap capital markets. Furthermore, structured finance enables DFIs to crowd in private commercial investors, complementing their own investment activities in microfinance. This potential has been realised by DFIs such as IFC, FMO and KfW through pioneering structured finance transactions, including MFI securitisations and structured MFI investment funds, as discussed below.

The family of securitisation instruments is diverse, including true sale securitisation instruments such as asset backed securities (ABS) and collateralised debt obligations (CDO), synthetic securitisation instruments such as credit linked notes (CLN) and credit default swaps (CDS), and future flow securitisations and similar transactions such as diversified payment rights (DPRs).[15] Indeed, structured finance can be thought of as deconstructed and reconstructed finance: structured finance transactions seek to isolate the cash flows as well as the risks of a pool of assets (or future assets) and reallocate these cash flows and risks to the parties most capable of managing them.[16]

---

[13] One of the most striking features of the development of regulated MFIs is their capacity to maintain healthy portfolio quality. For the Bolivian, Peruvian and Dominican cases see Calderon (2006).

[14] Even for mature MFIs, an average of only 15-25% of their liabilities consist of external debt. See USAID (2005), p. 3.

[15] For a definition of structured finance see Fender and Mitchell (2005), pp. 69-71.

[16] For an overview of the structured finance market see Frank J. Fabozzi, CFA, "The Structured Finance Market: An Investor's Perspective." *The Financial Analysts Journal.* May 2005, Vol. 61, No. 3: 27-40.

True sale securitisation in microfinance involves the disaggregation of the risks and the corresponding cash flows associated with the microloan portfolio on an MFI's balance sheet. The traditional true sale securitisation isolates credit risk through the sale of financial assets by an originator (here an MFI) to a special purpose vehicle (SPV). This sale separates or unbundles the credit risk of the assets from the corporate risks, e.g. in particular the insolvency risks of the originator, and removes the assets from the MFI's balance sheet. An arranger then structures the securities to be sold, based on the cash flows of the underlying financial assets. Securities are issued by the SPV and the proceeds from the sale of these securities are used to pay the originator for the sale of the financial assets to the SPV. Distilling securitisation to its lowest common denominator: relatively illiquid assets are converted into marketable securities by an originator who creates access to capital markets.[17]

Securitisation began in developed markets, but it has gained ground in emerging markets, most recently in the microfinance industry. In Asia, for instance, the overall volume of structured financing increased 600% from 1998 to 2003.[18]

Why Securitise?

Securitisation provides a way for MFIs in developing and transition countries to access capital markets directly, to diversify their funding sources and to improve liquidity, especially in local currency. The motives for securitisation are quite diverse depending on the growth and state of development of the MFI and the environment in which it operates. Most often, their strategies include:

- **Improving access to capital markets:** Many MFIs remain unrated despite the increasing professionalisation of microfinance rating agencies[19] and initial forays of mainstream rating agencies into rating MFIs. Even rated MFIs are perceived as inferior risks compared to financial institutions in the US and the EU, mainly because of the high country risk in which the typical MFI operates. This perspective inhibits MFIs from issuing securities, especially in international capital markets. By separating the credit risk of the MFI's loan portfolio, which is typically good, from the other business risks that contribute to the institution's rating, a securitisation may improve an MFI's capacity to issue securities in the capital market. Through portfolio tranching and subordination techniques, a securitisation transaction can be

---

[17] For a more detailed definition of securitisation see also Harald Hüttenrauch and Claudia Schneider "Securitisation: A Funding Alternative for Microfinance Institutions" in this publication.

[18] IFC. Global Securitisation Review. 2004/2005. Available online at http://www.ifc.org/ifcext/treasury.nsf/AttachmentsByTitle/MH_StructuredFinanceEuromoney/$FILE/Euromoney+Global+Securitisation+Review+-+Structured+Finance+in+Emerging+Markets.pdf.

[19] Sinha in this volume.

structured to provide different classes of notes, each with its own risk-return profile. Thus, even if the quality of the total securitised loan portfolio, including transfer and similar risks, is rated only slightly better than the MFI itself, a securitisation allows the MFI to attract new investors that invest only in prime assets.

- **Freeing up capital and increasing outreach:** Securitisation allows MFIs to leverage their regulatory and economic capital. This is achieved by removing loans from the balance sheet while keeping equity constant. Thus, more loans may be made based on a given amount of equity. This allows MFIs to expand their lending to existing clients, to serve new borrowers, or to develop new products, for example.

- **Diversification of funding sources**: The majority of micro loans issued by mature MFIs will be financed increasingly by deposits, but debt will remain vitally important. Estimates suggest that 15 to 25% of the liabilities of mature MFIs consist of external medium to long-term debt.[20] However, these funding sources may be concentrated geographically and by type of investor or creditor, as MFIs often rely on a small core group of investors and creditors that share their mission. By providing access to capital markets, securitisation may diversify MFIs' funding sources, reducing their refinancing risk and dependence on a core group of supporters. MFIs may also achieve geographical diversification of funding through off-shore securitisation.

- **Long term funding**: Through securitisation, relatively illiquid assets are converted into cash, immediately improving the liquidity on the balance sheet of the obligor. Given the typical MFI growth trajectory from non-deposit taking institutions to fully licensed financial institutions, the liquidity motive is especially relevant for more mature MFIs. As mature MFIs rely increasingly on deposits for their funding, the average maturity of their financing sources decreases. In many transition and developing countries, retail clients of banks and MFIs prefer to save short-term because of the volatile environment. In this situation, MFIs' ability to offer medium or long-term loans, such as for micro housing products, is limited. A securitisation transaction may enable the respective MFI to lengthen the average maturity of the loans in its portfolio. As the microfinance industry develops, this bodes well for the future of microfinance securitisation.

- **Reputation building:** Securitisation provides opportunities for MFIs to build a reputation in capital markets, particularly among accredited investors. Partners in a securitisation transaction, such as private commercial banks, pension funds, DFIs, rating agencies and law firms, may promote interest in the participating MFIs, extending beyond their typical supporters and

---

[20] See USAID (2005), p. 3.

investors. Many securitisations are rated: rating may generate additional name recognition, not only for microfinance as a new asset class but also for the MFI involved as a servicer of the transaction.

- **Developing the financial sector:** Securitisation plays an important role in developing local capital markets. Securitisation transactions reduce credit risks, contributing to a more stable banking sector. In addition, the banking sector becomes more transparent as securitisation brings more objective performance indicators into the market. Experience indicates that securitisation transactions align incentives that improve the technical performance of the originators.

Structured Microfinance: Basic Structures and Recent Examples

Securitisation Structures

The two most common forms of securitisation structures are true sale transactions and synthetic securitisations. In a synthetic securitisation the originator does not seek funding, but rather wants protection against default from a receivables pool. By using credit derivatives such as credit default swaps (CDS), only the credit risk of a portfolio is transferred to investors in capital markets. Similar to financial guarantees, CDS provide risk reduction and risk diversification for the originator as well as regulatory or economic capital relief. Since the assets remain on the balance sheet, synthetic securitisations are not a funding alternative for originators.

A major reason why originators in developed markets enter into synthetic securitisations is regulatory capital relief.[21] Synthetic securitisation allows the originator to expand its balance sheet, e.g. by making more loans with a given amount of capital. Synthetic securitisations have not yet been employed in microfinance, probably because they (a) do not provide additional funding, (b) allow for growth of the portfolio only if regulatory capital constraints were a limiting factor, and (c) require rather highly developed capital market legislation which permits a transfer of risks to reduce regulatory capital requirements. As synthetic securitisation is not yet used in microfinance, only true sale securitisations are dealt with in the remainder of this chapter.

A true sale structure entails the full sale of the originator's designated assets to a bankruptcy-remote special purpose vehicle (SPV). The SPV issues securities with principal and interest payments that match the principal and interest repay-

---

[21] As an example: enterprise loans according to Basle I standards carry a risk weight of 1.0, and thus have to be supported by the full 8% of regulatory capital. If a sovereign-guaranteed AAA institution with a zero risk weighting provides the CDS, the risk weight of the respective amount of assets such as enterprise loans is reduced to zero, requiring no underlying regulatory capital.

ments from the underlying assets. The sale of assets to the SPV removes them from the originator's balance sheet, constituting a true sale. This enables the originator to obtain additional funding. In microfinance, two forms of true sale securitisations have been used. In the case of microfinance collateralised debt obligations or CDOs, long-term loans to MFIs are securitised. In the case of a microfinance ABS, the MFI sells part of the loan portfolio.

A True Sale Securitisation by ProCredit Bank Bulgaria

A true sale securitisation of a portfolio of micro and SME loans by ProCredit Bank Bulgaria illustrates how basic securitisation structures can be designed to overcome the actual challenges of securitising the assets of an MFI.

In a transaction led by Deutsche Bank in April 2006, ProCredit Bank AD Bulgaria (PCB Bulgaria, an MFI) securitised part of its portfolio of loans to micro entrepreneurs and to small and medium enterprises. This first true sale securitisation in Bulgaria was facilitated by a credit enhancement provided pari passu by KfW and the European Investment Fund (EIF). While the initial securitised portfolio amounted to EUR 47.8 million, its targeted volume is EUR 100 million. After this build up phase, ProCredit Bank Bulgaria has the right to securitise loans on a revolving basis within an EUR 100 million limit. By securing funding for loans to micro entrepreneurs and small and medium sized businesses (SME), the transaction facilitates access to finance for new target group customers, especially in rural areas of Bulgaria where PCB is especially strong. Furthermore, the transaction allows PCB Bulgaria to tap indirectly into the international asset backed commercial paper market.[22]

The transaction also helped PCB Bulgaria to comply with recent changes in Bulgarian banking regulation. To curb inflation, the Bulgarian National Bank (BNB) limited credit growth to 6% per quarter for all banks. Growth exceeding this limit was subject to an additional minimum reserve (AMR) regardless of whether the credit growth was generated by competitive consumer finance or in the developing market for loans to micro and small enterprises. Depending on the degree the limit was exceeded, AMR of up to four times the excess had to be deposited with BNB.

Structuring the transaction as a true sale removed assets from PCB's balance sheet, reducing its total loan portfolio. This allowed PCB to serve their microentrepreneurs and SME clients without exceeding BNB's growth limit. Without this transaction the growth of micro and small enterprise in rural Bulgaria, or at least PCB's important contribution to it, would have been endangered. In the meantime, BNB has relaxed its reserve requirements on lending, while PCB continues to benefit from the release of economic and regulatory capital provided by the transaction.

---

[22] See Fitch Ratings (2006), p. 1.

In addition to promoting the sustainable growth of PCB Bulgaria, the transaction had an important systemic impact: improved access to financial services for microenterprises and SMEs, especially in rural areas, and corresponding improvements in employment, growth and poverty reduction. New efficiencies can translate into lower borrowing costs. Moreover, this transaction, as the first of its kind in Southeast Europe, has signalled to other originators the potential of such transactions. The funds mobilised can create about 24,000 jobs, contributing to the incomes of workers.

The innovative structure combined elements of a true sale securitisation and an asset-backed commercial paper (ABCP) programme. The originator, PCB Bulgaria, sold a portion of its SME and microenterprise loan portfolio on a continuing basis to a Bulgarian bankruptcy-remote SPV ("purchasing SPV") for loan proceeds with a revolving promissory note. The Dutch SPV may be used by other ProCredit banks as a conduit for similar transactions in the region, potentially reducing refnancing costs. The amount of the revolving promissory note is adjusted monthly to reflect the current balance of the securitised loan portfolio. The issuing SPV in turn refinances the notes through the issuance of Senior Notes, sold respectively to a Deutsche Bank ABCP (asset based commercial paper) conduit and through a subordinated loan by ProCredit Holding AG, the parent company based in Frankfurt. Through the conduit, Deutsche Bank then sells asset backed commercial paper to investors. An illustration is provided in the following diagram.

Several risk-mitigating features are worth noting:

- **Subordination:** The pool is structured into senior and junior tranches, comprising approximately 95% and 5% respectively at first closing.

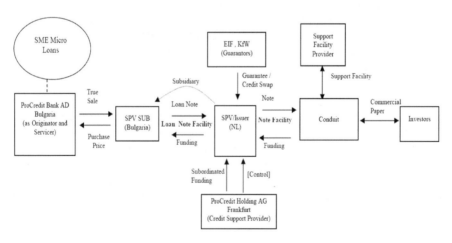

Fig. 1. Transaction structure of the PCB Bulgaria transaction

- **Guarantees:** EIF and KfW provided guarantees of principal and interest for the Senior Notes, raising their rating from BBB (by Fitch) to AAA. The Deutsche Bank ABCP conduit could buy notes only with the best credit quality and rating. The credit enhancements were essential to bridge the gap between the SPV owned by ProCredit Bank Bulgaria and the Deutsche Bank asset based commercial paper programme. Deutsche Bank was able to purchase the guaranteed senior tranche through an Irish conduit and sell commercial paper to investors.

- **Performance triggers:** A cumulative default trigger is activated whenever PAR > 90 days during the last 12 months exceeds 2.5% of the average portfolio. A delinquency trigger is activated when PAR > 1 day exceeds 1.5% of the portfolio. These rules mitigate credit risk in the event that portfolio quality declines. Accelerated maturity occurs if either of these thresholds is breached. The flow of funds into the portfolio is immediately suspended and the entire portfolio becomes due immediately. In this event, the bank would have to buy back the portfolio.

- **Portfolio concentration limits:** A loan to the end obligor may not exceed more than 6% of the total pool volume. New loans placed into the pool are regularly audited.

A precondition for implementation was the capacity of the originator's IT systems and credit technology to support the reporting requirements of the securitisation structure. In Bulgaria the legal system provided sufficient basis and comfort, e.g. bankruptcy remoteness of SPVs, taxation of SPVs, cession of loans and transfer of collateral. In many other transition countries the legal systems lack the framework for securitisation. The true sale operation in Bulgaria offers a model for MFIs that have high loan volume growth and that require equity relief as well as long-term funding. An adequate IT system and good credit technology must also be in place. Therefore, true sale transactions such as that of ProCredit Bank Bulgaria are suitable mainly for large, mature MFIs.

If small MFIs want to capture funds with long maturities at an attractive price, a CDO may be appropriate. Portfolios of different MFIs can be bundled, generating a sufficiently large volume that makes it economically worthwhile to securitise. The Opportunity Eastern Europe 1 transaction[23] and the Blue Orchard Microfinance Securities I, LLC[24] are examples of how microfinance CDOs can attract private investors for refinancing microentrepreneurs, small farmers and traders in developing and transition countries. Tranching and subordination are essential because microfinance markets are characterised by asymmetric information and market segmentation.

---

[23] See Annex 1.

[24] See Hüttenrauch and Schneider (2007) in this volume.

Microfinance Investment Funds (MFIFs)

Structured finance for microfinance is by no means limited to securitisation. The success of MFIFs requires financial structuring to create appropriate products. The financial tools used in securitisations to mitigate deal-specific risks can and have been applied to MFIFs.

A detailed description of the development of microfinance investment funds and the types of funds currently offered are beyond the scope of this paper. (See Ingrid Matthäus-Maier and J.D. von Pischke, eds. *Microfinance Investment Funds: Leveraging Private Capital for Economic Growth and Poverty Reduction*.) Instead, we begin with a discussion of the advantages of MFIFs and a brief overview of KfW's experience with microfinance funds. Using the European Fund for Southeast Europe as an example, we highlight the Fund's basic structure and its advantages.

MFIFs combine flexible management by private fund managers with elements borrowed from structured finance. MFIFs may offer a broad range of products and instruments, which allow their structures to be demand driven and adaptable to market conditions.

Risks are mitigated by the professional competence of the fund manager, by diversification (at the country and institution levels), by comprehensive investment and operational guidelines, and by sound governance structures with effective systems of checks and balances. Structural elements, such as waterfall structures (structuring investments in different risk classes and ratings) or reserve accounts may provide additional risk protection.

The flexibility of MFIFs allow them to mitigate risks and adapt to market demand, and their primary advantages include the benefits of coordination. Transaction costs are reduced by using a single platform to invest in different regions and MFIs, while having sufficient flexibility to manage the portfolio actively. Multiple donors may invest in a single fund with a fixed set of objectives, thereby harmonising regional activity. Donors and DFIs invest in the riskiest tranches. In this way they give private investors an incentive to join with the sources of scarce public funds, but in the less riskier classes. MFIFs monitor and guide risk management in the MFIs, adhering to the principles of socially responsible banking, transparency and good governance, thus contributing to better social and financial performance by the MFI and to the stability of the financial sector.

The European Fund for Southeast Europe (EFSE)

In 1998 a donor group established a revolving fund, the European Fund for Bosnia-Herzegovina (EFBH). The group included the European Commission, Austria, the German Ministry for Economic Cooperation and Development (BMZ) on behalf of the Government of Germany, and Switzerland. The fund refinances loans through local partner lending institutions (PLIs) for on-lending to micro and small enterprises, and low-income housing. PLIs were strengthened through technical assistance.

The first fund was extremely successful, encouraging the donor group to establish the European Fund for Montenegro, the European Fund for Kosovo and the European Fund for Serbia (together the "European Funds"), which are managed by KfW. Evaluations by donors and by third parties such as CGAP and SIDA have confirmed that these funds are extremely successful. From 1998 through June 2005, PLIs issued over 45,000 loans from these funds to their retail clients.

However, the funds were informal structures without legal persona. Based on their track records, and seeking to increase regional impact as well as operationing efficiency, the donors and the beneficiary countries decided to institutionalise the funds – that is, to place them in corporate structures with strong ownership, to enable the pooling of different sources of funds, to establish sound governance and most importantly, to leverage the funding by attracting private capital.

This was achieved in December 2005 when the European Fund for Southeast Europe (EFSE) was set up as an open-ended institutional fund under Luxembourg Law in the form of a SICAV (Variable Capital Investment Company). EFSE is a salient example of a public-private partnership (PPP) in microfinance, a flagship initiative of the European Commission and BMZ. To increase efficiency and to devise an efficient cost structure, service providers are outsourced: KfW acts as the structuring investor and promoter of the fund, Oppenheim Pramerica Asset Management is the fund manager, Bankakademie e.V. is the investment advisor, and Citibank International plc is the custodian and administration agent.

By applying structured finance elements, funds can attract private capital even for relatively risky countries or entities. In EFSE, this is achieved by issuing several risk tranches. The donor-financed portfolio of the European funds was trans-

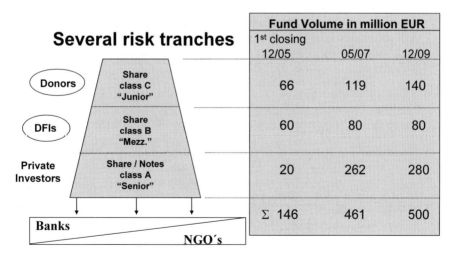

	Fund Volume in million EUR		
Several risk tranches	1st closing 12/05	05/07	12/09
Donors — Share class C "Junior"	66	119	140
DFIs — Share class B "Mezz."	60	80	80
Private Investors — Share / Notes class A "Senior"	20	262	280
Banks / NGO's	Σ 146	461	500

Fig. 2. Water fall structure, EFSE

ferred to EFSE, constituting the first loss tranche. DFIs including EBRD, IFC, KfW and FMO invested in the mezzanine tranche. The first loss tranche and the mezzanine tranche give risk protection for the senior tranche, comprised of private investors. Within its first year EFSE attracted EUR 172 million from purely private commercial investors, primarily Bankhaus Oppenheim, Deutsche Bank AG, Credit Cooperatíf and Tufts University.

A special challenge arises from the fact the funds of the first loss tranche are governed by bilateral agreements and therefore can be used only for a designated country. In order to maintain the national designations of the European Funds within a regional framework, the EFSE, as an umbrella fund, has national as well as regional sub-funds: These are combined via an innovative pooling mechanism (see annex).

Key characteristics of the fund include the following:

- **Subordination/waterfall payment structure:** EFSE's sub-funds are structured into senior, mezzanine and junior tranches, and the cascade of payments follows the subordination structure. The junior tranche, or C shares, are donor funds of unlimited duration. C shares are subordinate to B shares or the mezzanine tranche. These shares have a 10-year duration and are held by development finance institutions. A shares or A notes are mainly sold to private investors. They vary in duration and are issued only from regional sub-funds, which are discussed below.

- **First loss tranche:** C shares, held by donors, are a first loss tranche to provide a risk buffer for the A and B shares. They mitigate the credit risk of the underlying portfolio. No cross-collateralisation between the national C tranches is possible (see annex): country risk is assumed by all shareholders including A and B shares.

- **Active management:** Active management provides the flexibility to make new investments and reevaluate existing ones. The fund manager actively manages risk through investment decisions based on the underlying MFIs as well as on the vehicles (loans, securitisation structures, etc.) through which investments are made in MFIs.

- **Country pools:** Country and regional pools were established to attract investors interested in making commitments at a regional level as well as at the level of an individual country.

- **Technical assistance:** A technical assistance fund has been established alongside EFSE to provide assistance to MFIs in Southeast Europe. The main funding sources are contributions from EFSE's waterfall income.

- **Advisory Group:** The Advisory Group is composed of Central Bank Governors in the region. The Advisory Group gives EFSE a link with local concerns. The Advisory Group is not a decision-making body but provides valuable information to the board and fund manager.

Although still in the implementation phase, at the end of May 2007 EFSE had achieved very encouraging results. The Fund increased from EUR 146 million in December 2005 to EUR 461 million. The outstanding portfolio had increased from EUR 70 million to EUR 282 million. EFSE is active in nine European countries/entities. The average loan made by PLIs had decreased from EUR 6,000 to EUR 4,300.

EFSE is positioned for excellent results: the capitalisation target of EUR 500 million in 2009 would translate cumulatively into

- an estimated 120,000 loans to micro, small and rural enterprises and farmers,
- the creation of some 30,000 jobs, and
- 30,000 loans to families to rebuild or modernise their homes.

A striking feature of EFSE is the strategic use of public funds with a leverage factor of more than seven.

The Role of Donors in Structured MFI Refinancing

The use of structured financed in the MFI sector, as shown by the examples above, offers unique opportunities for grant-making donors, DFIs and private sector investors to combine their respective advantages and objectives.

Donors' initial role was as "venture capitalists" providing seed finance and technical assistance for setting up and supporting NGO MFIs. As microfinance has grown, donors have continued to play an essential role in providing financial services to the poor. Even for mature MFIs or large MFI groups (like ProCredit Holding), donors can retain a key role in furthering their growth and outreach through structured finance, operating in areas beyond the frontiers of DFIs or the private sector.

Donors and DFIs' Role in Microfinance Investment Funds (MFIFs)

In a unique PPP-approach, as demonstrated by the EFSE example above, donors providing capital – or existing loan portfolios – for a first loss tranche enable other investors with different views of risk and return to invest, based on the waterfall principle. For donors, "return" means achieving development impacts that are geared to their mission statements and investment policy through a structured microfinance fund. With its proven combination of development impact and financial sustainability, microfinance can meet or add to certain development criteria in the investment policy of a structured microfinance fund. It can do so without exceeding the limits of financial sustainability. By establishing proper development policies, and adhering to them through direct monitoring by a supervisory board,[25] donors can

---

[25] In the EFSE example, donors have assumed this direct supervisory role. While BMZ retains a permanent seat on the EFSE Supervisory Board, Austria (ADA) and Switzerland (SDC) hold a rotating seat.

mitigate the risks they face, i.e. the potential failure to achieve the desired development impact. Additionally, donor funds are continuously required for technical assistance to selected MFIs refinanced by such funds, for new programmatic approaches (e.g. new types of financial products or sub-sectors) or for impact analyses and evaluation.

Technical assistance for establishing and managing microfinance funds, and more importantly for strengthening the partner lending institutions, must be closely coordinated with the activities of the fund. They should be implemented under the direct supervision either of the fund's management or of a DFI that is a stakeholder in the fund. Supporting MFIs through TA builds stronger skills in microfinance by developing a highly trained and motivated pool of staff, streamlining internal procedures, elaborating risk assessment practices, or strengthening awareness and demand for rural finance as well as for savings mobilisation.

Through such a complememtary approach, TA can be a useful means of protecting the fund's financial investments, while the accompanying financial investments provided by the fund can ensure that TA for the MFIs is not considered as a theoretical exercise by the recipients. But trying to tightly coordinate TA provided by other donors or agencies with the financing activities of the fund is likely to produce inefficiencies (coordination costs) and adverse selection. Separate TA not managed by the fund or a DFI shareholder in the fund will tend to concentrate on weaker MFIs that are not likely to be eligible for funding. Nevertheless, this may create pressure on the fund and produce expectations on the part of the MFI that a funding relationship between the fund and the (weak) MFI will be concluded.

The same effect may occur when strong efforts are made by donors to "coordinate" or couple refinancing of MFIs while providing TA in the form of business advisory services (BAS). This may arise when the (micro) enterprises under the BAS programme are generally eligible for refinancing by the fund. EFSE in Kosovo[26] experienced these difficulties in coordination. A donor organisation that financed credit lines through the EFK and a BAS programme for enterprises in the horticulture sector found it hard to accept that enterprises assisted by the BAS programme were not automatically eligible for loans provided by financial institutions that had received credit lines from the EFK.

USAID also set up an MSE funding programme in Kosovo – Kosovo Business Financing Fund (KBFF) – which later became the American Bank of Kosovo (ABK). From the very beginning this venture was based on a TA programme for potential loan clients (a BAS model), which after having received advice were considered eligible for a loan from KBFF/ABK. With this inherent conflict of interest between the advisory function for BAS clients and the banking function of the bank or MFI, KBFF/ABK never achieved financial sustainability. After significant losses and with a very problematic loan portfolio, ABK was taken over by

---

[26] The European Fund for Kosovo (EFK) was a set of funds provided by Germany, the EU Commission and the Swiss Development Cooperation (SDC) managed as credit lines to banks and MFIs by KfW.

Raiffeisen Bank (Austria) in 2003. Information sharing between BAS programmes in the real sector and funding programmes in the financial sector are certainly useful. However, the autonomy of financial institutions in dealing with loan applications and their terms and conditions can best be safeguarded if the TA and the funding programme are both organised by the fund or a DFI supporting the fund, avoiding such conflicts of donor interests.

As discussed above, one of the main advantages of structured MFI refinancing is the reduction of transaction costs through volume and repetition. The wholesale refinancing role of microfinance funds, on a national or preferably a regional or global level, is consistent with the donors' rationale of better coordinating their efforts through programme-based or sector-wide approaches (SWAPs). In this way, regional funds are instruments for realising the donors' commitment to the Paris Declaration on Aid Effectiveness, creating stronger aid coordination while reducing transaction costs for the recipient countries.

When operating at a regional level, such as with EFSE or the Regional Micro-finance Fund for Sub-Sahara Africa (REGMIFA)[27] that is now being designed, an important collateral objective of donors' development policy can be pursued. This objective is to strengthen regional ties among developing countries as well as transition countries. Practical steps in this direction are illustrated by EFSE, despite the still unresolved and critical political situation the region faces. MFIs and microentrepreneurs from Serbia and Kosovo receive financing from EFSE, and representatives of the banking supervisory authorities of Serbia and Kosovo sit on EFSE's advisory board.

We believe that MFIFs supported by several donors working at a regional level can anchieve synergies in outreach and risk mitigation, and are therefore an appropriate tool for implementing the aims of the Paris Agenda on Aid Effectiveness, in this case through microfinance. The governments of the partner countries have an important role and therefore significant interest in such MFIF approaches.

DFIs such as KfW or IFC play a crucial role in structuring, launching and managing MFIFs. This role goes far beyond investing donor or own funds in the higher risk tranches which enables private capital to join in. This provision of tailor-made investments is of course extremely important. While donors' development orientation enables them to provide high risk or "first loss" funding, DFIs such as KfW have the capacity to incur higher risks than most institutional investors. This enables them to "close the gap" through mezzanine funding tranches that attract sufficient commercial investors based on these investors' risk perspectives.

But even more complex than providing the initial funding for MFIFs is the planning and structuring that requires expertise and – under most legal frameworks – a certified "standing" in capital markets. KfW, as demonstrated by EFSE for example, possesses these qualifications, which enabled it to be the official "promoter" re-

---

[27] REGMIFA was designed by the German Ministry for Economic Cooperation and Development (BMZ) and KfW while this article was being drafted.

quired under Luxemburg law to launch EFSE.[28] Furthermore, DFIs with their professional expertise and their ability to move easily among donors or charities and commercial investors, are ideally suited to serve on management or supervisory bodies of MFIFs in their own name as an investor or in trust for others. In sum, KfW and other DFIs can provide the necessary link between development-oriented donors and commercial investors. In this capacity they can set up structures, provide funds, assist in managing or supervision according to development and commercial criteria (i.e. financial sustainability) and further product development by putting into practice their ideas for new products and target groups.

Donors and DFIs' Role in Securitisations

The potential role of donors in structuring and supporting microfinance investment funds as described above is consistent with their role as DFIs in promoting and launching unique PPP approaches like EFSE. When supporting the securitisation of micro loans in developing and transition countries, donors can also use their technical competence and the banking licence of their national DFIs.

As the legal and regulatory environment in developing and transition countries often inhibits the development of local capital markets and especially securitisition transactions, donors and DFIs may jointly take the lead in initiating a policy dialogue with local ministries of finance, central banks or other supervisory agencies. However, the experience of KfW and other DFIs, as in the case of the securitisation of a microloan portfolio of BRAC (Bangladesh Rural Advancement Committee) or in the landmark transaction in Bulgaria described previously, have proved that for the donor-led policy dialogue to bear fruit, it should be linked to a concrete pilot transaction by a local financial institution.

When a country's initial securitisation of SME or microloans is contemplated, the local banks require advice, and DFIs often play the role of an honest broker. They are trusted by the potential local originators because of their know-how and experience. For example, local financial institutions and regulators have been interested in KfW's experience as the market leader in synthetic securitisations in Western Europe, even if they plan to develop true sale transactions first. Another reason for this trust is that DFIs like IFC, KfW and FMO do not compete with local financial institutions. Also, DFIs may provide technical assistance in the preparation of a pilot transaction. At this stage technical assistance helps all interested banks or MFIs to determine whether they are ready to participate in a securitisation. Finally, DFIs may guide local originators through the legal due diligence required for a transaction.

The high perceived risk of developing countries makes many international and local investors sceptical of securitisations with new structures or new asset

---

[28] Besides formulating the concept and convincing other donors and investors to participate, the promoter also has to assume some residual risks.

classes such as microfinance. As a result, the demand for lower rated tranches of microfinance securitisations is often limited, and microfinance institutions and local banks face difficulties in gaining access to the capital market. DFIs may help to bridge this gap by assuming risk via mezzanine or equity tranches. Investments in these tranches enable DFIs to leverage the investments of private institutional investors.

In some securitisation transactions, DFIs play an essential role as market catalysts by providing credit enhancements. Such instruments include full or partial credit guarantees which might be necessary to bring the credit quality of a senior tranche to a level that is acceptable to potential investors. Many institutional investors such as life insurance companies or pension funds are required to invest only in high quality assets. Likewise, asset backed commercial paper conduits usually have strict credit risk requirements. In cases such as these, a DFI can facilitate a securitisation by providing political risk insurance, protecting the investor against country risk.

The experience to date with securitisation transactions in developing and transition countries shows that donors – especially DFIs – are important catalysts, facilitators in negotiations or as structuring investors, standard setters and initial investors. The DFIs' mandate is developmental in nature. When a microfinance asset class is eventually well established, the DFIs will focus on new tasks. The involvement of KfW and other DFIs has proved effective in launching a number of pilot schemes and pioneering securitisations in countries that have not used such vehicles previously. This capacity should be further extended.

The Impact, Efficiency and Effectiveness of Structured Finance

Donors and DFIs are increasingly using structured finance instruments to support the development of microfinance and to promote financial sector development in developing and transition countries. The main objectives of financial sector projects and programmes are institution building, which consists of strengthening banks and microfinance institutions, while also creating a positive impact on the overall financial sectors in the selected developing and transition countries.[29] This positive impact includes the development of microenterprise financing as a sustainable source of business for MFIs. Structured microfinance funds, collateralised debt obligations (CDOs – securitisation of loans to MFIs) and asset backed securities (ABS, mainly securitisation of MFIs' loan portfolios) are relatively new instruments in the tool kits of donors and DFIs. Evidence is accumulating that these instruments have a range of impacts on financial institutions and on financial sectors.

---

[29] German Federal Ministry of Economic Cooperation and Development (2004): Sectoral Policy Paper on Financial System Development, Bonn 2004.

Table 1. Impact of structured finance instruments on financial intermediaries

Primary Impact	ABS	CDO	Funds
Increased outreach	Low	Low	Medium / High
Introduction of new financial products for target groups	Medium	Medium	High
Increased efficiency and productivity of MFIs/banks	High	Medium	Medium

Leaving aside the broad range of types of microfinance funds, structured funds are more suitable for helping MFIs to increase their outreach than are ABS or CDOs. Microfinance funds like EFSE include a technical assistance fund which enables them to offer an MFI a tailor-made package of funding together with technical assistance that is engineered to reach new client groups, for example in rural regions. ABS or CDOs are innovative funding tools, but have no technical assistance components directly tied to them.

All three forms of structured finance can help a bank or MFI to introduce new products for a target group. Many MFIs have difficulties in offering longer term loans, such as micro housing loans, because their deposits are mainly short term. ABS, CDOs and loans by microfinance funds can help MFIs raise long-term funding. However, only funds have the flexibility to combine their financing with technical assistance.

ABS transactions give the originator a very strong, market driven incentive to perform well. For example, an important pre-condition for a true sale securitisation of a loan portfolio is a standardised, efficient process of loan origination and monitoring. MFIs and banks that securitise their assets invest in up-to-date data processing and warehousing and in very efficient loan processing. They invest in their staff and internal processes to achieve the high standards which are required, and which are monitored quarterly or bi-annually by the rating agency that grades the transaction.

An ABS transaction removes loans from the balance sheet of the MFI. This enables the MFI to manage a larger loan portfolio without requiring more equity, which reduces the capital cost of lending. In addition, the MFI receives fee income for servicing the loan portfolio. Hence, ABS transactions can strongly increase the productivity and efficiency of the MFI.

CDO and structured funds can also increase efficiency. In the CDO case, the incentive to increase efficiency comes mainly from the reputational effect of participating in a CDO, as opposed simply to receiving a loan from a fund. However, funds like EFSE may provide grant funded technical assistance to help less mature MFIs increase their efficiency and productivity.

Recent studies of financial sectors in the EU confirm that ABS transactions have contributed to increased financial intermediation. The securitisation of loan portfolios by banks in the EU has increased banks' willingness to originate SME loans

Table 2. Impact of structured finance on financial sectors

Primary Impact	ABS	CDO	Funds
Increased financial intermediation	Medium / High	Low	Medium
Financial sector stability	Medium	Medium	Medium
Development of local capital markets	High	Low	Medium

because securitisation has enabled financial intermediaries to reduce their risk concentrations. This positive correlation between the introduction of ABS and financial intermediation is also likely to apply in a number of developing and transition countries. However, the correlation may not be as pronounced in less developed countries because of the absence of a secondary market for bonds and other securities. For these countries, structured funds might offer a better solution. This is especially so if, in addition to providing long-term funding to local banks, the transaction attracts local pension funds as investors, e.g. in the senior tranche.

The impact of CDOs on financial intermediation in emerging financial sectors is limited. Usually, CDOs bundle funding from different public and private investors in the North to banks and MFIs in the South. The contribution of structured finance to sustainability is measured by monitoring various benchmarks such as diversity of funding sources, the maintenance of the microfinance business after TA support is completed, the absence of mission drift, and the profitability of the MFI, among others.

Structured finance also contributes to financial sector stability. This is true for CDOs and funds because they provide long-term funding, in both foreign and local currency, to local financial intermediaries in developing countries. They make local banks and MFIs less susceptible to external shocks that could otherwise cause a sudden withdrawal of deposits. ABS transactions strengthen financial sector stability by distributing the credit risk of a loan portfolio over a large number of small investors. However, systemic risk may be increased by ABS transactions. This may occur if deficiencies in regulation and monitoring, which exist in many developing and transition countries, are used to deceive the ABS investors, causing a loss of trust. Therefore, it is essential that donors and DFIs support regulation and supervision simultaneously with early ABS pilot transactions. DFIs are diligent in structuring "transaction governance standards" and improving performance transparency.

By supporting ABS transactions, DFIs can make important contributions to the development of local capital markets. Asset backed securities offer local investors an opportunity to obtain excellent asset quality that is not otherwise available. If local insurance companies and pension funds invest in these securities – instead of investing, for example, in real estate in the capital city – this could help to create a more liquid and less volatile local bond market. The contribution of funds and CDOs in the development of the local capital market is less obvious. However, large structured funds like EFSE have high-level advisory councils where decision makers of the local central bank and other regulatory authorities are represented. In this way, structured funds may facilitate policy dialogue among DFIs, local regulators, MFIs and banks, supporting the development of the local capital market beyond plain vanilla refinancing lines. Even CDOs contribute to the development of local capital markets by increasing international investors' interest in developing and transition economies.

Conclusion

In the United States and Western Europe structured finance has a growing role, which is based on successful transactions. It consists of a set of instruments that provide both funding and risk management. These instruments therefore strengthen financial intermediation while maintaining and improving financial sector stability.

In developing and transition countries, microfinance – targeting small and very small entrepreneurs – is often of great importance. Its role in development was long neglected, but is now en vogue. Structured finance opens further new horizons in this drama because of its potential as an instrument to overcome barriers to funding microfinance institutions. Structured finance can provide access to capital markets for seasoned, financially sustainable MFIs. Moreover, it can free donor funds for new MFIs and promote microfinance in countries with nascent MFIs.

The direct development impact is clear: not only does funding MFIs improve microentrepreneurs' income levels, but it also enables MFIs to expand their outreach. More micro borrowers have access to capital for start ups and growth, which helps to raise the income levels of the poor. Second, funding for MFIs through structured finance transactions improves their financial flexibility. Transactions may remove loans from MFIs' balance sheets, enabling more loans to be issued; or they may lengthen maturity profiles of MFIs, permitting better long-term planning and broader product offerings. Third, structured finance makes the best use of scarce donor funds: through structuring, donor and IFI funds are leveraged to attract private capital. These transactions, in turn, may provide examples that will generate experience and lead to higher levels of investments in microfinance, attracting additional private investment.

For private investors the emerging microfinance asset class is especially attractive. MFI portfolios are performing extremely well due to the specialised credit technology which does not use scoring methods.

In the case of the securitisation of ProCredit Bulgaria, up to now no loan has been in arrears let alone in default. This is an outstanding model for microfinance securitisation operations which attracts private investment banks into microfinance.

Indirect effects are also important. Structured finance can contribute to financial sector growth and therefore general economic development. As demonstrated by experience in the US and Western Europe, structured finance is an important tool for strengthening financial intermediation, i.e. basically the allocation of savings to productive investment, while offering more choices to investors according to their risk appetites. Providing these opportunities and financial technology to developing and transition countries can contribute to the growth and stability of their financial sectors. At the same time, structured finance will enable developing and transition countries to attract more investments from international capital markets, in effect increasing their capacities to benefit from globalisation.

An important prerequisite for these developments is that transactions in structured MFI refinancing are supported by qualified and diligent DFIs in their capacities as pioneers in financial market innovation as well as in their capacity as donors. An example is the creation of regional arrangements to replace the classic form of bilateral contributions to specific partner countries. Another is that developing countries' "ownership" in MFIFs need not require a legal ownership stake but can also consist of political and regulatory support for the investments made by such MFIFs. We believe that donors embracing these innovations will reap the benefits of strong and sustainable impacts. They will also be recognised as constructive and creative innovators contributing to the Paris Declaration objective of coordination.

Annex 1: Microfinance Loan Obligations 1 (MFLO 1) – Opportunity Eastern Europe Securitisation: Asset-Backed Securities

International capital markets were opened for the first time to seven different MFIs in Russia and the Balkans, all members of the Opportunity International (OI) network, with the closing of the MFLO 1 securitisation in November 2005. A total of USD 32 million in refinancing credit lines were extended to the originating MFIs through a securitisation of their loan portfolios. This enabled further loan portfolio growth for these MFIs, as well as transferred management know-how, such as improved risk management procedures and systems and portfolio monitoring and reporting. This additional funding allowed the MFIs to disburse an additional 20,000 loans – over 60% of which benefit women.[30] Moreover, the link between improved access to credit for microentrepreneurs and SMEs is strong: for each new EUR 5,000 in credit extended in the region, one new job is created.

The Arranger was Symbiotics, the co-Arranger the European Investment Fund (EIF). The Issuer and Originator is a Luxembourg SPV, which extends the refinancing loans to the MFIs. These loans are financed through the issuance of an ABS.

The innovative deal structure incorporated a number of credit enhancement mechanisms:

---

[30] OI statistics. It is estimated that 60% of loans extended from the OI network's Eastern European branches go to female end-clieints.

- **Subordination:** The ABS was structured in three tranches: Senior Notes, comprising 75% of the loan portfolio, Junior Notes, comprising 20% of the securities, and First Loss Notes, comprising 5% of the securities. Accordingly, losses would have to amount to over 25% of the value of pool before the Senior Notes would incur a loss.

- **Reserve Account:** A cash reserve account, comprising 2.5% of the total deal value at closing, was established. The account was funded with the difference between the value of the issued securities and the refinancing lines extended to the MFIs, less the initial legal and administrative costs. Thereafter, the account would be replenished with funds generated from any excess spread, i.e. the difference between the weighted average of the interest payments received from the MFI loans and the weighted average of interest paid on the issued notes.

- **Performance Triggers:** Initially, MFI interest payments to the pool will be divided on a pro-rata basis between investors. Should pool performance deteriorate, however, interest payments would be redirected and paid out in order of seniority, i.e. investors in the senior tranche would be paid before investors in the mezzanine tranche, etc. For example, an MFI interest payment in arrears for greater than 3 days will trigger the redirection of the pool's interest payments. Additionally, excess cash in the reserve account would also be paid out according to seniority.

- **Guarantee:** The underlying MFI's had never been rated by an internationally-recognised rating agency. According to internally mapped ratings calculated by KfW, the average rating of the total pool was B+ at closing. Given the subordination structure and First Loss tranche, the Senior Notes would have been assigned a BB rating. The European Investment Fund (EIF), itself AAA-Rated, provided a guarantee of the timely payment of interest and principal for the Senior Notes. The guaranteed Senior Notes were assigned a AAA-Rating.

The structure of the pool combined with these credit enhancements enabled the provision of investment opportunities with varying risk/return profiles to investors. In the first and second closings, KfW made investments totalling EUR 11.8 million. In the third closing in October 2006, KfW made an additional investment of EUR 7.9 million, bringing KfW's total investment, and the total volume of the Senior Note, to EUR 19.7 million. The use of KfW's financial sector promotional funds is subject to certain criteria, including a minimum investment volume and good credit quality. The securitisation structure allowed KfW to provide refinancing lines to individual MFIs, which would not have been possible on a stand-alone basis given the minimum volume requirements. The EIF guarantee enabled KfW's investment in the Senior Notes: the lack of an internationally-recognised rating and the internally-assigned Senior Tranche BB rating would have made the required return on investment prohibitively high.

The driving force for the Opportunity network behind this transaction was the aspect of funding. The common bottleneck for MFIs is to capture funds with a long-term maturity at an adequate pricing. The described structure bundled portfolios of different MFIs in order to generate a sufficiently large volume making it economically worthwhile to securitise it. Through the issuing of ABS via the SPV, fresh funds with such a long-term maturity were generated. The resulting influx of funds enabled the participating MFIs to extend new long-term loans and refinance themselves matching these maturities thus strengthening the refinancing basis of the MFI in a sustainable way. In preparing the project KfW could draw on its experience it has gained in the cooperation with some OI-banks located in Eastern Europe. It has much facilitated the implementation of the project.

Annex 2: BlueOrchard Loans for Development 2006: Pass-Through Securitisation

BlueOrchard Loans for Development 2006 ("BlueOrchard II") closed in February 2006 with a total volume of USD 105 million.[31] This pass-through structure, which securitised 22 loans to MFIs in 17 different countries, is expected to enable these MFIs to reach 105,000 new end clients. Moreover, by extending the duration of their balance sheets, MFIs will be better able to plan their funding and may be able to expand their portfolio of product offerings.[32]

The notes, issued through a private placement by the SPV, BlueOrchard II, are based on principal and interest payments on the underlying loans. The final maturity of the notes is five years from their issuance; noteholders will not receive their principal payment until the underlying MFIs repay the principal of their respective loans. Noteworthy features of the deal include the following:

- **Subordination:** The deal is structured in two tranches. In contrast to the two deals outlined above, the senior tranche, Class A Notes, are not enhanced with a guarantee. Class B notes are subordinate to Class A notes. A waterfall payment structure is in place to ensure that senior note claims are paid out before subordinated claims.

- **Reserve Fund:** the reserve fund provides an additional risk buffer for the senior notes. Comprising 2% of the initial principal of the notes, the reserve fund is senior to Class B notes in the payment structure: interest and principal of the B Notes may only be paid after all reserve fund claims have been settled.

---

[31] BlueOrchard Microfinance Securities I, LLC, which closed in 2004, was the first securitisation of microfinance assets. See Hüttenrauch and Schneider, Chapter 17, for a description of this deal.

[32] Statistics from BlueOrchard Loans for Development 2006-1 S.A. Private Placement Memorandum.

- **Accelerator Provision:** Senior noteholders have the right to instruct the trustee of the fund to accelerate the notes, giving Class B noteholders the option to purchase all of outstanding Class A notes at par.

- **Currency Swap Agreements**: While loans issued to MFIs are denominated in U.S. Dollars, Mexican pesos, Russian rubles, Colombian pesos and euros, payments on the BlueOrchard II notes are primarily denominated in U.S. dollars and euros.[33] Therefore, the SPV is subject to exchange rate risk between U.S. dollars and euro on one hand and Mexican pesos, Russian rubles and Colombian pesos on the other. The fund will engage in currency swaps to mitigate exchange rate risk. Swap payments are second only to Class A Note claims according to the set waterfall structure.

Annex 3: EFSE Pooling Structure

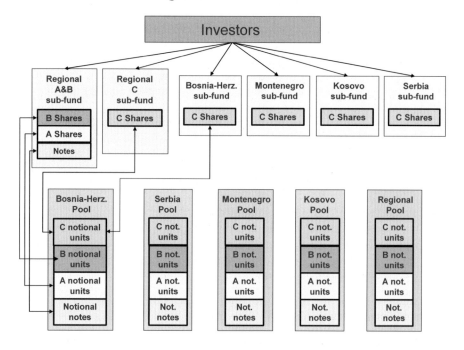

The two regional sub-funds pool their assets allocated to a particular nation or entity with the assets of the respective national sub-fund in national pools, each dedicated to a specific nation/entity.

---

[33] Loans extended to MFIs in Colombia are denominated in Colombian pesos, but payments of interest and principal to BlueOrchard II are denominated in U.S. dollars pegged to the Colombian peso.

The Fund operates similarly to a fund of funds from an accounting and an investment point of view, with the national and the regional sub-funds "investing" in national pools. However from a legal perspective, these national pools do not constitute separate entities and are not directly accessible to shareholders.

The above graph shows the flows, as detailed below, between the national pool from Bosnia-Herzegovina and the two regional sub-funds and the Bosnia-Herzegovina sub-fund. Similar flows would take place for the other nations/entities.

The investment in instruments of PLIs are made by each respective national pool. Each Participating Fund owns a portion of each asset of a national pool in proportion to the units such Participating Fund held in the national pool.

Within each national pool, the subordination waterfall is as follows:

- C notional units

  The C notional units will be owned by the C Shares of the Regional C sub-fund and by the C Shares of the respective national sub-fund.

  The C notional units will suffer in full the first losses for any loan loss provision required in accordance with IFRS accounting standards against defaults with respect to the investments made by such national pool.

  These loan loss provisions would decrease the value of the C notional units and would therefore decrease the value of the C Shares of the Regional C sub-fund and of the C shares of the respective national sub-fund in proportion to the ownership of such sub-funds in the national pool.

- B notional units:

  Each tranche of B notional units of each national pool is fully owned by, and will bear similar rights and obligations to, the respective tranche of B Shares of the Regional A&B sub-fund.

  The B notional units will only suffer a loss to the extent that the C notional units of the same national pool will have been depleted due to loan loss provisions required in accordance with IFRS accounting standards against defaults with respect to the investments made by such national pool.

  The B Shares of the Regional A&B sub-fund would only suffer a loss to the extent B notional units of a national pool will have suffered a loss.

- A notional units

  Each tranche of A notional units of each national pool will be fully owned by, and will bear similar rights and obligations to, the respective tranche of A Shares of the Regional A&B sub-fund

  The A notional units will only suffer a loss to the extent that the B notional units and the C notional units of the same national pool will have been depleted due to loan loss provisions required in accordance with IFRS accounting standards against defaults with respect to the investments made by such national pool.

The A Shares of the Regional A&B sub-fund would only suffer a loss to the extent A notional units of a national pool will have suffered a loss.

- Senior notional notes

The Senior notional notes of each national pool will be held by the Senior Notes of the Regional A&B sub-fund. They will bear similar rights and obligations to the Senior Notes.

These Senior notional notes benefit from the cash flows of the respective national pool in accordance with the priorities established in "Payment and Income Waterfall."

Risk ratios between the different classes will apply within each national pool:

o For each national pool, the B notional units will not exceed 100% of the C notional units.

o For each national pool, the sum of the Senior notional notes and of the A notional units will not exceed 250% of the sum of the C notional units and the B notional units.

References

Alles, Lakschman (2001): "Asset Securitization and Structured Financing: Future Prospects and Challenges for Emerging Market Countries." IMF Working Paper: WP/01/147. October 2001. www.imf.org.

American Securitization Forum (2003): "Statement of Cameron L. Cowan on Behalf of the American Securitization Forum," November 5, 2003. http://financialservices.house.gov/media/pdf/110503cc.pdf.

Basu, Sudiptu (2005): "Securitization and the Challenges Faced in Microfinance," April 2005. http://www.microfinancegateway.org/files/26257_file_26257.pdf.

BMZ (2004): "Sectoral Policy Paper on Financial System Development," Bonn.

Byström, Hans (2006): "The Microfinance Collateralized Debt Obligation: a Modern Robin Hood?" Working Paper, Department of Economics, University Lund, August 2006.

Calderon, Thierry Benoit (2006): Micro-bubble or Macro-immunity? Risks and Returns in Microfinance: Lessons from Recent Crises in Latin America; in: Ingrid Matthäus-Maier, J.D. von Pischke: Microfinance Investment Funds: Leveraging Private Capital for Economic Growth and Poverty Reduction, pp. 65–72.

Callaghan, Ian, Henry Gonzalez, Diane Maurice and Christian Novak, Morgan Stanley (2007): "Microfinance – on the Road to Capital Markets" in: Journal of Applied Corporate Finance, Vol. 19, No. 1, 2007, pp. 115–124.

CGAP (2004a): "CGAP/MIX Study on MFI Demand for Funding: Report of Survey Results," 2004. www.microfinancegateway.org.

CGAP (2004b): "Focus Note No. 25, Foreign Investment in Microfinance: Debt and Equity from Quasi-Commercial Investors," January 2004. www.cgap.org.

CGAP (2006): "Donor Brief No. 22, Maximizing Aid Effectiveness in Microfinance," February 2006. www.cgap.org.

CGAP (2006): "Focus Note No. 35, Aid Effectiveness in Microfinance: Evaluating Microcredit Projects of the World Bank and The United Nations Development Programme," April 2006. www.cgap.org.

De Sousa-Shields, Marc and Cheryl Frankiewicz, et al (2004): "Financing Microfinance Institutions: The Context for Transitions to Private Capital." USAID. Accelerated Microenterprise Advancement Project, December 2004. http://www.microfinancegateway.org/content/article/detail/23657.

Fabozzi, CFA, Frank J (2005): "The Structured Finance Market: An Investor's Perspective," Financial Analysts Journal, May 2005, Vol. 61, No. 3: 27-40.

Fender, Ingo and Janet Mitchell (2005): "Structured Finance: Complexitiy, Risk and the Use of Ratings," BIS Quarterly Review, June 2005, pp. 67-79.

Fitch Ratings (2006): "Credit Products/Bulgaria: New Issue: ProCredit Company B.V.;" Fitch Structured Finance, 15 May 2006, www.fitchratings.com.

Glaubitt, Klaus, Hanns Martin Hagen and Haje Schütte (2006): "Mainstreaming Microfinance Investments?" in: Ingrid Matthäus-Maier, J.D. von Pischke; Microfinance Investment Funds, Berlin, Heidelberg, New York.

Grameen Foundation USA and The Paul H. Nitze School of Advanced International Studies (2005): "Microfinance and Capital Markets Speaker Series," February-April 2005, published July 2005. http://www.gfusa.org/pubdownload/dl.php.

Hüttenrauch, Harald and Claudia Schneider (2007): "Securitisation: A Funding Alternative for Microfinance Institutions," in this publication.

IFC (2005): "Global Securitisation Review 2004/2005." http://www.ifc.org.

Littlefield, Elizabeth and Richard Rosenberg (2004): "Microfinance and the Poor." http://www.imf.org/external/pubs/ft/fandd/2004/06/pdf/littlefi.pdf

Littlefield, Elizabeth and Alexia Latortue et al (2004): "The Contribution of Microfinance to the Millenium Develoopment Goals," CGAP Focus Note 24.

Meehan, Jennifer (2004): "Tapping the Financial Markets for Microfinance: Grameen Foundation USA's Promotion of this Emerging Trend," October 2004. http://haas.berkeley.edu.

Siddiquee, Mohammad Moniruzzaman; Mohammad Farhad Hossain; Zahidul Islam (2006): "Asset Securitisation in Bangladesh: Practices and Impediments," in: The Cost and Management Journal, Vol. 34, No. 2, March/April 2006, pp. 19-38.

USAID (2005): "MFI Financing Strategies and the Transition to Private Capital," Micro Note No. 9, October 6, 2005.

World Economic Forum (2006): "Building on the Monterrey Consensus: The Untapped Potential of Development Finance Institutions to Catalyse Private Investment," Financing for Development Initiative, January 2006. http://site-resources.worldbank.org/INTINFNETWORK/Resources/CatalysingPrivInvest-ment.pdf

Unitus (2005): Annual Report 2005.
    http://www.unitus.com/sections/media/media_dl_main.asp

Index

M

Management information system
(MIS) 58, 121, 130, 131, 140,
174, 177, 183, 184, 187, 191, 192,
202, 204, 205, 318
Market transparency 5, 49
Marketing 86, 116, 131, 138, 140 –
142, 183, 215, 234, 250, 255,
258, 287, 292
McKinsey & Company 80, 82, 195,
300
Mezzanine tranche 306, 308, 309,
343, 362, 372
MFI 5, 17 – 19, 22, 25, 28, 29, 32,
34 – 38, 49, 50, 52 – 56, 58, 59,
62 – 71, 73 – 80, 82, 87 – 90,
92 – 94, 97, 99, 102 – 105, 107,
129 – 131, 133, 134, 136, 137,
141, 143, 152, 153, 164, 166, 181,
184, 191, 192, 198 – 200, 202,
203, 205, 247, 248, 250, 252, 253,
256, 257, 263, 271, 321 – 332,
334, 337 – 341, 349 – 357, 360,
363 – 365, 368 – 373, 377, 378
   MFI Equity 5, 18, 19, 22, 28, 29,
   69, 70, 73 – 79, 82, 103
   MFI Rating 49, 52, 56, 65, 66,
   324
Microcare 286, 288, 289, 292, 294,
298
Micro-Credit Ratings International
Limited (M-CRIL) 49 – 64, 66,
67
Microfinance 1, 2, 4 – 8, 10 – 13,
17 41, 47, 49 56, 58 60,
62 – 75, 78 – 83, 85 – 95, 97, 99,
100, 102, 103, 105 – 108,
111 – 114, 116, 117, 123, 126,
127, 129, 130, 132, 137, 139,
140, 142 – 145, 147 – 149, 154,
155, 158, 159, 165, 166, 171,
173 – 187, 189, 190, 195 – 200,
202 – 207, 222, 225 – 227, 234,

235, 239 – 244, 246, 249, 254,
258, 263, 266, 270, 282, 286, 287,
294, 297, 299 – 302, 306, 312,
321 – 335, 337, 339 – 347,
349 – 357, 359 – 361, 363 – 371,
373, 376, 377
Microfinance Investment Funds
(MFIF) 5, 12, 17, 19 – 21, 23, 24,
28, 31, 37, 47, 49, 73, 83, 91, 102,
108, 360, 363, 365, 376, 377
Microfinance providers 114, 116,
174, 179, 180, 184, 186, 187, 235,
282, 286, 294, 349
Microfinance rating 5, 17, 50, 51,
53, 60, 62, 65, 67, 352, 354
Microfinanza 51, 322
Microinsurance 5, 239, 264, 279 –
281, 283, 285, 287 – 293, 297,
298
Micropensions 5, 241 – 243, 249
MicroRate 31, 36, 50, 51, 53, 57,
58, 60, 66, 67, 322
MicroSave 171, 243, 251, 254,
263 – 265, 288, 298
MicroVest 29, 30, 53, 62
Migrants 113 – 119, 123, 125 – 127,
141, 144, 295, 311
Mobile banking 155, 160, 161, 166,
250
Money Transfer 5, 86, 111, 113 –
117, 119 – 127, 129, 130, 137,
141, 148, 150, 152, 156, 180
Money Transfer Organisation
(MTO) 131, 133 – 135, 137
MoneyGram 115, 119, 134 – 136
Monitoring 59, 62, 78, 87, 152,
159, 165, 216, 217, 273, 307, 318,
320, 360, 363, 368, 369, 371
Mutual Benefit Association (MBA)
264, 289, 291, 293, 294

Printing: Krips bv, Meppel, The Netherlands
Binding: Stürtz, Würzburg, Germany